RIZZOLI
NEW YORK

ROME

IN DETAIL

A Guide for the Expert Traveler

In Association with the

Herald INTERNATIONAL Tribune
THE WORLD'S DAILY NEWSPAPER

First published in the United States of America in 2003 by
Rizzoli International Publications, Inc.
300 Park Avenue South
New York, NY 10010

Library of Congress Control Number: 2002112220

ISBN: 0-8478-2462-4

Designed by Lisa Vaughn, Two of Cups Design Studio

Printed in China

Photo credits

Unless otherwise noted, all photos are by Aaron Gatti. Photo credits list the author and/or agency, the chapter in which the photo can be found, and the name of the photo.

Justine Kahn: "Quirinale," The Obelisk, Piazza del Quirinale.
Giovanni Latanzi: "Fora," Domus Aurea.
Andrea Rossi: "Laterano," San Giovanni in Laterano. "Quirinale/Tridente," Santa Maria in Via Lata; San Lorenzo. "Campidoglio," Il Gesù; Area Sacra di Largo Argentina. "Piazza Navona," Santa Maria della Pace; Chiostro del Bramante. "Trastevere/Gianicolo," San Pietro in Montorio; Tempietto di Bramante.

The following photos are © Azienda di Promozione Turistica di Roma (APT): "Fora," San Giorgio al Velabro; Michelangelo, *Moses*. "Laterano," Santa Maria degli Angeli; Scala Santa. "Quirinale," San Marco; Capuchin Crypt; Caravaggio, *Crucifixion of Saint Paul*. "Campidoglio," Interior, Pantheon; Sant'Angelo in Pescheria; Caravaggio, *Calling of St. Matthew*; *Bruto Capitolino*, Palazzo dei Conservatori; Sala degli Imperatori, Palazzo Nuovo. "Piazza Navona," Fiorenzo di Lorenzo, *San Sebastiano*; Palazzo Altemps. "Trastevere," San Crisogono; Cloister of San Giovanni; View of frescoes, Villa Farnesina. "Northern Rome," Bernini, *Pluto and Proserpina*; C. Carra, *Ovalle delle apparizioni*. "Southern Rome," Catacombe di Domitilla; View of vault, San Sisto Vecchio; Santa Balbina; Santa Prisca; San Saba; Model of Rome, Museo della Civiltà.

The following photos are © Photographic Archive of the Soprintendenza per il Patrimonio Storico, Artistico, e Demoetnoantropologico di Roma e Lazio, courtesy of APT: "Quirinale," *Cristo Pantocratore*. "Piazza Navona," Oratorio del Gonfalone.

The following photo is © Archivio Fabbrica di San Pietro in Vaticano, courtesy of APT: "Vatican," Michelangelo, *Pieta*; Necropolis.

The following photos are © Musei Vaticani, courtesy of APT: "Laterano," Interior, Santa Maria Maggiore. "Vatican," Raphael, *The Transfiguration*; *Laocoonte (Laocoön)*; Giovanni Bellini, *Deposition*; Nicolò e Giovanni, *The Last Judgment*.

The following photos are © Fondo Edifici di Culto, courtesy of APT: "Fora," Santi Giovanni e Paolo. "Laterano," Santa Pudenziana; Santa Prassede. "Campidoglio," Santa Maria in Aracoeli; Santa Maria Maddalena.

The following photos are © Foto Vasari, Roma, courtesy of APT: "Vatican," Raphael, *The School of Athens;* Octagonal Courtyard, Museo Pio-Clementino. "Northern Rome," Sant'Agnese.

Table of Contents

Foreword

By Fred Plotkin

There is a particular malady—not quite an illness but more of a chronic condition—that afflicts anyone who has ever visited Rome. In fact, it is an immediately recognizable ache shared by all who suffer from it. Perhaps it began when you turned your back to the Trevi Fountain and flung your arm high over your head to launch an old hundred *lire* coin to ensure you would return to the Eternal City once again. The little twinge you still feel, your Roman ache, is there to remind you that there exists a place where life is lived to the fullest.

Surely Rome was the most beautiful city in the world before the advent of the automobile. With its caressing breezes, splendid fountains and public squares, unmatched architecture, and a sensuality that few places can rival, Rome was an urban paradise. Vehicular traffic in the second half of the twentieth century gave Rome a grimy face, but all of this was wiped away as the city spruced up for the year 2000. Sections of the city's historical center are now closed to most auto traffic, so that the sights, sounds, and smells of an older Rome have returned. The city is better than ever.

Everything in Rome urges you to enjoy and embrace life: the eye is gratified with the boundless physical beauty of the city and its well-dressed natives; the nose and mouth delight in some of the lustiest food to be found in Italy, and in ice cream that is virtually unrivaled, even in Italy. Sounds, whether the hiss of an espresso machine or the kiss of a pair of lovers in the place that gave its name to romance, tickle the ear like an acoustic feather. And everywhere in Rome there is something gorgeous and often timeless to touch.

Too many visitors to Rome are occupied with a checklist of must-sees (the Sistine Chapel in the morning, the Forum in the afternoon, the boutiques at dusk, and Via Veneto by night), that they fail to indulge in the pleasurable Roman pursuits of strolling arm in arm, stopping to admire a thing of beauty or to stare just a little too intently at other people just being human. The secret to doing as the Romans do is to awaken your own dormant humanity.

The book you are now holding is not a guide for "checklist" tourists. Rather, it presents and explores Rome as Romans know it, unlocking doors and allowing you to enter the soul of the city that has perfected the art of living. If you have already been to Rome, this book will help you experience familiar sites anew as well as introduce you to more of its treasures. And if you have yet to visit the city that has beckoned travelers and pilgrims for two thousand years, you will encounter not only a place of incomparable grandeur and eroticism, but you will also find that elusive thing even the most experienced traveler can spend a lifetime trying to discover: one's self.

Fred Plotkin is a much admired expert on all things Italian. He is the author of *Opera 101, Classical Music 101, Italy for the Gourmet Traveler,* and four Italian cookbooks.

Introduction

Ancient Rome, medieval Rome, Renaissance Rome, baroque Rome, rococo Rome, and, of course, romantic Rome—no matter what your tastes or interests in art and architecture are, Rome can fulfill them like no other city in the world.

But, as Edith Wharton pointed out, each of these parts of Rome has a clearly visible "foreground"—the Colosseum, St. Peter's, the Trevi Fountain, the Spanish Steps—and a more concealed "background" of somewhat hidden jewels. The foreground is, of course, exceptional, the embodiment of over two thousand years of Western art and architecture; the background is the more intimate continuation of the city. The foreground is usually the province of the classic sightseeing tour and the conventional guidebook; the background is for the traveler interested in discovering the Rome known only to the real connoisseur and for the return visitor (and Rome is a city where visitors can return again and again and discover new, extraordinary corners each time).

There are many popular guides available on Rome, but none of them is specifically geared to the "background traveler." This is why we decided to publish this guide. And we do not believe there could have been a better combination than the Italian supplement of the *International Herald Tribune* and Rizzoli to write a guide that would open the doors to the often-overlooked sites of Italy's great capital.

We have divided the city into nine areas, not necessarily defined by the borders of the Roman districts, or *rioni*, but purely for the visitor's convenience. For each area we compiled a chapter with two major components:

Fundamentals—with descriptions of the better-known monuments and sites, accompanied by the very personal views of special observers, such as Henry James, Goethe, and Charles Dickens.

Walking Tours, Focuses, and Commercial Points of Interest—with less well-known cultural sites, and a selection of the best each area has to offer in terms of lodging, eating, and shopping.

Before you leave for Rome, we urge you to visit our web site—www. italyweekly.it—for additional information and an updated list and schedules of cultural events. And once there, remember that you can find the *International Herald Tribune* on most newsstands.

Claudio Gatti

John Moretti

How to Use This Guide

Rome in Detail is organized by neighborhood—nine in all—with cultural attractions featured in several sections within each chapter:

☛**Fundamentals**: Entries on major sites.

☛**Walking Tours**: Itineraries that take you to sites within the neighborhood that feature off-the-beaten-path treasures.

Within each **Walking Tour,** one site has been identified with our logo that we highly recommend. "**Our Pick**" sites are marked on the cultural maps in each chapter and on the map at the front of the book, so that you can easily make Rizzoli's favorite sites the focus of your trip.

☛**Focus:** Following each **Walking Tour**, a site from the tour is described in depth.

☛**Other Points of Interest**: Additional noteworthy cultural sites.

☛**Museums:** Museums of every type are featured, from the Vatican Museums to the National Pasta Museum (see Quirinale chapter).

☛**Commercial Points of Interest** sections feature **Hotel & Inns**; **Restaurants, Bars, & Cafés**; and **Specialty Shops**. In addition to the these listings, a **Profile** about an intriguing person whose work or shop is particularly unique and noteworthy is featured, such as the native Roman who creates facsimiles of famous works of art in mosaic, with techniques that go back to ancient Roman times.

☛**Our Critic's Favorite Restaurants**: Domenico Nucera, the well-known food critic for Italy's leading newspaper *Corriere della Sera*, offers his advice on the best restaurants in Rome.

A note about pricing: We have included approximate ranges of prices for Hotels & Inns and Restaurants. We have not included pricing information for cafés and bars.

Restaurants: All prices are for one.

€	Under 50
€€	50–75
€€€	75–100
€€€€	Above 100

Hotels & Inns: Prices are for double rooms. Unless noted with an *, hotels include breakfast.

€	Under 100
€€	100–200
€€€	200–300
€€€€	300 and above

At press time, the exchange rate for euros to American dollars was nearly equal, or $1 USD to € .99.

How to Use the Maps

Each chapter has one map marked with cultural sites and another marked with commercial points of interest. Each map has a key on the right hand side listing all of the entries alphabetically and each is assigned a number.

Commercial

Hotels & Inns
1   Hotel Turner

Restaurants & Cafés
2   Capo Boi
3   Ceppo

Shopping
52   Apolloni
53   Battistoni
54   Bomba

☞**Best of Rome:** An extensive "Best of" chapter features listings and descriptions of Rome's exceptional offerings in the following categories:

- Most Romantic Places
- Best Flea Markets
- Best Hotel Swimming Pool
- Best Vegetarian Restaurants
- Best Golf Courses and Ranges
- Best Gourmet Stores
- Best Salad Bars
- Best Bread
- Best Tea Rooms
- Best Chocolate
- Best Gelato
- Best Herb and Spice Stores

Each entry in this chapter lists the neighborhood where it can be found. Each "Best of" listing (with the exception of the golf courses which are all outside the maps) is marked on the commercial maps at the bottom of the key. If a listing appears in a particular chapter already as well as in the "Best of" chapter, an asterisk * will indicate that it can also be found in the "Best of" chapter.

Restaurants & Cafés

40	Gusto*
41	Il Leoncino
42	L'Osteria dell'Ingegno*
43	Matricianella
44	Nino Dal 1934
45	Osteria Margutta
46	Ristorante "34"
47	Ristorante Penna d'Oca
48	Roof Terrace of the Hotel Eden*
49	Rosati

Best of

74	Antico Caffè della Pace
75	Aureli Frutta e Verdura
76	Babington's English Tea Room
77	Carlo Gargani
78	Castroni, Via Flaminia, 28
79	Centro Macrobiotico
80	Ciampini
81	Ciampini
82	Dolci e doni di Loreti

TIME LINE

DATE	EVENT
753 B.C.	According to the legend, Romulus founds Rome. The circular marker Mundus is erected in the center point of Rome.
715–672	The Regia, said to have once housed the early kings, is built during the reign of Numa Pompilius.
673–642	The Comitium, a meeting place for the public assembly, is built under the reign of Tullus Hostilius.
640–616	The Carcer, a vaulted underground chamber used as the public jail and as a place for executions, is built during the reign of Ancus Marcius.
578–534	The city is divided into four "regions" and is enclosed by the so-called Servian Wall.
509	Roman Republic founded.
507–6	Latins and Etruscans declare war.
499	Romans defeat Latins at Battle of Lake Regillus.
434	Rome is at war again with the Etruscans.
390	Gauls sack Rome.
378	A new set of walls, nearly 7 miles long, is started.
312	First aqueduct is built.
264	Punic Wars against Carthage.
210	A fire burns the north and eastern ends of the Forum.
170	Basilica Sempronia, a covered columnar hall used for commercial and judicial purposes, is built by the censor Sempronius Gracchus.
148	The Regia is burned and immediately restored.
146	End of Punic Wars; Carthage is destroyed.
142	The Pons Aemilius, the first stone bridge in Rome, is built.
100	Julius Caesar is born.
80	Rome is estimated to have a population of about 400,000 people.
78	The Tabularium, a unique monumental public-records office, is built by consul Q. Lutatius Catulus.
60–50	First triumvirate: Caesar, Pompey, and Crassus.
54–46	The Basilica Iulia, a covered columnar hall used for commercial and judicial purposes, is built and dedicated, unfinished, by Caesar.
55–34	The Basilica Aemilia, a covered columnar hall used for commercial and judicial purposes, is constructed by Aemilius Paullus.
55	Caesar invades Britain.
51–50	Caesar crosses the Rubicon, marking the beginning of the civil war.
45	Caesar declared emperor.
44	The Curia Iulia, a monumental meeting room for Roman Senate, is dedicated.
44	Caesar killed by Brutus and Cassius.
43–32	Second triumvirate: Octavian, Mark Antony, and Lepidus.
31	Battle of Actium: Antony and Cleopatra are defeated by Octavian, who takes the title of Augustus and becomes sole ruler.
29	The Curia Iulia is completed by Augustus.
A.D. 14	Death of Augustus.
37	Caligula becomes emperor.

Date	Event
41	Caligula assassinated; Claudius takes his place.
64	Nero sets fire to city slums.
67	Saints Peter and Paul are martyred.
80	Colosseum inaugurated by Titus.
125	Pantheon rebuilt to designs by Hadrian.
141	Aedes Antonini and Faustinae, temple to the Imperial cult, is constructed by Antoninus Pius for his wife.
203	The Arch of Septimius Severus, a triple arch to honor Roman conquests in the East, is built and dedicated to Septimius Severus, Caracalla, and Geta.
217	The Baths of Caracalla are opened to the public.
270	Military disasters: Dacia lost to the Goths.
285	Diocletian splits empire into East and West.
313	Constantine proclaims Edict of Milan: Christians are free to practice their religion.
395	The empire is divided in two: the Eastern and the Western empires.
410	Alaric's Goths sack Rome.
476	The end of the Roman Empire with the deposition of Romulus Augustulus.
609	Pantheon is transformed into a church.
800	Pope crowns Charlemagne Holy Roman Emperor.
1084	Holy Roman Emperor Henry IV, followed by Robert Guiscard and the Normans, sack Rome.
1097	First Crusade begins.
1300	First Holy Year is declared. Giotto comes to Rome and paints the Stefaneschi Polyptich (in the Pinacoteca Vaticana).
1309	Pope Clement V moves the papacy to Avignon.
1347	Cola di Rienzo declares the Roman Republic.
1417	End of Great Schism in the papacy.
1425	Rome's population is about 20,000.
1481	First painting of the Sistine Chapel, by Perugino, Pinturicchio, Botticelli, and others.
1494	Charles VIII of France invades Italy.
1500	Michelangelo finishes the Pietà, his first work in Rome.
1508	Second painting of the Sistine Chapel, by Michelangelo.
1517–19	Raphael paints his Vatican *Stanze* or Raphael Rooms.
1526	The census counts 55,000 Romans.
1527	Sack of Rome by imperial army of Charles V.
1538	Pope Paul III moves the statue of Marcus Aurelius to Piazza del Campidoglio.
1542	Paul III starts the Congregation of Santo Uffizio, otherwise known as the Inquisition.
1555	Pope Paul IV orders the confinement of Roman Jews in the Ghetto.

Date	Event
1599	Caravaggio paints three canvases of Saint Matthew for the church of San Luigi dei Francesi.
1585	Sixtus V begins to change the layout of Rome.
1600	Philosopher Giordano Bruno is burned alive in Campo de' Fiori as a heretic.
1726	The Spanish Steps are built.
1762	Pope Clemens XIII inaugurates the Trevi Fountain.
1771	With the opening of the Museo Pio-Clementino, the Vatican palaces are transformed into museums.
1789	Antonio Canova completes his first work in Rome with the funereal monument to Pope Clemens XIV.
1798	French occupy Rome, exile the Pope, and declare Rome a Jacobin republic.
1800	The population of Rome reaches 150,000.
1808	Rome made "free city" in Napoleon's empire.
1815	After Napoleon's fall, Pius VII returns. The so-called Restoration begins.
1821	Death of Keats in Rome.
1848	Giuseppe Mazzini and Giuseppe Garibaldi found the Roman Republic; French troops occupy the city (until 1870) and restore the pope.
1870	Italian General Raffaele Cadorna enters Rome.
1871	Rome is proclaimed capital of a united Italy.
1874	The new Termini railroad station is inaugurated.
1881	The census shows that the population of Rome is 273,952. In that same year, the population of Naples is 535,206.
1901	The population of Rome has grown to 422,411 people.
1922	Mussolini marches on Rome; soon after King Victor Emmanuel III gives him the premiership.
1929	Lateran Treaty is signed creating the current Vatican State.
1931	The census counts 930,926 Romans.
1933	Mussolini opens the Via dei Fori Imperiali.
1944	In June Rome is liberated by the Allies.
1946	After a national referendum, Rome becomes the capital of the Republic of Italy.
1957	Common Market Treaty signed in Rome.
1960	Olympic Games held in Rome.
1978	Polish Cardinal Karol Wojtyla is elected Pope, first non-Italian in centuries.
1981	Pope John Paul II shot in Saint Peter's Square.
1990	Rome hosts the soccer World Cup Final.
2000	The Holy Year brings over 25 million pilgrims and tourists to Rome.

Editor's note: Each entry in this chapter has been marked on the commercial map for the neighborhood in which it can be found. See chapter and page numbers next to listing in parentheses.

Rome: The Capital of Romance

Public display of affection is the rule, not the exception, in Rome. Lovers sit intertwined on benches throughout the city. They smooch in front of monuments. And in the evenings the streets are full of starry-eyed *fidanzati* (boyfriends and girlfriends) meandering together, hand in hand. Rome, eternally lovely, plays Cupid with its millions of inhabitants and visitors; the city's ancient beauty quickens heartbeats and has inspired endless amorous proclamations and verses of poetry.

During the day Rome's romance is less apparent, veiled by raucous shouting in the marketplaces, chaotic traffic, and the bantering of boisterous Romans. But beginning in the late afternoon, when a golden light settles on its piazzas and murmuring fountains, the Eternal City slowly transforms into the Capital of Romance. Wandering the center as the sun sets, visitors will inevitably happen upon numerous romantic nooks, where words are whispered and loving looks abound.

There are countless itineraries for tourists in Rome—tours for those who want to see every piece of marble the baroque master Bernini ever touched, Gucci shopping tours, and tours of the damp, clammy catacombs. The following is a romantic itinerary of one of the world's most romantic cities. Visitors should keep in mind that this itinerary is not to be embarked upon in the heat of midday, hurriedly, or in a sour mood. The evening, early or late, is the ideal time for visiting these beautiful places that should be soaked in *con calma* (with calm), as Italians say.

Passeggiata from Trinità dei Monti to the Pincio

The early evening *passeggiata*, or stroll, used to be a fixture of daily Italian life. It has now become mostly a weekend activity,

particularly in busy Rome where the pace of life has accelerated in recent years. Yet, at sunset there are always people strolling along the well-worn road that stretches from the 15th-century French church of Trinità dei Monti, above the Spanish Steps, to the top of the Pincio Hill. Walking toward the Pincio Hill from the small piazza at the foot of the Trinità dei Monti, where artists sell watercolors of the city, strollers can envy some of the most beautiful terraces of Rome. The walls of Villa Medici, the exquisite home of the French Academy, rise on the right, lined with arching trees. Just in front of Villa Medici's vaulted entrance is a small pebbled area where you can pause for a moment to take in the sunset. The hum of the city below is drowned out by the sound of an overflowing fountain nearby.

Continuing along Viale Trinità dei Monti, a bright patch of bougainvillea marks the slight upward turn to the Pincio Hill. A broad area at the top of the Pincio overlooks the grand Piazza del Popolo, with Monte Mario and the Janiculum in the distance. This magnificent view is only lost on the many teenagers locked in long embraces, whose eyes see only each other. For those who would like to complete the *passeggiata* with a drink or dinner, there are two excellent options. The first one is to head back toward Trinità dei Monti, and go to Ciampini, a café/restaurant beautifully located on the side of the hill across the street from Villa Medici. In its outdoor garden you can enjoy great drinks—try the *Ciampini con spumante*, a fruit cocktail with sparkling white wine—and a very romantic view of the city.

The second option is to take the road that winds down the hillside of the Pincio Gardens to Piazza del Popolo and look for the Hotel de Russie, on nearby Via del Babuino (one of the three streets that leads into Piazza del Popolo). The hotel has an elegant bar in its internal courtyard. There are fountains, potted palm trees, plenty of shade, and a quiet, relaxed atmosphere. On an upper patio dinner is also served. The trees of the Pincio Hill serve as a backdrop to this charming place. Surrounded

on a weekday, the cost is slightly lower. At the ex-monastery of Via Valle delle Camene the ceremony costs €155 on weekdays, €258 on weekends; the Campidoglio's Sala Rossa costs €258.

For those who choose the Campidoglio, where it is extremely difficult to find parking for the "Just Married" get-away Rolls Royce, it is possible to obtain permission for two special city government parking places atop the Capitoline Hill.

For official arrangements:
Wedding Office, Municipality of Rome, Via Petroselli, 50; tel.: 06-67103066/67103782. (Campidoglio; see map pg. 160)

Best Flea Markets
People don't normally speak of Rome's markets with the reverence of Paris's famed Clingancourt or London's ramshamble Portabello markets, but the city is holding its own with the number and variety of venues for the collectibles crowd.

One of the most exciting events at Ponte Milvio, since the father of national unity Giuseppe Garibaldi blew it up in 1849, is the antiques market stretched along the Tiber every first Sunday of the month. The J4 express bus leads there from the center in less than 30 minutes. There's a plethora of choices here: small objects and collectibles, ephemera, vintage watches, linens, glassware, and some furniture.

Above the Spanish Steps, collectors climb to a cavelike market known as the Underground. Held on the first weekend of the month in a parking garage, the heart of this market is small antiques. Metal works are well represented in coins, medals, and odd tools, the uses of which sometimes remain a mystery to both buyer and seller.

Just off the Renaissance street of Via Giulia, another upscale market can be found on Vicolo della Moretta. Usually the site of a lone vegetable vendor during the week, the small lot hosts a tented market on the second and sometimes the first Sunday of the month. Uncrowded, unpretentious, and somewhat unpredictable, the fledgling market is a discovery one hesitates to share with others. The small antiques, including silver, European souvenir collectibles, and ephemera have a handpicked quality as if the vendors made rounds of the elegant palazzi on the Via Giulia just that morning.

The imposing Fascist loggia at Piazza Augusto Imperatore hosts a market every third Sunday. "Sotto i portici" as it is called, is a good escape from crowds and the ubiquitous pashmina purveyors. Market hounds will recognize many of the vendors from the Underground, and cultivating even the simplest of relationships can pay off with friendly service and prices.

There's somewhat of a luxurious melancholy about the Antiquariato a Piazza Verdi. The neighborhood, just a short distance from Villa Borghese, has the feel of a good cloth coat: warm, classic, and not too showy. And the market, on the fourth Sunday of each month, has the feel of an upscale porch sale. There are plenty of estate-quality collectibles, prints, jewelry, and antique watches, and restored furniture fit for a showroom. The prices reflect this well-heeled location, but most dealers will negotiate.

Il Mercatino del Borghetto Flaminio bills itself as the neighborhood garage sale, and—considering its location in a former bus depot—one might be tempted to pass by this market at full throttle. Doing so, you'd miss some of the best bargains in town. While there's a lot of kitsch and curiosities, there's a fair representation of the stuff that makes a serious collection.

Finally there is Porta Portese, Rome's largest and oldest flea market and once the premier place for antiques. Less about aesthetics and more about endurance, the market is crowded, competitive, and cluttered with knock-offs of everything from Lacoste to Levi's. The best goods are found by entering through Piazza Ippolito Nievo. Past the furniture forest, the offerings include Roman coins, paintings, silver, and unusual decorative papers such as 16th-century illustrated texts.

Antiquariato a Piazza Verdi (Northern Rome; see map pg. 254) Piazza Verdi; tel.: 06-8552773; open: fourth Sun. of the month 8 A.M.–7 P.M.; take bus #360 to Piazza Verdi.

Il Mercantino del Borghetto Flaminio (Northern Rome; see map pg. 254) Piazza della Marina, 32; tel.: 06-5880517; open: Sun. 10 A.M.–7 P.M.; take tram #19 to Via Flaminia/Piazza della Marina.

Ponte Milvio (Northern Rome; see map pg. 254) Lungotevere Capoprati; tel.: 06-9077312; open: first Sun. of the month through Feb., then the first weekend thereafter, Sat. 3–8 P.M., Sun. 8:30 A.M.–6 P.M.; take express bus #J4.

Porta Portese (Trastevere; see map pg. 238) Piazza Ippolito Nievo; open: Sun. 5 A.M.–2 P.M.; take tram #3 or 8 to Piazza Ippolito Nievo.

La Soffitta sotto i Portici (Quirinale; see map pg. 124) Piazza Augustus Imperatore; tel.: 06-36005345; open: third Sun. of the month 10 A.M.–sundown; take bus #913 to Piazza Augustus Imperatore.

The Underground (Quirinale; see map pg. 124) Via Francesco Crispi, 96; tel.: 06-36005345; open: first Sun. of the month and preceding Sat., Sat. 3–7:30 P.M., Sun. 10 A.M.–7:30 P.M.; take bus to Via del Tritone or Metro Barberini.

Vicolo della Moretta (Campidoglio; see map pg. 160) Via Giulia; open: first Sun. of the month 9 A.M.–8 P.M. (tel.: 06-8541461), second Sun., call for hours (tel.: 06-3720204 or 0339-7484573); take bus #116 to Via Giulia or #40 or #64 to Chiesa Nuova.

Best Hotel Swimming Pool

Rome has many public pools, but for those who prefer more selective pools, there is an alternative: the pools of top hotels. And some are open to a limited number of non-guests. The Aldovrandi Hotel Palace, located near Villa Borghese and the National Gallery of Modern Art has a beautiful pool, and from June to October it

is open to about twenty non-guests. The Grand Hotel Parco dei Principi also has a great pool, open until September, and on Sunday you can have brunch there. The pool of the Rome Cavalieri Hilton, a hotel also known for the top quality of its restaurant, has a breathtaking view of the city, and is also open until September. Children here will find a separate, smaller pool just for them.

Aldovrandi Palace (Northern Rome; see map pg. 254) Via Aldovrandi, 5; tel.: 06-3223993; pool open: 10 A.M.–6 P.M.

Parco dei Principi (Northern Rome; see map pg. 254) Via G. Frescobaldi, 5; tel.: 06-854421; pool open: July–Sept.

Rome Cavalieri Hilton (Vatican; see map pg. 212) Via Cadlolo, 101; tel.: 06-35091.

Best Vegetarian Restaurants

For those who are health conscious, Rome's offerings have increased over the years. According to Aloma Valentini, president of the Italian Centro Macrobiotico, or Macrobiotic Center on Via della Vite, "We don't offer trendy dishes but recipes that aim for a better nutritional balance."

Margutta Vegetariano's Mediterranean recipes include eggs and cheese, and the dishes are served in a dining room decorated with painting and sculpture.

Jaiya Sai Ma, managed by a native Neapolitan, offers tomatoes stuffed with rice, breaded artichokes, and eggplant parmesan in a much more ordinary atmosphere.

Arancia Blu prepares pasta dishes like saffron-tinted cannelloni stuffed with artichokes and offers a well-stocked cellar.

Arancia Blu (Laterano; see map pg. 84) Via dei Latini, 65; tel.: 06-4454105.

Margutta Vegetariano (all three are in Quirinale; see map pg. 124) Via Margutta, 118; tel.: 06-32650577. Via del Leoncino, 38; tel.: 06-6876581. Piazza Rondanini; tel.: 06-68134544.

Il Tiepolo (Northern Rome; see map pg. 254)
Via Tiepolo, 3–5; tel.: 06-3227449.

Centro Macrobiotico (Quirinale; see map pg. 122) Via della Vite, 14; tel.: 06-6792509.

Jaiya Sai Ma (Trastevere; see map pg. 238) Via Bargoni, 10–18; tel.: 06-5812840.

Insalata Ricca (Quirinale; see map pg. 124) Piazza Pasquino, 72–74; tel.: 05-68307881.

Best Golf Courses

Although golf has had a foothold in Rome since 1903 thanks to some enthusiasts at the English Consulate, it has only recently achieved more widespread popularity. And due to its temperate climate, the city is becoming a preferred destination for northern European golfers unable to tee off at home in the winter.

Rome's first golf course was built on the Torlonia princes' land at Acquasanta, in Via Appia Nuova, at the beginning of the last century, but the majority of today's courses were built in the 1980s, when the sport really took off. Today, Lazio, the region around Rome, boasts 6,500 players, making it the fourth largest concentration of golfers in Italy after Lombardy, Piedmont, and the Veneto.

All of the following courses and ranges are located outside our maps. Call individual courses for directions.

The Circolo Acquasanta is the oldest golf club in Rome. Via Appia Nuova, 716; tel.: 06-7803407.

The Circolo Castel Gandolfo is the most beautiful. Castel Gandolfo, Via Santo Spirito, 13; tel.: 06- 9312301.

The Circolo Golf Olgiata is possibly the most exclusive. Largo Olgiata, 15; tel.: 06-30889141.

The Circolo Marco Simone is currently the "hottest" course. It is owned by designer

Laura Biagiotti. Guidonia, Monte Celio, Via Marco Simone, 84; tel.: 0774-366469.

The Circolo Parco di Roma is the newest (with over 500 acres of land). Via Due Ponti; tel.: 06-3365339.

The Golf Club le Querce is managed by the Italian Golf Federation. Via Cassia (S. Martino Sutri); tel.: 0761-600489.

The Park Hotel dei Medici is primarily for the Sheraton's customers. Viale Parco dei Medici, 165/167; tel.: 06-6553477.

Best Golf Ranges
Appio Claudio
Via Ganiana, 45; tel.: 06-7187550.

Tevere Golf
Via del Balardo; tel.: 06-3337686.

Best Gourmet Stores

Nestled side by side with the "24/7" stores and standardized McDonald's of modern, globalized Rome, an older, more traditional Rome continues to defend the city's foods of "way back when." The latter includes 163 products from the region around Rome that experts have deemed worthy of "safeguarding," ranging from Maenza crepes; Cervara truffle; Ariccia porchetta, or roasted whole piglet; lentils from Ventotene Island; bread from Lariano; and wild strawberries from Nemi.

In recent years, Roman palates have become more demanding and the desire to rediscover traditional flavors and foods has grown. For over two decades, Valentino Belli and partner Renzo Fantucci have run La Tradizione, one of the city's gourmet stores most attuned to these demands. "Our job involves research and not just commerce," explains Belli, adding that, "after a period when uniformity and 'plastification' seemed to have taken over, in recent years more and more Romans and tourists have realized that the flavors and tastes of long ago cannot be beat and deserve to be preserved and enjoyed."

Aureli Frutta e Verdura (Quirinale; see map pg. 122) Via Flaminia, 50A; tel.: 06-3203456.

Carlo Gargani (Quirinale; see map pg. 122) Via Lombardia, 15; tel.: 06-4743710.

De Carolis (Vatican; see map pg. 212) Via Sabotino, 28; tel.: 06-3724050.

Ruggero Gargani (Northern Rome; see map pg. 254) Viale Parioli, 36B/38; tel.: 06-8079012.

Trimani (Northern Rome; see map pg. 254) Via Goito, 20; tel.: 06-4469661.

La Tradizione (Vatican; see map pg. 212) Via Cipro, 8; tel.: 06-39720349.

Volpetti (Southern Rome; see map pg. 280) Via Marmorata, 47; tel.: 06-5742352.

Volpetti (Quirinale; see map pg. 124) Via della Scrofa, 32; tel.: 06-6861940.

Best Salad Bars

Ancient Rome loved its salads, as Pliny's writings tell us. For some time now, salads have made headway in modern Rome, too. There are chains like L'Insalata Ricca, with salad restaurants throughout the city from Piazza Pasquino to Piazza Risorgimento. Another restaurant, La Pace del cervello, allows diners to choose among 40 different salads until 4 A.M. in the morning.

Another popular spot for nighthawks is Gusto, where the menu includes a marinated bass salad accompanied by bread baked in a wood-fired oven and stuffed with olives, vegetables, and aromatic herbs.

The wine bar Dolci e Doni di Loreti doesn't offer nearly as many selections but still has some truly original choices like arugula, pears, and Parmesan cheese with white truffle oil; smoked salmon and white celery topped with nonfat yogurt sauce and ginger; and tuna, tomato, green olives, and grated smoked fish roe.

L'Osteria dell'Ingegno offers nine different salads including the house specialty

"Olivia" with spinach, eggs, pecorino cheese, and crispy bacon. The "Americana," on the other hand, mixes apples, raisins, and grilled chicken breast.

Trimani and Tastevin offer other original and refined salads. Margutta Vegetariano's house salad combines Belgian endive, corn, olives, pickles, carrots, Pachino tomatoes, arugula, and olives, while the More touch salad restaurant offers cooked salads using eggplant, string beans, and bell peppers, as well as a fresh salmon salad.

Dolci e doni di Loreti (Quirinale; see map pg. 124) Via delle Carrozze, 85B; tel.: 06-69925001; closed: Mon.

Gusto (Quirinale; see map pg. 120) Piazza Augusto Imperatore, 9; tel.: 06-3226273.

L'Insalata Ricca (Campidoglio; see map pg. 160) Largo dei Chiavari, 85/86; tel.: 06-68803656.

Margutta Vegetariano (Quirinale; see map pg. 124) Via Margutta, 118; tel.: 06-32650577.

More touch (Quirinale; see map pg. 124) Via dei Pastini, 128; tel.: 06-69942160.

Nonna Papera (Quirinale; see map pg. 124) Zvicolo de' Modelli, 60; tel.: 06-6783510; closed: Wed.

L'Osteria dell'Ingegno (Quirinale; see map pg. 120) Piazza di Pietra, 45; tel.: 06-6780662; closed: Sun.

La pace del cervello (Fora; see map pg. 62) Via dei SS. Quattro, 63; tel.: 06-7005173.

Il Seme e la Foglia (Southern Rome; see map pg. 280) Via Galvani, 18; tel.: 06-5743008.

Tastevin (Vatican; see map pg. 212) Via Ciro Menotti, 16; tel.: 06-3208056.

Trimani (Northern Rome; see map pg. 254) Via Cernaia, 37B; tel.: 06-4469630.

Best Bread

Rome has an age-old relationship with bread. Roman emperors found that the best way to govern was with *panis et circensis,* or "bread and entertainment." Charred loaves of bread were even found at Pompeii. At the Largo Leopardi bread shop Panella, without a doubt the bakery most attentive to the history of Roman bread, patrons can find the same type of bread today that was sold in Pompeii's bakeries. Known as the *panis quadratus,* its name derives from the fact that before being placed in the oven, the baker made four incisions with a knife, dividing it into eight sections, or *quadre.* Panella also offers *panis siligeneo flore,* the best that imperial Rome had to offer and a favorite of Pliny the Elder.

The Renaissance's most famous *fornarina* (young baker), Raphael's lover and model—the daughter of a Roman baker—has been replaced by Antonella Citarella, a contemporary *fornarina* who sells bread and pizza at La Renella, a 130-year-old bakery at No. 15 Via de Moro. The stone-ground, whole-wheat flour used in the whole-wheat bread comes from an old-time mill outside Rome. The shop's pizza is made only with top-quality ingredients from the Pachino tomatoes to the water buffalo mozzarella to the arugula to the zucchini blossoms. The oven is fired by a cascade of hazelnut shells in place of wood, according to the traditions of Viterbo, a town north of Rome. Over 1,000 pounds of shells are burned every day in Massimo Arnese's stone-and-brick oven. Arnese, the last of three generations of bakers originally from Sicily explains, "It's all done by hand except for the kneading machine—everything else is by hand."

The bakery in Vicolo del Cinque named after owner Michele Tricario has patrons like Tyrone Power's daughter, Romina, who moved to Trastevere a few years ago. Specialties include the traditional *maritozzi,* now a rarity in Rome, as well as Terni-style salt-free bread and whole-wheat bread *in cassetta* (sliced). Open since 1906, the bakery makes traditional Roman pizza. Michele Tricarico explains that the secret is in the dough: "I make it the night before like in the old days, and the morning after I freshen it up. That way the bread comes out as good as back then."

Punturi on Via Flavia makes its breadsticks by hand, in addition to its 60 kinds of bread. In 1919 it was already a supplier for the Palazzo del Quirinale and the Italian Army.

Michele Tricarico (Trastevere; see map pg. 238) Vicolo del Cinque, 35; tel.: 06-5803886.

Panella (Laterano; see map pg. 84) Largo Leopardi, 4/10; tel.: 06-4872344.

Punturi (Quirinale; see map pg. 124) Via Flavia, 48; tel.: 06 4818225.

Forno La Renella (Trastevere; see map pg. 238) Via del Moro, 15; tel.: 06-5817265.

Best Tea Rooms

For the past few years, tea sommelier Yara Bitetti has presided over the afternoon tea service at the Riccioli Café on Piazza delle Coppelle from 4–7 P.M. Over 40 different varieties are available, ranging from Chinese, green, and black teas to semi-fermented, scented, Japanese green, and Indian blacks, as well as aromatic and African mint teas. Particular rarities include the Chinese White Silvery Pekoe variety and Japanese gyokuro.

Before Yara's arrival, however, tea in Rome was an exclusively English realm and since 1893 had been synonymous with Babington's English Tea Room, founded by Anna Maria Babington and Isabel Cargill. Today, Chiara Bedini, great-granddaughter of one of the founders, still offers over 30 varieties of English teas.

The tearoom at Caffè Greco, Rome's oldest café, is also English in style. As far back as 1742 it boasted a clientele that included Casanova and his Roman friends, and for centuries the café has attracted illustrious writers, musicians, and artists who come to sip English tea amidst the evergreen rooms of this elegant institution.

Near Piazza Farnese, Sciam, on Via del Pellegrino, serves tea from 2 P.M.–2 A.M., and is renowned for its mint, cinnamon, and rose teas and for the fact that these can be sampled through elegant narghiles, or water pipes.

Babington's English Tea Room
(Quirinale; see map pg. 122) Piazza di Spagna, 23; tel.: 06-6786027; open: 9 A.M.–8:30 P.M.; closed: Tues.

Caffè Greco (Quirinale; see map pg. 120)
Via Condotti, 86; tel.: 06-6785474/6791700; open: 8 A.M.–8:30 P.M.

Il Giardino del tè (Fora; see map pg. 62)
Via del Boschetto, 107; tel.: 06-4746888.

Sala da Tè del Riccioli Café (Quirinale;
see map pg. 124) Piazza delle Coppelle, 10A; tel.: 06-68210313; open: Tues.–Sat. 4 P.M.–7 P.M.

Sciam (Campidoglio; see map pg. 160)
Via del Pellegrino, 56; tel.: 06-68308957; open: 2 P.M.–2 A.M.

Best Chocolate
Rome has a half-dozen shops specializing in all varieties of chocolate. Among the best are the historic Moriondo e Gariglio on Via Piè di Marmo; Puyricard, the famed chocolatier from Provence offering only handmade, 100-percent pure chocolate; Gay Odin, the Rome branch of the Neapolitan institution; the Belgian chocolatiers Leonidas di Georgette, on Via Giolitti; and Godiva, in Piazza di Spagna.

The candied chestnuts and chocolates from Moriondo e Gariglio have a century and a half of history behind them and were one of poet Gabriele D'Annunzio's weaknesses. Another Moriondo e Gariglio specialty is *Solo per te,* chocolate candies wrapped in a little red box with golden writing, invented on the occasion of the engagement of Italy's last king and queen, Umberto II and Maria Jose. *Kri kri,* soft milk chocolates with toasted hazelnuts and a touch of rum, are also intriguing. In winter, the shop sells *Paisen,* a small cup of dark chocolate around a center of soft cream.

At the end of the 19th century in Naples, Isidoro Odin and Onorina Gay created a house of delicacies much loved by Oscar Wilde. Today, the same treats can be found in the Parioli neighborhood. The chocolate is made from a special mix of cocoas, and there are selections in every flavor. All products are handmade.

Leonidas offers its typical "coins" made with candied lemon and bitter chocolate, as well as 12 types of dietetic chocolate.

Godiva, in addition to pralines like "Le Comtesse," offers many other choices such as the exotic "Nippon," made principally from rice.

Gay Odin (Northern Rome; see map pg.
254) Via Stoppani, 9; tel.: 06-80693023; open: 10 A.M.–1:30 P.M., 4 P.M.–8 P.M.; closed: Sun. afternoon.

Leonidas di georgette (Laterano; see
map pg. 84) Via Giolitti, 10; tel.: 06-48930306; open: 8 A.M.–8 P.M.

Godiva (Quirinale; see map pg. 124)
Piazza di Spagna, 4; tel.: 06-69783318.

Moriondo e Gariglio (Piazza Navona;
see map pg. 188) Via Piè di Marmo, 21/22; tel.: 06-6990856.

Puyricard (Quirinale; see map pg. 124)
Via delle Carrozze, 26; tel.: 06-69202191; open: 10 A.M.–7:30 P.M.; closed: Sun. and Mon. morning.

Best Gelato
Since the early 1900s Giolitti has been making some of the best ice cream in Rome. One of the oldest ice cream shops in the city, its excellent reputation stems mostly from the quality of its ingredients.

San Crispino's forte, on the other hand, is pistachio ice cream made with Sicilian pistachios from Bronte. Other top flavors include meringue ice cream with chocolate and hazelnut ice cream made with Langhe hazelnuts from Piedmont.

Pellacchia is also famous for its hazelnut ice cream but perhaps even more so for its fruit flavors, including an unbeatable strawberry-and-lemon combination. The ice cream is all made by the house, without adding milk, under the supervision of Signora Maria. The store also supplies the surrounding restaurants and uses lemons delivered especially from Amalfi.

Chestnut ice cream with almond waffle cones is the specialty at San Filippo, while San Callisto specializes in chocolate, and Cecere, in Trastevere, in the *zabaione*, which is prepared from an old family recipe.

Bar Cecere (Trastevere; see map pg. 238)
Via S. Francesco a Ripa, 151; tel.: 06-58332404.

Ciampini (Quirinale; see map pg. 122)
Piazza S. Lorenzo in Lucina; tel.: 06-6876606.

Fragola e Limone (Quirinale; see map pg. 124) Via Giustiniani, 18A; tel.: 06-6896670.

Il Gelato di San Crispino (Southern Rome; see map pg. 280) Via Acaia, 56; tel.: 06-70450412.

Giolitti (Campidoglio; see map pg. 160)
Via Uffici del Vicario, 40; tel.: 06-6991243.

Ottaviani (Vatican; see map pg. 212)
Via Leone IV, 83; tel.: 06-37352003.

Pellacchia (Vatican; see map pg. 212)
Via Cola di Rienzo, 103/107; tel.: 06-3210807

San Filippo (Northern Rome; see map pg. 254) Via di Villa San Filippo, 2/10; tel.: 06-8079314.

Best Herb and Spice Stores

Enza Capozzoli, an expert in the oriental discipline of facial reflexology, which uses 500 facial signs to diagnose a problem or deficiency, is Rome's very own wizard of spice.

And at Albero del Pane, where Enza has worked for years, a huge assortment of spices is available for her to suggest. All are organic and make the store well worth a visit even for those who don't believe in facial reflexology.

For those interested exclusively in the culinary side of spices, one of the capital's top names is Mauro Berardi, who oversees a spice stand at the Campo de' Fiori open-air market. Among other things, he offers mixes for seasoning pasta, pizza, and many other dishes, all created by Berardi according to his own secret recipes.

Then, there are Rome's two oldest herbalists, which make for magnificent visits if only for their well-preserved premises and historic atmosphere. The Pontificia Erboristeria, founded in 1780, is managed today by Sergio Bellanza, whereas the Antica Erboristeria Romana is run by Paolo Ospici and offers herbs, spices, and centuries-old recipes.

Albero del Pane (Campidoglio; see map pg. 160) Via S. Maria del Pianto, 19/20; tel.: 06-6865016.

Antica Erboristeria Romana (Campidoglio; see map pg. 160)
Via Torre Argentina, 15; tel.: 06-6879493.

Banco Spezie di Mauro Berardi (Campidoglio; see map pg. 160) Campo de' Fiori market, Piazza Campo de' Fiori

Castroni (Vatican; see map pg. 212)
Via Cola di Rienzo, 196; tel.: 06-6874383.

Castroni (Quirinale; see map pg. 122)
Via Flaminia, 28; tel.: 06-3220857.

Pontificia Erboristeria (Quirinale; see map pg. 124) Via Pozzo delle Cornacchie, 26; tel.: 06-6861201.

Fora/Monti/Celio

By Ruth Kaplan

The highest concentration of ancient Rome's archaeological riches is in the **Foro Romano**, or **Roman Forum**, and the various fora that were cobbled onto it over the centuries. The best approach is from the **Colosseo**, Vespasian's oval amphitheater built in A.D. 72 and inaugurated in A.D. 80. Gladiatorial fights, wild animal combats, and naval battles (for a short time) were held here as frequently as every other day, for the pleasure of about 70,000 spectators. Next to it is the carved marble **Arco di Costantino**, dedicated in A.D. 315 to celebrate the Christian emperor's victory over Maxentius. Enter the Forum beyond the arch on the Via Sacra, still paved with its original grooved flagstones. Spanning the Via Sacra is the **Arco di Tito**, erected in A.D. 81 to celebrate Titus's victory in Judea. The raised lawn extending out to the right, ringed with columns, was the site of the **Tempio di Venere e Roma**, for the goddess who personified the city. Behind it is the 9th century church, **Santa Francesca Romana**, with its Romanesque bell tower and baroque interior. The three enormous coffered barrel vaults on the Forum's edge here belonged to the **Basilica di Costantino e Massenzio**, built in the 4th century A.D. The giant marble head, hand, and foot of Constantine at the Capitoline Museums came from a 39-foot statue of the emperor that once decorated the central vault.

Downhill on the right is the round, domed **Tempio di Romolo,** or **Temple of Romulus** (see Santi Cosma e Damiano), built in the 4th century to honor not the founder of Rome, but an emperor's son with the same name. Its original bronze doors are still in place. Now it serves as a vestibule for the attached church, **Santi Cosma e Damiano**. Still on the right, the imposing square colonnade of the 2nd-century **Tempio di Antonino e Faustina** is now the portico of the church, San Lorenzo in Miranda. Facing these buildings is the delicate shell of the circular Temple of Vesta, which used to have an eternal flame devoted to the goddess of the hearth. The priestesses who tended the sacred shrine lived in the spacious, rectangular **Casa delle Vestali** behind.

The western end of the Forum has spectacular colonnades that mark the spot of the it's oldest temples. The eight prominent columns and entablature of the **Tempio di Saturno** also date back to the 5th century B.C. The triumphal **Arco di Settimio Severo** is in its shadow, covered with friezes celebrating the emperor's war victories. The rebuilt brick **Curia Iulia** commemorates the site where the Roman Senate used to meet.

Across the modern Via dei Fori Imperiali are a string of forums built by emperors Augustus, Nerva, and Trajan. The **Colonna Traiana**, wrapped with a finely carved continuous bas-relief, marks the end of the excavations.

Left, Colosseo

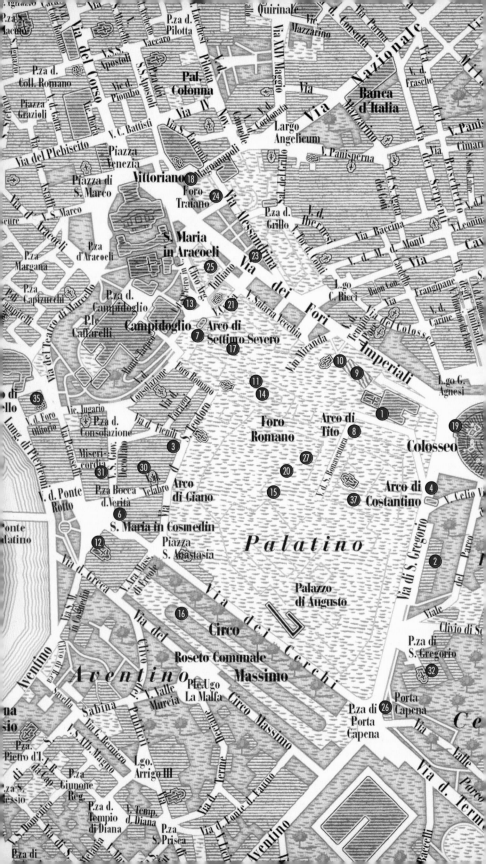

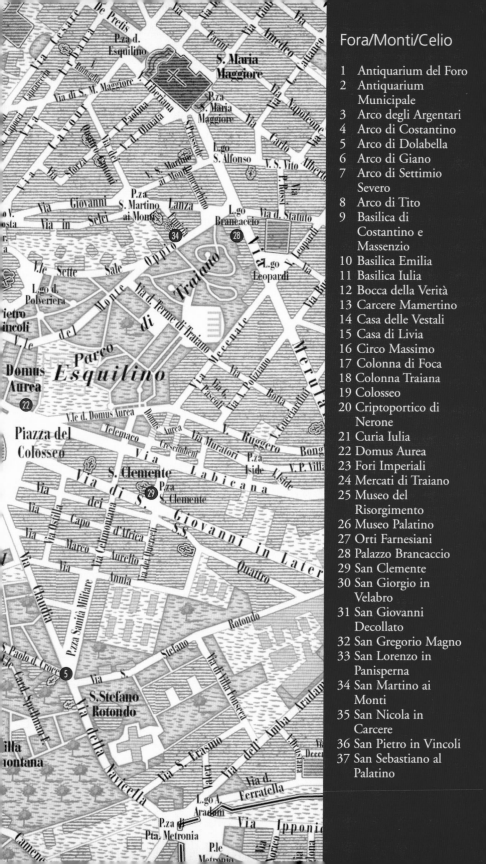

Fora/Monti/Celio

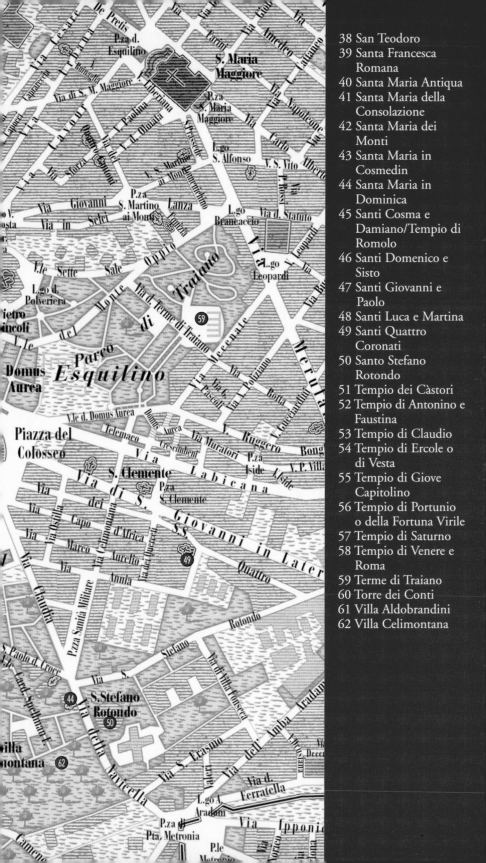

Arco di Costantino

ARCO DI COSTANTINO (ARCH OF CONSTANTINE)

Between Via di San Gregorio and Piazza del Colosseo

➢ Considered Rome's best-conserved and most spectacular arch, the Arch of Constantine was built in A.D. 315 to commemorate Constantine's victory over coemperor Maxentius, his political rival.

It actually consists of three separate arches, and incorporates spoils of other monuments, as the builders introduced the practice of plundering older monuments. Much of the upper relief work comes from the Arch of Trajan, as do some of the sculptures. The eight fluted Corinthian columns, made of *giallo antico* marble, come from a monument built under Domitian, which was destroyed as a response to Domitian's anti-Christian persecutions.

The Arch of Constantine spanned the Via Triumphalis, or Triumphal Way, the site of victorious military processions. Named after the first Christian emperor, it offers a march through ancient Roman history, commemorating Rome's imperial past, its Christianization, and its decline. During the Middle Ages the arch was incorporated in the Frangipane Fortresses and thereby survived several attacks on Rome. In 1804, the surrounding buildings were demolished.

BOCCA DELLA VERITÀ (MOUTH OF TRUTH)

Piazza della Bocca della Verità, 18; tel.: 06-6781419; open: daily 9 A.M.–6 P.M. (summer), 9:30 A.M.–5 P.M. (winter).

➢ To the left, under the portico of the Church of Santa Maria in Cosmedin, is the most famous ancient Roman drain cover. It is known as the *Bocca della Verità*, or the Mouth of Truth, and has no connection with the church. A large stone disk, it represents the face of an ancient god and, according to medieval legend, will chop off the hands of those who lie or who dare to insert their hands in its mouth.

Between 1796 and 1864, heads, not hands, rolled by the Bocca della Verità, as the area became a site for public executions. In those years, G. B. Bugatti, known as Mastro Titta, the most active Vatican executioner, managed to behead 516 people.

CARCERE MAMERTINO (MAMERTINE PRISON)

Clivio Argentario, 1; tel.: 06-6792902; open: daily 9 A.M.–12:30 P.M., 2:30–6:30 P.M. (summer), 9 A.M.–noon, 2–5 P.M. (winter); admission: offering.

➢ In the northern part of the Forum, where the Temple of Concord used to stand, is the Mamertine Prison. This ancient prison consisted of two subterranean dungeons, one below the other, with only one round aperture in the center of each vault, through which light, air, food, and men could pass. No other means of ventilation, drainage, or access existed. The walls of large stone blocks had rings fastened into them for securing the prisoners, but many inmates were laid on the floor with their feet fastened in stocks. The upper dungeon is mentioned by Livy as having been made by Ancus Martius, the fourth king of Rome, in c. 640 B.C. An inscription on the front records that the building was restored in the 1st century A.D. The lower dungeon, a dark, gravelike room, was called Tullianum, perhaps from Servius Tullius, who, according to Varro, excavated it out of the solid rock in 578 B.C. Saints Peter and Paul are thought to have been cast into the lower dungeon during Nero's persecution of Christians in A.D. 65 or 66, and are said to have lain here eight or nine months, bound to the wall with chains.

CASA DI LIVIA (HOUSE OF LIVIA)

Entrance on Via di San Gregorio and near the Arch of Titus on Via Sacra; tel.: 06-39749907; open: daily 9 A.M.–7 P.M. (4 P.M. in winter); closed: public holidays; admission: €7 (includes entry to the Palatine Museum).

➢ This 1st-century-B.C. house is possibly the best-preserved house on the Palatine Hill. It was part of the home of Emperor Augustus, where he lived with his second wife, Livia, for 40 years. He most likely slept in the small bedroom. The house now lies on the ground level of the Palatine Hill. To reach the house's courtyard, it is necessary to walk down some steps and along a paved corridor. In the middle of the three reception rooms are frescoes including a scene with ancient gods, quite faded now. In the room to the left are frescoes of griffins and other beasts, while the room to the right has frescoes of cityscapes and colorful landscapes. The floor is in mosaic with black-and-white tiles.

Bocca della Verità

CIRCO MASSIMO (CIRCUS MAXIMUS)

Via del Circo Massimo

➤ Originally built in the 4th century B.C. and repeatedly destroyed and rebuilt, the Circus Maximus has been the site of races and festivities since the time of Caesar. Augustus added the imperial stand and then the obelisk (now in Piazza del Popolo). After the big fire of A.D. 64, Trajan rebuilt the circus bringing its capacity to almost 300,000 spectators. In 357 Emperor Constans II brought an obelisk from Thebes (now in the Piazza del Laterano). The last races were held here in 549.

On the south side of the circus there is still a tower, the Torre della Moletta, which was once part of a medieval fortification system that included the Colosseum and the Arch of Titus. During the 16th century the side facing the Aventine Hill was used as a Jewish cemetery.

COLONNA TRAIANA (COLUMN OF TRAJAN)

Via dei Fori Imperiali

➤ The Column of Trajan, erected by the Senate and people of Rome in 113, is composed of 34 blocks of marble, and is covered with a spiral band of high reliefs describing the fortunes of the Dacian wars. It was an innovative concept in the history of Roman monumental architecture. The column was not meant to be observed from far away; rather, it was meant to be read like a marble parchment from the adjacent buildings. The 23 spirals of bas-reliefs had 2,500 figures, originally painted in color. It was formerly crowned by a statue of Trajan holding a gilt globe (which fell from its pedestal). It is now alighted by a figure of Saint Peter, commissioned by Sixtus V. The Senate and Emperor Hadrian decided to deposit Trajan's ashes underneath the column, in an urn of solid gold, which was never found. Inside the column, a small staircase with 185 steps leads to the top.

COLOSSEO (COLOSSEUM)

Piazza del Colosseo; tel.: 06-7004261; information and reservations: 06-39967700; open: 9 A.M.–1 hour before sunset, Sun. 9 A.M.–1 P.M.; admission: €5.

➤ This is one of the most striking and longest-lasting of Roman monuments. Begun by the Emperor Vespasian in A.D. 72 and finished by his son Titus in 80, the stadium was the work of captive Jews, who were brought to Rome after the destruction of Jerusalem.

Originally known as the Flavian Amphitheater, it was built on the site of Nero's man-made lake. The dedication lasted a hundred days, killing several thousand gladiators and 5,000 wild beasts. In 313, Emperor Constantine issued a decree forbidding gladiatorial shows, but they continued. In 404 Emperor Honorius decided to stop them forever, but it wasn't until 432 that gladiatorial combat was truly abolished, by Valentinian III. The last contests of wild animals on record were held in 523.

It first earned its name during the Middle Ages, from a huge gilt-bronze statue of the Roman emperor Nero, known as the *Colossus*, which stood near the amphitheater.

The outline of the building is elliptical, 607 feet in length and 512 feet across. It rises four stories, to a height of 159 feet, with a facade made entirely from travertine stone. The structure is made up of three circular tiers, each of which has 80 immense arches. The lower tier arches, the *vomitoria*, doubled as doorways for the spectators.

The arena itself is 253 by 153 feet, and covers extensive substructures for the needs and machinery of gladiatorial displays. Beneath were tunnels, with underground rooms and three-sided cages holding wild animals. A winch system (an early type of elevator) brought the caged animals up to the arena level, where a trap door would release them directly into the battle zone.

A system of awnings (called *velarium*) shaded the stands. It is estimated that the Colosseum provided seats for 55,000–85,000 spectators. The exterior of the building is faced with travertine; the interior is built of brick and covered with marble. A sophisticated entry system allowed separate access to reserved seats and ensured that different social classes were kept apart. The emperor and other notables, segregated from ordinary specta-

COLOSSEO

It is no fiction, but plain, sober, honest Truth, to say: so suggestive
and distinct is it at this hour: that, for a moment—actually in
passing in—they who will, may have the whole great pile before
them, as it used to be, with thousands of eager faces staring down
into the arena, and such a whirl of strife, and blood, and dust
going on there, as no language can describe. Its solitude, its awful
beauty, and its utter desolation, strike upon the stranger the next
moment, like a softened sorrow; and never in his life, perhaps, will
he be so moved and overcome by any sight, not immediately
connected with his own affections and afflictions . . . to climb into
its upper halls, and look down on ruin, ruin, ruin, all about it; the
triumphal arches of Constantine, Septimus Severus, and Titus; the
Roman Forum; the Palace of the Caesars; the temples of the old
religion, fallen down and gone; is to see the ghost of old Rome,
wicked, wonderful old city, haunting the very ground on which its
people trod. It is the most impressive, the most stately, the most
solemn, grand, majestic, mournful sight, conceivable. . . . Standing
there, a mountain among graves: so do its ancient influences outlive
all other remnants of the old mythology and old butchery of Rome.

—Charles Dickens, *Pictures from Italy*

tors, watched the games from a marble
podium, where they had a perfect view of
the arena.

This gigantic structure was so well built
that it still stands proudly today, nearly
2,000 years after its construction, despite
earthquakes, fires, war, and plundering.

In early medieval times, churches and
oratories were erected in the Colosseum.
In the 11th century the building became
a fortress, and two rival families, the
Frangipani and the Annibaldi, fought
over ownership until it became the
property of the Roman Senate and the
people of Rome in 1312. By 1381 the
part facing the Celian Hill had collapsed, and the rest was transformed
into a hospital.

During the Middle Ages the Colosseum
faced regular ransacking and was used primarily as a quarry for building materials.
It furnished materials for the Palazzo di
Venezia, the Pons Aemilius (Il Ponte
Rotto), the Palazzo della Cancelleria, and
the Palazzo Farnese. One of the last edifices built with its travertine was the
Palazzo Barberini, and this wanton spolia-
tion suggested the caustic remark: "Quod
non fecerunt Barbari fecerunt Barberni,"
or "What barbarians did not do, the
Barberini did."

During the 8th century, the Venerable
Bede wrote his famous proverb on the
Colosseum: "QUAMDIU STAT COLISAEUS,
STABIT ET ROMA: QUANDO CADET
COLISAEUS, CADET ET ROMA; QUANDO
CADET ROMA, CADET ET MUNDUS" [If the
Colosseum stands, so does Rome. If the
Colosseum collapses, so will Rome. And
when Rome collapses, the world will too].

CRIPTOPORTICO DI NERONE

In the Palatine, entrance on Via di San
Gregorio or near the Arch of Titus; tel.:
06-6990110/39749907; open: daily 9 A.M.–
7 P.M. (4 P.M. in winter); admission: €7
(includes entry to the Palatine Museum).
➤ The Criptoportico di Nerone is a subterranean passage, which Nero built to
connect the palaces of Augustus, Tiberius,
and Caligula to his majestic Golden
House.

Foro Romano (Roman Forum)

• Arco di Settimio Severo (The Arch of Septimius Severus)

Roman Forum, entrance on Largo Romono e Remo (Capitoline Hill) or on Via della Curia; tel.: 06-39749907; open: daily 9 A.M.–1 hour before sunset; closed: Jan 1, May 1, Dec. 25.
➤ Erected by the Senate in A.D. 203 and adorned with three barrel vaults, four free-standing composite columns on each facade, and bas-reliefs relating the victories of the emperor, this arch was built to celebrate Septimius Severus's 10th anniversary as emperor.

The four relief panels above the two lateral barrel vaults narrate victories in Parthia (modern Iran), as do the inscriptions on the upper part of the facades. This technique of the figurative relief recalls that of Marcus Aurelius's column, even though the narration here is simpler and more schematic.

When it was built, the arch was crowned by a large bronze group, with a carriage drawn by four horses and figures of Severus and his two sons, Caracalla and Geta. In 212, after Caracalla killed his brother Geta, he had his name erased from the inscription.

• Arco di Tito (Arch of Titus)

Roman Forum, entrance on Via Sacra; tel.: 06-39749907; open: daily 9 A.M.–1 hour before sunset; closed: Jan. 1, May 1, Dec. 25.
➤ Near the Church of Santa Francesca Romana is the Arch of Titus, a monument of Pentelic marble, built in A.D. 81 by the Roman Senate and by Domitian in honor of his brother Titus. It was erected to commemorate the victory of Titus and Vespasian over the Jews, which culminated in the destruction of Jerusalem.

One of the bas-reliefs depicts a triumphal march with Jewish captives and soldiers bearing the Golden Table; the seven-branched candlestick, or menorah; two censers; and other spoils of the Temple of Jerusalem. Titus brought these sacred spoils to Rome, and Vespasian placed them in his Temple of Peace.

During the Middle Ages the arch was turned into a tower, called Turris Chartularia, which was part of the Frangipane Fortress. In 1821 the fortress was taken down and the arch restored by Giuseppe Valadier, who integrated the

Arco di Tito

Basilica di Costantino e Massenzio

missing parts with travertine. Notwithstanding the heavy restorations of the 19th century, the Arch of Titus is one of the best-preserved monuments in Rome.

• BASILICA DI COSTANTINO E MASSENZIO (BASILICA OF CONSTANTINE AND MAXENTIUS)

Roman Forum, entrance on Largo Romolo e Remo or Arch of Titus on Via Sacra; tel.: 06-39749907; open: daily 9 A.M.–1 hour before sunset; closed: Jan 1, May 1, Dec. 25.

➢ The Basilica of Constantine and Maxentius, one of the most impressive ruins in the Forum, was begun by Maxentius and completed by Constantine (after he killed Maxentius) in the early 4th century A.D.

With a large interior set on a 70,000-square-foot platform, the basilica was divided into three separate aisles: two side aisles divided into three transversal chapels, each covered by a coffered barrel vault, and a central aisle covered by a cross vault. Its majestic proportions inspired many Renaissance artists, including Michelangelo, who may have been inspired by it for the plan of Saint Peter's.

The visible ruins belong to the north aisle, and one can still see the apse, which Constantine later added to the basilica. The apse, on the west end, was deeply recessed and housed a colossal statue of Constantine. The head, arms, and legs of the statue were made of white marble; the remaining parts were probably made of gilded bronze. The remains of the statue were found here and moved to the Palazzo dei Conservatori, in the Musei Capitolini. The podium at the center of the apse might indicate that the basilica was used as a seat of the *Praefectus Urbi* (law court) and the headquarters of Constantine. Eight colossal columns once decorated the interior, but Pope Paul V removed the last surviving one and placed it in front of Santa Maria Maggiore.

• BASILICA EMILIA

Roman Forum, entrance on Largo Romolo e Remo; tel.: 06-39749907; open: daily 9 A.M.–1 hour before sunset; closed Jan. 1, May 1, Dec. 25.

➢ Built in 179 B.C., facing the central piazza of the Roman Forum, the Basilica Emilia was one of the most ancient and richest basilicas in Rome. It was named after Marco Emilio Lepido, who restored it in 78 B.C. A large portico made a grand transition from exterior to interior, which included a large room used for the administration of justice and public affairs. Augustus rebuilt it after a fire, but it was permanently destroyed by another fire after the sack of Alaric in A.D. 410.

Tempio di Antonino e Faustina

• BASILICA IULIA

Roman Forum, entrance on Largo Romolo e
Remo or Via del Foro Romano; tel.: 06-
39749907; open: daily 9 A.M.–1 hour before
sunset; closed Jan. 1, May 1, Dec. 25.

➤ The side of the Forum just below the
entrance in Via del Foro Romano is dominated by the disinterred remains of the
Basilica Iulia, begun by Julius Caesar on
the remains of the Basilica Sempronia and
finished by Augustus. It was restored first
by Diocletian and then by G. Vettius
Probanus in A.D. 146. The plan was rectangular with a broad central nave separated from the side aisles by rows of columns.
Over the four side naves were galleries. At
the extremity farthest from the chief
entrance was a raised tribune, where the
Roman praetor or judge sat with his coun-
cillors, and which, in the adaptation,
became the sanctuary of the church. The
basilica served as a hall of justice or court
of law, and the bar at which the criminal
was arraigned was known as the *cancelli*.
The pillage of its material was so thorough
that all that remains of the original building is the pavement of the central room.
On the steps of the side of the basilica facing the Forum piazza, there are traces of
carved game boards on which the ancient
Romans used to play checkers and similar
games.

• CASA DELLE VESTALI (HOUSE OF THE VESTAL VIRGINS)

Roman Forum; entrance on Largo Romolo e
Remo; tel.: 06-39749907; open: daily
9 A.M.–1 hour before sunset; closed: Jan 1,
May 1, Dec. 25.

➤ This building was the home of the
vestals, the only order of priestesses in
Rome, chosen by the high priest as children and asked to remain virgins for 30
years. Their main task as vestals was to
guard the flame in the Temple of Vesta, the
goddess of the hearth and home. A vestal
who lost her virginity would be buried
alive with a loaf of bread and an oil lamp.

The stakes were high, but the vestals
were well rewarded for their chastity.
Unlike other women, vestals were allowed
to attend political meetings and trials and
sat in honorary places at gladiatorial
games. After the 30 years of service, they
were allowed to marry, but most did not.
(At that time, the average life span was 40
years.)

The building, discovered in 1883, consists
of a rectangular atrium surrounded by a
two-story portico. At the end of the great
hall were the rooms of the house and at the
long sides of the building were the sleeping
quarters. Some of the rooms had splendid
mosaics and pavements of multi-colored
marbles arranged in geometrical figures.

Between the pillars near the atrium stood the statues of the *Vestales Maximae,* the head vestals, which contained inscriptions recording the vestal virtues on their pedestals.

After the great fire in A.D. 64, Emperor Nero rebuilt the house and later continued to enlarge it. Christian Emperor Theodosius closed the temple in 394 as part of his campaign against Roman paganism.

• COLONNA DI FOCA (COLUMN OF PHOCAS)

Roman Forum; entrance on Largo Romolo e Remo.

➤ This column was erected in 608 to honor Constantinople Emperor Foca in gratitude for his donation of the Pantheon to Pope Bonifacius IV. This act probably saved this most exceptional Roman monument from being destroyed or dismantled for spoilage in the following centuries. The column was the last monument to be erected in the Forum.

• CURIA IULIA

Roman Forum, entrance on Largo Romolo e Remo; tel.: 06-39749907; open: daily 9 A.M.–1 hour before sunset; closed Jan. 1, May 1, Dec. 25.

➤ The Curia Iulia was built by Caesar as the seat of the Roman Senate, to replace the Curia Hostilia, which was destroyed by fire. It was completed by Augustus in A.D. 29 and was renovated by Domitian in 94. The present structure dates from the time of Diocletian, who ordered its reconstruction after the devastating fire of Carinus (283). Its bronze doors were used for the Basilica of San Giovanni in Laterano. The interior still has the extraordinary original marble floor. Two huge marble reliefs represent scenes of daily life and events during the reign of Trajan.

• SANTA MARIA ANTIQUA

Roman Forum; closed to the public, open on request (Soprintendenza Archeologica; tel.: 06-6990110).

➤ In 1900 the Church of Santa Maria Liberatrice, which stood just above the House of the Vestal Virgins, was taken down, and beneath it, serving as its foundation, were found the splendid remains of a Christian basilica that was already called old, *antiqua,* in the 7th century.

The basilica is adorned with frescoes of the Crucifixion, angels, saints, and *Our Lady and the Divine Child,* all of which are beginning to fade from exposure. The church was built in a part of Domitian's palace at the foot of the Palatine, and was destroyed by an earthquake in the middle of the 9th century.

• TEMPIO DEI CÀSTORI (TEMPLE OF CASTOR)

Roman Forum, entrance on Largo Romolo e Remo or Via del Foro Romano; tel.: 06-39749907; open: daily 9 A.M.–1 hour before sunset; closed: Jan. 1, May 1, Dec. 25.

➤ This very ancient temple, inaugurated in 484 B.C., was rebuilt in 117 B.C. and again in A.D. 6 by Tiberius, who covered it entirely in marble. All that remains now are three slim Corinthian columns. A block of marble from this temple was used by Michelangelo to build the base of Marcus Aurelius's equestrian statue in Piazza del Campidoglio.

• TEMPIO DI ANTONINO E FAUSTINA (TEMPLE OF ANTONINUS AND FAUSTINA)

Roman Forum; entrance on Largo Romolo e Remo, near the Arch of Titus on Via Sacra; open: daily 9 A.M.–1 hour before sunset; church open: Thurs. 10 A.M.–noon (ring the bell); closed: Jan. 1, May 1, Dec. 25.

➤ The temple was originally dedicated to Faustina, the wife of the emperor Antoninus Pius, in A.D. 141. Twenty years later, following the emperor's death, it was also dedicated to him, hence the two names. The magnificent portico and frieze are very well preserved. The ten huge columns, approximately 52 feet high, are made from a cipollino marble. The diagonal grooves visible on the upper part of the columns were carved to fasten ropes in a vain attempt to bring down the building to reuse its building materials. The podium, on which the temple rests, is still in its original form but the steps leading up to the temple have been reconstructed. The temple later became a church, probably in the 7th century. It was named after San Lorenzo in Miranda, who was sentenced to death there. In 1602, the church was rebuilt, and a baroque facade was added by Orazio Torriani behind the columns of the old temple. Two damaged statues, probably representing the emperor and his wife, were found underground during construction, and were then placed in the pronaos. On the left side of the building, the frieze, with griffins, acanthus scrolls, and candelabra, is still visible and well preserved.

• Tempio di Saturno (Temple of Saturn)

Roman Forum, entrance on Capitoline Hill or Largo Romolo e Remo; tel.: 06-39749907; open: daily 9 A.M.–1 hour before sunset; closed: Jan. 1, May 1, Dec. 25.

➤ The first temple dedicated to Saturn was here as early as 497 B.C. Originally built in Ionic style, it was rebuilt several times. Today's temple dates back to 42 B.C. and it is the most noticeable ruin between the Forum and Capitoline Hill. It presents a high platform, eight columns, and a section of entablature. The friezed architrave blocks were posed in 30 B.C. As the different colors of the columns testify, the Temple of Saturn is a splendid example of *spolia*, the practice of recycling materials or elements from more ancient buildings. From the earliest time, the temple had housed the public treasury. Saturn was by far the most popular god in Rome as he was thought to have presided over a long period of prosperity, peace, and civil freedom. He was thus feted, for a week, at the end of December. Family members and friends exchanged gifts, and his statue was draped and carried in procession through the city.

• Tempio di Venere e Roma (Temple of Venus and Rome)

Roman Forum, entrance near the Arch of Titus on Via Sacra; tel.: 06-39749907; closed to the public, open only on request (Soprintendenza Archeologica).

➤ The Temple of Venus and Rome was erected by Emperor Hadrian in A.D. 121 to honor the goddess Venus, mother of the Julio-Claudian dynasty, and founder of the empire and Rome. It was the largest temple in Rome. In order to build it, Hadrian had the colossal statue of Nero moved to the side of the Flavian Amphitheater (which, because of this statue, became known as the Colosseum). The highly original plan, with two tangential *cellae* facing opposite directions, is a creation of Hadrian's genius. The temple was completed by Antoninus Pius and was restored by Maxentius in 307, after a fire damaged it. In the 8th century the vestibule dedicated to the goddess Roma was converted into a church initially dedicated to Saints Peter and Paul, subsequently to Santa Maria Nova, and finally to Santa Francesca Romana.

Orti Farnesiani

Fori Imperiali (Imperial Fora)

Main entrance on Via dei Fori Imperiali, a short walk from Piazza Venezia; tel.: 06-6990110; information and reservations: 06-39967700; open: daily 9 A.M.–1 hour before sunset; closed: Jan. 1, May 1 and Dec. 25; admission: €6 (Roman Forum free of charge).

• Mercati di Traiano and Fori Imperiali (Markets of Trajan and Imperial Fora)

Via IV Novembre, 94; tel.: 06-6790048; open: 9 A.M.–6:30 P.M. (summer), 9 A.M.–4:30 P.M. (winter); closed: Mon.; admission: €6. ➢ With the construction of the new forum, Julius Caesar, like many victorious generals of the late Republic, intended to celebrate his political importance while at the same time emphasizing the divine favor he enjoyed from Venus, the mythological progenitor of the family of the *gens Iulia*.

Adjacent and connected to Caesar's Forum is the Augustan Forum, built by Augustus on an area purchased with his own funds. The complex is bordered by the densely populated Suburra neighborhood where a high wall still intact served to protect it from fire. Inaugurated in the year A.D. 2, the Temple of Mars the Avenger (Marte Ultore) backs up onto the rear wall. A small square flanked by porticos decorated with caryatids stood in front of the temple. The northern, left-hand portico opens onto the Aula del Colosso, restored with its original colored marble floors and walls. A base at the rear once supported a colossal statue probably depicting the emperor's protective divinity, or *genio*. The southern portico hosted statues of the *summi viri*, the most important protagonists in Rome's history, whereas the northern portico hosted statues of the members of the *gens Iulia*. In the square's center stood a statue of the emperor on a triumphant, four-horse chariot.

Domitian later erected the Arch of Titus and began construction of a new forum inaugurated by and named after Nerva in A.D. 97. Three times as long as it is wide, it stretched approximately 150 yards from the Temple of Minerva to the Roman Forum. It also became known as the Forum Transitorium, because it served as a passageway to the Roman Forum. The Forum of Nerva consisted of an oblong rectangular square closed on the short end by the temple dedicated to Minerva. Because of a lack of space, columns extending just beyond the walls took the place of the porticos and were topped by a decoration of female figures in high relief representing the myth of Athena and Aracne. Located behind the temple was the Porticus Absidata, a semicircular structure of various orders of pilasters that served as the monumental entrance.

In the second century, Rome had reached its height of urban expansion and exceeded a million inhabitants. The emperor Trajan not only restored the fora of Caesar and Augustus, but also began construction of the grandest imperial forum—Trajan's Forum, which was inaugurated between A.D. 112 and 113. Boasting the most articulate plan of all, it is chronologically the last of the imperial fora. A square flanked by side porticos hosted an equestrian statue of the emperor. The Basilica Ulpia, with its colonnaded facade and five-naved interior, closed off the rear. Behind the basilica, Trajan's Column rose from a narrow courtyard paralleled by the libraries with their porticoed facades. There was also a temple dedicated to the "Divo" Trajan and "Diva" Plotina, as both the emperor and empress were deified after their deaths. The area used for the Forum was created by digging out a portion of the ridge that probably connected the Quirinale and the Capitoline Hills. The cost of the colossal endeavor was covered by the spoils that came with the conquest of Dacia—today's Romania—led by Trajan between A.D. 101 and 106. The decorations of the entire complex and, in particular, the frieze that runs along the column, celebrate this glorious military campaign as the justification of the emperor's apotheosis. The complex of the Forum of Trajan was intended as a monument to the self-assertion of a monarch in his capitol, a permanent emblem of his political propaganda.

The Markets of Trajan, as they are known today, refer to a series of buildings constructed on various levels at the same time as Trajan's Forum. The lower portion includes the greater semicircle, articulated on three floors, and the lesser semicircle, also articulated on three floors. The upper and lower portions are separated by an actual city street that in the late empire was called the Via Biberatica. Along its way taverns—stores—line the third story of the greater semicircle. On the opposite side stands the central complex with additional taverns at ground level along the Via Biberatica and another three stories that include more architecturally elaborate structures complete with niches and apses.

ORTI FARNESIANI (FARNESE GARDENS)

Entrance and ticket kiosks: Via di San Gregorio and near the Arch of Titus on Via Sacra; tel.: 06-39749907; open: daily 9 A.M.– 7 P.M. (4 P.M. in winter).

➤ The gardens were designed by Vignola for Cardinal Farnese between 1520 and 1589. Pope Paul III decorated them with statues moved from ancient monuments in the vicinity. They were turned into a villa when the two large bird cages over the nymphaeum were fused into a small house.

SANTA FRANCESCA ROMANA (OR SANTA MARIA NUOVA)

Piazza di Santa Francesca Romana; tel.: 06-6795528; open: daily 9:30 A.M.– noon, 4–7 P.M.

➤ This church, built by Saint Leo IV in 850, replaced the ancient Santa Maria Antiqua in the Roman Forum. Its name was changed from Santa Maria Nuova to Santa Francesca after the saint's canonization in 1608. In 1216 it was destroyed by fire. The only part spared was the tribune, or sanctuary, with its mosaics and the ancient picture of the Virgin Mary. Pope Honorius III restored the church in 1220, and Paul V modernized it giving it its present white travertine facade in 1615. The 12th-century bell tower is decorated with majolica pieces. The altar of the *Confession* was designed by Bernini in c. 1640. The "Tempietto" is rich in bronzes, marbles, jasper, and other precious stones. The marble group of *Saint Frances and the Angel* is by G. Meli (1866). The tomb of the saint, who died in 1440, is located in the crypt. The remarkable mosaic in the apse dates from 1160 and is comparable to those in San Clemente and Santa Maria in Travestere. The Virgin and child, on wood, is from the 13th century. During

the restoration of 1949, a precious 7th-century icon, the *Madonna Glycophilousa,* was found under the painting and is now in the sacristy. In the wall of the right transept is the stone that, according to legend, retains the impression of Saint Peter's knees. In the left transept is a handsome marble ciborium in the style of Mino da Fiesole.

SANTI COSMA E DAMIANO/ TEMPIO DI ROMOLO (TEMPLE OF ROMULUS)

Via dei Fori Imperiali, 1; tel.: 06-6991540; open: daily 9 A.M.–1 P.M., 3–7 P.M.

➤ The approach to this ancient church is by a side street near the Forum end of the Via Cavour. It was originally the Library of the Forum of Peace (Biblioteca Forum Pacis), where the archives of the census taker, the municipal plans, and registration lists were probably kept. Adjoining it and forming part of the present church is a circular temple erected by the Emperor Maxentius for his son Romulus. The two temples were transformed into a church in 527, and dedicated to Saints Cosmas and Damian, two martyrs who were killed in the persecution of Diocletian. In 780 the church was restored. In c. 1633 the floor, considerably beneath the level of the soil, made the church damp and unhealthy. Pope Urban VIII raised the level of the floor so as to be even with the ground, and thus an upper and lower church were formed; beneath the latter is an ancient crypt.

SANTI LUCA E MARTINA

Via della Curia, across from Mamertine Prison; tel.: 06-39749907; open: daily 9 A.M.–1 hour before sunset; closed: Jan. 1, May 1, Dec. 25.

➤ Close to the Mamertine Prison is the Church of Santi Luca e Martina, built originally in the 7th century on the ruins of the Secretarium Senatus, the closed-door criminal court instituted in A.D. 412. It was restored in 1256, and rebuilt from the designs of Pietro da Cortona in 1634. In 1588 Pope Sixtus V granted the church to the artists' academy, the Accademia Nazionale di San Luca. The luminous interior, in the form of a Greek cross, is adorned with columns and pilasters. The marble statue of Saint

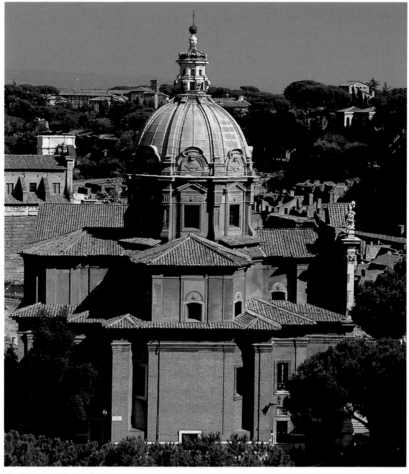

Santi Luca e Martina

Martina, under the altar, is much admired. The beautiful octagonal Chapel of the Crypt is decorated with polychrome marbles in sharp contrast to the whiteness of the church above. It was also designed by Pietro da Cortona as a receptacle for the shrine of the saint.

TEMPIO DI ERCOLE O DI VESTA (TEMPLE OF HERCULES OR VESTA, OR ROUND TEMPLE)
Piazza della Bocca della Verità
➤ This perfectly preserved temple is the oldest surviving marble structure in Rome. Erroneously considered to be dedicated to Vesta, this temple, designed by the architect Hermodorus from Salamina, was erected in the 2nd century B.C. with the spoils of the victorious campaigns against Greece by L. Mummius, the destroyer of Corinth. The *cella* is surrounded by 20 columns with Corinthian capitals in the Hellenistic style. An inscription on the base of the statue recalls the name of the sculptor Skopas.

The upper part of the building was entirely lost and the sloping roof is modern. During the restorations undertaken by Tiberius in A.D. 15, nine columns and 11 capitals were redone in Luna marble (Carrara). In the 12th century the temple was converted into the Church of Santo Stefano delle Carrozze and later into Santa Maria del Sole (16th century). The frieze on the walls dates from the 15th century. The interior contains a 15th-century Roman school fresco, the *Virgin and Child with Saints*.

TEMPIO DI GIOVE CAPITOLINO (TEMPLE OF JUPITER)

Via del Tempio di Giove (Capitoline Hill)

➤ Inside the Palazzo dei Conservatori, a solid basement of *cappellacio* tufa blocks is visible. The wall was one side of the podium of the Temple of Jupiter. The temple was the center of Roman religion and politics. It presented a six-columned facade that was oriented toward the Forum. According to legend, it was erected by Tarquinius Priscus and completed by his son Tarquinius Superbus in 509 B.C. The style was Etruscan but its size was far greater than usual canons: the podium was 175 by 200 feet and 18 impressive stone columns (69-feet tall) formed the porch. Behind the porch were three *cellae* dedicated to Jupiter (center), his wife Juno (left), and Minerva (right). The roof was wooden, a common feature of the center-Italian architecture of that time, and decorated with terra-cotta polychrome. The sculptural decoration had been executed by artists from Etruria, perhaps Veio, and belonged to the school of Vulca, the most important sculptor of the time. The temple went through three fires (83 B.C., A.D. 69, and A.D. 80) and it was rebuilt by Silla, Vespasian, and Domitian. On the left of the entrance of Palazzo Caffarelli are several ruins of the temple.

TEMPIO DI PORTUNIO O DELLA FORTUNA VIRILE (TEMPLE OF PORTUNUS OR OF FORTUNA VIRILIS)

Piazza della Bocca della Verità

➤ The Temple of Fortuna Virilis, situated in a grassy enclave beside the Tiber, dates from the 2nd century B.C. A very well-preserved monument of the Republican era, it consists of a rectangular building, set on a podium, with four travertine columns to the front, two on the sides, and 12 columns embedded inside the wall of a room. This room is known as the *cella* and housed the image of the god of rivers and ports, Portunus. The Ionic capitals are made of stucco-covered travertine. During the Middle Ages the temple was reconsecrated as a church of Santa Maria de Gradellis and, during the Renaissance, rededicated to Santa Maria Egiziaca, or Saint Mary Egyptian.

TERME DI TRAIANO (BATHS OF TRAJAN)

Parco del Colle Oppio

➤ Apollodorus of Damascus, Trajan's favorite architect and the designer of the Forum, designed Trajan's Baths. They were built in just five years on the ruins of Nero's Domus Aurea after the fire of A.D. 104. They were the first imperial baths to be so large and became the model of the Baths of Caracalla, Decius, Diocletian, and Constantine. The main bath block measured 600 by 450 feet and presented a linear sequence made of an open-air Olympic-size swimming pool (*natatio*), covered cold hall (*frigidarium*), some small intermediary warm rooms (*tepidarium*), and huge hot hall (*caldarium*). The baths were richly decorated with works of art that had been taken from the Domus Aurea, such as the famous *Laocoön* found here in 1506. The facilities included libraries, shops, and a stadium. The main body was surrounded by a larger order of columns measuring some 100 by 750 feet which, in turn, were flanked by gardens and storage. Today visitors can still see a semicircular terrace at the southwest side of the platform, a semicircular *exedra* in brick-faced concrete at the western corner of the precinct, two walls of the central bathing block, and a semicircular fountain house at the eastern corner. Water was supplied by a cistern known as the "Sette Sale" (seven rooms) located outside the compound of the baths and still perfectly preserved. (To visit, contact the Sovrain-tendenza del Comune di Roma, tel.: 06-67103819.)

Walking Tour 1:

Revisiting Early Christianity in Il Velabro

By Ruth Kaplan

Formerly a low-lying swamp area, Il Velabro is tucked between the Capitoline Hill, the Roman Forum, the Palatine Hill, and the Tiber. Remarkably quiet considering its central location, this area is one of Rome's oldest. Romulus and Remus are said to have been suckled here by the she-wolf before the founding of Rome. Later came the city's central grain and cattle markets. By the 7th century A.D., this stretch of the Tiber's edge was known as the *ripa graeca*, or the Greek bank, after a heavy influx of Greek Christian refugees settled here and started work on many of the area's churches.

The **Church of San Nicola in Carcere** is one of Rome's most overt examples of the city's architectural layering. Located on the corner of Via del Teatro di Marcello and Via di Monte Savello, the church's outer walls incorporate original columns from three Republican-era temples. The right brick wall is built around seven exposed peperino columns with Ionic capitals from the Temple of Janus. More chunks of fallen marble litter the grass lawn in front of it. Six taller, travertine columns with Ionic capitals show through the left outer wall, remnants of the Temple of Spes. The peperino column included on the left of the facade of the church and the fragment of the podium, protruding from the frontal section, are part of the temple dedicated to Juno Sospita over which the church was built. Remains of the fourth temple, dedicated to Pity, have been discovered recently and are visible in the area of the Theater of Marcellus.

Rome's Greek community built this church, dedicated to Saint Nicholas of Myra. It took the name *in carcere*—"in prison"— because the grounds

San Nicola in Carcere

San Teodoro

were formerly used as exactly that. The building dates back at least to the later part of the 9th century, when it was first mentioned in church records. After being restored in 1090 and 1128, Giacomo Della Porta touched up the church in 1599, adding a rectangular off-white facade with two classical columns in relief. The pilasters and walls inside the boxy nave are done in convincing faux marble, and colorful frescoes cover the upper walls. Two rows of mismatched ancient columns split the nave into three parts. Lorenzo Costa's painting on wood of the Ascension sits high at the end of the left aisle. The green porphyry urn on the altar contains the remains of various Christian martyrs.

Diagonally across the street from San Nicola in Carcere is the large Area Sacra di Sant'Omobono with the excavated remains of temples dating back at least to the beginning of the Republican era. Continue along Vicus Iugarius, which opens up into a large piazza at the foot of Santa Maria della Consolazione, an aging early baroque church sitting atop a tall marble stair- case. To the left of the piazza is the Tarpeian Rock, the cliff-like edge of the Capitoline Hill where ancient Romans once threw traitors to their deaths.

Built in 1470, **Santa Maria della Consolazione** was named for a paint- ing of Mary underwritten by a rich man condemned to death, to serve as consolation for other prisoners in their final moments. In the late 16th century the church was reconstructed and the intricately carved facade was added.

A few points of interest are spotlighted in the church's dark interior. The first chapel on the right was frescoed by Taddeo Zuccari in 1556. The paintings depict the life of Christ using large figures, with a fine sense of form, perspective, and movement, especially in the Flagellation and Crucifixion scenes. The intri- cately vaulted chapel ceiling is fully painted, too. Over the altar is the church's namesake fresco, the 14th-century *Madonna della Consolazione,* repainted by Antoniazzo Romano two centuries later. Despite the touch-up job, the painting renders a delicate image of Mary draped in blue with a curious-eyed Christ child in her lap, holding a sphere in his hand. Raffaello da Montelupo's 1530 marble relief of the *Marriage of Saint Catherine* is located in the first chapel on the left.

Turn the corner onto Via di San Teodoro, with a thick line of trees blocking off this neighborhood from the Forum down below. As the street curves right again, massive brick ruins of the Palatine Hill rise up on the left, and continue until the street ends at the Circus Maximus. Halfway down the street, recessed into the Palatine's lap, is the **Church of San Teodoro**. The small, barrel-shaped church was built in the 6th century, a period of heavy Byzantine influence in Rome—Saint Theodore himself was a Christian soldier from the Eastern church. This site had already been used as a Christian welfare center before the church was built. Called *diaconia*, these community centers were established by the church between the 6th and 8th centuries to compensate for the declining presence of civil government and social services in the city. (The *Lupa* is an Etruscan bronze from the 5th century B.C.; *Romolo e Remo* is a Renaissance addition.)

A 6th-century mosaic remains in the apse, but the present church was built in 1453, when the cupola was added. Two curving staircases lead down from the street into a recessed courtyard designed by Carlo Fontana in 1705.

Continue down Via di San Teodoro and turn right onto Via del Velabro, passing the Church of San Giorgio in Velabro on your right (see Focus). Turn right again onto Via di San Giovanni Decollato, home to the splendid **Oratory of San Giovanni Decallato**, packed with 16th-century frescoes by the Roman mannerists. The church-oratory-cloister complex was built in 1488–1504 by a Florentine confraternity devoted to the confession and burial of prisoners condemned to beheading. The oratory is not open to the public but visits can be arranged by calling in advance; ring the "Arciconfraternita" buzzer at No. 22 to be let in.

Expansive and expressive frescoes by mannerist painters Jacopino del Conte, Francesco Salviati, and Pirro Ligorio cover the walls of the oratory of San Giovanni Decollato, dominating the rectangular space with vivid oversized figures engaged in scenes from the life (and gruesome beheading) of Saint John the Baptist. The church is also covered with frescoes and fine stucco decoration done in the late 16th century.

Pomarancio's oil painting of the Visitation is the third on the right side of the nave. The main altar holds Vasari's crisp *Beheading of Saint John*. A fragment of a stylistically older Mother and child fresco hangs in the first niche on the left, a hold-over from the 12th-century church that used to stand on this ground.

Seven white carved marble discs line the walkway around the small, tree-filled cloister: they mark the group graves of the executed, six for men and one for women, whose bones remain buried here.

OUR PICK

Finally, there is **Santa Maria in Cosmedin**, the area's greatest repository of medieval art. Before approaching the church, take a look at its elegant bell tower, a light, seven-tiered structure built in 1123. By the time the bell tower came around, Santa Maria in Cosmedin was already more than 300 years old, built in the 8th century by Pope Adrian I and assigned to Greek refugees from Constantinople. Various elements of the site's previous buildings were incorporated into the church: the foundations of an imperial market inspector's office, the side walls of an early *diaconia*, and the floor plan of an early temple of Hercules. The present church is the result of a radical restoration campaign in the 19th century that erased most of the post-medieval structures. The liturgical furnishings were recovered, the ceiling was removed so that fragments of a fresco cycle with episodes from the Old Testament (1123) were revealed on the upper walls, and the three apses were repainted in the style of the period. The few remaining patches of the 12th-century frescoes constitute one of the most important examples of the Romanesque classic-inspired painting. The church's brick portico is the unlikely home of the Bocca della Verità, the Mouth of Truth, the famous Roman drain cover (see page 28).

The first piece of medieval art you encounter is a framed chunk of an 8th-century mosaic of the Adoration of the Magi, hanging on the wall of the sacristy. Next comes the chapel off to the right, with its spotlighted *Madonna and Child*, complete with Greek writing across the bottom from the 15th century.

The small, darkened nave balances an inventive Cosmati floor made of multicolored marble chips with the simplicity of plain cement-colored walls. Much of the nave is taken up by the intricately carved marble choir. The equally filigreed Gothic altar is cordoned off from the body of the church by a line of thin, raised marble columns. The stone bishop's throne, with a Cosmatesque colored target high on its back and arms made of fat carved lions, faces the altar's centerpiece, a baldacchino (canopy) composed of four red Egyptian-granite columns supporting the vertical marble Gothic structures inlaid with intricate mosaics on a gold ground.

Santa Maria in Cosmedin

FURTHER INFORMATION

San Giovanni Decollato
Via di San Giovanni Decollato, 22; tel.: 06-6791890; open: call in the morning to organize a visit.

San Nicola in Carcere
Via del Teatro di Marcello, 46; tel.: 06-68307198; open: Mon.–Sat. 7:30 A.M.–noon, 4–7 P.M., Sun. 10 A.M.–1 P.M.

Santa Maria della Consolazione
Piazza della Consolazione, 84; tel.: 06-6784654; open: daily 7 A.M.–noon, 3:30–6:30 P.M.

Santa Maria in Cosmedin
Piazza della Bocca della Verità, 18; tel.: 06-6781419; open: daily 9 A.M.–1 P.M., 2:30–6 P.M. (5 P.M. in winter).

San Teodoro
Via di San Teodoro; tel.: 06-6786624; open: daily 10 A.M.–6 P.M. (but currently closed for restorations).

FOCUS: SAN GIORGIO IN VELABRO

Via del Velabro, 19; tel.: 06-6793335; open: daily 10 A.M.–12:30 P.M., 4–6:30 P.M.

By Ruth Kaplan

By the time Pope Gregory IV completely rebuilt this church in the 9th century, its location had already been well-known for over a millennium. It used to be the heart of the *velabrum*, the fluvial swamp where, according to the legend, Romulus and Remus were found being fed by a she-wolf. As early as the 5th century, Rome's Greek community had built a church here to worship Saint George, a Christian martyr from Cappadocia (modern-day Turkey).

Renovations in the 12th century added the brick bell tower. The handsome brick portico decorated with marble columns and assorted Latin inscriptions has survived a series of disasters. A plaque records the high water mark from an 1870 flood, which reached about three-feet high in the portico alone—deeper still inside the church itself. And on the night of July 27–28, 1993, a car bomb attributed to the Mafia exploded in the piazza in front of the church, blowing off the entire portico. It has since been carefully reconstructed using original columns and bricks found in the rubble. Photographs in the back right corner of the church document the reconstruction.

Three steps lead down into the wide, stone-floored nave. The columns separating the two side aisles are particularly interesting, being a mix of fluted and flat granite plus some darker columns taken from ancient monuments. The nave is slightly trapezoidal, narrowing toward the altar and subtly lengthening the space.

Pietro Cavallini's 1295 apse fresco, *Christ and the Virgin Mary*, is the only decorative painting in the church. It was repainted in the 16th century. The 13th-century marble altar and canopy are the real visual focus of the church. Four columns surround the altar, supporting a square colonnade of miniature columns no more than eight inches tall. Two smaller octagonal colonnades slope upward toward the peak.

Attached to the church is the Arco degli Argentari, an elaborately carved square arch erected in A.D. 204. It was built by the city's *argentari*, or money changers, to honor the emperor Septimius Severus and his family. Basreliefs of the imperial family on the inner walls took a beating after Septimius Severus's son Caracalla rose to power by killing his brother Geta, who is noticeably missing in the carved family portrait.

San Giorgio in Velabro

Walking Tour 2:

Il Celio

By Ruth Kaplan

Hiding just across the street from the Colosseum is one of the few authentic neighborhoods in Rome that is also studded with world-class churches, quiet ancient streets, shady parks, and excellent, unpretentious restaurants. No more than a three-by-four grid of one-way streets, Il Celio exudes a relaxed coziness thanks to its borders: the Colosseum to the west, an ancient Roman retaining wall rising uphill to the south, a military hospital and a fortresslike monastery to the east, and the Colle Oppio park to the north.

An ideal place to shift gears from the Colosseum's swarm of traffic and tourists is the Colle Oppio park, a slanted sprawl of stone-paved walking paths and clumps of pine trees rising up on the ridge just north and east of the Colosseum. The iron-gated entrance leads to the park's tree-lined pedestrian main drag, which is usually invaded by toddlers and dogs during daylight hours. The canopy of tall trees at the far end of the park houses a pleasant outdoor café offering cappuccinos and pastries or gin and tonics and chips, depending on the time of day.

The stairs south of the café lead out to Via Labicana. Just to the left across the street, taking up a whole oblong block, is **San Clemente**, whose plain, pious-looking exterior plays down its dazzling Byzantine mosaic and multiple layers of rich underground excavations. The church's main entrance leads straight into the side of the peaceful, colonnaded nave, naturally lit by an adjoining open courtyard at its far end. Its buckling floor is inlaid with the swirling, multicolored marble patterns typical of Rome's medieval churches (much of San Clemente's ground level was built in the 12th century), and the odd gray paving stone is carved with incomplete Latin inscriptions.

A striking gold-encrusted Roman mosaic covers the apse with a complex iconography of the Tree of Life that originates from the blood of Christ and alludes to the Church. Christ is flanked by "Agios Petrus" and "Agios Paulus"—that is, Saints Peter and Paul, with their names written in an unusual hybrid of transliterated Greek and Latin. The 12 disciples sit equally spaced in a ring framing the mosaic's bottom edge, mirrored by twelve sheep on a gleaming gold-tiled background.

In the chapel near the side entrance of the church, there are frescoes by Masolino da Panicale representing scenes from the life of Saint Catherine of Alexandria and Saint Ambrose. The frescoes are among the most important executed in Rome during the 15th century and clearly show the close tie between Masolino and his pupil Massaccio, to whom the paintings were formerly attributed.

Despite the balanced beauty of the ground level, the real attraction of San Clemente is in its sprawling undergrounds. Before entering the gift shop/ticket office for the ruins, take a look at the exposed ancient Roman brick arches reaching their peak at eye level: these are the tops of the tall arches that form the structural support of the Christian basilica built around the 4th century that occupied this space when Rome's ground level was about 15 feet lower than it is now.

A well-lit staircase leads down to the cool, spacious depths of the old basilica. Its earth walls are caked with an odd collection of Roman column capitals, angry marble faces and unidentifiable carved body parts, and other decorative sculpture fragments found on the site by excavators in the 19th century. Frescoes of Saint Clement and other lesser-known Christian figures dating back to as early as the 6th century remain intact, making the space feel more like an art gallery than an ancient basilica.

Another two-dozen steps lead to the second underground layer, a labyrinth of small, oddly shaped rooms jutting off a series of jagged, cramped,

San Clemente

but well-lit hallways. In the 3rd century this area was a Mithraeum, a place of worship of the Persian god, Mithras, as well as a school for training in the practices of the Mithraic cult, whose presence was not uncommon in Rome in the years before Christianity took root. The winding, sometimes shoulder-width hallways echo the flowing sounds of a natural spring that pours into one of the far rooms, which kept the Mithraeum almost completely flooded with water until 1912, when it was drained.

After exiting San Clemente through the palm-spotted courtyard, walk uphill to Via dei Santissimi Quattro, where you will find Il Celio's fruit and vegetable market (open: Mon.–Sat., 8 A.M.– 1 P.M.). It's the neighborhood's only source of fresh produce

Arco di Dolabella

within comfortable walking distance, and the half-dozen stands are well stocked and definitely worth a look for their color and variety, if not to buy a pound of whatever fruit is in season.

Keeping the Colosseum behind you, take the short uphill walk up Via dei Santi Quattro. Once you pass the car mechanics' shops that line the first intersection, the street is indistinguishable from how it looked in the 1600s: lush ivy spills down the tall stone walls that line the street, beaten-up wooden doors hang in their sagging frames, and there are no parked cars in sight—not even a *motorino*—thanks to the narrowness of the street as it rises uphill.

As the street flattens out at the top of the hill, you'll find yourself across from the entrance of the **Santi Quattro Coronati**, the church and monastery whose barrel-like fortified foundations loom over the eastern edge of Il Celio's residential streets. The main door leads into a sort of fortified piazza/parking lot adjoined to a sun-baked colonnaded courtyard. The only sound you're likely to hear is the murmur of a few of the Augustinian nuns who live there or a stray tourist admiring the church's prize, locked in a small chapel off the courtyard, a wildly Byzantine-influenced fresco cycle from the 13th century depicting the life of Constantine. The nuns will hand over the key upon request; a small contribution is expected afterward.

The fresco's ten well-preserved (and recently restored) panels are painted in meticulous detail. One panel shows a horse and rider levitating through a medieval arched city gate, with five wonderfully out-of-proportion onlookers looming over the cityscape behind. Other highlights are Constantine suffering from leprosy, with orderly arranged red boils equally spaced all over his face; and his baptism, which shows the Christian emperor squeezed into a baptismal font while his attendants tower over him holding his crown, robe, and matching striped umbrella.

Head back down the way you came, and turn left up the main commercial strip, Via Celimontana, continuing uphill until it merges with Via Claudia, and on Via della Vallicella enter the iron gates of the well-kept **Villa Celimontana**, a 16th-century estate whose grounds are now a public park. The villa itself is closed to the public, but the park unfurls in both directions over the Celian Hill, which was originally inhabited by, and named by, the ancient Etruscans. Its grassy slopes and lawns are used as soccer fields, while joggers and other pedestrians weave their way through the villa's packed-dirt walkways. There are plenty of shade-covered spots and benches, a small Neo-Gothic temple, a well-kept Japanese-style corner garden, and a few fish-filled round fountains. From the southern reaches of the park, you can see the remains of the ancient Aurelian Wall, the Baths of Caracalla, and, on a clear day, the Appenine Mountains rising up in the distance. An excellent jazz concert series is held here from June through August.

Coming out of the park, go back down toward the Colosseum and take the first left under the remains of the travertine **Arco di Dolabella** (**Arch of Dolabella**), used by Nero for his aqueduct feeding the Palatine Hill, onto Via di San Paolo della Croce, a secluded, countrylike road lined by garden walls fencing in tall Italian pines and palm trees. The steep, three-minute walk downhill leads under a series of arches that used to be part of original Roman shops and houses. The cobblestone street flattens out across from the foot of the Palatine Hill, where passing trams and traffic clearly delineate the calm of Il Celio from the rest of Rome.

Further Information

Arco di Dolabella (Arch of Dolabella)
Via S. Paolo della Croce at Piazza Celimontana.

San Clemente
Via di San Giovanni in Laterano or Piazza San Clemente; tel.: 06-70451018; open: Mon.–Sat. 9 A.M.–12:30 P.M., 3–6 P.M., Sun. and holidays open at 10 A.M.; admission: €3, for underground section.

Santi Quattro Coronati
Via dei Santi Quattro Coronati, 20; Capella di San Silvestro (which houses the medieval fresco cycle of the life of Constantine); open: Mon.–Sat. 9:30 A.M.–noon, 4:30–6 P.M., Sun. and holidays 9–10:40 A.M., 4–5:45 P.M.

Villa Celimontana
Piazza Santa Giovanni e Paolo delle Navicella; open: sunrise to sunset.

FOCUS: Domus Aurea

Viale della Domus Aurea (in the Colle Oppio); tel.: 06-39967700; open: 9 A.M.–7:45 P.M., Sat. (June 15–Sept 15) closes at 10 P.M.; closed: Mon.; admission: €6; advance booking required.

By Ruth Kaplan

Built on the Palatine Hill, the Domus Tiberiana was the first imperial Roman palace, home to the Julio-Claudian dynasty. But for Nero, it was not enough; after the fire in July of A.D. 64, he decided to build a new residence in the space created after the central Roman neighborhoods were totally gutted. The Domus Aurea, conceived by architects Severus and Celer, was a grandiose project.

The complex of buildings extended from the Palatine to the Esquiline and Celian Hills. Gardens and woods surrounded a great artificial lake, all of which were part of the imperial complex. But the sumptuous villa lasted as an imperial residence for less than four decades. In fact, in 104, Trajan built his baths on top of it, incorporating Nero's structures into the foundations.

Today, the great pavilion directly underneath the Trajan's Baths is the only surviving building of the Domus Aurea. A long structure, it consists of 150 rooms "rediscovered" in the 15th century that once boasted marble-covered walls and exquisitely painted and stuccoed vaults. In addition to the painting and stucco work, the rediscovery of the Domus Aurea uncovered sculptures such as the bronze originals of the *Gaul Committing Suicide*, the *Dying Gaul*, and, above all, the *Laocoön*, clearly indicating that the sculptural decoration must have included the greatest masterpieces of Nero's time.

Still, a visit to the Domus pavilion provides an idea of what Nero's imperial residence once was like. The floor plan is divided into two wings: a western wing where the rooms surround a vast courtyard and an eastern wing built around a central octagonal room. The western wing is home to the complex of the Nymphaeum of Odysseus and Polyphemus, one of the pavilion's most interesting architectural elements. Today, only the central round remains of the mosaic that once covered the vault and the upper section of walls of the nymphaeum. It depicts Odysseus, standing, as he hands a lounging Polyphemus a goblet of wine, a drink unknown to the Cyclops that would prove fatal. Polyphemus proceeded to become drunk and Odysseus was then able to blind him. This is the oldest surviving figurative mosaic image.

Other excerpts from Homer's epics inspired the decoration of the rooms. The farewell of Aeneas and Andromache and Achilles on Scyrus are also featured. Without a doubt, this was due to Nero's specific request. After all, the emperor himself was both a poet and singer and had even performed on stage in Naples.

The nymphaeum leads to the eastern wing, where every room is decorated differently with colors, including the costly purple red that was so precious and sought after in ancient times. The visit continues along the hallway that opens to the left into the main rooms of the first courtyard. The largest of these is named the Room of the Golden Vault. Its decoration made it one of the most important rooms in the pavilion and with its discovery in the 15th century, the course of decorative painting was changed.

Because the complex was buried, it was "rediscovered" in the 15th century by Renaissance artists who entered through holes made in the vaults. These cavelike openings led to naming the ancient rooms of Nero's palace "grottoes." The frescoes of the Domus Aurea became objects of admiration and imitation by the greatest artists working in Rome at the time, such as Pinturicchio and Raphael, who were working at the Vatican on the *Stanze* (Rooms) and the loggias. Today only the background colors remain of the once-lavish ancient decoration, but 16th-century drawings and paintings still provide an idea of what Nero had willed.

Domus Aurea

Walking Tour 3:

Climbing up the Three Hills of Monti

By Margaret Stenhouse

There's nothing boastful about Rome's No. 1 district. Rione Monti, the first of the 22 *rioni* that carve up the historic center of the Eternal City, is for the most part a little-known maze of quiet, old streets, wedged between the busy thoroughfares of Via Nazionale and Via Cavour.

Since its boundaries are marked by some of Rome's most popular sights—the Roman Forum, the Colosseum, and the Basilica of Santa Maria Maggiore—most tourists simply pass through it, with little more than a perfunctory glance at the monuments, churches, old buildings, and piazzas.

Everyone has heard of rollicking Trastevere, Rome's good-time district over the Tiber, but Monti, which has been Trastevere's rival since the days when unruly gangs of Monticiani and Trasteverini youths broke staves over each others heads amongst the ruins of imperial Rome, is largely unknown. If you want to savor the true flavor of Rome, Monti is the place to find it.

The area is packed with vestiges of every phase of Roman history, from the times when Augustus built the massive stone wall to protect his forum from the fires that often broke out in the plebian Suburra, which sprawled up the slopes of the Viminale, Quirinale, and Esquiline Hills, to pre–World War II, when Enrico Fermi was working out how to split the atom in his lab in Via Panisperna.

Monti has always been the home of artists and craftsmen. Bernini sculpted his *Apollo and Daphne* in his workshop opposite Santa Maria Maggiore, and in nearby Via San Martino ai Monti, No. 20, an inscription on the wall recounts that Domenico Zampieri Bolognese, better known as Domenichino, took refuge here from the "implacable envy" of his enemies.

Nowadays, it is one of the last bastions of the old, traditional arts and crafts. Carpenters, picture framers, gilt and silverware restorers, cobblers, decorators, printers, and leatherworkers are all busily plying their trade in dark, little *botteghe*, or shops, opening directly onto fascinating old streets like Via Urbana (named after Pope Urban VIII) and Via dei Zingari. Gypsies used to camp here when this was open land around the cow shed where the miraculous image of the Madonna dei Monti was discovered in 1579.

At the bottom of Via Cavour, overlooking the Roman Forum, the landmark 13th-century **Torre dei Conti** guards the entrance to one of Rome's most picturesque corners. The tower is one of many dotted throughout the *rione*. Once a grim reminder of the turbulent past, it is now the Monti senior citizens' recreational center. Peek in the gate as you go by and you'll see the old folks gossiping in the garden that borders on, appropriately, the remains of Nerva's Forum of Peace.

Via Torre dei Conti, with its fascinating old votive shrines draped with silver hearts and dried flower posies, is straight out of a Pinelli print. It runs along the side of the Suburra wall to the medieval House of the Knights of Rhodes. The house is private but the magnificent Hall of Honor and the Chapel of Saint John the Baptist can be viewed by prior arrangement.

A gate (always open in the daytime) leads onto a suspended walkway that runs around the side of the house and overhangs the adjoining Trajan's Forum. Camera buffs will enjoy the angle they can get toward the Forum floor—usually full of sun-basking cats—as well as the spectacular three-tiered, hemicycle-shaped market and the sculpted column, where the emperor's ashes were once kept in a golden urn.

Carrying on up Via Torre dei Conti, there are other, lesser-known Monti "sights," such as the palace of the Marquis del Grillo, a notorious 18th-century prankster, the site of the original Propaganda Fide printing works (Salita del Grillo, No. 17), and the grating through which you can observe artist Saverio Ungheri's moving sculptures (No. 21). At the top of the hill stands the **Church of Santi Domenico e Sisto**—a little-known

jewel of Counter-Reformation architecture, with its voluptuously curving staircase and a tympanum crowned with eight flaming torches carved in stone. The church, with a single, very tall nave and three chapels per side, is inside the grounds of the Angelicum Catholic University. Ask at the university office to be admitted to see the magnificent Bernini chapel and main altar, the *Noli Me Tangere* sculpture group by Antonio Raggi, and the Madonna and child, attributed to Benozzo Gozzoli. The monastery has an ample and shiny cloister with porticos attributed to Vignola.

From the top of the church steps, look across into one of Rome's secret gardens, the lovely **Villa Aldobrandini**, perched on a spur of rock at

Church of Santi Domenico e Sisto

the bottom of Via Nazionale. It's an ideal place to relax, in the shade of the cypresses and orange trees. The entrance is on Via Mazzarino.

The best stopping-off place, however, is Piazza Madonna dei Monti at the bottom of Via dei Serpenti—believed to be named after a painting of the *Laocoön* sculpture that once decorated a house wall. This charming little square, with its Giacomo Della Porta fountain, is the true pulsing heart of Rione Monti. Have some ice cream at one of the outdoor cafés and watch the Monticiani locals meeting up, chatting, and feeding the pigeons, as they will in any other village. The adjacent **Church of Santa Maria dei Monti**, always called simply "Madonna dei Monti," is a Giacomo Della Porta masterpiece. The venerable image of the Virgin and child, found inside the walls of the barn that originally stood on the spot, has pride of place above the main altar. Note the surrounding frame, with the *rione* coat of arms—a trio of triple humps, symbolizing the three hills in Monti territory. The *Monticiani* are very proud of this, their very own Madonna, who is credited with many miracles. They parade her triumphantly through the streets each year on April 26.

Since this was originally one of Rome's poorest areas, where Christianity took an early hold, Monti possesses some of the world's oldest churches. At the top of the Esquiline Hill, near the Basilica of Santa Maria Maggiore, the **Church of San Martino ai Monti** dates back to the first half of the 3rd century. An inscription inside recounts that Pope Sylvester I held two councils on this spot, in 324 and in 325, with the emperor Constantine and his mother, Saint Helena, present.

The original Roman house where early worship took place can be visited under the crypt (admission: €1). The church has been rebuilt several times over the ages and was radically modified by Pietro da Cortona, who designed the present facade. Most of the internal decoration dates from the 16th to 17th centuries, including the magnificent wooden ceiling, which was donated by Saint Carlo Borromeo, and the interesting wall paintings in the naves. The paintings include a series of landscapes by Gaspard Dughet—unusual for the period—and two unique renderings of the original interiors of Saint

Santa Maria dei Monti

Peter's and the old San Giovanni in Laterano. The half-moon crypt with its monumental stairway was also designed by Pietro da Cortona and is considered one of the finest examples of the baroque style. It contains the bones of Popes Sylvester and Martin and numerous early Christian martyrs, brought here from the Catacombs of Priscilla.

Just around the corner, on Via Merulana—a busy, tree-lined thoroughfare linking San Giovanni in Laterano with Santa Maria Maggiore—stands the imposing **Palazzo Brancaccio**. This now houses the National Museum of Eastern Art.

Originally it belonged to a late-19th-century New York socialite, Mary Elisabeth Bradhurst Field, whose daughter Elisabeth married Prince Brancaccio. Designed by architect Gaetano Koch, the building was called Palazzo Field and was celebrated for its glittering receptions and soirées. The collection is laid out in some of the lavishly decorated salons where the Brancaccio and Field family once lived, including Princess Elisabeth's bedroom, now known as Room XV, full of stuccoed angels, gilt embellishments, and intarsia.

FURTHER INFORMATION

Palazzo Brancaccio
Viale del Monte Oppio–Largo Brancaccio. 82/a; Ufficio Commerciale; Largo Brancaccio, 82; tel.: 06-4873177, 06-4873139, 06-4742235; website: www.palazzo brancaccio.com; e-mail; palazzo brancaccio@palazzobrancaccio.com

San Martino ai Monti
Viale del Monte Oppio, 28; tel.: 06-4784701; open: daily 9 A.M.–noon, 4–5:30 P.M.

Santa Maria dei Monti
Via Madonna dei Monti, 41; tel.: 06-485531; open: Mon.–Sat. 7 A.M.–noon, 5–7:30 P.M., Sun. 8:30 A.M.–1:30 P.M., 5–7:30 P.M.

Torre dei Conti
Largo Angelicum, 1; tel.: 06-67021; open: by appointment only; closed: July–Sept.

Santi Domenico e Sisto
Largo Angelicum.

Villa Aldobrandini
The entrance to the park is on Via del Mazzarino.

FOCUS: SAN PIETRO IN VINCOLI

Michelangelo, Moses

Piazza di San Pietro in Vincoli; tel.: 06-4882865; open: daily 7 A.M.–12:30 P.M., 3:30–7 P.M. (Oct.–Mar. closes at 6 P.M.).

By Margaret Stenhouse

The Basilica of San Pietro in Vincoli is one of Rome's oldest and most venerable basilicas. Tourists flock to see Michelangelo's *Moses*, but its hallowed relics also draw millions of pilgrims. A bronze and crystal casket on the main altar contains a double set of chains which Catholics believe bound the apostle Peter during his imprisonment in Palestine and, later, in Rome. According to tradition, these two sets of chains welded themselves miraculously together. In the Middle Ages, they were used to exorcise devils, as illustrated in the enormous fresco by Parodi (1706) on the ceiling.

San Pietro in Vincoli is also known as the Basilica Eudossiana, after the wife of the Byzantine emperor Valentiniano III, who brought the first set of chains over from Jerusalem. The church was consecrated by Pope Sixtus III around 439, and despite various alterations carried out over the centuries, it is still one of the best examples of an early Christian church in Rome.

The vast interior has none of the baroque opulence of most Roman churches. The walls are mostly unembellished, and the nave is lined with a row of unadorned Doric columns from the ancient imperial Prefecture, where Christians were held for trial at the time of the persecutions. The focus is on the relics, with a backdrop of frescoes by Giacomo Coppi (1577) illuminating the presbytery. From the door, you can't even see Michelangelo's monument, which is in the right transept.

The star attraction is, of course, the *Moses*, which was intended to be part of Pope Julius II's mausoleum, a grandiose project involving 40 major sculptures. The pope lost interest and forced the protesting artist to decorate the Sistine Chapel ceiling instead. This single completed side, with the colossal figure of the patriarch, flanked by Rachel and Leah, was placed in this church by Pope Paul III. At the moment, it is undergoing major restoration. Details of the project are available in Italian and English on touch screens inside the church, as well as on the internet at www.progettomose.it.

Other things to look out for: *The Liberation of Saint Peter* by Domenichino (in the ante-sacristy); a 7th-century Byzantine mosaic of Saint Sebastian (in the left nave); the Tomb of Cardinal Cusano with bas-relief by Andrea Bregno; and, near the door, the funeral monument of the 15th-century Florentine artists Antonio and Piero del Pollaiuolo.

Other Points of Interest

Arco degli Argentari (Silver Changers Arch)

Via del Velabro, between Via Giovanni Decollato and Via di San Teodoro, right next to the Church of San Giorgio in Velabro.

➢ At the left of the Church of San Giorgio in Velabro is the Silver Changers Arch built in A.D. 204 in honor of Septimius Severus and his family. Its pilasters are marked by several holes, believed to be the result of a search for hidden silver treasures in the Middle Ages.

Arco di Giano (Arch of Janus)

➢ The Arch of Janus is a four-faced marble arch, built in the 4th century in honor of Emperor Constantine or perhaps Constans II. In the niches next to the arcades were once 12 small statues of gods. Now, only small figures of the goddesses Roma, Juno, Minerva, and Ceres are visible above the arches. The monument also originally had an attic, that was accidentally destroyed in the Middle Ages, when the Frangipane family added a tower to the arch. The Frangipane tower was demolished soon after it was built.

San Gregorio Magno

Piazza di San Gregorio, 1; tel.: 06-7008227; open: daily 8:30 A.M.–12:30 P.M., 1:45–6:30 P.M.

➢ This church was erected in the Middle Ages on the site where Pope—and later Saint—Gregory the Great had turned his family home into a monastery. The exterior was restored by G. B. Soria, who designed the white facade in 1629–1633, while the interior was remodeled, following baroque lines, by Francesco Ferrari between 1725 and 1734. At the peak of the spectacular stairway is, preceded by a broad portico, the imposing facade whose material (travertine) and design recalls the Church of San Luigi dei Francesi. The columns of the portico come from the previous church. The portico hosts several burial niches. The interior, mainly baroque, presents three aisles separated by 16 ancient columns and pillars. The mosaic floor is also ancient. At the end of the right aisle is an altar whose frontal bas-reliefs depict the 30 masses of the saint. In the predella are the Umbrian-school paintings *Saint Michael Archangel Subjugating Lucifer* and *Saint Anthony and Saint Sebastian*. Before the main altar are the statuettes of Saint Andrew and Saint Gregory the Great, which date back to the 15th century. Francesco da Volterra designed the Cappella Salviati (to visit it, ask at the

Arco di Giano

monastery), which was completed by Carlo Maderno in 1600. The marble altar on the left is by Andrea Bregno. The white facade of the church turns a sweet golden hue at sunset. Behind the church is a complex of shady gardens, with walking paths and chirping birds. The monks here sell handmade herbal and gastronomic delicacies.

On the left of the staircase leading to the church, amid the cypresses of a former cemetery, is a little square containing three oratories erected in the late 17th century by the cardinal Baronio. The oratory of Saint Andrew has Guido Reni's *Saint Andrew Being Led to His Martyrdom* (left), Domenichino's *Flagellation of Saint Andrew*, Pomarancio's *The Virgin Mary and Saint Andrew and Saint Gregory* (at the altar), and Giovanni Lanfranco's *Saint Sylvia and Saint Gregory* (counter facade). The oratory of Saint Sylvia has an amazing wooden ceiling and, in the apse, is Reni and Baldocchio's *Concert of Angels* (1608–1609). Saint Barbara's oratory contains frescoes by Antonio Viviani and, at the center, an ancient marble table on which Saint Gregory served 12 poor men daily.

San Lorenzo in Panisperna

Via Panisperna, 90; tel.: 06-483667.

➤ This church was built in the 8th century on the supposed site of Saint Lawrence's martyrdom. Saint Gregory of Tours, who visited Rome in the 11th century, spoke of it as one of the richest

churches in the city. It was rebuilt in 1300 and restored as it is at present by Francesco da Volterra in 1576. Its bell tower is one of the very rare Renaissance varieties in Rome. The name of the church comes from an old tradition of its friars, who distributed bread and ham—*panis et perna*, in Latin—to the poor of the neighborhood. Over the altar is a large fresco of the martyrdom of Saint Lawrence by Pasquale Cati, a pupil of Michelangelo.

San Sebastiano al Palatino

Via San Bonaventura, 1; tel.: 06-6784236; open: Mon.–Sat. 9 A.M.–2:30 P.M., 4–7:30 P.M.

➤ San Sebastiano al Palatino, built in the 10th century over the ancient Temple of Heliogabalus, was completely restored by Pope Urban VIII in 1630. The frescoes in the apse are all that remain of the old church.

Santa Maria in Dominica

Piazza della Navicella, 12; tel.: 06-7001519; open: daily 9 A.M.–noon.

➤ The 16th-century reconstruction of this church is credited to Andrea Contucci da Monte San Savino, a.k.a. Sansovino, who worked on the structures of an existing place of worship called *dominicum,* built at the end of the 7th century. The church itself overlooks Piazza della Navicella, or piazza of the "little boat," from a Roman stone boat made into a fountain by Pope Leo X. The boat was likely a votive offering from a camp of non-Italian soldiers. The church still maintains the basilica form of the 9th century, with a nave and two side aisles divided by 18 columns of gray granite. Below the 16th-century coffered ceiling is a frieze painted by Perin del Vaga and designed by Giulio Romano. The triumphal arch, flanked by two porphyry columns, and apse are decorated with Byzantine mosaics that depict Christ with two angels and the apostles and, in the semi-dome, the pope at the feet of the Virgin and child. The Virgin is surrounded by angels and holds a handkerchief in the style of a fashionable lady at a Byzantine court. The wooden, gilded ceiling was redone in 1566. The crypt of the church contains Roman sarcophagi, remains of a 9th-century *plutei,* and a 17th-century altar.

San Gregorio Magno

San Lorenzo in Panisperna

Santi Giovanni e Paolo

Piazza Santi Giovanni e Paolo, 13; tel.: 06-7005745; open: Mon.–Sat. 8:30 A.M.–noon, 3:30–6:30 P.M., Sun. 8:30 A.M.–12:45 P.M., 3:30–7 P.M.; to visit the Case Romane beneath the basilica, call 06-7216601.

➤ Saint Pammachius, a wealthy senator, erected the Church of Santi Giovanni e Paolo in 410 above the Roman homes in which, according to tradition, the officers John and Paul were martyred in 361. The basilica was restructured in the 11th century by Pope Paschal II, who erected the bell tower and the portico at the front. The gallery above the porch was built in 1216. In 1718 the interior was radically modified.

In the right nave is the noteworthy altarpiece by Marco Benefial, *Saint Saturninus Destroying the Idols*. The altar has beautiful columns of Egyptian alabaster and an altarpiece from the 18th century. A large urn of porphyry beneath the altar contains the bodies of the two saints. In the apse *Christ in Glory* (1588) is by Niccolò Pomarancio, and the Virgin and Child among Saints in the sacristy is by Antoniazzo Romano. The exterior of the apse of the church, with the gallery and pensile arches, dates from the 13th century. It is the only example of Lombard Romanesque in Rome.

The Roman homes beneath the church have been recently reopened to the public after a careful restoration. The frescoes provide a vivid impression of daily life in Rome between the 2nd and 4th centuries.

In the summer, wedding parties descend on the church three times a day, with cars beeping in rhythm with white ribbons flying from their antennas.

Santo Stefano Rotondo

Via di Santo Stefano Rotondo, 7; tel.: 06-70493717; open: Tues.–Sat. 9:00 A.M.–1 P.M., 2–4 P.M., Mon. 2–4 P.M., in summer: daily 3:30–6 P.M.; closed: public holidays.

➤ This is the oldest church with a circular plan in Rome. It dates back to the 5th century and the reign of Pope Saint Simplicius. The original structure included two concentric porticoes intersected with a Greek cross inscription, probably taken from Eastern models such as the Church of the Holy Sepulcher in Jerusalem, and ancient Roman buildings. The church was

View of apse, Santi Giovanni e Paolo

modified by the addition of an entrance portico in the 12th century and by the removal—under Bernardo Rossellino's supervision in the 15th century—of the outermost circular colonnade and three arms of the Greek cross. The round inner area is surrounded by 34 granite and marble columns on the outside and 22 supporting columns on the inside, with two Corinthian columns in the center and two pillars supporting three arches recently covered in bright white plaster. The high drum in the center is 72-feet high and exactly the same measurement in width. It is lit by a series of windows, 22 in all. The outside wall is frescoed with 34 scenes of the *Martirologio*, a history of the martyrs, painted by Niccolò Pomarancio, Antonio Tempesta, and assistants, which graphically represent the tortures to which the Christian martyrs were subjected. On the left of the entrance is an antique Roman throne, allegedly belonging to Saint Gregory. In the first chapel to the left of the entrance is a 7th-century mosaic of Christ with San Primo and San Feliciano, retaining some of the medieval decor. Underneath the church is a 2nd- or 3rd-century Mithreum.

SANTI GIOVANNI E PAOLO

No spot in Rome can show a cluster of more charming accidents [than the piazzetta of the church of San Giovanni e Paolo.] The ancient brick apse of the church peeps down into the . . . little walk before the neighboring church of San Gregorio; and a series of heavy brick buttresses . . . overarches the short, steep, paved passage which leads into the small square. This is flanked on one side by the long medieval portico of the church of the two saints, sustained by eight columns of granite and marble. . . . The place always seems to me the perfection of a out-of-the-way corner—a place you would think twice before telling people about, lest you should find them there the next time you were to go.

—Henry James, *Italian Hours*

TEMPIO DI CLAUDIO
Piazza Santi Giovanni e Paolo

➤ Empress Agrippina dedicated this great temple to her husband, who died in A.D. 54. It was completed in 69 by Vespasian. All that remains are a few arches incorporated in the foundations of the convent of Santi Giovanni e Paolo, at the base of the church's bell tower, and the great brick wall of excellent quality with semicircular and rectangular niches along the Via Claudia.

Museums

ANTIQUARIUM DEL FORO (ANTIQUARIUM OF THE FORUM)
Piazza Santa Maria Nova, 53; tel.: 06-6990110; open: 9 A.M.–2 hours before sunset; admission: free.

➤ Houses finds coming from the Forum excavations and frescoes once on the walls of the churches of Santa Maria Antiqua and Sant'Adriano.

ANTIQUARIUM MUNICIPALE (MUNICIPAL ANTIQUARIUM)
Via Parco del Celio, 22; tel.: 06-7001569.

➤ Household objects from the 6th century B.C. to the time of the barbarian invasions. The Municipal Antiquarium includes the famous doll with jointed limbs that was part of the funeral accoutrement of Crepereia Tryphaena.

MUSEO DEL RISORGIMENTO (MUSEUM OF ITALIAN RISORGIMENTO)
Via San Pietro in Carcere; tel.: 06-6780664; open: 10 A.M.–6 P.M.; closed: Mon.; admission: free.

➤ The collection includes paintings, sculptures, and drawings related to Italian history from the Risorgimento to World War I.

MUSEO PALATINO (PALATINE MUSEUM)
Via di San Gregorio, 30; tel.: 06-6990110; open 9 A.M.–2 hours before sunset; admission: €6.

➤ Materials coming from the Palatine excavations.

Fora/Monti/Celio

Hotels & Inns
1 Hotel Borromeo
2 Hotel Casa Kolbe
3 Hotel Celio
4 Hotel Duca d'Alba
5 Residence Palazzo al
   Velabro

Restaurants & Cafés
6 Alvaro al Circo
   Massimo
7 Caffè Brasile
8 Cavour 313
9 Fienile
10 Il Giardino del Tè*
11 Le Tavernelle
12 Magna Roma
13 Osteria del
   Campidoglio
14 Trattoria San
   Teodoro

Shopping
15 Arte Colosseo
16 Centro Stampa Forti
17 Gutenberg al
   Colosseo
18 Immagini
19 La Bottega del
   Cioccolato
20 L'Alternativa
21 Libreria Archeologica
22 Longobardi
23 San Bernardo
24 Zadig

Best of
25 La pace del cervello

HOTELS & INNS

Hotel Borromeo

Via Cavour, 117; tel.: 06-485856/4882541; e-mail: borromeo@travel.it; category: ★★★; number of rooms: 35, including 4 suites; credit cards accepted: all major; facilities: parking (€15 a night); access to internet: direct-line (US, UK) telephone jack in all rooms; most beautiful rooms:104, 115, and 302; €€–€€€.

☞Located between the principal Termini train station and the Imperial Forum, this hotel sits amidst a neighborhood strewn with small artisan shops and merchants, and renowned for its hard-core Roman character. The ornately decorated lobby and public rooms are pleasant. A roof garden affords a lovely view of the city's rooftops. The recently renovated rooms are small to medium in size, with newly fitted bathrooms, all with bathtubs. There is a comfortable breakfast room but no real lounge. Staff is helpful.

Hotel Casa Kolbe

Via di San Teodoro, 44; tel.: 06-6794974/5 or 06-6798866; category: ★★; number of rooms: 63; credit cards accepted: all major, except Diner's Card; access to internet: none; €*.

☞Tucked away right across from the Palatine Hill, this hotel is an excellent value for its location. Rooms are simple, but all have bathrooms and TV. Many look out over the shady, grassy back garden, with some tables and chairs for reading. Visitors are mostly groups, but the price is the same for individuals. Lunch and dinner are available in the barebones dining room.

Hotel Celio

Via dei Santi Quattro, 35/C; tel.: 06-70495333/7096377; e-mail: info_htl.sstefanel@tin.it; website: www.charmingrome.com; category: ★★★; number of rooms: 22, including 2 suites; credit cards accepted: all major; facilities: parking (€25 a night); access to internet: direct-line (US, UK) telephone jack in all rooms; most beautiful rooms: Michelangelo, Julius Caesar, and Nero; €€–€€€.

☞Charming, in a restored 19th-century palazzo. The lounge is elegant, the rooms comfortable.

Hotel Duca d'Alba

Via Leonina, 14; tel.: 06-484471/4884840; e-mail: info@hotelducadalba.com; website: www.hotelducadalba.com; category: ★★★; number of rooms: 27; credit cards accepted: all major; facilities: parking (€25 a night); access to internet: direct-line (US, UK) telephone jack in all rooms; €€.

☞Small and comfortable, not far from the Forum and the Colosseum. The rooms are soundproofed and have electronic safes.

Residence Palazzo al Velabro

Via del Velabro, 16; tel.: 06-6792758; e-mail: velabro@velabro.it; website: www.venere.it/roma/velabro; category: ★★★★; number of rooms: 25; credit cards accepted: all; access to internet: direct-line telephone jack in all rooms; most beautiful rooms: 36, 37, 46, 47; €€*.

☞A peaceful setting and tasteful decorations make this residence an ideal place to spend a long stay in Rome. All suites include a sitting room, fully furnished kitchenette, and air conditioning. Minimum stay of seven nights. Friendly and attentive staff. Central location.

RESTAURANTS & CAFÉS

Alvaro al Circo Massimo

Via dei Cerchi, 53; tel.: 06-6786112; open: 12:30–3:30 P.M., 7:30–11:30 P.M.; closed: Mon.; credit cards accepted: all major; €.

☞If you're not put off by the smell of fresh fish sitting in the glass cases by the entrance, this restaurant offers a wide selection of fish and seafood dishes at reasonable prices in a relaxed atmosphere. Dishes that branch out from the norm include linguine with lobster sauce and risotto with truffles. Grilled porcini mushrooms and a dozen meat dishes are available as second courses.

Caffè Brasile

Via dei Serpenti, 23; tel.: 06-4882319; open: Mon.–Sat. 6 A.M.–8:30 P.M., Sun. noon–8 P.M.

☛One of Rome's last-remaining traditional coffee shops where they roast on the premises. Pope John Paul II took his morning espresso here when he was a student at the nearby Angelicum University. This friendly and unpretentious little café, run by Sergio and Giusy Tiradritta, has had other illustrious customers in the past, like Enrico Fermi and Guglielmo Marconi.

Fienile

Via del Fienili, 54; tel.: 06-6790849; open: 8 A.M.–7:30 P.M.; closed: Sun.

☛A small coffee bar/wine bar/lunch spot with nice homemade sandwiches and pastries. A good 20 wines are available by the glass, with an unusual focus on those from in and around Naples. The sidewalk tables offer good people-watching opportunities in the middle of the day, when Rome's city administrators come down from the Capitoline Hill for lunch.

Il Giardino del Tè

Via del Boschetto, 107; tel.: 06-4746888; website: www.ilgiardinodelte.it.

☛This tiny tea shop is unique in Rome, with specialty teas and infusions from all over the world, as well as special arabica coffee blends with cinnamon, vanilla, chocolate, and cherry flavors. Ask owner Carmen Marcat to help you with your choice.

Magna Roma

Via Capo d'Africa, 26; tel. 06-7009800; open: daily 12–2 P.M., 8:30–11:30 P.M.; €€€€

☛When in Rome, do as the Romans, or at least eat like their ancient ancestors. At Magna Roma, a mere stone's throw from the Colosseum, it's possible to get a first-hand taste of some archaeological gastronomy. The inside of the restaurant is meant to resemble a *thermopolium*, or ancient Roman *taberna*, from Hadrian's reign, around the year A.D. 123, the period of Magna Roma. Archaeologist Franco Nicastro, the *Magister Cena*, or master of ceremonies, will be present to provide priceless gastronomic and archaeological elucidation throughout the evening, and to guide guests through the intricacies of ancient Roman cuisine. The unique epicurean experience looks to original recipes found in the writings of Cato, Lucullus, and Varro and from *De Re Coquinarua,* a ten-volume cookbook written by Marcus Gavius Apicius. Using only ingredients that the Romans would have known, several ten-course menus, served by toga-clad *ancillae,* have been cooked up. The menus change weekly. An excellent website, www.magnaroma.com, has information on the restaurant and its food.

Osteria del Campidoglio

Via dei Fienili, 56; tel.: 06-6780250; open: noon–3:30 P.M., 7:30–11:30 P.M.; closed Sun.; credit cards accepted: all major; €.

☛Both the outdoor area overlooking Santa Maria della Consolazione and the cozy, brick-faced dining room go well with the classic Roman food served here. In addition to the standard favorites like *bucatini all'amatriciana,* the menu offers rarer treats like *spaghetti alla gricia* dressed with sautéed pancetta, parmesan, and black pepper. Second courses include tripe or cod in a light tomato sauce. Over 150 wines from all over Italy.

Trattoria San Teodoro

Via dei Fienili 49-50-51; tel.: 06-6780933; open: 12:30–3:30 P.M., 7:30–12:30 A.M.; credit cards accepted: all major; €€.

☛Creativity and freshness are the focus of this restaurant, with a menu that changes every week, revolving around whatever ingredients are in season. Eighty percent of the offerings are based on fish or seafood, like spaghetti with shrimp tails, aged pecorino, and zucchini flower strips, or tuna flavored with oranges, capers, and olives. One-of-a-kind desserts include pure chestnut gelato and wild fennel sorbet. One hundred ninety wines and a vast selection of grappa. Beautiful outdoor patio.

Arte Colosseo

Via S. Giovanni in Laterano, 58; open: Tues.–Sat. 10 A.M.–8 P.M., various hours Sun. and Mon.
☞A small gallery selling original Italian and European prints, mostly bucolic cityscapes, dating as far back as the 17th century. A rotating collection of contemporary Italian paintings and a case of choice antique watches and jewelry round out the offerings.

Centro Stampa Forti

Via Madonna dei Monti, 67; tel.: 06-4744 633; website: www.centrostampaforti.it.
☞Traditional family-run printers inside a 13th-century house in one of the oldest parts of Rome. Riccardo Forti and his son, Fabio, do everything from traditional hand typesetting to digital printing techniques.

Gutenberg al Colosseo

Via S. Giovanni in Laterano, 94; open: Tues.–Sat. 10 A.M.–1 P.M., 4–8 P.M., Mon. open afternoons only.
☞The walls of this quirky used bookstore are littered with framed, coaster-sized prints delicately depicting various areas of Rome as it was centuries ago. The shop specializes in classics and sells texts dating back to the 17th century, plus a small collection of foreign-language books.

Immagini

Via dell'Angeletto, 12; tel.: 06-47825562; open: 9 A.M.–1 P.M.; 4–8 P.M.; closed: Sun.
☞A variety of paper, books, period postcards, and stamps, including some signed by Garibaldi.

La Bottega del Cioccolato

Via Leonina, 83; tel.: 06-4821473.
☞You feel as if you were stepping into a chocolate box when you enter this small, specialty boutique, entirely lined in red. Choose from a vast variety of fillings, like rose- or violet-flavored treats. An elegant gift for Italian hosts—or sweet memories to take home, in the form of a chocolate model of the Colosseum—all gift wrapped with a smile.

L'Alternativa

Via S. Giovanni in Laterano, 24; open: Mon.–Sat. 10 A.M.–7 P.M.
☞Flashy espresso-makers, chrome orange juicers, and sets of glasses especially for *limoncello* (lemon liqueur) and grappa are highlights of this fun household design shop. Fun watches, pens, and jewelry are also sold.

Libreria Archeologica

Via S. Giovanni in Laterano, 46; tel.: 06-77201395; open: Mon.–Fri. 10 A.M.–7 P.M., Sat. 10 A.M.–1:30 P.M.
☞A well-stocked bookstore specializing in ancient Roman and Greek art and archaeological sites, plus frame-worthy maps, teach-yourself-ancient-Greek books.

Longobardi

Via dei Fienili, 43/A; tel.: 06-6781104; open: Mon. 3:30–7:30 P.M., Tues.–Sat. 9:30 A.M–7:30 P.M.; closed: Sun.
☞A small boutique specializing in hand-worked silver and gold, from elaborate tableware and picture frames to a range of jewelry. All items are made in Italy, with the exception of some English antiques. The owner, Mr. Longobardi, is well versed in Roman history and loves to discuss it with visitors.

San Bernardo

Via dei Fienili, 61; tel.: 06-6794231; open: Mon.–Fri. 9 A.M.–7 P.M., Sat. 9 A.M.–1 P.M.
☞This small organic grocery store carries imported fresh meat, whole wheat pastas and breads, and organic dairy products and snacks. Most of their business seems to come from the lunchtime rush on the deli counter, which is stocked with a great selection of cheeses, cured meats, salads, and bread.

Zadig

Via dei Fienili, 42/E-G; tel.: 06-69925176; open: Mon.–Sat. 10 A.M.–8 P.M.
☞This beautiful store displays and sells handmade crafts from the Middle and Far East, from 100-year-old ceramics to carved wooden farming implements from central Turkey and golden silk ceremonial robes from Turkmenistan, plus clothing by contemporary designers from Nepal, Egypt, and Korea. In addition to running this sort of contemporary anthropological museum, the Zadig cultural association also organizes classes and dinners on Eastern themes.

PROFILE

Glass and Coke

By Margaret Stenhouse

Domenico Passagrilli is a well-known figure in Via del Boschetto, one of Monti's most interesting streets for crafts, restaurants, and specialty shops. In La Vetrata, his cramped workshop at No. 94, he turns out original stained-glass panels, bowls, lamp bases, and screens, using techniques he has developed over half a lifetime of experimentation.

A Monti resident for almost 30 years, Passagrilli was first drawn to the area by a small workshop in Via Baccina that created stained-glass windows for churches and other buildings. At that time, there were only three places in Rome making leaded panes and stained glass.

Passagrilli became interested in glass as an art after a friend went to San Francisco to study the technique. He was fascinated by what his friend told him and decided to make glass-making his life's work.

His most striking creations are his glass 20-by-24-inch "pictures." These are translucent panels, glowing with delicately tinted mottled bands and rays, designed to be mounted with a light shining discreetly behind them to show off their beauty. The fascinating kaleidoscopic effects are obtained by fusing various substances between two or three sheets of glass. He has created all kinds of unexpected patterns and images by experimenting with different materials like sugar, petroleum, silver foil—and even Coca-Cola.™

The art of glass, he believes, is still appreciated more by northern Europeans and Americans than by Romans. Many of his orders, in fact, come from abroad. One of his most important recent works, however, was in the heart of Rome, near the Spanish Steps. This was an entire glass wall for the reception room of the Spanish Embassy to the Holy See, to commemorate the millennium Jubilee year.

OUR CRITIC'S FAVORITE RESTAURANTS

Cavour 313

Via Cavour, 313; tel.: 06-6785496; closed: Sun. at lunch.

☛The cellars of this historic wine bar on Via Cavour accommodate over 1,200 different labels from Italy and around the world. In addition to offering a vast assortment of wines by the glass, the excellent menu includes regional Italian recipes and products—from salads to soups, cheeses and cured meats and salamis. The atmosphere plays its role too, with wood furnishings and bottles decorating the premises.

Le Tavernelle

Via Panisperna, 48; tel.: 06-4740724; closed: Mon.; €€

☛In the 1930s this traditional old restaurant was a favorite spot of the so-called "Via Panisperna boys," the group of Italian nuclear scientists lead by Enrico Fermi. Over the decades, the atmosphere has remained pleasant and informal, with a menu varying according to the seasons. Favorite first courses include the ricotta cheese and spinach *ravioli alla zarina*, as well as the pasta with porcini mushrooms. Second courses range from *orata* prepared with Vernaccia wine to a rich buffet of seafood and vegetables. Delicious house desserts.

Laterano/ Esquilino/Termini

By Ruth Kaplan

Rome has about 650 churches (about 350 in the center of the city), a handful of which are designated as the Major Basilicas. One of these is "the mother of all churches," **San Giovanni in Laterano**. It is Rome's first Christian basilica, built by Constantine in the 4th century. The adjoining Lateran Palace was the official papal residence until it moved to Avignon in 1309.

Next door is the beautiful 13th-century **cloister**, carefully restored in the 19th century. Twisted marble columns and inlaid marble line the walking path around the garden. The octagonal, domed **baptistery** dates back to Constantine's time and has served as a model for baptisteries all over the world. It is located in a separate small building along with the Chapel of San Venanzio, which is plastered with 7th-century mosaics.

Across the street is the **Scala Santa**, a 28-step staircase believed to have been walked on by Christ during the Passion. Pilgrims still climb it on their knees. It leads to the **Sancta Sanctorum**, also known as the Cappella di San Lorenzo, which once served as the pope's private chapel. The wealth of relics that earned it its name as the "holiest place on Earth" are now in the Vatican Museums.

Not far from San Giovanni is **Santa Maria Maggiore**, another giant and ritually important basilica. Dating from the 5th century, Santa Maria Maggiore successfully integrates additions and decorations from the early medieval period through the baroque. Southeast of here is another one of the "Seven Churches" of Rome, **Santa Croce in Gerusalemme**. Legend says it was founded by Saint Helena, Constantine's mother. It was probably built as early as the 3rd century, but was rebuilt and modernized in the 18th century. Santa Croce has a unique, showy facade and oval vestibule. The Chapel of Saint Helena has a beautiful 15th-century mosaic. Pieces of what are believed to be of the True Cross are preserved along with other venerated relics in the next chapel.

San Lorenzo fuori le Mura, another of Rome's pilgrimage churches, is located in the neighborhood named after the church's name, San Lorenzo, on the other side of Rome's Termini Station. It is a composite building, created by combining the 4th-century church devoted to the martyr with an adjacent 5th-century church devoted to the Virgin Mary. The cloister leads to the Catacombs of Saint Ciriaca, where Saint Lawrence's body was said to be buried after his death. His remains now rest in the choir added to the church in the 6th century.

Left, Scala Santa

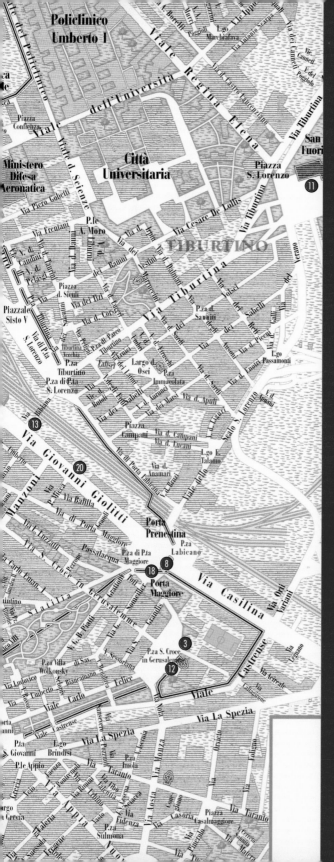

SAN GIOVANNI IN LATERANO

As to the great front of the church overlooking Porta San Giovanni . . .
the architecture has a vastly theatrical air. It is extremely imposing—
that of Specter's alone is more so. . . . The view from the great space
which stretches from the church steps to the city wall is the very prince
of views. . . . The charm of charms at St. John Lateran is the admirable
twelfth-century cloister. . . .[From there] you may look up and see a
section of the summit of the great facade of the church. The robed and
mitred apostles, bleached and rain-washed by the ages, rose into the
blue air like huge snow figures. . . . If there were no objects of interest
at all in the Lateran, the palace would be worth walking through every
now and then, to keep up one's idea of solid architecture.

—Henry James, *Italian Hours*

SAN GIOVANNI IN LATERANO

Piazza di San Giovanni in Laterano, 4; tel.: 06-
69886452; open: church and cloister:
7 A.M.–7:30 P.M., museum: Sat. and first Sun.
of month 9 A.M.–1 P.M.; admission: €2.

➢ The original palace belonged to a
wealthy family, the Laterani. Platius
Lateranus, head of the family, was put to
death by Nero in A.D. 67. The palace
became an imperial residence when a member of the family, Fausta, became the
second wife of Constantine. The emperor
eventually donated the building to the
church, and the popes set up residence here
after the Edict of Milan legalized
Christianity in the Empire. It remained the
papal residence until Sixtus V decided to
build the new Vatican complex at the end of
the 16th century.

The basilica was first erected by
Constantine between 314 and 318, but in
the 5th century it suffered so much damage
from the Vandals that it had to be restored.
In the 8th century, Adrian I (771–795)
repaired it with great splendor. After nearly
being destroyed by an earthquake, it was
completely rebuilt in 904. In 1288–1292, it
was restored; the mosaics of the apse belong

San Giovanni in Laterano

San Giovanni Cloister

sent the events from the life of Constantine. The pope alone may say Mass at the main altar. Its splendid Gothic canopy was erected by Giovanni di Stefano for Urban V about 1371. Above the altar the heads of Saints Peter and Paul are preserved, enshrined in silver gilt busts. In the left transept, the four Corinthian columns of gilt bronze are said to have belonged to the palace of Constantine. One tradition claims that Titus brought them from Jerusalem.

• THE CLOISTER
➢ This courtyard was built between 1215 and 1227, and formed part of the monastery founded at the end of the 6th century by Benedictines from Monte Cassino. The low arches rest on twisted columns inlaid with mosaic, above which is a frieze of colored marble. In the cloister are many interesting monuments, and many architectural remains from the old basilica.

• THE OBELISK
➢ The obelisk in the center of the piazza is the tallest and oldest in Rome, said to date from the reign of the Pharaoh Thutmosis III, in the 15th century B.C. It is composed of red granite, is covered with hieroglyphics, and originally stood before the Temple of Ammon in Thebes (Karnak). It was brought to Alexandria by Constantine, who intended it for Constantinople, but his son Constantius II presented it to the Roman Senate, which placed it in the Circus Maximus. Pope Sixtus V moved it to its present site in 1588.

• THE SCALA SANTA (HOLY STAIRCASE)
➢ According to tradition, these are the 28 marble steps from the palace in Jerusalem that Jesus had to climb to reach Pontius Pilate. The steps are now covered by protective wood and lead to the Sancta Santorum, so called for the numerous holy relics kept here. The steps are said to have been brought from Jerusalem in 326 by Saint Helena, mother of Constantine. They formerly stood to the right of the portico of the ancient Lateran basilica. Pope Sixtus V moved them to their present site in 1589.

to this period. (The medieval apse was destroyed in the course of enlarging the choir, so the mosaic visible now is a copy, faithful only in its iconography, and executed between 1883 and 1884.) In 1361 the basilica was burned down, and until 1364, it lay in utter ruin. It was rebuilt by Martino V, its walls frescoed by Gentile da Fabriano and Pisanello. Nothing is left of these paintings. The transept was redone and frescoed by the Cavalier d'Arpino on the occasion of the Jubilee of 1600. The central nave was given its current appearance by Borromini after 1644.

The present eastern facade, looking toward Santa Croce, was erected from the designs of Galilei in 1734. The central nave still conserves a beautiful Cosmatesque floor. In the other naves there is a series of funerary monuments and a fresco representing Pope Boniface VIII calling the first Jubilee, traditionally attributed to Giotto. The two columns of *giallo antico*, flanking the northern entrance, are said to have belonged to the Lateran Palace, which Constantine gave to the pope. The Tomb of Innocent III (1198–1216), restored by Leo XIII, is in the right transept. The frescoes in the transept represent

SCALA SANTA

Beyond the great alcove of mosaic, is the Scala Santa, the marble
stair case which (says the legend) Christ descended under
the weight of Pilate's judgment, and which all Christians must
for ever ascend on their knees.

—Henry James, *Italian Hours*

• THE SANCTA SANCTORUM

➤ At the head of the Holy Staircase, passing through an iron gate, visitors can see the Sancta Sanctorum, private oratory of the popes before 1308, and the only part of the Lateran Palace that escaped the great fire of that year. In this chapel, also known as the Cappella di San Lorenzo, the heads of Saints Peter and Paul were discovered by Urban V in 1367. The interior, from floor to ceiling, was entirely decorated by the Cosmati, with the exception of the frescoes, executed by an anonymous Roman artist, which are masterpieces of medieval art. According to tradition, the *Acheropita* image above the altar was painted by a divine hand.

• THE BAPTISTERY
Open: daily 9 A.M.–12:30 P.M., 3:30–7 P.M.

Interior, San Lorenzo fuori le Mura

➤ San Giovanni in Laterano has the first baptistery of the Christian world, an architectural prototype for those that would follow. It's an octagonal building detached from the basilica. Inside, the eight large porphyry columns are said to have been the gift of Constantine, who founded the baptistery in a former nymphaeum of the Laterani-family complex. Adjoining the baptistery are four ancient chapels. The Chapel of Saint John the Baptist, on the right, was built in the 5th century, and has two bronze doors, allegedly brought from the Baths of Caracalla: when opened and closed slowly, they have the sound of a powerful organ. The Chapel of Saint John the Evangelist on the left was also built in the 5th century, and has bronze doors wrought during the papacy of Celestine III (1191–1198). The vaulted ceiling is covered with 5th-century mosaics. The Chapel of Saints Rufina and Secunda was originally the atrium of the baptistery. The 5th-century mosaic in the small apse was the Roman model of the mosaic in San Clemente. The Oratory of San Venanzio (Saint Venantius) was built in 640. The mosaics date to the 7th century.

SAN LORENZO FUORI LE MURA
Piazzale del Verano, 3; tel.: 06-491511; open: daily 6:30 A.M.–12:30 P.M., 3:30–7 P.M. (7:30 P.M. in summer).

➤ San Lorenzo fuori le Mura is one of the designated patriarchal basilicas of Rome, with high altars reserved for the pope and Holy Doors to be open in Jubilee years.

The name of the church means "Saint Lawrence outside the walls." The saint, who was burned to death in A.D. 258, was one of the most revered Roman Christian martyrs. The church was originally built as a cemetery church in A.D. 300 and then rebuilt by Pope Pelagius II, in a location that ran par-

Santa Croce in Gerusalemme

allel to the original building. The patriarchal basilica was renovated over the centuries and was part of the citadel Laurentiopolis. The portico, possibly built by Pietro Vassalletto in 1220, has a trabeation decorated by a frieze, and the remains of mosaics. To its left is the 12th-century bell tower. Following the Allied bombing of the San Lorenzo neighborhood in July 1943, the church had to be reconstructed. The inside of the church clearly represents the two very different phases of construction. The basilica Honoriana dates back to the 13th century, and has a nave and two side aisles separated by medieval columns. The older basilica, Pelagiana, from the 6th century, has been incorporated into the presbytery occupying the nave. Inside, the baldacchino of the Tomb of Cardinal Guglielmo Fieschi is worth noting, along with the floor, the two ambos, and the paschal candelabrum. The underground chapel, Cappella Sottoterranea di Santa Ciriaca, is reached from the left aisle through a door flanked by the Tombs of Gerolamo Aleandri and Bernardo Guglielmi, both by Pietro da Cortona. In the presbytery, a remarkable trabeation is supported by 6th-century columns. The ciborium is the oldest signed work by Roman marble carvers. The bishop's throne, dating from 1254, has elegant mosaics. The adjoining cloister, from the late 12th century, contains fragments of classical and medieval sculpture that still decorate the walls. From there you can go down into the Catacombs of Saint Ciriaca.

SANTA CROCE IN GERUSALEMME (THE BASILICA OF THE HOLY CROSS)

Piazza di Santa Croce in Gerusalemme,12; tel.: 06-7014769; open: daily 7 A.M.–7 P.M.

➤ Santa Croce in Gerusalemme is one of the seven patriarchal basilicas in Rome. It was founded by Saint Helena, the mother of Constantine, and may have been originally one of the halls of the Sessorian Palace, from where it derives its title of Basilica Sessoriana. Saint Helena built or adapted it as a church in 320 to receive the large relic of what is thought to be Jesus' cross, brought by her from Jerusalem. The basilica was restored in 720 and again in 975, when the adjoining monastery was erected. In 1144 the tall Romanesque bell tower was erected. In 1492 there was another restoration and then a final one in 1741–1744. Little is left of the old edifice, except the subterranean Chapel of Saint Helena, the pillars of the nave, part of the mosaic floor, and the medieval bell tower. The nave is divided from the aisles by eight large columns of Egyptian granite. The ancient mosaic pavement is preserved in part, and probably dates to the 13th century. The splendid frescoes in the vault of the apse, representing the discovery of the Holy Cross by Saint Helena and its recovery from the Persians by the Byzantine emperor Heraclius, are traditionally attributed to Antoniazzo Romano, but more likely originate from an Umbrian workshop active around 1490. Two passages, one on each side of the sanctuary, lead down to the underground chapels. The chapel to the left is dedicated to Saint Gregory. Opposite it is the Chapel of Saint Helena; this, the most ancient part of the building, was erected by the saint herself. The ceiling was adorned with mosaic figures on a gold ground by Melozzo da Forlì in c. 1484 and restored in the 16th century by Baldassare Peruzzi.

SANTA MARIA MAGGIORE

Piazza di Santa Maria Maggiore; tel.: 06-483195; open: daily 7 A.M.–7 P.M.

➢ The Basilica of Santa Maria Maggiore was built by Pope Sixtus III in A.D. 432–440 on the highest point of the Cispian Hill. The building is 279-feet long and has a basilica plan with a nave, two side aisles, and an apse. Originally, the sanctuary was probably preceded by an atrium, the design and dimensions of which are unclear. The 36 columns of Hymettian marble and four of granite all have Ionic capitals over which is an architrave decorated with mosaics from the 5th century. The mosaics on the triumphal arch, with the rare iconography of the childhood of Christ, are from the same period.

In the course of time, the basilica was changed, restored, and extended by various popes. In the mid-12th century the present Cosmatesque pavement was added. In the following century, the 5th-century half-dome and ambulatory were replaced with the current apse by Nicholas IV (1288–1292), who also commissioned Jacopo Torriti to add the mosaic showing the Coronation of Mary. The 246-foot bell tower next to the basilica was begun in 1375–1376 and finished in the middle of the next century. The ceiling of the nave was coffered and, according to tradition, gilded with the first gold brought back from the New World, donated to the Spanish pope Alexander VI by Ferdinand and Isabella. The obelisk behind the apse was erected in 1587 by Sixtus V, who had it moved from the Mausoleum of Augustus. Many chapels were added later along both side aisles, substantially changing the original appearance of the church. The most notable of these are the Sistine Chapel, or Chapel of the Holy Sacrament, designed by Domenico Fontana in 1584–1587 (off the right aisle); and the Borghese Chapel built by Pope Paul V in 1605–1611. In 1614, in the piazza in front of the church, Pope Paul V erected a colossal Corinthian column taken from the Basilica of Maxentius. The column supports a bronze statue of the Virgin Mary. Finally, Pope Benedict XIV (1740–1758), commissioned architect Ferdinando Fuga to build the present facade and to modify the interior.

Interior, Santa Maria Maggiore

Walking Tour

Around Rome's Termini Station

By Ruth Kaplan

Everybody who's been in Rome for any length of time has probably seen the **Baths of Diocletian**, but wouldn't say so if asked. The enormous brick remains of these ancient baths are the anchors of Rome's Termini Station area, and dictate the layout and traffic flow of the whole area around Piazza della Repubblica without attracting much notice. In fact, the train station takes its name from these thermal baths, the Terme di Diocleziano, which were Rome's largest.

These baths were not always so inconspicuous—Emperor Diocletian destroyed an entire neighborhood between A.D. 298 and 305 just to build them. Political prisoners were mostly responsible for building them, especially early adherents of Christianity. Three aqueducts kept fresh water flowing in. The baths have been reinvented many times over the years: as a storage center for grain and oil, a hospital, a cotton refinery, and a brewery, among other things.

Take a walk around the perimeter of the ruins, starting from Piazza dei Cinquecento in front of the station. This section of the ruins has been revamped to hold a wonderful collection of ancient art, the Museo Nazionale Romano. Continue clockwise around the gated brick ruins, which give way to the circular Piazza della Repubblica, formerly known as Piazza Esedra. This square takes its more traditional name from the *exedra* that used to be here—a semicircular atrium that functioned as a gathering place for bathers. This edge of the baths has since been reconverted into the Basilica of Santa Maria degli Angeli.

Pass the church and take the first right on Via Cernaia, offering the best views of the ruined baths on both sides of the street. The high inner brick walls remain intact, some with tall curved niches. From here you can see down into the back courtyards of the museum, with its carefully pruned orange trees and fragments of ancient sculpture dug up from this area. Unfortunately, the ruins of the baths are not open to visitors.

After making the full circle back to the station, enter through the museum to get into the spectacular inner courtyard, the **Chiostro della Certosa**, also called the Michelangelesque cloister, based on a design by Michelangelo. It is an enormous square courtyard ringed by short, two-story buildings, and occupies a space already delineated by the ruins of the baths. Its name comes from the silent order of Certosa monks who inhabited the rooms facing onto the cloister.

The cloister is ringed by 100 travertine columns. The walkways have white painted walls and a white vaulted ceiling. The walls are lined with innumerable ancient statues, from fat cherubs to goddesses missing heads and limbs. Many have accompanying tags explaining when and where they were found. A surprisingly large number were found in the 19th and 20th centuries on streets whose names are instantly recognizable and now heavily developed.

The cloister's most striking features are the boulder-sized horse and oxen heads that peek out from the bushes at the meeting of the four paths that lead to the central fountain. The best time to visit is an hour or two before sunset; the sun's low rays warm up the pumpkin-and-brick-colored, ivy-covered buildings beyond the cloister.

Make your way back to the brick-fronted **Santa Maria degli Angeli**. Michelangelo designed this unusual building in the 1560s, along with the Chiostro della Certosa behind it. Its tall brick facade is concave, taking its shape from the baths' *exedra*. Michelangelo converted the bath's

Santa Maria degli Angeli

tepidarium into a long hall with an entrance at the foot, near the train station. What used to be the nave became the transept in 1749, when Vanvitelli built a new entrance to the church at Piazza Esedra.

The unusual layout has a humbling effect. The entrance takes you into a round, domed vestibule with an expansive, shiny marble floor. Walking though this space takes you into the transept, Michelangelo's nave. It's a vast open space with the clear, glinting marble floor of a skating rink or ballroom. Enormous vaults secure the towering ceiling. The eight pink-granite columns leading from here into the altar area measure about 45-feet high. The sheer size and lack of clutter makes Santa Maria degli Angeli dwarf Rome's other churches, and gives it a definite sense of purpose, similar to the feeling of awe created by a Gothic cathedral.

Unfortunately, the most interesting paintings are on the walls in the altar area, which is closed off. They are *The Martyrdom of Saint Sebastian* by Domenichino and *The Baptism of Our Lord* by Carlo Maratta.

An interesting strip of inlaid numbers and zodiac symbols runs from near the altar to the back right corner of the transept. It's a solar clock that was built in 1702 and used to calibrate Rome's clocks until 1846. Sunlight enters the room through a tiny but visible hole in the upper edge of the right wall. A daily announcement is posted on a bulletin board predicting at exactly which time of day the sun will cross the meridian (solar noon). A second notice excuses the slight variation from this formula—the hole was tampered with a few years ago and has thrown off the clock's precision.

Back over by the Termini Station is the **Palazzo dell'ex Collegio Massimo**, another branch of the Museo Nazionale Romano. The 16th-century palazzo was renovated in 1995 and 1998 to improve the look of the museum's impressive collection of ancient Roman art. The pieces are arranged on three levels and make use of the inner courtyard's natural lighting. Republican-era busts and full portraits are one of the museum's strong points. Other sculptures to look for are the statue of the *Discobolo Lancellotti* (Discus Player), whose focused concentration and swinging motion are reflected in every inch of marble muscle. It is a Roman copy of an earlier Greek original, as is the strange *Sleeping Hermaphrodite,* thought to have originally decorated a private garden. You can trace the development of Roman sculpture through early Christian times with one particularly rich statue of *Christ the Teacher,* made in the 3rd century A.D. The earlier glorification of human anatomy peters out in this era, when figures are clothed and carving becomes more streamlined.

Palazzo Massimo has a collection of Roman frescoes, friezes, and mosaics taken from the area's villas for preservation. A guide will accompany you on this part of the visit, but serves more as a guard than a source of background information.

Walk down the busy Via Cavour to Piazza dell'Esquilino and go one block downhill to catch Via Urbana. Close to the corner on the right is the recessed **Church of Santa Pudenziana**, built in the 4th century. Sources differ on whether or not Saint Pudenziana actually existed. Some say that this was the site of the house of Pudens, a Roman senator who once hosted Saint Peter and his two daughters, Pudenziana and Praxedes (the nearby church of Santa Prassede is devoted to her). Others say "Pudenziana" is a derivation of "Pudens" and was simply the name that the building kept when it was transformed into public baths some time between the 1st and 4th centuries A.D.

Two staircases lead down to the rectangular courtyard. A brick-tiered campanile was added in the 13th century and is visible from the street level. Various

Terme di Diocleziano

renovations throughout the centuries have left their marks, including two levels of medieval carved detailing and brightly colored frescoes covering the facade. Inside, some parts of the walls reveal the original brick, with ancient gray columns holding up the wall's reinforcing arches.

The 4th-century apse mosaic is the real artistic focus of the church. It has been heavily restored, with arguable success, but still conveys an unusually complex approach to composition, with toga-clad apostles facing different directions. There is also a highly developed sense of three-dimensionality in the roof tiles and cityscape behind the figures. This mosaic is one of Rome's few surviving Christian mosaics that shows no influence of the later, flatter Byzantine style.

Santa Pudenziana

In a small room upstairs and behind the apse, 11th-century frescoes demonstrate a heavy Byzantine influence. The main panel shows Mary and Jesus with Saint Pudenziana and her sister, while the two side frescoes show Saint Paul baptizing Pudenziana's brothers and preaching to the masses. The room is usually closed to the public, but you may convince the groundskeeper to let you in.

Some niches and stretches of original flooring are visible in the curved chamber behind the apse. The Caetani Chapel on the left of the nave is the church's largest. Its altar displays Pier Paolo Olivieri's 16th-century bas-relief, *The Adoration of the Magi,* plus two funeral monuments by Maderno and statues of the cardinal virtues by pupils of Bernini. The round stone barrel covering near the chapel is said to be the opening of the well where Saint Pudenziana buried the bones of 3,000 martyrs—a story that sounds suspiciously like the tale of her sister, Saint Praxedes (see Focus).

FURTHER INFORMATION

Palazzo dell'ex Collegio Massimo/ Museo Nazionale Romano (see also museum entry)
Largo di Villa Peretti, 1; tel.: 06-48903500.

Santa Maria degli Angeli
Piazza della Repubblica; tel.: 06-4880812; open: 7 A.M.–6:30 P.M., Sun. 8 A.M.–7:30 P.M.

Santa Pudenziana
Via Urbana, 160; tel.: 06-4814622; open: weekdays 8 A.M.–noon, 3–6 P.M., Sun. 9 A.M.–noon, 3–6 P.M.

Terme di Diocleziano/Museo Nazionale Romano (Baths of Diocletian) (see also museum entry)
Via Enrico De Nicola, 78; tel.: 06-39967700; open: 9 A.M.–7:45 P.M.; closed: Mon.

FOCUS: SANTA PRASSEDE

Via Santa Prassede, 9A; tel.: 06-4882456; open: daily 7 A.M.–NOON, 4–6:30 P.M.

By Ruth Kaplan

View into a vault, Santa Prassede

Santa Prassede is not one of Rome's most visited churches, but it should be. Some of Rome's most striking Byzantine mosaics are here, and the floors, ceilings, and myriad decorative surfaces are clean and bright, showing little effects of aging.

Saint Praxedes, after whom the church is named, was an early Christian saint who lived in this area. An early oratory had already developed on this ground, a transformation of a 2nd-century-A.D. apartment block, when the site was overhauled to build the current structure in A.D. 822. The renovations were carried out in conjunction with the transfer of the bones of 2,000 martyrs from the catacombs, where they were no longer safe due to Saracen invasions. Saint Praxedes is said to have gathered those martyrs' bones and buried them here.

The simple Romanesque entrance leads into the right side of the high-ceilinged nave. A small chapel immediately to its right contains some decorative carvings from the earlier oratory. Moving down toward the rear of the nave brings into view the extensive 9th-century mosaics covering the presbytery and apse. In bold, colorful strokes they show Saints Peter and Paul introducing Praxedes and her sister, Saint Pudenziana, to Christ. Pope Paschal I, who was largely responsible for the church's construction, is in the background holding a model of the building. The arches leading out toward the nave are done in colorful mosaic depicting the elect being led into the Eternal City by angels.

The Chapel of San Zenone off the right aisle, nicknamed "The Garden of Paradise," offers an incredible chance to see 9th-century mosaic work—in strict Byzantine style—up close: it is little more than a stuffy, closed room, totally encrusted in tile. The chips have kept their intense orange, rust, and teal colors, and are arranged to show four large angels holding a disc with the bust of Jesus. Off to the side in a reliquary is a two-foot-high black-and-white marble column supposedly used in the flagellation of Christ. Bernini's first tomb, done in black stone, is in the chapel next to San Zenone.

Cosmati floorwork is almost ubiquitous in Rome's medieval churches, but here it's a bit different; tiles were machine-cut and convincingly arranged in 1917.

Two rows of carved columns split off the side aisles from the main nave. Mannerist frescoes cover the walls above them in large, colorful panels. Under the red marble steps leading up to the altar are the two inlaid tombs of Saint Praxedes and her sister, Pudenziana.

Other Points of Interest

AUDITORIO DI MECENATE (AUDITORIUM OF MAECENAS)

Largo Leopardi, 2; tel.: 06-4873262; open: Tues.–Sat. 9 A.M.–7 P.M., Sun. 9 A.M.–1 P.M.; admission: €2.

➤ The Auditorium of Maecenas is the ancient Roman summer dining room, or nymphaeum, of the Horti Maecenas, the imposing villa of Maecenas. There are fragments of frescoes depicting landscapes and gardens, as well as mosaic floors and painted floors. Usually there are very few visitors to this hall where Virgil and Horace once read poetry to their patron, Maecenas.

PORTA MAGGIORE

Piazza di Porta Maggiore

➤ The Porta Maggiore stands at one of the tallest parts of the Esquiline Hill, where eight of the eleven Roman aqueducts met. This monumental gate was built by Claudius in A.D. 82, utilizing the arches of his aqueduct that crossed the Prenestina and Labicana roads.

PORTA MAGICA

Piazza Vittorio Emanuele II

➤ In the 18th century, the former queen of Sweden attracted many artists and intellectuals to Rome—and also a circle of alchemists. The latter group used to meet in the villa of Marquis Massimiliano di Palombara, near Piazza Vittorio Emanuele II. It was the marquis who built the Porta Magica, or Magical Gate, in what was then the garden of his villa and is now the center of the piazza. Twin statues of the Egyptian god Bes stand guard on the sides. In the inscriptions above and to the sides, the marquis sculpted what some consider the magic formula to turn metal into gold. According to legend, the marquis found it in an ancient book. He was unable to decipher the formula, but nonetheless decided to have it sculpted in stone.

SANTA BIBIANA

Via Giovanni Giolitti, 154; tel.: 06-4461021; open: daily 7:30–11 A.M., 4:30–7:30 P.M. (call before going).

➤ Built in the 5th century over the buried remains of 11,266 Christian martyrs, the church was restored in 1626 by Gian Lorenzo Bernini, who added its current facade and two lateral chapels, redefined the apse, and redesigned the main altar. In the main altar, an alabaster basin holds the remains of three martyrs—Bibiana, Dafrosa, and Demetria.

SEPOLCRO DI EURISACE (OR TOMBA DEL FORNAIO)

Piazza di Porta Maggiore

➤ This unusual funerary monument was built by Eurisace, a slave-turned-baker, to celebrate himself, his social ascent, and his profession. It was erected in the last days of the Roman Republic (around the year 30 B.C.).

TEMPIO DI MINERVA MEDICA (TEMPLE OF MINERVA)

Via Giolitti

➤ The name of this temple derives from a statue of Minerva with a snake, the symbol of medicine, found here. This great hall with twelve sides, each provided with a niche, is probably a nyphaeum of the Horti Liciniani, the large villa of the emperor Licinio Gallieno (260–269).

Museums

MUSEO DEGLI STRUMENTI MUSICALI (MUSEUM OF MUSICAL INSTRUMENTS)

Piazza S. Croce in Gerusalemme, 9/A; tel.: 06-7014796; open: 8.30 A.M.–7:30 P.M.; closed: Mon.; admission: €2.

➤ A collection of instruments of great historic value that belonged to tenor Evan Gorga and to Benedetto Marcello.

Porta Magica

Tempio di Minerva Medica

Museo nazionale d'Arte Orientale (National Museum of Eastern Art)

Via Merulana, 247; tel.: 06-4874415; open: 9 A.M.–2 P.M., Sun., Mon., Thurs. 8:30 A.M.– 7:30 P.M.; closed: 1st and 3rd Mon. of each month; admission: €4.

➢ The most important Italian collection of Eastern art, consisting of finds from excavations of the archaeological missions of the Italian Institute for the Middle and Far East.

Aula Ottagona/Museo Nazionale Romano (Octagonal Hall)

Via G. Romita, 8; tel.: 06-4880530; open: 9 A.M.–2 P.M., holidays 9 A.M.–1 P.M.; closed: Mon.; admission: free.

➢ The splendid hall is an integral part of the Baths of Diocletian. It holds important sculptures from Roman bath complexes.

Palazzo dell'ex Collegio Massimo/Museo Nazionale Romano

Largo di Villa Peretti, 1; tel.: 06-48903500; open: 9 A.M.–6:45 P.M.; closed: Mon.; admission: €6.

➢ The completely restored building holds important statues and splendid floor mosaics from Roman villas, as well as a reconstruction of a completely frescoed room belonging to the Villa of Livia. It's extremely rich numismatic collection is not to be missed.

Terme di Diocleziano/ Museo Nazionale Romano (Baths of Diocletian)

Viale Enrico De Nicola, 79; tel.: 06-4880530; open: 9 A.M.–7:45 P.M.; closed: Mon.; admission: €4.

➢ Features an archaeological collection of funerary engravings and remains of the Roman baths, including parts of wall decorations.

Museo Storico della Liberazione di Roma (Historic Museum of the Liberation of Rome)

Via Tasso, 145; tel.: 06-7003866; open: Tues., Thurs., Fri. 10 A.M.–12:30 P.M., 4 P.M.– 7 P.M., Wed. 10 A.M.–12:30 P.M.; Sat., Sun. 9:30 A.M.–12:30 P.M.; closed: Mon.; admission: free.

➢ The building was once the headquarters of the SS Kommandantur, where members of the anti-fascist movement and the Roman Resistance were interrogated, tortured, and imprisoned.

Museo Storico Vaticano (Vatican History Museum)

Palazzo Apostolico Lateranense, Piazza di San Giovanni in Laterano; tel.: 06-69884947; open: Mon.–Fri. 8:45 A.M.–3:20 P.M., Sat. and the last Sun. of every month 8:45 A.M.– 12:20 P.M.; closed: public and religious holidays; admission: €3.

➢ Visit the Papal apartment and chapel. In the museum, there are collections of weapons and two sections on the iconography of the popes and papal ceremonial objects.

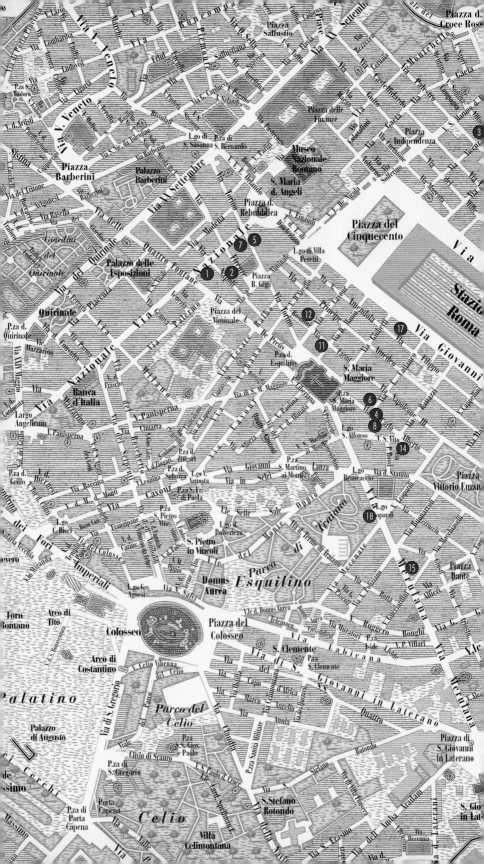

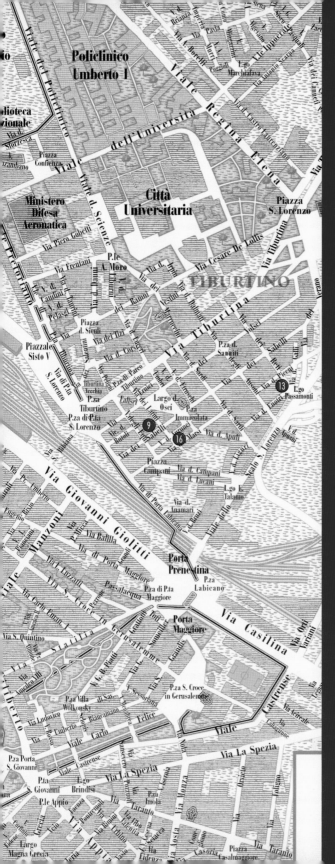

Laterano/Esquilino/Termini

Hotels & Inns
1. Hotel Artemide
2. Hotel Britannia
3. Hotel Canada
4. Hotel Mecenate Palace
5. Hotel Mondial
6. Hotel Montreal
7. Hotel Quirinale

Restaurants & Cafés
8. Agata e Romeo*
9. Il Dito e la Luna
10. Il Palazzo del Freddo
11. Monte Caruso "Il Cicilardone"
12. Pizzeria Gallina Bianca
13. Tram Tram
14. Trattoria Monti

Shopping
15. Panella: L'Arte del Pane

Best of
16. Arancia Blu
17. Leonidas di georgette
18. Panella

HOTELS & INNS

Hotel Artemide

Via Nazionale, 22; tel.: 06-489911/4899 700; e-mail: hotel.artemide@tiscalinet.it; category: ★★★★; number of rooms: 85; credit cards accepted: all major; access to internet: direct-line (US, UK) telephone jack in superior rooms or use of a free internet station in the hotel; most beautiful room: penthouse; €€€€.

☞This five-story late-19th-century palazzo has been completely renovated with Liberty-style furnishings. All the rooms are quiet and newly furnished with a mini-bar. The larger rooms all have a VCR and couch. Non-smoking rooms are also available. A handsome restaurant on the lower level is open for lunch and dinner, with good food. A busy café with lighter fare is open all day and evening.

Hotel Britannia

Via Napoli, 64; tel.: 06-4883153/ 4882343; e-mail: info@hotelbritannia.it; website: www.hotelbritannia.it; category: ★★★★; number of rooms: 33, including 1 suite; credit cards accepted: all major; facilities: free parking, air conditioning, babysitting services; access to internet: direct-line (US, UK) telephone jack in all rooms; most beautiful room: 402; €€–€€€.

☞Hotel Britannia is located in the center of Rome in an old palazzo once owned by the aristocratic Orsini family. The entryway may be small, but the rooms are comfortable and snazzily decorated, with interesting photomontages on the walls, good lighting, TVs, and safes. All bathrooms have bronzing lamps. Soundproofed rooms are available. Some rooms have balconies. Located on a side street, this family-run hotel is quite peaceful, even though it's only a one-minute walk to Via Nazionale.

Hotel Canada

Via Vicenza, 58; tel.: 06-4457770/4450749; e-mail: info@hotelcanadaroma.com; website: www.hotelcanadaroma.com; category: ★★★★; number of rooms: 70; credit cards accepted: all major; access to internet: direct-line (US, UK) telephone jack in all rooms; most beautiful room: 322; €€.

☞This family-run hotel is housed in an elegant, old building near the Termini railroad station. There are period furnishings and paintings and an attentive and responsive staff.

Hotel Mecenate Palace

Via Carlo Alberto, 3; tel.: 06-44702024/ 4461354; e-mail: info@mecenatepalace. com; website: www.mecenatepalace.com; category: ★★★★; number of rooms: 62, including 3 suites; credit cards accepted: all major; facilities: parking (€25 a night); access to internet: use of one computer in the lobby; most beautiful rooms: 323 (double), 557 (suite); €€-€€€€.

☞Located on one of Rome's rare wide, tree-lined streets in front of the Church of Santa Maria Maggiore. Rooms are welcoming, with wall-to-wall carpeting and new bathrooms. Some rooms have an excellent view of the church. The roof terrace offers spectacular views in all directions. In the summer a bar operates there, and breakfast is served all year round.

Hotel Mondial

Via Torino, 127; tel.: 06-472861/4824822; e-mail: md3058@mclink.it; website: www.hotelmondialrome.com; category: ★★★★; number of rooms: 84; credit cards accepted: all major; access to internet: direct-line (US, UK) telephone jack in all rooms; €€€–€€€€

☞In a 19th-century building not far from the Termini railroad station and the Santa Maria degli Angeli church, this family-run hotel has a friendly and attentive staff.

Hotel Montreal

Via Carlo Alberto, 4; tel.: 06-4457797/ 446514; e-mail: info@hotelmontreal roma.com; website: www.hotelmontreal roma.com; category: ★★; number of rooms: 22; credit cards accepted: all major; access to internet: direct-line (US, UK) telephone jack in almost all rooms; most beautiful rooms: rooms on the first floor, especially 107; €–€€.

HOTELS & INNS

Hotel Quirinale

Via Nazionale, 7; tel.: 06-4707/4820099; e-mail: booking@hotelquirinale.it; website: www.hotelquirinale.it; category: ★★★★; number of rooms: 204, including 13 suites; credit cards accepted: all major; facilities:

parking in nearby garage (€25 a night); access to internet: free access from lounge, €€€.

☞Retro atmosphere with period furnishings. It has its own private garden.

RESTAURANTS & CAFÉS

Agata e Romeo

Via Carlo Alberto, 45; tel.: 06-4466115; closed: Sat., Sun.; credit cards accepted: all major; €€€€ (special tastings menu with wine).

☞A Rome institution run by Agata Parisella and Romeo Caraccio, who married some 30 years ago. Their shared passion for popular cuisine is showcased at this elegant restaurant, founded by Agata's grandparents 80 years ago as a neighborhood osteria. Still mom-and-pop in feel, the menu is based on simple ingredients, heavy flavors, and massive portions. Dishes include *fusilli con radicchio e speck, risotto zizzania,* and *budino al parmigiano con funghi.* Under the dining room is a basement where local wines were once funneled into oversized storage barrels. Now the cantina houses some of the world's best bottles.

Il Palazzo del Freddo

Via Principe Eugenio, 65/67; tel.: 06-4464740; credit cards accepted: all major.

☞Run by local personality Giovanni Fassi—and sometimes just referred to as "Fassi's place"—this is one of the capital's best gelaterie. The century-old ice cream factory serves colorful and varied flavors, including rice, coconut, kiwi, white chocolate, and marzipan.

Monte Caruso "Il Cicilardone"

Via Farini, 12; tel.: 06-484436; open: noon– 3 P.M., 7:30 P.M.–midnight; closed: Mon. lunch and all day Sun.; credit cards accepted: all major; €.

☞The menu here is limited in size, but with a good balance between Roman standards, like fettuccine with meat sauce, and

one-of-a-kind first courses, like *ciabatte,* a small pasta prepared with soft cow's milk cheese, or the *panchilose,* pappardelle pasta with eggs, peas, bacon, mushrooms, and grated cheese. Second courses include roast veal with truffle cream, stuffed zucchini, and *pezze pezze,* thinly sliced beef with peppers, oregano, garlic, and oil.

Pizzeria Gallina Bianca

Via Antonio Rosmini, 9; tel.: 06-4743777; always open; credit cards accepted: all major; €.

☞Possibly the home of Rome's best pizza served in a friendly, homey atmosphere, this pizzeria offers traditional toppings— from mozzarella to mushrooms—on a crust that is rolled slightly thicker than the norm in Rome. Unlike many other pizza joints, Gallina Bianca's pies are grease-free and light on the stomach. Start with the excellent house antipasti.

Trattoria Monti

Via San Vito, 13A; tel.: 06-4466573; closed: Sun. night and Mon.; credit cards accepted: all major; €.

☞Run by the Camerucci family and nestled away on the road between Santa Maria Maggiore and Piazza Vittorio is this tiny culinary gem. Specializing in traditional cooking from the Marche region, the chef is especially proud of *tortello di rosso d'uovo,* or pasta stuffed with ricotta cheese and spinach then oven roasted with hard-boiled eggs inside. Another mouthwatering delicacy is *coniglio tartufato,* or rabbit stuffed with pork and spices, drenched in truffle-based olive oil and served with roasted potatoes.

A Tiara Fit For a Queen

By Margaret Stenhouse

There is nothing showy about Mimmo and Danilo Ranati's costume jewelry business on Via Merulana, the tree-lined avenue on the slopes of the Esquiline, which Pope Sixtus V built to connect the two basilicas of Santa Maria Maggiore and San Giovanni in Laterano. However, for the past 36 years, Dierre Bijoux, with its display windows and cramped workshop tucked away inside the gray portal of No. 165, has been a Roman institution and a pillar of Italian couture.

In a typical day's work, Mimmo and his son, Danilo, will be taking orders for diamanté belts to grace the catwalk at the next Milan showing, and helping a customer rake through boxes of beads and baubles to embellish the collar of a homemade party dress.

The little workshop/showroom, piled from floor to ceiling with cases of designer buttons, colored glass beads, crystal droplets, sequins, gilt chains, links and clasps, and delicate rhinestone bridal diadems, is decorated on its one free wall with photos of some of the business's most illustrious clients, like Swedish movie star Anita Ekberg, stylists Franco Litrico and Sorelle Fontana, and a series of radiant Miss Italia winners, bearing Ranati tiaras and scepters.

Mimmo created the regalia for the Miss Italia pageant for over ten years. A photo of him standing beside one of the leggy title-bearers graces the wall of his shop. When the store was larger, he displayed the regalia there.

Authentic works of art, the regalia take weeks to make. The tiara for the 1992 pageant weighed over two pounds and was decorated with more than 800 different colored rhinestones and crystals. The scepter, which was even more ornate, weighed over three pounds.

The Ranati art adorns the haute couture creations of designers like Gattinoni and Gai Mattioli, but their workshop draws customers from every walk of life. Like all true dedicated craftsmen, Mimmo and Danilo treat all alike and will happily spend hours helping a modest home dressmaker choose a set of buttons.

Dierre Bijoux, Via Merulana, 165; tel. and fax: 06-70494695.

SPECIALTY SHOPS

Panella: L'Arte del Pane

Via Merulana, 54/55; tel.: 06-4872651; open: 8:30 A.M.–1:30 P.M., 5 P.M.–8 P.M.; closed: Thurs., Sun. afternoons.

☛One of Rome's most celebrated bakeries, stuffed with sweet and savory goodies, melt-in-your-mouth cakes, and sophisticated party takeout. Admire the magnificent bread sculptures on display. A favorite with locals for Sunday morning aperitifs. Just next door to the Auditorium of Mecenate.

OUR CRITIC'S FAVORITE RESTAURANTS

Il Dito e la Luna

Via dei Sabelli, 49/51; tel.: 06-4940726; closed: Sun.; €.

☛When the finger—*il dito*—points to the moon—*la luna*—only the imbecile watches the finger. So goes an old saying that seems to inspire this trattoria. Here, however, all eyes are on the dinner plate, which comes topped with exquisitely prepared delicacies from southern Italy, like the tasty Tropea red onion flan or seafood in a potato crust. Extensive wine list. Reservations required.

Tram Tram

Via dei Reti, 46; tel.: 06-490416; closed: Mon.; €.

☛While the streetcars rambling by seemed to be a disadvantage at first, they have become an endearing characteristic of this pleasant restaurant, which owes its name to the tram that crisscrosses the San Lorenzo neighborhood. At the bar, demanding wine connoisseurs can order by the glass from a substantial wine list. The dining room, on the other hand, can accommodate up to 50 patrons more interested in tasting well-prepared regional specialties like lamb with potatoes, *pasta alla Norma* (with eggplant), *orecchiette* with broccoli and clams, and stewed calamari. Reservations required.

Quirinale/Tridente

By Ruth Kaplan

ome grandeur tends to blend in around the architecturally crowded Via del Corso area, but some researched wandering can lead you to the best of the city's modern monuments. In Piazza Santi Apostoli, the sprawling 15th-century **Palazzo Colonna** arches over into the villa and gardens to its east and houses both a church and the **Galleria Colonna**, with collections of Renaissance painting and Roman sculpture. Narrow streets lead to the grandeur of the **Fontana di Trevi**, which has been stealing attention from neighboring buildings since being installed by Nicola Salvi in 1762. The carved A.D. 180 **Colonna di Marco Aurelio** decorates the square across Via del Corso and one block up, with intricate reliefs winding up its 100 feet. It faces **Palazzo Chigi**, the 16th-century palace that has been used since the end of World War II to house the offices of Italy's 40-some prime ministers. Italy's lower house of Parliament meets in the nearby **Palazzo Montecitorio**, a spacious 17th-century building designed by Bernini with a self-confident, slightly curved facade. In the piazza is a 6th-century-B.C. Egyptian **obelisk** brought to Rome by Augustus, who used it as the arm of a sundial in a nearby piazza until it was moved here. The ancient **Ara Pacis**, or Altar of Peace, is just north, sandwiched between the Tiber and Via del Corso. The Senate commissioned the carved marble monument in 13 B.C. to applaud Augustus's act of bringing peace to the Mediterranean.

Via del Corso terminates at the vast **Piazza del Popolo**, an important medieval point of entry into the city. The **Pincio Gardens** overlook the piazza and offer an impressive panorama of Saint Peter's dome. On the gardens' edge is the slightly crumbling 19th-century **Casina Valadier**, whose café used to be a hot spot for famous visitors, from Gandhi to Mussolini. The Pincio Gardens blend into the grounds of the elegant 16th-century **Villa Medici**.

The curvy cascade of stairs by the Church of Trinità dei Monti are the famous **Spanish Steps**. The boat-shaped fountain at the base of the stairs spouts drinkable water. An informative museum of English Romantic poets has been set up in the **Keats-Shelley Memorial House** here, where Keats spent his last years.

Southeast of here, Bernini's **Fontana del Tritone** marks Piazza Barberini. Farther up is **Palazzo Barberini**, which houses the **Galleria Nazionale di Arte Antica**, one of the city's most impressive art collections.

Take a right on Via del Quirinale to skirt the enclosed gardens of the **Palazzo del Quirinale**, built on one of the city's seven hills in the 16th century as the pope's summer residence. Today it is the official home of Italy's president.

Left, Fontana del Tritone

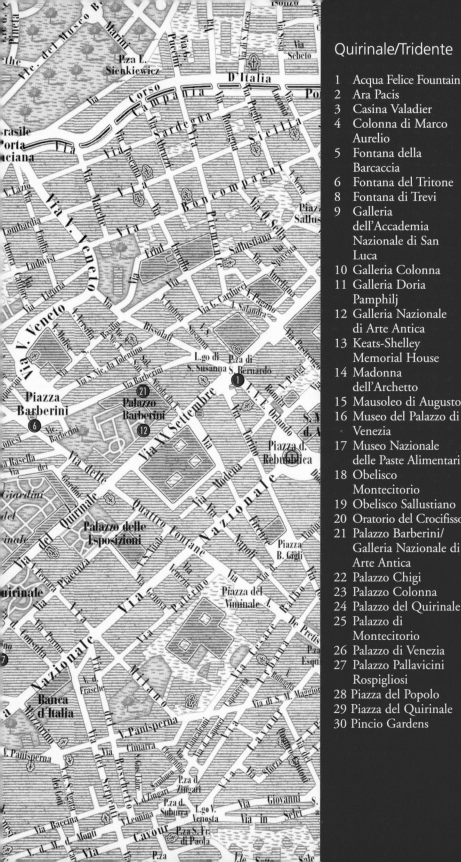

Quirinale/Tridente

Quirinale/Tridente

Ara Pacis (Altar of Peace)

Lungotevere in Augusta; tel.: 06-68806848.

➤ Reconstructed over a period of many years, at great expense, the Ara Pacis, or Altar of Peace, is a highly significant monument of ancient Rome, probably the most significant from the reign of Augustus. In 13 B.C. the Senate commissioned the monument and it was completed four years later. It was positioned in such a way that the shadow of the huge obelisk arm of the sundial on the Campus Martius (a field named after Mars, the god of war) would fall on the monument on Augustus's birthday. It symbolizes the rise of peace created by Emperor Augustus's victorious campaigns in Gaul and Spain, and throughout the Mediterranean. In the 16th century the first marble panels that surrounded the altar were unearthed. In the 19th century archaeologists became aware of the real significance of what had been discovered accidentally. The walls are decorated with magnificent friezes and reliefs of rare elegance in the Hellenistic tradition, carved in Carrara marble. On the base itself, an account of the emperor's political career is engraved with the text "Res Gestae Divi Augusti." On the north and south walls, the reliefs depict a procession that took place in 13 B.C. on July 4. Members of the emperor's family can be identified, ranked by their position in the procession.

Casina Valadier

Pincio Gardens

➤ This neoclassical café has played host to the famous, including Richard Strauss, Benito Mussolini, King Farouk, and Mahatma Gandhi. It is named after its architect. The huge terrace on the left, high above Piazza del Popolo, offers a spectacular panoramic view of Rome.

Colonna di Marco Aurelio (Column of Marcus Aurelius)

Piazza Colonna

➤ At 137 feet, the Column of Marcus Aurelius is the tallest column in Rome. It was erected after the death of Marcus Aurelius in A.D. 180, to celebrate the emperor's victories over the Germanic populations of eastern Europe.

The column was constructed in marble, is almost 12 feet in diameter, and has a staircase of 201 steps. Like Trajan's Column, it is decorated by a continuous frieze, which narrates war events in a bold and simple carving style. However, the events are represented with more violence and cruelty than in Trajan's Column; the action looks almost like a continuous battle. A statue of the emperor once stood on top of the column, but it was plundered in the Middle Ages.

In 1588–1589 Domenico Fontana rebuilt the basement and added a statue of Saint Paul to the crown. An inscription on the column wrongly attributing it to Emperor Antoninus Pius gave it the nickname *colonna antonina*.

Fontana della Barcaccia (Barcaccia Fountain)

Piazza di Spagna

➤ Commissioned by Pope Urban VIII, the Barcaccia Fountain was built in 1629 by Pietro Bernini, with the help of his promising son Gian Lorenzo, to commemorate the disastrous flood of the Tiber River in 1598. It depicts a symmetrical, half-sunken boat.

Colonna di Marco Aurelio

The street-level basin, thought up by the young Gian Lorenzo, was supposed to resolve the difficulty of poor water pressure. The sun and bees are the coat of arms of the Barberini house, Pope Urban VIII's family. In the 17th century, two countries battled for cultural supremacy in this piazza. The French dominated the northern part, above the Spanish Steps, with Trinità dei Monti and Villa Medici, and the Spanish dominated the southern part, where the Spanish ambassador resided, giving the piazza its name.

FONTANA DEL TRITONE (FOUNTAIN OF THE TRITON)
Piazza Barberini
➤ Bernini created the travertine Fountain of the Triton for Pope Urban VIII in 1642, just as construction of the nearby Palazzo Barberini was drawing to an end. It was Bernini's first public fountain. In it he experimented with architectural techniques that would later be used in his Fountain of the Four Rivers in Piazza Navona. The fish that grow out of the four-lobed basin throw their tails upward, toward the unmistakable coat of arms of the Barberini family, the bees. A triton is seen blowing through the conch with all his might, spraying water over the entire sculpture. The fountain is a beautiful example of Roman baroque style.

FONTANA DI TREVI (TREVI FOUNTAIN)
Piazza di Trevi
➤ Pope Nicholas V first built a fountain here in the middle of the 15th century to celebrate the reactivation of an ancient Roman aqueduct, which Agrippa once constructed in order to bring water to his baths near the Pantheon.

In 1733 Nicola Salvi began work on a new, much more ambitious fountain, which eventually became one of the most well-known symbols of baroque Rome. His design was original and striking. It was built like the stage of a huge open-air theater, with a triumphal arch, two orders of four columns, and a balustrade with four statues representing the benefits of water. In the center of the arch is a huge statue of *Ocean*, standing on a shell-shaped carriage being pushed by two seahorses and pulled in front by two tritons, works of Pietro Bracci. On the sides are *Abundance* and

Health, sculpted by Filippo della Valle.

The Trevi Fountain was inaugurated in May 1762. The water, called *acqua vergine*, once considered the best in Rome, was, and still is, conveyed by subterranean aqueducts fourteen miles in length.

OBELISCO DI MONTECITORIO (MONTECITORIO OBELISK)
Piazza Montecitorio
➤ The obelisk of Psammeticus II (594–589 B.C.), made of red granite and 30-yards tall, was moved to Rome from Heliopolis. Augustus wanted it as a pointer of a sundial in the Campus Martius, thus its nickname of Obeliscus Solaris. It crumbled in the 11th century when the Normans sacked the city. Giovanni Antinori rebuilt it in 1792, using parts from the Column of Antoninus Pius, under the auspices of Pius VI. The pope decided to restore it as a solar clock, by adding the papal sigil as pointer. Its hieroglyphics are considered technically perfect. Antinori added a globe with a hole in the center on top of the obelisk.

PALAZZO BARBERINI (SEE GALLERIA NAZIONALE DI ARTE ANTICA IN MUSEUMS)
Via delle Quattro Fontane, 13; tel.: 06-4824184.
➤ Palazzo Barberini was designed and started by Carlo Maderno, at the request of Pope Urban VIII, but completed by Bernini and Borromini.

Maderno began building a unique and bold design on the site of another palazzo, the villa of Cardinal Francesco Barberini. The wings of Palazzo Barberini extended into the existing villa gardens, blending in with the shape of the traditional aristocratic palazzo.

After Maderno's death, Bernini and Borromini added to and somewhat transformed the design. Bernini was responsible for a glassed-in loggia and the stairway with a square stairwell. Borromini built the oval, spiral staircase, and the twin columns to the right side of the building's elevation.

Originally, the top palazzo floor held the library of Cardinal Barberini, with 60,000 volumes and 10,000 manuscripts. The Vatican Library bought it in 1900, with the original bookshelves designed by Bernini.

In the palazzo, an extravagant and lavish room known as the Gran Salone has a

PALAZZO AND PIAZZA BARBERINI

The portrait of Beatrice di Cenci, in the Palazzo Barberini, is a picture almost impossible to be forgotten. Through the transcendent sweetness and beauty of the face, there is something shining out, that haunts me. . . . She has turned suddenly towards you; and there is an expression in the eyes—although they are very tender and gentle—as if the wildness of a momentary terror, or distraction, had been struggled with and overcome, that instant; and nothing but a celestial hope, and a beautiful sorrow.

—Charles Dickens, *Pictures from Italy*

beautiful ceiling fresco, *The Triumph of Divine Providence*, by painter and architect Pietro da Cortona. The fresco scene portrays a dramatic celebration of Pope Urban VIII and his family.

The building was purchased by the Italian state in 1949 to house the Galleria Nazionale di Arte Antica, which contains extraordinary artwork, including *La Fornarina* by Raphael, and *Judith and Holofernes* and *Narcissus* by Caravaggio.

PALAZZO CHIGI
Piazza Colonna

➤ At Palazzo Chigi, now home to Italy's prime minister, was first built by Matteo da Città di Castello in 1580 for the Aldobrandini family. The Chigi family purchased the building in 1659, later adding a courtyard, adorned by an elegant and original square stucco scheme, as well as a stairway, decorated with antique sculptures. The Chigis, a family of bankers from Siena, were well known for their enthusiastic patronage of the arts. In the 18th century, G. B. Contini finally completed the palazzo, adding a portal overlooking Piazza Colonna and redecorating the interior.

Some of its rooms are still decorated with furniture, mirrors, and paintings from the Chigis' collection. In 1917 the palace was sold to the Italian State and in 1961 it became the seat of the prime minister.

PALAZZO COLONNA
(SEE GALLERIA COLONNA IN MUSEUMS)
Via della Pilotta, 17; tel.: 06-679436; website: www.galleriacolonna.it; to visit the private Princess Isabella Apartment, tel.: 06-6784350.

➤ Palazzo Colonna originated with a 15th-century building, which Pope Martin V, of the Colonna family, commissioned next to the Santi Apostoli basilica. Over the next two centuries, the Colonnas introduced new additions to the building, until the current complex was completed in 1730.

In 1654–1665 Cardinal Girolamo Colonna established the galleria, which contains a spectacular group of paintings from the 14th to 18th centuries, as well as Roman statues.

The Sala della Colonna Bellica is named after the *rosso antico* marble column that stands in the center. In the vault are the *Apotheosis of Marcantonio II*, a fresco by Giuseppe Bartolomeo Chiari (1689– 1702), and paintings hanging on the walls by Dosso Dossi, Bronzino (*Venus, Cupid and Satyr*), Michele di Ridolfo del Ghirlandaio (*Venus and Adonis*), and Jacopo Tintoretto (*Narcissus at the Spring*).

The upper hall is separated from the lower one by a pair of Corinthian columns of *giallo antico*. Seven steps, decorated with stuccoes, large mirrors, and frescoes, lead into the Sala Grande. The cannonball embedded in the marble steps recalls the French bombing at the time of the Roman Republic. Worth noting are the canvases by Guido Reni (*Saint Francis with Two Angels*) and Francesco Salviati (*Adam and Eve*). The vault, painted by Giovanni Coli and Filippo Gherardi in 1678, depicts the Battle of Lepanto, mostly celebrating Marcantonio Colonna. The fresco is one of the best examples of the Roman decorative baroque tradition. The magnificent hall was the setting for the famous final

The Obelisk, Piazza del Quirinale

• Princess Isabella Apartments

➤ Ten 15th-century rooms of what is still today the Colonna family's extraordinary private residence, inside the so-called Palazzo Vecchio, are open to visitors, featuring hosts of paintings and antique furniture. The palazzo's richest and most important hall is the Sala della Fontana, which houses frescoes by Pinturicchio.

Palazzo del Quirinale

Piazza del Quirinale; tel.: 06-46991; fax: 06-46993125; www.quirinale.it; open: Sun. 8:30 A.M.–12:30 P.M.; closed July, Aug.; admission: €5; credit cards accepted: none.

➤ The Palazzo del Quirinale exemplifies baroque Rome as well as political power. Begun in 1574, it was used for papal conclaves until 1846, and was a favorite summer residence of the popes. In 1870 it was taken over by the king of Italy, and in 1948, by the president. Built between the late 16th and mid-18th centuries on the site of a 15th-century villa, the palazzo was enlarged and embellished by the most important architects of the Counter-Reformation and the baroque period, including Ottavio Nonni, known as Il Mascherino; Domenico Fontana; Flaminio Ponzio; Carlo Maderno; and Gian Lorenzo Bernini.

The Gardens of the Quirinale, open to the public every year on June 2 for the celebration of the Italian Republic, offer a beautiful view. The trim box hedges and clipped avenues remind one of Pliny's account of the gardens in his villa outside the city.

The palazzo stands in a piazza, commissioned by Gregory XIII and Pius IX, that offers one of the most stunning views of the city. The two-level, late-Renaissance facade was designed by Fontana in 1589. On top of the entrance portico, decorated by two statues of Saints Peter and Paul, is Bernini's

scene of the movie *Roman Holiday*, with Audrey Hepburn and Gregory Peck.

Beyond the Sala dei Paesaggi (Hall of Landscapes), is a case made from sandalwood and precious stones and one made of ebony with carved ivory panels. The Sala dell'Apoteosi di Martino V, named after the painting by Benedetto Luti (1720), has the *Bean-Eater* by Annibale Carracci, and the *Portrait of the Gentleman* by Paolo Veronese. The Sala del Trono still displays the throne itself, turned around toward the wall to recall the absence of the ruling pope or as a protest against the unification of Italy, which deprived the Church of its temporal power. The Sale dei Primitivi contains artwork from the 15th and 16th centuries, as well as the pretentious *Resurrection of Christ* and *Members of the Colonna Family*, by the young Pietro da Cortona.

PALAZZO CHIGI

I have seen the column of Antoninus and the Chigi Palace by moonlight. To take in even a small part of everything there is to see here would take a lifetime or, rather, the return of many human beings learning from each other in turn.

—Goethe, *Italian Journey*

Loggia delle Benedizioni (1863). A circular tower on the left, also by Bernini, lends a certain rhythm. At the end of the courtyard, whose severe portico by Fontana (1589) is a masterpiece of Counter-Reformation architecture, stands the 16th-century *palazzetto* built by Mascherino. The yard and the *palazzetto* are used by the president to welcome heads of state. On the landing of the Scalone d'onore, designed by Ponzio in 1611–1612, is a very important fresco of the Ascension by Melozzo da Forlì (1472), which formerly adorned a side chapel in the Basilica of Santi Apostoli. The Sala Regia is 190-feet long. Here, the cardinals met for papal elections. The floor is inlaid with precious marble, and the richly gilt ceiling is adorned with frescoes of scenes from the Old and New Testament by Lanfranco and Agostino Tassi. The Paolina Chapel, as large as the Sistine Chapel in the Vatican, was stuccoed by Martino Ferrabosco, while the Sala del Diluvio was frescoed by Antonio Carracci. The private chapel of the popes, known as the Cappelle dell'Annunciata, erected by Paul V, contains a picture of the Annunciation by Guido Reni.

Palazzo di Montecitorio

Piazza Montecitorio tel.: 06-67601; open: guided visits only, first Sunday of the month 10 A.M.–6 P.M.

➢ The palazzo was designed and built by Gian Lorenzo Bernini in 1653 on the site of the Palazzo Gaddi. After several restorations, it later became the headquarters of the State Tribunal of Pope Innocent XII. Since 1871 it has been the site of the lower house of the Italian Parliament. Between 1903 and 1927 the architect Ernesto Basile added a cherry wood hemicycle, which hosts the Parliament. The glassed ceiling is covered by a canvas that narrates the most important events of Italian history and the virtues of the Italian people. The basement and the first floor are decorated with ancient and modern works of art such as *The Marriage of Cana* by the school of Paolo Veronese, Carlo Carra's *Winter on the Iseo Lake*, Giorgio de Chirico's *Gladiators*, and Renato Guttuso's *Sicilian Barrows*.

Piazza del Popolo

➢ Since the early Middle Ages, Piazza del Popolo has been the main entrance point for visitors and pilgrims coming from the north. The renewal of this piazza and the surrounding area was the most significant urban-renewal work of the 19th century in Rome. The final project, by Giuseppe Valadier, was completed between 1818 and 1824. In the center of the piazza, the existing fountain was dismantled and substituted with four round basins with four marble Egyptian lions. On the hill facing the piazza, Valadier created a panoramic terrace with a large garden. Three main avenues— Via del Corso, Via di Ripetta, and Via del

View of the terrace in Piazza del Popolo

Spanish Steps

Babuino—form an area called Tridente and lead to Piazza del Popolo, where, in addition to the fountain, there are three churches and an obelisk. The interior facade of Porta del Popolo was designed by Gian Lorenzo Bernini on the occasion of the arrival of the freshly converted Catholic, Queen Christina of Sweden, in 1655. The "twin" churches—Santa Maria dei Miracoli and Santa Maria di Montesanto—were originally designed by Carlo Rainaldi and Carlo Maderno to look very similar, but they were later modified to offer a better perspective. Therefore, the first has a circular plan and an octagonal dome, while the second has an elliptical plan and a dodecagonal dome.

Piazza del Quirinale
➢ In the center of Piazza del Quirinale, the Fountain of Monte Cavallo has two colossal statues of Castor and Pollux holding back their horses. They are copies of a Greek statue from the 5th century B.C. Originally they were at the entrance of the Baths of Constantine. In 1588 Pope Sixtus V asked architect Carlo Fontana to place them in the piazza, thus giving it the familiar name of Horse Hill. In the following century Bernini was asked by Pope Urban VIII to enlarge the piazza. In 1783 Pope Pius VI had them moved in order to erect between them an obelisk taken from

the Mausoleum of Augustus. The massive granite basin, which used to be a cattle trough in the Forum, was added in 1818.

Pincio Gardens
Piazza del Popolo
➢ The Pincio Gardens extend over the remains of the villa of the Pincii family, after whom it was named. It starts in Piazza del Popolo and is delimited by the Aurelian Wall and the Villa Medici. It was designed by architect Giuseppe Valadier in 1811 as an embellishment to the city. The gardens include staircases, niches with allegorical classic-style statues, perspective games, and a small neoclassical villa, the Casina Valadier. Dispersed throughout the Pincio are about 230 busts of famous Italians. This project started during the days of the short-lived Roman Republic in 1849. In 1851 Pope Pius IX decided that the faces of atheists, heretics, or revolutionaries were to be taken back to the stonecutters and changed into the faces of people more acceptable to the Church.

Spanish Steps
Piazza di Spagna
➢ The triumphal yet sober *scalinata*, or outdoor stairway, is possibly the most outstanding urban setting of the baroque period in Rome. It was designed and built, after several decades of proposals, by the architect Francesco De Sanctis between 1723 and 1726. The stairway was aimed at bridging the gap between Piazza di Spagna and the church, thus replacing tree-lined paths. It immediately became popular as a major spot for summer nightlife, with balls and concerts held at the top. On the right, at the beginning of the steps, is the Casina Rossa, where the poet John Keats lived and died in 1821. Since the beginning of the 20th century, it has hosted the Keats-Shelley Memorial House (see Museums), whose library holds one of the most complete collections of works from the English Romantic period.

Villa Medici
Accademia di Francia a Roma, Viale della Trinità dei Monti, 1; tel.: 06-67611.
➢ Between 1564 and 1575 Nanni di Baccio Bigio and Francesco Salviati transformed this villa, previously owned by the

Villa Medici

Crescenzi family. In 1576 Cardinal Ferdinando de' Medici purchased it, embellishing and enlarging it, particularly the western side, to which he added a statue gallery. The Florentine architect Bartolomeo Ammannati designed the new apartment, subsequently decorated with frescoes and canvas paintings by Jacopo Zucchi. Ammannati also designed a new layout for the garden, providing it with a small pavilion with frescoes simulating a bower inhabited by exotic birds, a vestibule with grotesque elements, and an allegory of *Aurora*. In 1804 Napoleon decided that it should house the French Academy, where French artists could refine their talents by studying and living in the Roman environment. In front is a fountain whose water comes from a big stone ball. It is said that this cannonball was shot by former Queen Christina of Sweden from Castel Sant'Angelo. There are two alleged explanations: that she was shooting at a former lover hiding in Villa Medici, or that it was her way of keeping her word to the owner of the villa that one day she would knock at his door to invite him hunting.

VILLA MEDICI

Perhaps on the whole the most enchanting place in Rome. I should name as my own first wish that one didn't have to be a Frenchman to come and live and dream and work at the Académie de France. Can there be for a while a happier destiny than that of a young artist conscious of talent of no errand but to educate, to polish and perfect it, transplanted to these sacred shades? . . . The blessing in Rome is not that this or that or the other isolated object is so very unsurpassable; but that the general air so contributes to interest, to impressions that are not as any other impressions anywhere in the world. And from this general air the Villa Medici has distilled an essence of its own—walled it in and made it delightfully private. The great facade on the gardens is like an enormous rococo clock-face all incrusted with images and arabesques and tablets. What mornings and afternoons one might spend there, brush in hand, unpreoccupied, untormented, pensioned, satisfied.

—Henry James, *Italian Hours*

Walking Tour 1:

Going to Church on Via del Corso

By Ruth Kaplan

Rome's main north-south backbone, Via del Corso, has undergone some considerable personality changes since its construction in ancient times. During ancient Roman rule, when it was known as Via Flaminia, it flaunted the triumphal arches of Marcus Aurelius, Domitian, Claudius, and Gordian. Starting in 1468, horses used to race wildly down the straight, mile-long street as part of Rome's Carnival celebrations, supposedly egged on by mixtures of boiling paste. The annual race gave the street its current name: the street of the race, or the run.

Today, Via del Corso is best known as a pedestrian-clogged commercial strip. But take away the 20th-century overlay of traffic, shopping, and fast food, and the street is an excellent showcase for the evolution of Roman church architecture and art, from the medieval bell tower of San Silvestro in Capite to the baroque fixation on gold leaf in the interior of Santa Maria in via Lata.

Hundreds of years of Renaissance aesthetics are brought together in the **Church of Santa Maria del Popolo**, located in the northeast reaches of Piazza del Popolo, the northern terminus of Via del Corso. Its flat, dirtied facade was built by Andrea Bregno in the 1470s and echoes the simplicity of the period, with one round window above the modestly adorned main door. The light-filled, spacious interior shows signs of a series of decorative overhauls executed after the

Caravaggio, Crucifixion of Saint Paul, *Santa Maria del Popolo*

building was erected in 1099, the most recent being Bernini's 1655 attempt to spruce the place up for a visit by Queen Christina of Sweden.

Pinturicchio's delicate fresco, *The Nativity with Saint Jerome*, provides a classic Renaissance focus for the della Rovere chapel, the first on the right. The late-1480s painting contains the balance of colors and form, the precision and severity of facial features, and the background cityscape and hills typical of Renaissance frescoes.

The adjoining Cybo chapel jumps 150 years forward into the visual turbulence of the baroque. At least ten different colors of marble cover the floor and walls, and Carlo Maratta's 17th-century *Immaculate Conception* oil painting sits on the altar, notable for Mary's look of focused communication with the divine.

The gems of Santa Maria del Popolo are two paintings by Caravaggio, located in the dark chapel to the left of the main altar: *The Crucifixion of Saint Peter* and *The Conversion of Saint Paul*, executed in 1600–1601. Even at first glance, one can sense Caravaggio's rule-breaking new approach to visual images: he shoots his subjects in prone positions and from revealing angles, catching Saint Peter struggling to keep his head up while being turned upside down for crucifixion, and Saint Paul flat on the ground, his face turned away from the viewer.

A five-minute stroll down Via del Corso, just after crossing Largo dei Lombardi, is the ornate baroque **Church of Santi Ambrogio e Carlo al Corso**. The site was given by the pope to expatriate Lombards in 1471, who built a church here to honor Saint Ambrose of Rome—more famous and meaningful to the Lombards as an important bishop of Milan. The current church, begun in 1612 and finished in 1672, is cavernous and looms disproportionately over the tightly packed buildings that surround it.

The generous size and shape of the cream-colored facade are hard to appreciate in the tight quarters offered by Via del Corso. Inside, decoration follows baroque tastes: gold trim shines on moldings, golden bas-reliefs adorn the niches and unused space between the walls and the ceiling. The high cupola was designed by Pietro da Cortona, and has been celebrated for its sheer size, one of the biggest in Rome. At the altar is Carlo Maratta's painting, the *Gloria dei Santi Ambrogio e Carlo,* a large canvas notable for the full-spirited

Church of Santi Ambrogio e Carlo al Corso

San Lorenzo in Lucina

hope expressed in the saints' faces. A copy of Maratta's painting at Santa Maria del Popolo hangs in one of the large side chapels.

After another few minutes' walk south, the wedge-shaped Piazza San Lorenzo opens off to the right, providing a good view of the shaded, porticoed entrance of **San Lorenzo in Lucina**. The traditional medieval campanile and non-flashy entryway recall the church's first major rebuilding in the 12th century, though underground excavations have shown that this space has been inhabited since the 3rd century B.C., and used as a place of Christian worship since the 4th century A.D. Inside, the boxy nave and chapels twinkle with silver; one of the small, domed chapels is devoted to the sacred heart of Christ, the walls hung with embossed heart ornaments that pop up in other corners of the church. Filigreed silver reliquaries adorn almost every chapel, and a dozen of them are amassed on the main altar, displaying a wide assortment of human bones. All of the chapels were built in the 17th century. Bernini carved the bust in the far corner of the fourth right chapel, showing a figure leaning out from the wall, his attention focused on the altar. Bernini's contemporary, Guido Reni, painted the Crucifixion over the church's main altar.

Two blocks down Via del Corso, turn left toward the **Church of San Silvestro in Capite**, whose soothing, peach-colored entrance faces the piazza, one of Rome's main bus terminals. The church was built between 752 and 757 over the ruins of Emperor Aurelian's Temple of the Sun, entirely redone at the end of the 16th century, and redecorated in heavy Roman baroque style in the 17th. More than its neighbors, San Silvestro successfully creates an atmosphere of a microcosm lifted out of central Rome's chaos.

The main entryway leads to a beautiful square, brick-paved courtyard. The church facade and contiguous three residential walls are painted a warm brick red, richer than Rome's usual russet tone. Chips of marble inscriptions and hefty bas-reliefs recall the site's ancient use as a pagan

Church of San Silvestro in Capite

temple, while a handful of leafy palm trees create an out-of-place tropical atmosphere. A seven-tiered square campanile remains from the 12th century, with mismatched colored marble posts holding up its layers of double arches. The oval dome was designed by Francesco da Volterra and painted in 1690 by Cristoforo Roncalli, also known as il Pomarancio, while the main altar has a rich tabernacle by Carlo Rainaldi (1667).

The church's prize relic is the head (or *capite*, in Latin) of Saint John the Baptist, a dark brown, skull-shaped lump on display in the side room to the left of the entrance. San Silvestro officially belongs to the English Catholics, and English mass is held here regularly.

Continuing south, Via del Corso opens up onto Piazza Colonna, which takes its name from the 99-foot Column of Marcus Aurelius from the 2nd century A.D., decorated with carvings honoring the emperor's military victories. Italy's prime minister's office, the 16th-century Palazzo Chigi, sits on the north side of the square.

Another five-minute walk down Via del Corso leads back into the baroque at the **Church of San Marcello al Corso**, redesigned by Jacopo Sansovino in 1519 after a devastating fire completely destroyed the original 4th-century place of worship. In 1683 Carlo Fontana added the white concave facade, which rises up above the surrounding buildings. Its fluted edges are punctuated by a few simple columns and some statues standing in niches. Inside, San Marcello has a cathedral-like feeling, with an unencumbered nave and very high ceiling. The five chapels on each side are characterized by a decorative richness that is otherwise restrained in the building's main body. Floor inlays, decorative columns, and sculptural elements are done in heavily veined marble ranging in color from dusty blue to black green to burnt orange. The second chapel on the right (devoted to Saints Degna and Merita) has the carved torsos of the chapel's patrons popping out of the walls, staring at the action in the altar painting. In the third chapel on the right, the 17th-century frescoes by Giovanni Battista Ricci da Novara are still richly colored and worth a look, though the cycle covering the vault and the side walls borrows conspicuously from Michelangelo's Sistine Chapel ceiling. The Cappella del Crocifisso has a highly venerated 15th-century wooden crucifix. The Cappella di San Paolo was painted by Taddeo and Federico Zuccari.

Slightly south, on the other side of Via del Corso, is the compact, dark **Santa Maria in Via Lata**, which took its present form in the 15th century and afterward. Pietro da Cortona built the unspectacular facade and vestibule that lead into the dimly lit, oppressively ornate belly of the church. Gold paint adorns everything: decorative trim, column capitals, fat cherubs hanging out of the walls. Deep red marble columns line the nave. What really attracts your attention in the dark space, though, is the main altar, designed by Bernini. It consists of a small, Byzantine-looking panel of the Madonna, dwarfed by a complex series of silver and gold frames expanding to fill the

whole front of the church. The lower level, which is unfortunately closed to visitors, was once a large Roman building, most likely a warehouse, which was converted into a Christian chapel and welfare center in the 5th century. Christian murals from the 7th to 9th centuries were discovered there during excavation work.

But did Renaissance residents of Via del Corso really spend all their time in these churches? Take a look down the alleylike Via Lata to see the remnants of a totally different face of the city's history: the Fontana del Facchino, or Porter's Fountain, built into the side of a building. The male figure holding a still-spouting barrel represents one of the water carriers who roamed the city in the 15th century, when the ancient

Santa Maria in Via Lata

Roman aqueducts were in heavy disrepair. At the time it was built, this Renaissance fountain was one of Rome's "talking fountains," which locals would use as a bulletin board to anonymously air their more subversive thoughts—the ones that the all-powerful Church made it impossible for them to express freely in public. The model for the carved figure is thought to be a heavy-drinking local character named Abbondio Rizio, though some argue that he is a satirical caricature of Martin Luther—a hypothesis that fits well with the rebellious spirit of this meeting spot.

Fontana del Facchino

Further Information

San Lorenzo in Lucina
Via in Lucina, 16A; tel.: 06-6871494; open: 8:30 A.M.–noon, 4:30–7:30 P.M.

San Marcello al Corso
Piazza San Marcello, 5; tel.: 06-6780888; open: Mon.–Sat. 7 A.M.–noon, 4–7 P.M., Sun. opens at 8:30 A.M.

San Silvestro in Capite
Piazza San Silvestro; tel.: 06-6797775; open: Mon.–Sat. 7 A.M.–7:15 P.M.; closed: Sun. from 1–3 P.M.

Santa Maria del Popolo
Piazza del Popolo, 12; tel.: 06-3610836; open: Mon.–Sat. 7 A.M.–1:30 P.M., 4–7 P.M., Sun. 7:30 A.M.–7:30 P.M.

Santa Maria in Via Lata
Via del Corso, 306l; tel.: 06-6796190; open: 5–10:45 P.M.

Santi Ambrogio e Carlo al Corso
Via del Corso, 437; tel.: 06-6878332; open: 7:30 A.M.–12:30 P.M., 5–7 P.M.

Piazza Venezia, 48; tel.: 06-6795205; open: 7:30 A.M.–12:30 P.M., 4–7 P.M.; closed: Tues. morning and Thurs. afternoon.

By Ruth Kaplan

Pope Marcus founded the Basilica of San Marco in Piazza Venezia in A.D. 336 in honor of his namesake, Mark the Evangelist. In its early days it housed a *diaconia*, or Christian welfare center. What's visible today, though, are additions made from the 9th century onward.

The two-story facade consists of a travertine portico and loggia, each with three wide arches. It lines up snugly with the two brick buildings on either side, and seems to tower over the small grassy piazza in front. The 15th-century architect Leon Battista Alberti is thought to have designed this facade. The portico walls are hung with inscriptions, from scribbled Greek to cleanly cut and polished baroque plaques. Two marble lions guard the entrance, the symbol of both Pope Paul II and of the Venetian community to which Pope Paul dedicated the church in the 15th century. The 12th-century brick bell tower behind the loggia can only be seen from across the street.

Inside, the decoration turns to pure late Roman baroque madness, with nothing left undecorated. Filippo Barigioni packed into the smallish church ten caramel-streaked jasper columns per side, creating rounded arches that separate the aisles. Gilding is everywhere, from the Corinthian-style column capitals to the stucco work covering the arches and the blue-and-gold coffered ceiling, dating from 1468. The upper walls have alternating panels of frescoes and deep white plaster reliefs. Pietro da Cortona designed the chapel to the right of the altar. Inside is a 15th-century painting of Pope Marcus by Melozzo da Forlì. Stretches of original Cosmati tilework cover the floor in front of the chapel and extend to the area around the altar.

The only significant remnant of the 9th-century church is the brilliantly colored mosaic in the apse, showing, among others, Pope Marcus himself in a scene with Christ and the saints. Dark lighting, combined with the splendor of the multicolored marble altar, downplay the mosaic's decorative importance.

Apse mosaic, San Marco

San Marco's lateral walls are lined with elaborate tombs. Each one displays the bust of the deceased. Decorations range from carved skulls to flying angels blowing golden trumpets. Ask to see the sacristy, which has a painting of Saint Mark the Evangelist by Melozzo da Forlì, along with a fragment of a Crucifixion painting by Pietro Cavallini.

Walking Tour 2:

The Quirinale

By Margaret Stenhouse

Via del Quirinale, from the crest of the Quirinale Hill to Via XX Settembre, where Garibaldi's troops entered Rome in 1870, is an epic thoroughfare, the fulcrum of two centuries of power and glory. This street is lined with magnificent baroque churches—showpieces of the Counter-Reformation—and monumental late-19th- and early-20th-century buildings, symbols of the new order that came in with the unification of Italy and the end of papal reign.

Halfway along the "Long Sleeve," as the Romans call the monotonous right flank of the presidential palace, an elegantly curving flight of steps leads up to **Sant'Andrea al Quirinale**, built between 1658–1671. Gian Lorenzo Bernini considered this his finest work and refused payment for it. The site available was limited in size, so he conceived a revolutionary elliptical design, with the high altar on the short axis, immediately in front of the entrance. The

dazzling interior is rich with marbles, gilt, and stuccoes, the altar a blaze of gilded bronze and lapis lazuli, flanked with red-veined marble columns. Antonio Raggi, Bernini's most gifted pupil, sculpted the gigantic statue of Saint Andrew hovering above the pediment, as well as the cavorting cherubs around the dome.

Bernini's rival, Borromini, has his own masterpiece just along the same road. This is the oval **Church of San Carlo alle Quattro Fontane**, which was commissioned by the Barefoot Trinitarians of the Redemption of Spain in 1638. Borromini worked on it for 30 years, doing almost all the inside decoration as well. The church is so small that it is nicknamed "San Carlino," and it is said that it could fit inside one of the supporting pillars of Saint

Sant'Andrea al Quirinale

Peter's dome. Don't forget to take a good look at the facade. This was Borromini's last work and it was only completed after his death. High and curving, it is covered in a wealth of architectural detail, with columns, niches, and sculpted figures. The image of Saint Charles over the main door is by Antonio Raggi.

By contrast, the church is refreshingly unadorned inside. The plain white walls enhance the harmony of the artist's oval design, crowned with the beautiful elliptical dome. On the left of the altar is the Barberini chapel, belonging to Pope Urban VIII's powerful family. Look out for the unusual depiction of the Barberini bees (the family coat of arms) hovering on the flowers at the base of the columns. A door on the right of the altar leads to the sacristy and the charming, octagonal cloister, considered another Borromini masterpiece. It is small and narrow, but with perfect proportions. The center is marked by a well, sealed with antique majolica tiles.

San Carlo stands on the corner of the **Quattro Fontane** crossroads, a key feature of the grand city plan drawn up by the energetic Sixtus V, who revolutionized Rome in his short five-year reign. The intersection is a unique vantage point, with four famous landmarks crowning the horizon in each direction: the Quirinale obelisk and fountain, with the historic Porta Pia gate across from it; and the Trinità dei Monti obelisk opposite the Santa Maria Maggiore bell tower.

Pope Sixtus V originally wanted four saints on the corners, but the four reclining figures that Domenico Fontana eventually set up are of pagan, rather than Christian, inspiration. There is some doubt as to what they actually represent, except for the allegory of the Tiber on the Via XX Settembre corner, with the she-wolf lurking by his side. The other male figure is thought to be the Aniene (a Tiber tributary) or the Arno. The remaining two fountains feature female goddesses, though some experts believe they are actually the Christian virtues of Faithfulness and Fortitude. One is set into the side of the imposing Palazzo del Drago, on Via delle Quattro Fontane, which was begun by Domenico Fontana in 1587 and completed by Alessandro Specchi.

Via XX Settembre, the continuation of Via del Quirinale, is lined with a succession of massive stone fin-de-siècle edifices, many of which now belong to departments of the Ministry of Defense, which explains the presence of submachine-gun-toting guardsmen. A brisk walk, however, soon takes us into more peaceful territory at Piazza di San Bernardo, which is surrounded by three celebrated churches and one of Rome's famous fountains.

In Roman times, the Baths of Diocletian covered most of the area and, in fact, the little circular Church of San Bernardo alle Terme, on the far side of the square, is built in one of the old rooms. Opposite stands the American Parish Church of Rome, **Santa Susanna**, with its Carlo Maderno travertine facade. It is the first autonomous masterpiece by Carlo Maderno, who would later design the imposing facade of Saint Peter's. Although the present church dates from the Counter-Reformation, Santa Susanna is of very ancient origin. In 1990 excavations among the ruins of what is believed to be Susanna's house underneath the adjacent Cistercian convent revealed a Roman sarcophagus containing a male skeleton, covered with 7,000 fragments of an 8th-century mural. This has now been laboriously pieced together and can be viewed by ringing the bell at the nuns' door in the left nave. The church contains many works of art, including a series of frescoes by Baldassarre Croce, the Saint Lawrence Chapel by Domenico Fontana, and Maderno's lavishly gilded ceiling.

Santa Susanna has many other attractions, including coffee for parishioners and visitors after Sunday mass, a lending library, which is a godsend to the English-speaking community, and daily Gregorian chant for early birds at the seven A.M. mass.

On the corner opposite stands another great Counter-Reformation church. **Santa Maria della Vittoria** was built between 1608 and 1620, not long after Santa Susanna. Giovanni Battista Soria's facade is, in fact, an imitation of Maderno's showpiece. The victory alluded to in the name of the church commemorates the Battle of White Mountain near Prague, when Catholic troops routed Protestant forces, thanks to the help of a miraculous image of the Virgin and child. This church is world famous for its Cornaro Chapel, entirely designed by Bernini. The chapel contains his masterpiece Saint Teresa in Ecstasy, but look out, too, for the Chapel of Saint Francis with the last Roman works of Domenichino.

R
OUR PICK

The monumental "Moses Fountain" fills one end of the Piazza San Bernardo. Its real name is the **Acqua Felice Fountain**, in honor of Pope Sixtus V (Felice Peretti), who had included a new aqueduct in his plans for the new city. This was Rome's first monumental fountain. In spite of being designed by the great Domenico Fontana, it is considered one of Rome's least attractive fountains, mainly because of the stodgy figure of the prophet Moses in the middle. Depending on the sources, this figure is attributed to two different sculptors, Prospero da Brescia and Leonardo Sormani. Legend has it that when it was unveiled, it was ridiculed so much that Prospero da Brescia killed himself. Perhaps the most interesting features are the four lions at the base, which

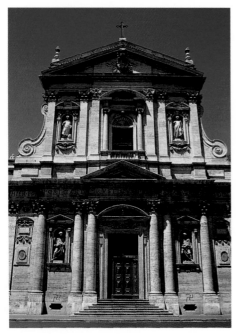

Santa Susanna

are copies of Egyptian originals brought by Pope Gregory XVI to the Vatican Museums.

The old Borgo district, which clustered around the protective skirts of the papal palace on the Quirinale Hill, is full of lesser-known treasures. A maze of picturesque alleyways lead off from the steep flight of steps on the left side of the Quirinale Square going down toward the Trevi Fountain. By taking a detour through Vicolo Scanderbeg and Vicolo dei Modelli (where the artists' models once hung out), you can take in the charming little Pasta Museum and Via dei Panettieri, where the papal bakeries once stood. The massive door of No. 15 conceals the Antamoro Fountain. This is arguably Bernini's least-known work,

Acqua Felice Fountain

a fountain-nyphaeum decorated with two sea monsters. The monsters blow into a small shell while opening the valves of a gigantic shell, with water gushing into a basin decorated with two dolphins. Bernini installed it here in 1657 or 1658. The courtyard is private, so you will have to ask the doorman on duty for admittance.

Follow Via della Stamperia, on the right side of the Trevi Fountain. Valadier designed the imposing building on the left (No. 6), which now houses the Calcografia, founded in 1738. This museum houses an enormous collection of 20,000 copper plate engravings, including a vast collection of Piranesi.

The palazzo was designed by leading 16th- and 17th-century artists Giacomo Della Porta and Francesco Borromini, who planned the internal oval ramp and the loggia on the ground floor. Since 1932, it has housed the National Academy of San Luca and its collection of art. The **Gallery of the National Academy of San Luca** has an important collection of works by artists who belonged to the historic academy, including Zuccari, Algardi, and Guido Reni.

FURTHER INFORMATION

Acqua Felice Fountain
Piazza San Bernardo, on Via Vittorio Emanuele Orlando.

Galleria dell'Accademia Nazionale di San Luca (Gallery of the National Academy of San Luca)
Piazza dell'Accademia di San Luca, 77; tel.: 06-6798850.

Quattro Fontane
On the four corners of Via Quattro Fontane and Via del Quirinale.

Sant'Andrea al Quirinale
Via del Quirinale, 29; tel.: 06-48903187; open: Wed.-Mon. 8 A.M.–noon, 4–6 P.M.; closed: Tues.

San Carlo alle Quattro Fontane
Via del Quirinale, on the corner with Via Quattro Fontane.

Santa Maria della Vittoria
Via XX Settembre, 17 and Largo di Santa Susanna; tel.: 06-42740571; open: during masses, daily 8:30–11 A.M., 11:30 A.M–noon, 3:30–6 P.M.; on Sun.: only in afternoon.

Santa Susanna
Via Settembre, 14; tel.: 06-42014554; open: 9 A.M.–noon, 4–6 P.M.; holidays: 10 A.M.–noon, 4:30–7 P.M.; mass given: Mon.–Sat. 6 P.M.; Sun.: 9:30 A.M. and 10:30 A.M.

FOCUS: SANTA MARIA DELLA CONCEZIONE

Via Veneto, 27; tel.: 06-4871185; open: 7 A.M.–7:30 P.M., 3:45–7:30 P.M., crypt: Fri.–Wed. 9 A.M.–12 P.M., 3–6 P.M.

By Amelia Cleary

Capuchin Crypt

The Church of Santa Maria della Concezione (Saint Mary of the Immaculate Conception) was built in 1626–1631 for the cardinal Antonio Barberini. The second chapel on the left has two famous 17th-century paintings: *Saint Michael the Archangel* by Guido Reni and *Christ Mocked* by Gherardo delle Notti. The church is perhaps better known, however, for the crypt beneath.

Until 1870, the papal states permitted burials in and under churches. Over a period of 100 years, the bones of nearly 4,000 Capuchin monks piled up in the crypt under the Church of the Immaculate Conception in Rome. In 1631 the Capuchin monks moved to a new friary, at the foot of what is now the bustling Via Veneto. They brought the remains of their deceased brothers and buried them under the new church in earth they had taken from the Holy Land. As more monks died, bones were exhumed to make space for new ones. Legend has it that in the late 1700s the monks offered a fugitive artist refuge in the crypt. He spent his years there decorating the walls with the accumulated bones, creating what is now one of the most macabre settings in the city: the Capuchin Crypt, where shoulder blades join together to form wings and bones dangle under vertebrae flowers as chandeliers. At least that is one theory. Another account says French Capuchins fleeing France during the revolution created the morbid baroque chapels while in retreat.

Friar Alberto Cimini, the Capuchin who oversees the crypt, doesn't believe either of these hypotheses. He is convinced that the Roman Capuchins were responsible for the embellishment, not in the name of art, but for practicality. The crypt is only 105-feet long, and there were so many skeletons that they piled up along the walls. Cimini said that with no room to walk, the monks decided to arrange the bones on the walls to get them out of the way.

Cimini is convinced that the monks simply organized the bones into symbolic shapes as a "meditation on life." This meditation is repeated throughout the crypt. A shoulder-blade winged hourglass advises viewers that time flies, while a large, bone-drawn heart is a reminder that love conquers all. Three skeletons of young noble children warn that death has no preferred age; skull-bone scales symbolize that good and evil deeds will eventually be judged. Finger bones are the numbers on a vertebrae clock, suggesting the ticking of time.

About 120,000 visitors come each year, so it can be crowded during the busy tourist season. Morning is the best time to visit.

Other Points of Interest

Madonna dell'Archetto

Via S. Marcello, 41 (near Piazza Venezia);
open: Mon.–Sat. 7–8 P.M., Sun. 6:30–8 P.M.

➢ In 1796, the year Napoleon Bonaparte's forces pillaged Rome, some locals claimed they witnessed a miracle: A small painting of the Madonna hanging under the arch of a narrow alley moved its eyes. Today this image is venerated in the smallest church in Rome dedicated to the Virgin Mary, the Church of Madonna dell'Archetto. A narrow passageway lined with potted plants leads into the tiny nave that can accommodate about 30 worshippers. The altar nearly falls out of the apse and into the lap of the congregation, offering an intimacy rarely felt in many of the awe-inspiring basilicas around the city. The gilded apse, where the miraculous painting hangs as an altarpiece, reflects the golden twinkle of the prayer candles. Stucco angels stand below the minute dome, which is adorned in its center by an encaustic fresco of the Immaculate Conception surrounded by angels. Playful cherubs seem to dance in a ring around this image. The frescoes just under the dome are of four allegorical figures representing the four virtues of the Madonna.

Mausoleo di Augusto (Mausoleum of Augustus)

Piazza Augusto Imperatore; tel.: 06-67103819;
open: Sat., Sun. 10 A.M.–12:30 P.M., Tues., Fri. guided visits (only in Italian) at 9:30 A.M., Fri. or Sat. (depending on the month) guided visits (only in Italian) at 8 P.M.

➢ Rome's much-loved Emperor Augustus and his family were buried in the center of this 1st-century-A.D. barrel-like tomb.

Its entrance once had two obelisks, one on each side (now moved to Piazza del Quirinale and in the back of Santa Maria Maggiore). On top of the mausoleum, surrounded by evergreens, there was a statue of the emperor.

Its series of circular walls are now sunken far below street level. The entrance through a tall, dark archway leads inside the first ring, where boulder-sized chunks of stone and cement have crumbled over the years and lay scattered. The darkened, hushed inner burial chamber is sparsely decorated, spotlighted with an occasional shaft of sunlight. Photographs at the entrance show the monument's use through the years as a fortress, amphitheater, and concert hall.

Obelisco Sallustiano (Sallustian Obelisk)

Piazza Trinità dei Monti

➢ This obelisk is a Roman imitation of Egyptian ones built during the 2nd or 3rd century. Some of its hieroglyphics are similar to those of the obelisk in Piazza del Popolo, but the Roman stonecutter made a few mistakes and sculpted some signs upside down. It is located in front of the Church of Trinità dei Monti. It was discovered in an underground site of the vast Roman garden Horti Sallustiani, the Villa of Sallust, hence the origin of its name. In 1789 the neoclassical architect Giovanni Antinori moved the obelisk to its present-day position, at the request of Pope Pius VI. At the time, many Romans were afraid the obelisk would tumble, while others feared its position would damage the appeal of the area. However, both were unfounded concerns, since the obelisk still stands, and the area, at the top of the Spanish Steps, is one of the most popular in Rome.

Oratorio del Crocifisso (Oratory of the Crucifix)

Piazza dell'Oratorio

➢ The Oratory of the Crucifix was

Oratorio del Crocifisso

designed by Giacomo Della Porta with a Mannerist-style facade. Inside lies a captivating rectangular hall, frescoed by a number of artists, including Niccolò Pomarancio, Paris Nogari, and Giovanni de' Vecchi.

PALAZZO PALLAVICINI ROSPIGLIOSI

Via XXIV Maggio, 43; Palazzo Pallavicini: closed to the public; Casino Pallavicini: tel.: 06-4827224; open: first day of each month, 10 A.M.–noon, 3–5 P.M.; closed: Jan. 1; admission: free.

➤ The original villa was built between 1611 and 1616 for the wealthy art lover, Cardinal Scipione Borghese. The site on the top of the Quirinale Hill was covered by the ruins of the Baths of Constantine and it was, of course, conveniently situated near the papal palace.

In the cardinal's day, the villa was known as the Palace of Montecavallo (the Mount of Horses), because of the Dioscuri sculpture group, which was found on the spot. The Pallavicini-Rospigliosi family acquired the property in the 18th century.

The villa is best known for the Casino Pallavicini, the ornate pavilion which the cardinal erected on the grounds as a place to entertain special guests in the summer. In 1614 Borghese called in one of the top artists of the day to provide the decor. The result was the *Apollo's Chariot*, which covers the ceiling of the main salon. Guido Reni depicts the procession of Apollo driving the chariot of the sun across the sky. He is preceded by a floating Dawn and surrounded by a flock of pretty dancing girls, who symbolize the Hours. This painting had an enormous influence on the neoclassical art of the 18th and 19th centuries.

The loggia which gives onto the charming walled garden has a frescoed ceiling by Gentileschi and Tassi, while the garden itself is set off by the Water Theater, with sculptures of the river gods Tiber and Arno. This feature was probably designed by Vasanzio.

The Pallavicini-Rospigliosi family were great art collectors. The gallery on the first floor of the villa holds works by artists like Rubens, Luca Signorelli, van Dyck, Lorenzo Lotto, and Domenichino, as well as paintings attributed to Titian and Caravaggio.

PALAZZO DI VENEZIA (SEE MUSEUMS)

Via del Plebiscito, 118; tel.: 06-696999431; open: Tues.–Sun. 9 A.M.–2 P.M.; closed: Jan. 1, May 1, and Dec. 25.

➤ Cardinal Pietro Barbo began the Palazzo di Venezia in 1455, enlarging it between 1465 and 1468, when he was elected Pope Paul IV. Until 1560 the palazzo served as the summer papal residence; afterward it became the home of the Venetian Embassy. Palazzo di Venezia was passed over to France in 1797 and then to Austria in 1814. In 1916 the Italian government reclaimed the building, and Mussolini used its small balcony to preach to the crowds during the Fascist era.

The structure incorporates into its design an older medieval tower (on the left end). The Sala del Mappamondo, or The Globe Room, was decorated by Andrea Mantegna with his typical perspectives.

Next to the main building is a smaller one, the Palazzetto Venezia, which was once in the center of the piazza, but was moved in the middle of the 19th century.

Cristo pantocratore, *Museo del Palazzo di Venezia*

San Silvestro al Quirinale

SAN SILVESTRO AL QUIRINALE (CURRENTLY CLOSED FOR RESTORATION)

Via XXIV Maggio10; tel.: 06-6790240.

➤ When the road now known as Via XXIV Maggio (the date commemorates Italy's entrance into World War I) was built at the end of the 19th century, the Church of San Silvestro on the Quirinale Hill was unfortunately in the way. A chunk of it had to be demolished and a new facade was constructed. The church, which dates back to the Dark Ages, has therefore been significantly altered since it was rebuilt in the 16th century, when the great Michelangelo came to call on the poet, Vittoria Colonna in the garden next door.

In many ways, San Silvestro al Quirinale can be regarded as a showpiece of late Renaissance and early-17th-century art, with works by many of the major artists who served the popes of that period. The first chapel on the left is decorated with della Robbia tiles with the Medici coat of arms, which came originally from the Loggia of Raphael in the Vatican. The two frescoes on the sides of the altar, representing Mary Magdalene and Saint Catherine of Siena, are by Polidoro da Caravaggio, who also painted the landscapes, with scenes from the lives of the saints, with the help of Maturino. These frescoes are the first examples of autonomous landscape painting known in Renaissance art

history. The baseboard on the walls is decorated with a monochromatic frieze with putti. The ceiling is frescoed with the story of Saint Stephen, by Cavalier d'Arpino.

The octagonal Bandini Chapel in the transept dates from 1585 and was designed by Mascherino. The cupola is decorated with frescoes by Domenichino, while the stucco statues of Mary Magdalen and Saint John are probably Algardi's first Roman works. Note the two funeral monuments on the back wall. One commemorates Monsignor Prospero Farinacci, who acted as defense counsel for Beatrice Cenci, executed in 1618 after being accused of plotting the assassination of her father; the other, by Domenico Fontana, commemorates Cardinal Federico Cornaro.

A side door gives access to the little hanging garden where artists and intellectuals gathered, under the patronage of the aristocratic poet, Vittoria Colonna.

SANTA MARIA DI LORETO

Piazza della Madonna di Loreto; tel.: 06-22484297.

➤ The Confraternity of Bakers started building the Church of Santa Maria in Loreto in 1507. The project might have been designed by Donato Bramante. In 1576 Jacopo del Duca designed the dome and bell tower; the interior was redone in the 17th century. Del Duca's great octagonal dome rising above the building in the shape of a die, *dado* in Italian, culminates with an exceptional hollow lantern, the only one of its type in Rome. The marble composition in the portal, with the Virgin and the House of Loreto, may be by Andrea Sansovino. Inside, there is a chapel decorated by Niccolò Pomarancio and some large paintings by Cavalier d'Arpino. The beautiful *Santa Susanna* by Francois Dusquenoy (1633) illustrates the trends in 16th-century Roman sculpture that departed from Bernini's style.

SANTA MARIA IN TRIVIO

Piazza dei Crociferi

➤ Santa Maria in Trivio is just around the corner from the Trevi Fountain. According to tradition, it was founded by the Byzantine general Belisarius, who freed Italy from the Goths in 537. Belisarius subsequently tarnished his reputation by plotting to depose Pope Silverius, who died in exile. The repentant general built the church as an act of atonement.

Originally, it was known as Santa Maria in Xenodochio, because of the adjacent hospice for pilgrims and sick people, and it kept this name until the 16th century.

Between 1573 and 1575, thanks to the patronage of Pope Gregory XIII and a large donation from Venetian cardinal Luigi Cornaro, the church was enlarged and embellished by Jacopo Del Duca, Michelangelo's favorite pupil. The elegant Del Duca facade was restored to its original glory in 1998–1999.

Of note inside is the magnificent ceiling *Stories of the Virgin Mary*, by Antonio Gherardi, considered one of the finest examples of a painting cycle from the Roman seicento. The same artist also created the gilt-and-stucco Triumphal Arch, which highlights the vista of the main altar.

The third chapel from the left is dedicated to the fearless Saint Gaspare Del Bufalo, who preached to bandits and was imprisoned for defying Napoleon. One of Rome's best-loved modern saints, he was canonized in 1954. His remains are enclosed in an urn inside the life-size gilded bronze statue underneath the altar, by sculptor Aurelio Mistruzzi.

The third chapel on the right displays a magnificent wooden crucifix painted in Venice in the 14th century. The much-venerated *Virgin and Child* above the main altar dates from the 15th century.

From the sacristy, you can pop into the small, quadrangular cloister, where there is an interesting curiosity. A door in the wall once led into the oratory of the wine sellers' guild. Their coat of arms and the inscription, VINEA NOSTRA FLOUIT ("Our vine has flourished") is carved on the lintel, dated 1856.

SANT'ANDREA DELLE FRATTE
Via Sant'Andrea delle Fratte, 1; tel.: 06-6793191; open: daily 6:30 A.M.–12:30 P.M., 4:30–7 P.M.

➤ The construction of the present church started in 1612, over a much older church mentioned in 12th-century documents. In 1653 Francesco Borromini took charge of the project. His most evident legacies here are the apse, the tambour that wraps up the dome, and the bell tower, designed with an unusual square plan and known in Rome

for a different reason: it oscillates when the bells sound. The two angels to the sides of the main altar were originally sculpted for the Ponte Sant'Angelo, but were moved here to protect them from the weather. Records say one of them is by Gian Lorenzo Bernini's son, Paolo Valentino. But art historians believe they are both by the father, who tried to give his not-so-talented son credit for beautiful work. The convent next door has an elegant and peaceful cloister built in 1604 with a small domed bell tower and an old clock on one side.

SANTI XII APOSTOLI
Piazza Santi XII Apostoli, 51; tel.: 06-6794085.

➤ The oldest part of the Basilica of Santi XII Apostoli dates back to the 4th century. The church was rebuilt in the 15th century and subsequently altered a number of times. The 15th-century portico was designed by Baccio Pontelli, and the balustrade with the statues of Christ and the 12 apostles was added in the 17th century by Carlo Rainaldi. In 1702–1708 the church was completely renovated by Francesco Fontana and, after his death, by his father, Carlo Fontana. Giuseppe Valadier then added the neoclassical exterior. In the apse the church holds the largest altar painting in Rome, an oil painting by Domenico Maria Muratori (1704). The Funerary Monument of Clemens XIV is the first Roman work of Canova.

TRINITÀ DEI MONTI
Piazza della Trinità dei Monti; tel.: 06-679417; open: daily 9:30 A.M.–12:30 P.M., 4–7 P.M.

➤ The platform on the stairway of the Church of Trinità dei Monti offers such a beautiful view of Rome that visitors often ignore the church itself. They shouldn't.

In 1495 Charles VIII began building the church alongside a French convent of the order of Minims, and in 1587 the architect for Pope Sixtus V built a double staircase with two separate flights here. The church was consecrated in 1595. A single nave divided by a grille at the height of the third chapel inside still retains some of its Gothic style, particularly in the triumphal arch, the presbytery, and the transept.

The artwork inside is worth noting too: The *Assumption* by Daniele da Volterra, a pupil of Michelangelo, in the Cappella della

Rovere, the third chapel on the right; *Deposition*, a muscle-bodied artwork influenced by Michelangelo, in the second chapel on the left; and artwork by Perin del Vaga in the Cappella Pucci, in the seventh chapel on the left. Del Vaga also began the Cappella Massimo, but the brothers Taddeo and Federico Zuccari later completed it.

Museums

GALLERIA COLONNA (COLONNA GALLERY)

Via della Pilotta, 17; tel.: 06-6784350; fax: 06-6794638; e-mail: galleriacolonna@tin.it; website: www.galleriacolonna.it; open: Sun. 9 A.M.–1 P.M.; closed: month of Aug. (on written request, tours of the gallery and private apartments are available every day, including in Aug.); admission: €5.

➢ Holds the collection of Italian and foreign art of the Colonna family. Includes works by Melozzo da Forlì, Michele di Ridolfo del Ghirlandaio, Veronese, Palma il Vecchio, Tintoretto, Carracci, and Guercino.

GALLERIA DELL'ACCADEMIA NAZIONALE DI SAN LUCA (GALLERY OF THE NATIONAL ACADEMY OF SAN LUCA)

Piazza dell'Accademia di San Luca, 77; tel.: 06-6798850.

➢ Collection of the work of artists belonging to the historic academy, including that of Zuccari, Algardi, and Guido Reni.

GALLERIA DORIA PAMPHILJ

Piazza del Collegio Romano, 1A–2; tel.: 06-6797323/6794365; website: www.doria pamphilj.it; open: 10 A.M.–5 P.M.; closed: Thurs.; admission €7, with audioguides.

➢ The Doria Pamphilj collection is one of the most important private collections in Rome. Begin the visit of the painting gallery in the 15th-century rooms on the far end of the main hall, which contain a handful of European medieval paintings, then continue to the 16th-century rooms, with portraits by Raphael and Tintoretto, a seductive *Salomé* by Titian, and an anomalous winter landscape with ice skaters by Brueghel. Some of the gallery's other highlights include Velasquez's focused, intense portrait of the Pamphilj Pope Innocent X, a

papal bust by Bernini, a small Madonna and child by Parmigiano, and Caravaggio's *Rest during the Escape from Egypt*, with an angel playing the violin with his back to the viewer. Flemish and Dutch painters are particularly well represented in the collection.

GALLERIA NAZIONALE D'ARTE ANTICA (NATIONAL GALLERY OF ANCIENT ART)

Via Barberini, 18; tel.: 06-4824184; website: www.ticketeria.it; open: 9 A.M.–7 P.M.; closed: Mon.; admission: €6; note: it is advisable to book the visit to the 18th-century apartment beforehand (tel.: 06-328101).

➢ The building was designed by Maderno and finished by Bernini. The ceiling of the central hall is decorated with an allegorical painting by Pietro da Cortona. It features 12th- to 18th-century paintings, furniture, majolica, and porcelains.

MUSEO DEL PALAZZO DI VENEZIA (MUSEUM OF PALAZZO VENEZIA)

Via del Plebiscito, 118; tel.: 06-69994318; open: 8:30 A.M.–7:30 P.M.; closed: Mon.; admission: €4.

➢ Thirteenth- to 18th-century paintings, marble sculptures, wood carvings, bronzes, terra-cotta pieces, pottery, and tapestries.

KEATS-SHELLEY MEMORIAL HOUSE

Piazza di Spagna, 26; tel.: 06-6784235; e-mail: info@keats-shelley-house.org; website: www.keats-shelly-house.org; open: Tues.–Fri. 9 A.M.–1 P.M., 3–6 P.M., Sat. 11 A.M.–2 P.M., 3–6 P.M.; closed: Sun.; admission: €3.

➢ The Romantic poet Keats lived here in the fall of 1820 and the winter of 1821. He was already very ill by the time he came to Rome, and he died from consumption here in February 1821. Autographed documents and memoirs of English Romantic poets Shelley and Byron.

MUSEO NAZIONALE DELLE PASTE ALIMENTARI (NATIONAL PASTA MUSEUM)

Piazzetta Scanderbeg, 117; tel.: 06-6991119; open: 9:30 A.M.–5:30 P.M.; admission: €8.

➢ Utensils and objects documenting the history of pasta, from the Etruscans to the present.

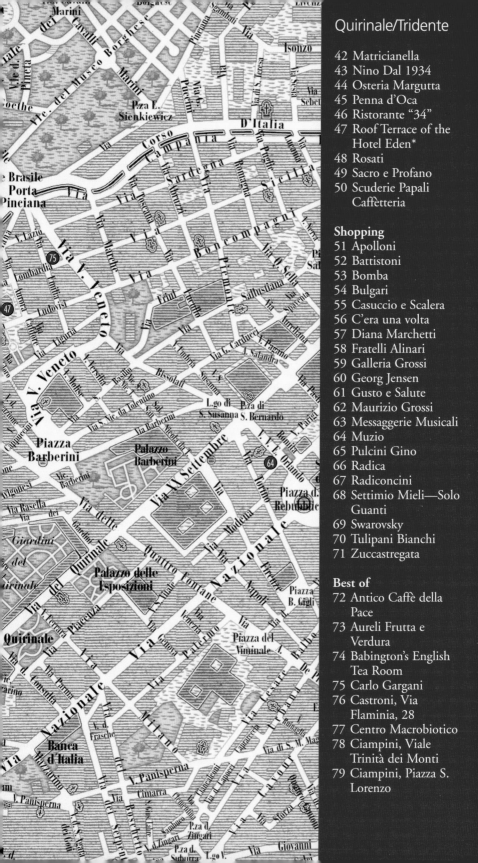

Albergo Fontana

Piazza di Trevi, 96; tel.: 06-6786113/6790024; website: www.fontanahotel.com; category: ★★★; number of rooms: 25; credit cards accepted: all major; access to internet: none; most beautiful rooms: 105, 302; €€.

☛Across from the Trevi Fountain, even though, unfortunately, the loveliest rooms are on the opposite side. They feature beamed ceilings and upholstering with floral fabrics on yellow backgrounds. Breakfast and cocktails are a must, served in a room looking over the fountain.

Hotel Accademia

Piazza Accademia di San Luca, 75; tel.: 06-69922607/6785897; e-mail: accademia@travelroma.com; website: www.accademiahotel.com; category: ★★★; number of rooms: 58; credit cards accepted: all major; access to internet: direct-line (US, UK) telephone jack in all rooms; most beautiful rooms: the rooms on the second and third floors have been renovated recently; €€.

☛Situated in an enviable position in the heart of the Eternal City, the Accademia Hotel is only a few steps away from the Trevi Fountain. Piazza di Spagna and Via Veneto are not far.

Hotel Augustea

Via Nazionale 251, tel.: 06-4883589/4814872; e-mail: infoaugustea@hotelpatria.it; category: ★★★; number of rooms: 30; credit cards accepted: all major; access to internet: direct-line (US, UK) telephone jack in all rooms; €€.

☛Busy Via Nazionale doesn't interfere with the tranquility of this small hotel, which occupies the second and third floors of a distinguished late-19th-century palazzo. Not far from Via Veneto, the renovated hotel still maintains the homelike atmosphere of the past with its pink-tinted walls, period furniture, armchairs, and sofas that make the guest rooms both well furnished and inviting. Bathrooms are medium sized. Simple meeting rooms are available.

Hotel Baglioni

Via Veneto, 72; tel.: 06-421111/42012130; e-mail: regina.roma@baglionihotels.com; website: www.baglionihotels.com; category: ★★★★★; number of rooms: 130; credit cards accepted: all major; access to internet: direct-line (US, UK) telephone jack in all rooms; most beautiful room: 303; €€–€€€€.

☛This hotel offers a luxurious mix of modern comfort and old-world class, with period furnishings, frescoed walls, and spacious bedrooms. Although located on Via Veneto, the windows are double-glazed to block out the street noise.

Hotel Bernini Bristol

Piazza Barberini, 23; tel.: 06-4883051/4824266; website: www.berninibristol.com; e-mail: sina@italyhotel.com; category: ★★★★★; number of rooms: 125; credit cards accepted: all major; facilities: fitness club with gym, steam-bath, sauna, and hydromassage-tub; access to internet: direct-line (US, UK) telephone jack in all rooms; €€€–€€€€.

☛Built in the late 19th century and recently restored, the Bernini Bristol maintains the atmosphere of that era. The lounges, with a view over the Fountain of the Triton, feature antique furnishings and 18th-century tapestries. The rooms and the suites are decorated with taste and elegance, and are sound-proofed to ensure privacy. The terraces of the suites offer enchanting views of the Eternal City. You can either request a room with a view of Piazza Barberini or you can have a quieter room at the back of the hotel.

Hotel dei Borgognoni

Via del Bufalo, 126; tel.: 06-69941505/69941501; e-mail: reservation_hir@charminghotels.it; website: www.hotelborgognoni.it; category: ★★★★; number of rooms: 51; credit cards accepted: all major; access to internet: direct-line (US, UK) telephone jack in all rooms; most beautiful rooms: 109, 110, 112, 114 (with terraces); €€€.

☛The elegant and exclusive Hotel dei Borgognoni is located between Piazza di Spagna and the Trevi Fountain, in a small palazzo dating from 1800. Right in the center of the city's historic, artistic, and commercial center, the hotel exudes the charm and atmosphere of a secret Rome. The hotel welcomes its guests with the hospitality of the best tradition of Italian hotels and includes an American bar, an internal garden, and a private garage.

Hotel Carriage

Via delle Carrozze, 36; tel.: 06-6990124/ 6788279; e-mail: hotel.carriage@alfanet.it; website: www.hotelcarriage.net; category: ★★★; number of rooms: 24; credit cards accepted: all major; access to internet: direct-line (US, UK) telephone jack in all rooms; most beautiful rooms: 501, 601; €€€.

☛A charming hotel, near Piazza di Spagna. The entire ground floor is decorated with 18th-century furnishings. Rooms 501 and 601 have terraces with great views of Rome's rooftops. If you fail to get those rooms you can still enjoy breakfast in the common terrace, which also features a lovely view.

Hotel Casa Howard

Via Capo delle Case, 18; tel.: 06-69924555/ 6794644; e-mail: casahowardroma@yahoo.com; website: www.casahoward.com; number of rooms: 5; credit cards accepted: all major, except American Express; facilities: massages available; access to internet: fast, DSL line from cable TV in all rooms, some rooms have a PC; most beautiful rooms: *"Verde"* and *"Rossa"* ; €€*.

☛In the heart of the city, only 100 yards from Piazza di Spagna. This is an English-style guesthouse inside a historic building. Casa Howard, named after its British owner, Jennifer Howard, has five rooms with wooden floors and coffered ceilings. Breakfast is fresh from a Tuscan farm owned by Ms. Howard. Excellent service. It's a home more than a hotel, and guests are usually introduced by other guests.

Hotel Cesari

Via di Pietra, 89/A; tel.: 06-6792386/ 6790882; e-mail: cesari.booking@albergocesari.com; website: www.venere.com/it/roma/ cesari; category: ★★★; number of rooms: 47; credit cards accepted: all major; access to internet: direct-line (US, UK) telephone jack in all rooms; €€–€€€.

☛Inaugurated in 1787, the hotel sits in the Colonna area, or *rione*, in the heart of the city. The *pietra*, or stone, to which the street name refers is that of the columns of the temple of Hadrian, later incorporated by baroque architect Carlo Fontana into the facade of the building that once housed the stock exchange. Though completely renovated in 1999, the hotel still boasts the charm of older establishments. Spacious and tastefully decorated rooms have double-paned windows. Bathrooms are new.

Hotel Eden

Via Ludovisi, 49; tel.: 06-478121; 167-820088; fax: 06-4821584; e-mail: reservation@ hotel-eden.it; website: www.hotel-eden.it; category: ★★★★★; number of rooms: 118, including 30 suites; credit cards accepted: all major; access to internet: direct-line (US, UK) telephone jack in all rooms; €€€€*.

☛The Eden is over 100 years old and one of the most luxurious hotels in Rome. It is surrounded by the parks of the Ludovisi, Borghese, and Malta Villas, and is situated between the famous Via Veneto and the Spanish Steps, leading to the Trinità dei Monti. It has been renovated to keep up with modern standards. Enjoy the view of Rome from their terrace restaurant or have a drink in the piano bar.

Hotel Fontanella Borghese

Largo Fontanella Borghese, 84; tel.: 06-68809504/6861295; e-mail: fontanella borghese@interfree.it; website: www.fontanellaborghese.com; category: ★★★; number of rooms: 29; credit cards accepted: all major; access to internet: direct-line (US, UK) telephone jack in all rooms; most beautiful rooms: 102, 209, 213; €€.

☛Located in a historic palazzo that once belonged to the Borghese princes. The hotel's lobby and breakfast room are bursting with various marbles, while the guest rooms boast coordinated fabrics and antiques, as well as the occasional, original black-and-gray checked flooring.

Hotel Grand Hotel Palace

Via Veneto, 70; tel.: 06-478719/47871800; e-mail: reservation@palace.boscolo.com; website: www.boscolohotels.com; category: ★★★★; number of rooms: 95; credit cards accepted: all major; facilities: sauna, pool; access to internet: direct-line (US,UK) telephone jack in all rooms; most beautiful room: 110, €€€€.

☛In the heart of Via Veneto, the Hotel Grand Hotel Palace was designed in the 1920s. The walls of the Art Deco lobby are frescoed.

Hotel Gregoriana

Via Gregoriana, 18; tel.: 06-6794269/ 6784258; category: ★★★; number of rooms: 19; credit cards accepted: none; facilities: parking (€25 a night); access to internet: direct-line (US, UK) telephone jack in all rooms; most beautiful room: "R"; €€€.

☛Above the Spanish Steps, but on a quiet street. Unusually decorated, with a mix of Art Deco and Asian furnishings and pictures, but elegant and very, very friendly. Some rooms have a view of the rooftops of the city.

Hotel Hassler

Via Trinità dei Monti, 6; tel.: 06-699340/ 6789991; e-mail: hasslerroma@mclink.it; web site: www.hotelhasslerroma.com; category: ★★★★★; number of rooms: 100; credit cards accepted: all major; access to internet: direct-line (US, UK) telephone jack in all rooms and access to a business center with copy machine, fax, and computer with internet; most beautiful rooms: 403, 505, 608 (doubles), 701 (super-deluxe); €€€€*.

☛Considered one of the finest hotels in the world, the Hassler, located in a former Medici palace, overlooks Rome from atop the Spanish Steps at Trinità dei Monti. Operating since 1885, it features frescoes, antique furnishings, marble baths, and works of art in the suites. Each room is individually decorated. You have a choice of dining in the courtyard with stone walls, statues, and flowers, or one can have dinner on the terrace with one of the finest views of Rome. They also offer a Sunday buffet brunch with magnificent views.

Hotel d'Inghilterra

Via Bocca di Leone, 14; tel.: 06-699811/ 6798601; e-mail: information.hir@ royaldemeure.com; website: www.charming hotels.it; category: ★★★★; number of rooms: 98; credit cards accepted: all major; access to internet: direct-line (US, UK) telephone jack in all rooms; €€€€*.

☛Right in the center of Rome, walking distance from the Spanish Steps, this 17th-century building opens out onto a quiet pedestrian side street lined with boutiques. Inside, the rooms are lavish and carefully decorated, with full carpeting and dark wooden furniture as well as period paintings and prints. The marble-paneled bathrooms are decorated with fresh orchids. The hotel has a snazzy restaurant and room service, in addition to a bar and café.

Hotel Inn at the Spanish Steps

Via dei Condotti, 85; tel.: 06-69925657/ 6786470; e-mail: info@atspanishsteps.com; website: www.atspanishsteps.com; number of rooms: 24; credit cards: all major; access to internet: direct-line (US, UK) telephone jack in all room; €€€–€€€€.

☛This 17th-century private residence, right off the Spanish Steps, where Hans Christian Andersen lived for years, was transformed into a very intimate hotel that still looks and feels like a home. The rooms are decorated with antique furniture and period drapes but offer the modern comfort of Jacuzzi tubs. With a charming veranda and a beautiful terrace.

Hotel Locarno

Via della Penna, 22; tel.: 06-3610841/ 3215249; e-mail: info@hotellocarno.com; category: ★★★; number of rooms: 60, including 4 deluxe rooms and 1 suite; credit cards accepted: all major; facilities: parking nearby (€25 a night); free bicycles; access to internet: direct-line (US, UK) telephone jack in all rooms, business center with copy machine and computer with internet; most beautiful rooms: 201 (double), 602 and 606 (deluxe); €€–€€€.

☛There is a unique Art Deco flavor to the entrance of this small hotel tucked behind

Piazza del Popolo. The magnificent green ground-level garden with a small fountain is open all day, as is the roof terrace that looks out toward the Tiber. The dining room and the bar have a fireplace. The rooms are all different but equally charming, with high ceilings and wooden floors. The upper floors of the building are still private apartments, as were all the rooms until the hotel's opening in 1925. It's a real find.

Hotel Majestic

Via Veneto, 50; tel.: 06-421441/4880984; e-mail: hotel_majestic@flashnet.it; website: www.hotelmajestic.com; category: ★★★★★; number of rooms: 99, including 5 suites; credit cards accepted: all major; access to internet: direct-line (US, UK) telephone jack in all rooms; €€€€*.

☛In a beautiful historical building in Rome, the Majestic was the first luxury hotel to open its doors on Via Veneto. The lobby is decorated with antique furnishings and fresh flowers. The rooms are medium-sized and richly decorated with antiques. The bathrooms have white Carrara marble. Breakfast is served at La Veranda restaurant, with a terrace overlooking Via Veneto.

Hotel Manfredi

Via Margutta, 61; tel.: 06-3207676/ 3207736; e-mail: hmanfredi@tiscalinet.it; website: www.hmanfredi.com; category: ★★★; number of rooms: 18; credit cards accepted: all major; access to internet: direct-line (US, UK) telephone jack in all rooms; most beautiful room: 104; €€–€€€.

☛The Manfredi is a pleasant hotel situated in a 16th-century building on Via Margutta, a street known for its art and antique galleries. Renovated in 1999, it offers the charm and pleasure of staying in a stylish residence. The 18th-century furnishings create welcoming surroundings. Much attention has been paid to the rooms, and the upholstery is done in pastel shades of pink, green, and light blue.

Hotel Mozart

Via dei Greci, 23/B; tel.: 06-36001915/ 36001735; category: ★★★; number of rooms: 56; credit cards accepted: all major; access to internet: direct-line (US, UK) telephone jack in all rooms; most beautiful rooms: 25 and 31; €€–€€€.

☛Between Piazza del Popolo and the Spanish Steps, this hotel is situated across from Rome's Conservatory of Music. The hotel is therefore provided with a steady soundtrack of live classical music during the academic year. It has a welcoming atmosphere, with rooms painted cream yellow with sky blue decorations, and a friendly staff. Large windows in the rooms bring in lots of light. Ask for a fifth-floor room with a balcony. The roof garden with a view of Trinità dei Monti and the Pincio is open late.

Hotel Parlamento

Via delle Convertite, 5 (right off Piazza S. Silvestro); tel.: 06-6792082/69921000; e-mail: hotelparlamento@libero.it; website: www.hotelparlamento.it; category: ★★; number of rooms: 23; credit cards accepted: all major; facilities: air conditioning in 17 rooms (€11 a night); access to internet: computer in the lounge (€3 for 15 minutes); most beautiful rooms: 76, 82, 108; €–€€.

☛In the third and fourth floor of a 17th-century palazzo, near the Italian Parliament building. Decoration and furnishings are sober but stylish, with a few antique pieces. The lobby is decorated with a trompe l'oeil of the skyline of Rome. If you are interested in the room with a terrace, No. 108, you have to book it far in advance. If you can't reserve it, you can still enjoy the common terrace.

Hotel La Residenza

Via Emilia, 22; tel.: 06-4880789/485721; e-mail: hotel.laresidenza@venere.it; category: ★★★★; number of rooms: 29, including 5 suites; credit cards accepted: all major; facilities: limited parking (€5 a night); access to internet: one direct-line telephone jack in the hotel; most beautiful rooms: 26 (double), 25 (suite); €€.

☛A former private villa near Via Veneto.

The hotel has a small courtyard and an elegant lobby, decorated with antique furniture and interesting paintings. Very charming.

Hotel Romantik Barocco

Via della Purificazione, 4 (Piazza Barberini); tel.: 06-4872001/485994; e-mail: info@hotel barocco.com; website: www.hotelbarocco.com; category: ★★★★; number of rooms: 37; credit cards accepted: all major; access to internet: none; €€–€€€.

☛An intimate and charming hotel not far from Via Veneto. Decorated with lots of cherry wood and murals with scenes of Rome. The rooms have large mirrors that make them look very spacious.

Hotel de Russie

Via del Babuino, 9; tel.: 06-328881/ 32888888; e-mail: reservations@ hotelderussie.it; website: www.rfhotels.com; category: ★★★★★; number of rooms: 129, including 20 suites; credit cards accepted: all major; access to internet: direct-line (US, UK) telephone jack in all rooms; most beautiful rooms end in 23 on each floor: 123, 223, 323, and so on; €€€€*.

☛The Hotel de Russie, reopened in 2000 by Rocco Forte Hotels after a 60-year interval, still exudes the aura of its impressive past. In 1816 it was designed as an upscale hotel by architect Giuseppe Valadier. From early on, the Hotel de Russie was an institution for dignitaries and blue bloods.

Just a few paces past the doorman is a tranquil courtyard facing a romantic, terraced garden that climbs the Pincio Hill. Contact with the bustling outside world, whether it's the non-stop traffic on Via del Babuino or the ambient noise of Piazza del Popolo, is shut out by high walls and muffled by the garden.

The bedrooms have been fitted with stylish, modern furnishings and decorated with a hodgepodge of clever touches: baroque headboards, Georgian chairs, and postmodern tables—all of which reflect the city's layer-upon-layer of past and present. There are marble mosaic tiles in the bathrooms and linen sheets on the beds.

Hotel Scalinata di Spagna

Piazza Trinità dei Monti 17; tel.: 06-69940896 /69940598; e-mail: info@hotelscalinata.com; website: www.hotelscalinata.com; category: ★★★; number of rooms: 16, including 1 suite; credit cards accepted: all major; access to internet: direct-line (US, UK) telephone jack in all rooms; most beautiful room: 15; €€€.

☛This 16-room hotel has an unpretentious, bed-and-breakfast feel. Most rooms have a bird's-eye view of Piazza di Spagna, if not a terrace overlooking it. Luxurious drapes, big windows, and handsome furniture make for a rich setting, though the rooms are not huge. Breakfast is served on the trellis-covered terrace, weather permitting. Room 15 is by far the best with French fabrics in blues and yellows, a small but comfortable bath, and a private terrace with a view of Rome—perfect for eating breakfast in pleasant weather. There is excellent service and a rooftop terrace, where you can have breakfast or enjoy the sunset. It has a great view of one of the most beautiful piazzas in Rome.

Hotel Valadier

Via della Fontanella, 14; tel.: 06-3612344/ 3201558; e-mail: info@hotelvaladier.it; website: www.hotelvaladier.com; category: ★★★★; number of rooms: 60, including 6 suites; credit cards accepted: all major; access to internet: direct-line (US, UK) telephone jack in all rooms; most beautiful room: 312; €€–€€€€.

☛The Art Deco furnishings, country tiles, and wooden ceilings are somewhat out of place in this typical, old Roman palazzo, but the Hotel Valadier is elegant and cozy. Its fifth-floor roof garden is small but offers a great view of the roofs of the Eternal City, including the cupola of one of the two twin churches of Piazza del Popolo. The hotel sells wonderful bath oils made by a local craftwoman.

Hotel Westin Excelsior

Via Veneto, 125; tel.: 06-47081/4826205; website: www.westin.com or www. luxurycollection.com/ExcelsiorRome; number of rooms: 321, including 29 suites; credit cards accepted: all major; facilities: parking

HOTELS & INNS

(€30 a night); access to internet: direct-line (US, UK) telephone jack in all rooms; €€€€*.

☛The hotel of the dolce vita right in Via Veneto. It features the largest suite in Europe. Known as the Villa La Cupola, the 12,000-square-foot accommodation includes a Jacuzzi pool, two uniformed butlers, bottles of champagne, a screening room, and an immense terrace overlooking the roofs of Rome. They have recently added a Sunday buffet brunch, which includes wonderful salmon, vegetables, and desserts. The service is impeccable.

Hotel White

Via in Arcione, 77; tel.: 06-6991242/ 6788451; e-mail: white@travelroma.com; website: www.whitehotel.com; category: ★★★★; number of rooms: 44, including 8 suites; credit cards accepted: all major; access to internet: direct-line (US, UK) telephone jack in all rooms; most beautiful room: 102; €€.

☛The four-star Hotel White opened in September 1993 in a 19th-century building. It is situated 110 yards from the Trevi Fountain and Piazza di Spagna. The rooms have air conditioning and satellite TV. A buffet breakfast is available for guests and the cigar bar is open late.

RESTAURANTS & CAFÉS

Al Moro

Vicolo delle Bollette, 13; tel.: 06-6783495; open: 1–3:30 P.M., 8–11:30 P.M.; closed: Sun. and month of Aug; €.

☛Just minutes from Montecitorio with Italian country atmosphere and fine Roman cuisine, including *spaghetti alla Moro* (a lighter version of carbonara), baked salt-cod, and beef *alla Checca*.

Caffè Dagnino of Palermo

Galleria Esedra (entrances at Via V. Emanuele Orlando, 75 and Via Torino, 95); tel.: 06-4818660.

☛One of the few authentic Sicilian bakeries in Rome, with ricotta-filled cannoli, single-serving cassata cakes, marrons glacés, candied fruits, and almond paste shipped in from Palermo. Sicilian-style gelato is made on the premises. A full offering of Sicilian foods are available for take-out or for lunch or dinner, including beautifully gift-wrapped biscuits, baked pasta casseroles, vegetable sides, and *arancini*, fried balls of rice with a rich meat sauce inside. Seating is available inside on two levels or in the covered shopping strip outside the entrance.

Caffè Greco

Via dei Condotti, 86; tel.: 06-6791700; open: 8 A.M.–8:15 P.M.

☛In Via Condotti, long-time haunt of European intelligentsia. Goethe, Casanova, Wagner, Liszt, Stendhal, Baudelaire, Leopardi, and Byron all felt at home in its intimate rooms adorned with 18th- and 19th-century Italian landscapes. Still excellent are the hot croissants and hot chocolate with whipped cream.

Caffètteria Barcaccia

Piazza di Spagna, 71; tel.: 06-6797497; open: daily 7 A.M.–10 P.M.

☛Named after the nearby Barcaccia Fountain, designed by Bernini senior, father of the more famous Gian Lorenzo. The delightful, relaxing tearoom upstairs has a great view. Window tables look directly onto the Spanish Steps, the Church of Trinità dei Monti, and the Keats-Shelley Memorial House, where poet John Keats spent his last days.

Canova

Piazza del Popolo, 16

☛One of two historic cafés located in Piazza del Popolo at the beginning of Via del Babuino. It serves a wide assortment of *panini*, pastries, and drinks. Popular on-the-go lunch place for the area's upwardly mobile working crowd. In fact, the crowded chaos at Canova's bar during peak eating hours can resemble the stock market floor.

Dal Bolognese

Piazza del Popolo; tel.: 06-3611426; open: 12:45–3 P.M., 8:15–11 P.M.; closed: Mon.; credit cards accepted: all major; €€.

☛One of Rome's most elegant restaurants, featuring the hearty, meaty foods of the Emilia-Romagna region. Interesting antipasti include smoked duck breast, while pastas include the classic *tortellini al bolognese*. The menu has a strong emphasis on fish, and it changes with the seasons.

Enoteca Antica di Via della Croce

Via della Croce, 76/B; tel.: 06-6790896; open: daily noon–1 A.M.; credit cards accepted: all major.

☛Thirty or so wines are available by the glass at this wine bar/restaurant near the Spanish Steps, with hundreds more available by the bottle. Typical *enoteca* fare such as cheeses, cured meats, and smoked fish is available, as well as heartier dishes such as sliced beef braised in Barolo wine and roast veal with potatoes. Appetizers, pastas, and second courses all run about €10–30. The vaulted dining area is tastefully frescoed with images of a cherubic Bacchus.

Enoteca Buccone

Via di Ripetta, 19; tel.: 06-3612154; open: Mon.–Thurs. 9 A.M.–8:30 P.M., Fri., Sat. 9 A.M.–midnight, Sun. 10 A.M.–5 P.M.; credit cards accepted: all major.

☛Just off Piazza del Popolo, this favorite wine bar of directors Bernardo Bertolucci and Ettore Scola is located in an old carriage house that once belonged to the marquis who inhabited the 18th-century palazzo. With dark wood tables and shelves, the bar offers a huge selection of labels from all over the world—by both the bottle and the glass—and hot and cold snacks to accompany the wines.

Gran Caffè La Caffettiera

Via Margutta, 61A; tel.: 06-3213344; open: Tues., Wed., Sun., 9 A.M.–9 P.M., Thurs., Fri., Sat., 9 A.M.–midnight; live music (jazz and American piano bar classics) Thurs., Fri., Sat. 9:30 P.M.–11:30 P.M.

☛This café has a delightful Art Nouveau decor, with painted ceilings of grotesques, evoking the Belle Epoque in Via Margutta, the traditional artists' street, where Fellini used to live. Live music on weekends.

Gusto

Piazza Augusto Imperatore, 9; tel.: 06-3226273; open: always; €.

☛The venue, in which food of all varieties is offered, includes an excellent restaurant, a pizzeria, a wine bar, a bookstore, and a kitchen utensils store. Chef Marco Gallotta works with Mediterranean flavors and exotic fragrances, producing dishes such as couscous tart, salmon eggs with heart of mozzarella burrata, *tagliolini* with smoked pigeon salad and flavored with green tea, spaghetti with vegetables and ginger stir-fried in a wok pan; Cajun-style tuna with fennel and citrus-fruit oil. The restaurant also offers a selection of 70 types of cheese from Italy and France. At the end of the meal, do not miss the chocolate tart with a spicy center. The wine selection spans over 1,000 labels. Brunch available on Sundays and, at night, live music (Bill Clinton once played his sax here).

Il Leoncino

Via del Leoncino 28; tel.: 06-6876306; open: 8–11 P.M.; closed: Wed., Sun., and month of Aug.; €€.

☛The pizza is very good, and that's why it is often difficult to find a table.

Matricianella

Via del Leone, 4; tel.: 06-6832100; open: 12:30–3 P.M., 7:30–11 P.M.; closed: Sun. and two weeks in Aug.; €.

☛*Bucatini all'amatriciana* and other classics of Roman cuisine, in one of the most renowned areas of Rome. Good wine selection.

L'Osteria dell'Ingegno

Piazza di Pietra, 45; tel.: 06-6780662; open: 12:30–3 P.M., 7:30–midnight; closed: Sun.; credit cards accepted: all major; €.

☛Located in Piazza di Pietra, this restaurant offers a strictly regional cuisine that is low in fat with an accent on vegetables: puree of Castelluccio lentils with black truffle, excellent eggplant moussaka, and homemade desserts. Homemade salamis and cheese served with wine after midnight.

Penna d'Oca

Via dell'Oca, 53; tel.: 06-3202898.

☛A small place, right off Piazza del Popolo, almost in front of Hotel Locarno. Outdoor service, weather permitting. Very good and creative takes on Sardinian and Sicilian cuisine. The husband-and-wife owners are often there, adding their courteous and friendly touch to the excellent service.

Ristorante "34"

Via Mario dei Fiori, 34; tel.: 06-6795091; open: 12:30–3 P.M., 7:30–11 P.M.; closed: Mon.; credit cards accepted: all major; €.

☛One of Rome's standbys for traditional, hearty, local food. The enormous menu offers over 40 pastas, 20 meats, and 20 fish dishes, in addition to a wide array of appetizers and desserts. A row of outdoor tables faces an ivy-covered wall across the way.

Rosati

Piazza del Popolo, 4/5A; tel.: 06-3227378.

☛Ever since Piazza del Popolo was closed to traffic, the view from this historic café, strategically located at the edge of the piazza opposite the Pincio, has become much more beautiful. More refined than its competitor across the piazza, Rosati has a literary past—the Roman author Alberto Moravia and his circle of friends used to spend many an evening there.

Scuderie Papali Caffètteria

Via XXIV Maggio, 16; tel.: 06-696270; open only during exhibition hours for exhibition visitors: Sun.–Thurs. 10 A.M.–8 P.M., Fri., Sat., 10 A.M.–11 P.M.; closed: Mon.

☛Recently opened café inside the new state-of-the-art exhibition venue created by architect Gae Aulenti inside the former papal stables. From the windows over the Quirinale Square there is a magnificent view of the presidential palace and the twin gods fountain.

Specialty Shops

Apolloni

Via del Babuino, 133; tel.: 06-36002216; open: 9:30 A.M.–1 P.M., 3:30–7:30 P.M.; closed: Sat. afternoon and Sun.

☛An antique shop dealing only in high-quality pieces of Italian furniture, 17th-century paintings, and rare antique silver.

Battistoni

Via dei Condotti, 61A; tel.: 06-6786827; open: Tues.–Sat. 10 A.M.–7 P.M., Mon. 3–7 P.M.; closed: Sun.; credit cards accepted: all major.

☛Two thousand types of fabric, cashmere sweaters, and ties designed by artists.

Bomba

Via dell'Oca, 39/41; tel.: 06-3203020; open: 11 A.M.–7:30 P.M.; closed Sun. and Mon. morning.

☛Textile expert Luisa Cevese creates orig-

inal items from handbags to shoes—all handmade. Large collection of shawls and scarves, and many one-of-a-kind pieces in cashmere and silk.

Bulgari

Via dei Condotti, 10; tel.: 06-6793876; open: Tues.–Sat. 10:30 A.M.–7 P.M.; closed: Sun. and Mon. morning; credit cards accepted: all major.

☛Andy Warhol defined it as the "most important museum of modern art in Europe." Since 1884, when Sotirio Bulgari arrived in Rome from Epirus, Greece, it has represented the height of Italian jewelry. Its Renaissance-inspired pieces are famous the world over.

Casuccio e Scalera

Via Frattina, 47; tel.: 06-6794302; open: daily 9 A.M.–2 P.M., 3–7:30 P.M.

☛One of Rome's most exclusive shoe stores.

C'era una volta

Via Angelo Brunetti, 40; tel.: 06-3203019; open: daily 9 A.M.–1 P.M., 4:30–7:30 P.M.

☛Handmade candles of every kind.

Diana Marchetti

Via Vittoria, 28; tel.: 06-3220916; open: 9:30 A.M.–7:30 P.M.; closed: some Sun. and all Mon. mornings.

☛This store specializes in decorative prints, principally of floral subjects, from the 17th to early 20th centuries. It also features views of Rome and prints of cats and dogs.

Fratelli Alinari

Via Alibert, 16A/B; tel.: 06-6792923; fax: 06-69941998.

☛This photographic art bookstore features books and photographs of the world from the 1850s until today.

Galleria Grossi

Via Margutta, 109; tel./fax: 06-36001935; website: www.marble.8m.com; open: Mon.–Sat. 10 A.M.–7:30 P.M.

☛Maurizio Grossi specializes in tasteful marble and mosaic reproductions of classic works of art, as well as original souvenirs, like his life-size marble fruits and vegetables, which make stunning table decorations. The figs and peaches look so real you'll want to eat them! Maurizio has also written a short history of the Via Margutta, Rome's traditional artists' quarter, which he sometimes gives to customers with their purchases.

Georg Jensen

Piazza di Spagna, 77; tel.: 06-69924869; open: 10 A.M.–7:30 P.M.; closed: Sun. and Mon. morning.

☛Danish silversmith featuring Venini vases and dishes and sterling silver services, like the Bernadotte pattern with plain, grooved handles or the Cactus pattern, inspired by the plant.

Gusto e Salute

Via della Panetteria, 8; tel.: 06-6796259; open: Mon.–Sat. 9:30 A.M.–7:30 P.M., Wed. 9:30 A.M.–2:30 P.M.

☛You can smell the freshly baked cookies before you come through the door. Everything in this prettily decorated specialty store, crowned with a spreading candelabra of leafy branches, is organic—from the cereals, flour, olive oil, and dairy products to the wines, fruit juices, and lemonade. Owner Liliana Fabbro, a brisk and knowledgeable native of Turin, was a pioneer in the field some 30 years ago, when she and some friends opened Rome's first organic grocery store near the Pantheon.

Maurizio Grossi

Via Margutta, 109; tel.: 06-36001935; open: 10 A.M.–7:30 P.M.; closed: Sun.

☛Ancient-style marble busts, bas-reliefs, and mosaics are sold here, created by various contemporary Roman artists. Some are recognizable renderings of famous monuments, while others are original designs. Larger objects like tables and obelisks are available as well.

Messaggerie Musicali

Via del Corso, 473; tel.: 06-684401; open: Mon.–Sat. 10 A.M.–11 P.M., Sun. 11 A.M.–9 P.M.

☛You can listen to Italy's Top 40 pop hits at the entrance to this music superstore. A large selection of sheet music is available, including songbooks by Italy's best-loved rock stars. The jazz, classical, and world music sections have headphones with at least a dozen current releases to sample. There's even a station where you can test out DVDs. There's a travel agent, concert box office, and decent-sized bookstore, as well.

Muzio

Via Vittorio Emanuele Orlando, 77 (entrance to the Galleria Esedra); tel.: 06-4883529; fax: 06-48919798; open: daily 9:30 A.M.–8 P.M.

☛Muzio's toiletries and gadgetry is a Roman institution. Vast selection of every kind of knife, including Swiss army knives and chefs' knives, as well as tableware, shaving mirrors, perfume bottles, giant bottle openers for magnums, and hair-brushes. Also specializes in top-quality, genuine badger hair shaving brushes.

Pulcini Gino

Via del Lavatore, 93 (corner Via della Panetteria, 1/c); tel.: 06-6794739.

☞One of Rome's most famous gold- and silversmiths. Selection of cameos featuring cats and dogs. Corals and custom-made jewelry.

Radica

Via di San Giacomo, 14; tel.: 06-36005583; open: 9:30 A.M.–1 P.M., 3:30–7:30 P.M.; closed: Sun. and Mon. morning.

☞All kinds of burl products.

Radiconcini

Via del Corso, 139; tel.: 06-6791807; open: 9:30 A.M.–1:30 P.M., 4–7:30 P.M.; closed: Sun., Mon. morning, and Sat. afternoon; credit cards accepted: all major.

☞In Via del Corso, this milliner's hats define two centuries of history, from famous Montechristi panamas, sold in traditional balsa wooden boxes, to Borsalinos. Also available are ties, walking sticks, and smoking jackets that evoke cozy living rooms with fireplaces, scented by wood and tobacco.

Settimio Mieli—Solo Guanti

Via di S.Claudio, 70; tel.: 06-6785979.

☞As the name suggests, this small store sells only gloves. But there is a great selection of wonderful leather gloves for all tastes.

Swarovsky

Via della Fontanella Borghese, 39–40; tel.: 06-68192600; open: 10 A.M.–7:30 P.M.; closed: Sun.

☞All kinds of crystals, from jewelry and glasses to a collection of colored crystals. Also available are chalices, candleholders, and the classic miniature animals.

Tulipani Bianchi

Via dei Bergamaschi, 59; tel.: 06-6785449; open: 9 A.M.–1 P.M., 3:30–7 P.M.; closed: Sun. and Mon. morning; credit cards accepted: all major.

☞Florist Franz Steiner, a former Swiss guard at the Vatican, is famous worldwide for his Art Nouveau bouquets of tulips and Coburg roses as well as camellias, ivy, and thyme, yellow Iceland poppies, and arrangements with seeds and twisted hazelnut branches.

Zuccastregata

Via Belsiana, 70; tel.: 06-6793460; open: 10 A.M.–7:30 P.M.; closed: Mon. morning.

☞Household items, plus wallets and key chains.

Silver Nutmegs and Golden Pears
By Margaret Stenhouse

The golden apples and the silver boughs of ancient myth materialize here in Natura & Argento, Silvana Papette's delightful little store, situated a couple of blocks away from Rome's Piazza del Popolo. Papette has created a dazzling botanical garden of gilded and silvered fruits, flowers, leaves, and seedpods, which she fashions into pendants, brooches, table ornaments, and various objets d'art.

A former mathematics teacher, Papette started her business nine years ago. She began with seashells, then gradually applied her skills to perishable things, like flowers and vegetables.

By dint of experimentation, she perfected techniques that allow her to preserve even the most fragile and difficult materials, such as sprays of mimosa, artichokes, pomegranates, whole pumpkins, long-stemmed sunflowers, and winged sycamore seeds. Her creations range from small and reasonably priced earrings and other pieces of jewelry to large dining-room centerpieces, such as a candleholder made from a cluster of silver barnacles. The most surprising pieces are the gold and silver pinecones, lavender springs, and anise florets, which have all retained their original fragrance.

Each item can take weeks of preparation. First, it must be treated with a special fixing agent to stop the decomposition process. It then has to dry out completely—an operation that can take from a few hours to several weeks, or even months. The objects are all coated in copper before the final pure gold and silver leaf finish is applied.

Many of Silvana's customers come back regularly to commission custom-designed pieces, which may have originated as something growing in their garden. Her creations have attracted celebrities like ballerina Carla Fracci and movie stars Vittorio and Alessandro Gassman.

Natura & Argento; Via del Vantaggio, 41A; tel.: 06-3219384.

OUR CRITIC'S FAVORITE RESTAURANTS

Café Romano

Via Borgognona, 4/M; tel.: 06-69981500; open: daily 10 A.M. until late, after-theater dining possible; €.

☛The interior design echoes this gesture by offsetting arches, columns, Pompeii-red barrel vaulting, and marble floors with a collection of works by young contemporary artists. Chef Alessandro Morelli offers patrons a culinary tour that steps from *spaghetti con bottarga* (grated, cured red mullet roe) to *confit de canard*, moussaka, seafood couscous, Lebanese mezzeh, Chicago rib-eyes, chicken with green curry, salmon teriyaki, and myriad salads. The large dessert selection includes chocolate mousse, Catalan flan, apple strudel, and cheesecake. A solid wine list offers domestic and foreign labels. Tables are set with fine china, sterling, and crystal, and outdoor dining is possible in Via Borgognona, weather permitting.

Nino Dal 1934

Via Borgognona, 11; tel.: 06-6795676; fax: 06-6786752; €.

☛Amidst Rome's Tridente neighborhood, Nino offers down-to-earth traditional Tuscan cooking. Starters include mixed *crostini* and a spinach-and-chicken liver torte, followed by *ribollita* (the classic Tuscan cabbage and bread stew), polenta with wild boar sauce, or *pappardelle* with wild rabbit, grilled quail, and spicy steaks. Homemade apple cake tops the dessert list, whereas the sound wine list favors Tuscan labels.

Osteria Margutta

Via Margutta, 82; tel.: 06-3231025; closed: Sun.; €.

☛A cross between a painter's studio and an art gallery, Osteria Margutta lives up to its location in one of Rome's most bohemian streets and the historic home of the capital's artistic community. On the menu, a combination of classic and regional dishes include tonnarelli Margutta and Mediterranean-style spaghetti alla chitarra, as well as the house's special, Danish beef fillet. On Tuesdays and Fridays the chef offers fresh seafood dishes only.

The Roof Terrace of the Hotel Eden

Via Ludovisi 49; tel.: 06-478121; open: always; €€€€.

☛Enrico Derflingher has worked for Elizabeth, Queen of England, and will work for you if you visit the splendid terrace of the Eden, with its exceptional view of the roofs of Rome. The menu includes dishes in the Mediterranean tradition, modernized with a delicate touch: codfish pancakes with pecorino cheese; chicken liver; tagliolini with shrimp, zucchini, and tomato sauce; risotto with peas, goat cheese, and marjoram; and green gnocchi with scorpion fish ragout. A good choice for a second course is the tuna with eggplant and bacon. For dessert, try the bittersweet chocolate mousse with celery sauce. The wine selection is carefully put together.

Sacro e Profano

Via dei Maroniti, 29; tel.: 06-6791836; always open; €.

☛Meals start with a flurry of appetizers from Calabria-like baby sardines, to soppressata and capocollo, cured pork specialties. Afterward, diners at Sacro e Profano can delve further into their gourmet journey through this southern Italian region with *maccarruni a ferretti*, a pasta prepared with Sila mountain mushrooms, or be tempted by local cheeses, marinated vegetables, or ice creams delivered directly from Pizzo Calabro. Among the homemade desserts, do not pass up the *Pittanchiusa*. The atmosphere of the restaurant, set in a desecrated Maronite church from 1190, is no less inspiring. The wine list includes a selection of Calabrian labels.

Campidoglio/ Ghetto/Pantheon

By Ruth Kaplan

The five busy roads feeding into Piazza Venezia have turned the once-quiet square into the quintessential vortex of nonstop Roman traffic, but have also made it a useful reference point for exploring this area of central Rome. The massive white marble **Vittoriano** anchors the south side of the piazza, with the **Capitolium**, or Capitoline Hill, hidden behind it. Important temples and administrative buildings have been located here since the 6th century B.C., and Rome's city government is still located in the square's central **Palazzo Senatorio**, known for its unique Renaissance bell tower. Michelangelo was responsible for the look of the piazza, from the building facades to the choice of statuary. The **Statue of Marcus Aurelius** (see Capitolium entry) seated on a horse is a copy of one of the few ancient bronzes to survive the Middle Ages intact. The original, along with scores of other masterpieces of Roman statuary, are on display at the **Musei Capitolini**, located in the two buildings on either side of the square. Michelangelo's wide, gently sloping staircase—the Cordonata— leads down out of the piazza. A steep staircase rising up next to it leads to the ancient **Santa Maria in Aracoeli**, the church on the highest point of the Capitoline Hill.

Down the street from the Capitoline Hill are the white travertine arches of the **Teatro di Marcello**, a 15,000-seat theater built by Emperor Augustus. Skirting the edge of the Jewish Ghetto, you arrive at **Il Gesù**, a heavily decorated Jesuit church built in the 16th century. Saint Ignatius, the founder of the Jesuit order, is buried there. North of Il Gesù is **Santa Maria sopra Minerva**, a church rebuilt over an ancient temple of Minerva and modeled on Florence's Santa Maria Novella. In the next piazza is the **Pantheon**, Rome's best-preserved ancient monument. Hadrian built and probably designed the circular walls and enormous poured concrete dome, which, as its name denotes, was once a temple devoted to all the gods.

Near the Pantheon are two Renaissance palazzos that have been taken over by the Italian Senate. **Palazzo Giustiniani** was built in the 16th century, with some work done by Borromini. **Palazzo Madama** is the Senate building, built as the home of the Medici family in the 16th century.

Left, Interior of the Pantheon

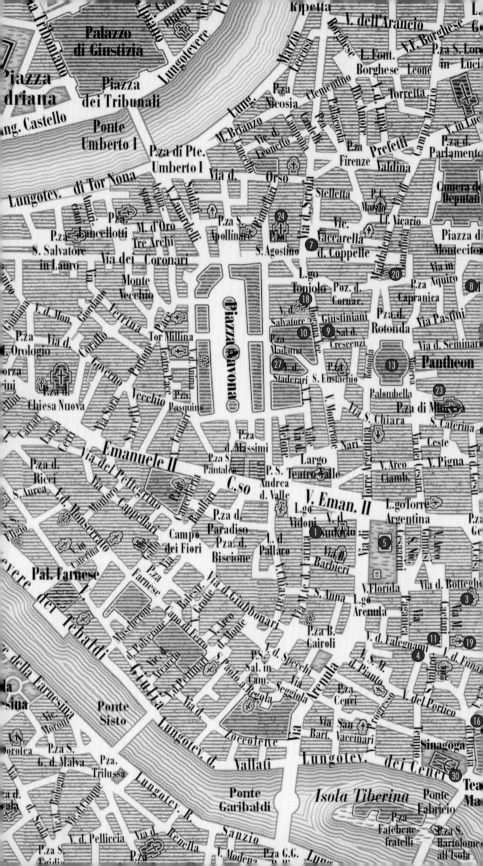

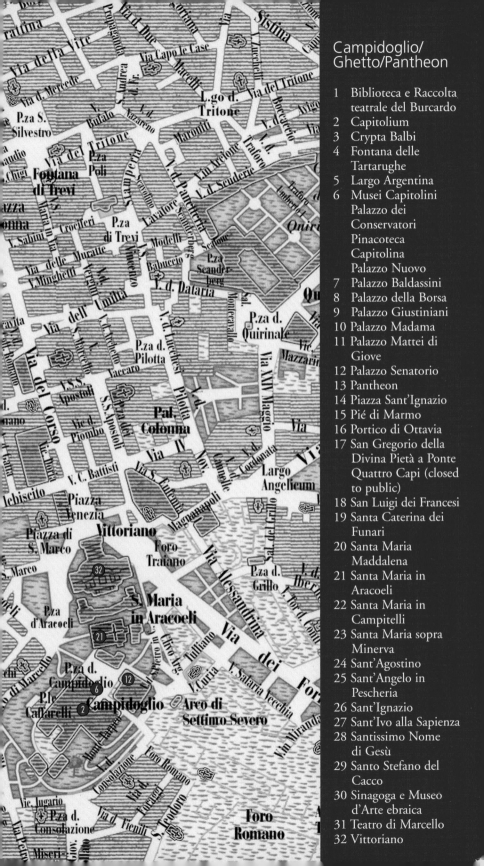

CAPITOLIUM
Piazza del Campidoglio

➤ The Capitolium, now the site of Rome's city hall, is, at 131-feet tall, the shortest of the city's seven hills but the most sacred and revered. It was the home of the Temple of Jupiter and the Temple of Juno Moneta (Juno the Admonisher), which held the Roman mint. Consequently, with time, the word *moneta* became synonymous with money. The large staircase that ascends to the capitol was first opened in 1536, on the occasion of Charles V's visit to Rome. The two lions at its foot are copies of two Egyptian statues now in the Capitoline Museum, which were found near Santo Stefano del Cacco, and probably belonged to the ancient Temple of Isis and Serapis. At the head of the staircase are colossal statues of Castor and Pollux, also trophies of imperial times. The center of the square is occupied by a copy of the famous bronze equestrian statue of Marcus Aurelius, transferred from the Lateran Piazza in 1538 (now in the Palazzo Nuovo). It owes its preservation in medieval times to the fact that it was supposed to be a statue of Constantine, the emperor that legalized the Christian church. Originally gilt, it stood in front of the Arch of Septimius Severus, and was removed to the Lateran Piazza by Sergius III (905–912). The building in front, erected by Michelangelo, fills the site of the ancient *Tabularium*, or Roll Office (city archive), of the Roman Republic and Empire.

PALAZZO GIUSTINIANI
Via della Dogana Vecchia, 29, at Via Giustiniani

➤ The building, begun by Giovanni and Domenico Fontana in 1585, was later taken over by Carlo Maderno and Girolamo and Carlo Rainaldi, and finally completed by Francesco Borromini in 1672. The structure itself stands over the ancient Nero Baths. Today, the palazzo is the house of the president of the Senate.

The sober facade presents an elegant main door that stands between two columns supporting a balcony. The outstanding Sala delle Colonne was designed and built by Borromini and frescoed by Antonio Tempesta and Matteo Zaccolini.

The Constitution of the Italian Republic was signed here in 1947.

PALAZZO MADAMA
Corso del Rinascimento; tel.: 06-6706;
open: first Sat. of the month 10 A.M.–6 P.M.

➤ Since 1871, Palazzo Madama has been home to the Italian Senate. It was first built in 1503, by Giovanni de' Medici, on an existing 15th-century structure and enlarged in 1512. The present-day look is

Statue of Marcus Aurelius, Piazza del Campidoglio

the work of Paolo Marucelli, 1637–1642, although further transformations were made by Pope Benedict XIV and Pope Pius IX in the 18th and 19th centuries.

The palazzo is named after "Madama" Margherita d'Austria, widow of Alessandro de' Medici. Palazzo Madama was the residence of the Medici cardinals, Giovanni and Giuliano, who later became popes, Leo X and Clement VII, respectively.

The facade has a portal set on columns surmounted by a balcony, which was once used every Saturday at noon for the Roman lottery. The Senate chamber was built in the courtyard of the old papal post office. Extensive art collections and a valuable library still belong to the palace.

PALAZZO SENATORIO
Piazza del Campidoglio

➤ For centuries, the Palazzo Senatorio was a work in progress. In medieval times, a complex of public buildings was slowly built over the ancient Roman Tabularium, and at the end of the 13th century, Pope Boniface VIII constructed a large loggia facing the piazza. Over the course of the next two centuries, various builders added towers. Michaelangelo completely restored the building in the process of his renewal of the piazza.

The fountain, underneath the staircase, is a collection of ancient remains, including a statue of Minerva as the goddess Rome in the center and two fluvial (river) gods (the Nile and the Tiber), that were removed from the Baths of Constantine.

Today, the Room of Julius Caesar on the second floor is used for the meetings of the city council. The statue of Caesar, which gives the room its name, is the only ancient Roman statue of Caesar. It dates from the Trajan period.

PANTHEON
Piazza della Rotonda; tel.: 06-68300230; open: 8:30 A.M.–7:30 P.M., Sun. 8:30 A.M.– 6:30 P.M., holidays 9 A.M.–1 P.M.; admission: free.

➤ One of the most remarkable architectural structures in the world, the Pantheon was built in 27 B.C. by Marcus Agrippa, the intimate friend and counselor of Augustus, as a temple in honor of Jupiter the Avenger and of Mars and Venus, the tutelary deities

of the Julian house. In A.D. 118 Emperor Hadrian completely rebuilt it. In 609 Pope Saint Boniface IV, with the permission of the Emperor Phocas, consecrated it as a Christian church (Saint Mary and all the Martyrs). In 663 the bronze tiles of the roof were carried off by Emperor Constans II to be used in a building in Constantinople, but they fell into the hands of the Saracens at Syracuse. The Pantheon was then used as a fortress in the Middle Ages, and in 1625 it was dismantled by Pope Urban VIII of the Barberini family. He removed the bronze sheeting of the portico beams to build the cannons of Castel Sant'Angelo— inspiring the famous saying, "What the Barbarians didn't destroy, the Barberini did"—and the baldacchino, a canopy over the altar of Saint Peter's. In 1870 the Pantheon was made sacred to the kings of Italy and was restored, by demolishing the infamous bell towers—called *orecchie d'asino*, or "donkey's ears," because of the way in which they stuck out at the front of the building—and eliminating the gates. The pronaos, a huge vestibule, has a total of 16 monolithic columns. Each one is 43-feet high and made of gray and pink granite. The bronze doors of the portals date back to a reconstruction carried out at the time of Pope Pius IV. On either side are two niches that were probably intended for the statues of Augustus and Agrippa. The rotunda has 20-foot-thick brick walls, and the 141-foot-diameter dome, the largest dome ever built in classical times, precisely equal to its height, is made from concrete. The interior is made up of seven semicircular- and rectangular-shaped niches. There are two marble columns on the front, almost 30-feet high, while the far niche is surmounted by an arch that lies in perfect symmetry with the arch over the entrance. The only high opening in the building, an oculus of nine feet in diameter, is in the vault. The marble floor, with its geometrical pattern of squares and circles, is mainly original. The tympanum was formerly adorned with bronze reliefs representing Jupiter hurling down the Titans. The ancient inscription on the frieze, reading M. AGRIPPA L. F. COS. TERTIUM FECIT is Hadrian's and recalls the commissioner of the first Pantheon.

SANTA MARIA IN ARACOELI

Piazza d'Aracoeli (entrances via Aracoeli
Staircase and door behind Palazzo Nuovo); tel.:
06-6798155; open: daily 7:00 A.M.–6:00 P.M.

➤ Santa Maria in Aracoeli, or Saint Mary
of the Altar in Heaven, stands on what was
once the Temple of Juno, on the northern
end of the Capitoline. The church was
built between 1251 and 1300. The beautiful Savelli chapel in the right transept was
erected in the year of its completion. The
final phase of construction may have been
directed by Arnolfo di Cambio, the greatest architect of the time.

The huge flight of steps was built in
1348, to thank the Virgin Mary for saving
Rome from the plague. Until the 19th
century, some Romans would go up the
124 steps on their knees, reciting the Ave
Maria, in the belief that they would
then win the lottery. The interior is majestic, with 22 columns taken from old
Roman buildings. In the first chapel to the
right there are frescoes by Pinturicchio
(1486). Over the huge main altar there
is a Byzantine image of the Virgin, an
11th-century painting on wood. The
interior includes works by Donatello
(*Tombstone of Giovanni Crivelli*, on the
wall to the right of the main entrance),
Benozzo Gozzoli (*Saint Anthony*, third

Il Gesù

left chapel), Francesco Amadori and
Michelangelo (*Tomb of Cecchino Bracci*, on
the right-hand door), and Pietro Cavallini
(*Virgin Mary with Child and Saints,* left
transept). The church is also known for the
Santo Bambino, a 15th-century, olive-
wood baby Jesus kept in the sacristy and
believed to have miraculous powers. The
figure was cut out of a tree from the hill in
Jerusalem where Christ was crucified. The
Santo Bambino figure was recently stolen,
but the church still contains splendid
Cosmatesque decorations visible in the pulpit, in the floor, and in the interesting
funerary monuments such as the Tomb of
Cardinal Alessandro Crivelli (1571) in the
left transept. The church was almost
destroyed in the 1880s, when the huge
monument to Vittorio Emanuele was being
built. Its old sacristy and convent perished.

SANTA MARIA SOPRA MINERVA

Piazza della Minerva, 42; tel.: 06-6793926;
open: daily 7 A.M.–7 P.M.; cloister open:
Mon.–Sat. 8 A.M.–1 P.M., 4–7 P.M.

➤ Santa Maria sopra Minerva, the head
church of the Dominicans in Rome, was
probably begun about 1285, by two
Dominican friars, architects of Santa
Maria Novella in Florence. It was completed in 1370, and is particularly famous
for Michelangelo's statue of Christ that
stands on the left of the sanctuary. The
Cristo Risorto was sculpted completely
naked, but a high prelate commissioned a
bronze loincloth for "decency." When it
became clear that the faithful were damag-
ing the foot with their touches, the church
decided to add a gilded bronze sandal.

Santa Maria sopra Minerva is the only
Gothic church in Rome. It stands on the
site of a temple to Minerva, erected by
Pompey as a memorial of his victories in
Asia. The exterior is plain, and the visitor
is unprepared for the interior, with its
imposing dimensions, its numerous
chapels, its rare sculptures, and remarkable
frescoes. In these chapels many noble families—the Caffarelli, the Aldobrandini, the
Altieri, the Giustiniani—have their sepul-
chral monuments. The Room of Saint
Catherine of Siena, near the sacristy, is
adorned with paintings by Antoniazzo
Romano. The room the saint died in was

IL GESÙ

A great mise-en-scène, the church is gorgeous; late Renaissance, of great proportions, and full, like so many others . . . of seventeenth and eighteenth century Romanism. It doesn't impress the imagination, but richly feeds the curiosity, by which I mean one's sense of the curious; suggests no legends, but innumerable anecdotes à la Stendhal. There is a vast dome, filled with a florid concave fresco of tumbling foreshortened angels, and all over the ceilings and cornices a wonderful outlay of dusky gildings and moldings. There are various Bernini saints and seraphs in stucco-sculpture, astride of the tablets and door-tops, backing against their rusty machinery of coppery nimbi and egg-shaped cloudlets. Marble, damask and tapers in gorgeous profusion. The high altar a great screen of twinkling chandeliers. The choir perched in a little loft high up in the right transept, like a balcony in a side-scene at the opera, and indulging in surprising roulades and flourishes.

—Henry James, *Italian Hours*

transported here in 1637. The Tomb of Fra Angelico is in the bay to the left of the sanctuary, near the side entrance. The Chapel of Saint Thomas of Aquinas in the right transept, has frescoes by Filippino Lippi, follower of Botticelli. The painting of the Annunciation in the fifth chapel, right aisle, is by Antoniazzo Romano. In the same chapel Pope Urban VII is buried. His papacy was the briefest of any pope: from September 15 to September 25, 1590. He was killed by malaria, the Roman scourge of those days. In this church, the Inquisition held the ritual of Public Abjuration by heretics and schismatics, including the trial of Galileo Galilei. The obelisk in front of the church comes from Egypt and is the shortest in Rome. The little elephant that supports it was added by Bernini. In the 17th and 18th centuries, it was known in Rome as the "piglet of the Minerva."

SANTISSIMO NOME DI GESÙ (IL GESÙ)

Piazza del Gesù; tel.: 06-69700; open: daily 6 A.M.–12.30 P.M., 4 P.M.–7:15 P.M.

➤ Dating from 1568, Il Gesù was the first Jesuit church built in Rome. Its proper name is Santissimo Nome di Gesù (Holiest Name of Jesus). Its design epitomizes Counter-Reformation baroque architecture and has been much imitated throughout the Catholic world.

Architect Jacopo Barozzi da Vignola (better known as Vignola) designed the church, but Giacomo Della Porta, one of his students and a follower of Michelangelo, completed it. Della Porta also designed the facade, which was constructed entirely in travertine and has three entrances and twin Corinthian columns at the nave.

The interior is exceedingly rich and ornate; the profusion of decoration in marble, bronze, gilding, and fresco painting are somewhat bewildering. It coupled religious requirements—a large nave with side pulpits for preaching to large crowds, and a principal altar as a centerpiece to celebrate the mass—with an elongated design. The ceiling, dome, and apse glow with frescoes, the best work of Giovanni Battista Gaulli, known as Baciccia; its altars are adorned with rich bronzes and sculptures; its walls are encrusted with costly marbles; its pavement is inlaid with porphyry and other precious stones.

Among its principal treasures is the Altar-Tomb of Saint Ignatius of Loyola, in the left transept, said to be the richest altar in Rome. The steps are of porphyry; the *predella*, a panel at the bottom of an altarpiece, is of Florentine mosaic, richly inlaid with agates, lapis lazuli, and porphyry; the four fluted columns that support the entablature of gilded bronze are lined with lapis lazuli;

Vittoriano or Altare della Patria

the bases and capitals are of bronze; the pilasters are of black-and-white marble, the pedestals and entablature of *verde antico,* adorned with reliefs and foliated ornaments of bronze. These reliefs illustrate incidents in the life of Saint Ignatius. The summit is crowned by the figures of the Three Divine Persons (Trinity) in white marble encircled by rays of glory. Between the Father and the Son is a large globe of lapis lazuli.

The high altar is a mass of very rare marble. The four large columns are of *giallo antico.* The frontal, or antependium, consists of four large slabs of Egyptian fluorite (*fiorito antico*), which was muchprized in the baroque era.

In Via degli Astalli is Casa Professa with the Rooms of Saint Ignatius, frescoed by Andrea Pozzo with an interesting trompe l'oeil.

Teatro di Marcello (Theater of Marcellus)

Via del Teatro di Marcello; tel.: 06-67103819.

➤ The Theater of Marcellus, the only surviving ancient theater in Rome, was erected on a site traditionally dedicated to stage representations. It was initiated by Julius Caesar and continued by Augustus. In 11 B.C. the theater was dedicated to Marcellus, the emperor's beloved nephew. During the 4th century it underwent successive structural transformations. The theater was grandiose —427 feet in diameter, with a capacity of around 15,000 spectators. It was a model for the later

Flavian Amphitheater, also known as the Colosseum. The facade, in travertine, presents three orders. The arches of the two lower orders were decorated by colossal marble masks. The stage, of modest depth, was decorated by columns and statues made up of colored marble. The theater was abandoned in the 5th century, and subsequently used as quarry, fortress, and eventually as a residential palazzo by Baldassarre Peruzzi.

Vittoriano (Monument to Vittorio Emanuele II, also known as Altare della Patria)

Piazza Venezia; tel.: 06-6991718; open: 10 A.M.–6 P.M. (summer), 10 A.M.–4 P.M. (winter); closed: Mon.; admission: free.

➤ The monument to Vittorio Emanuele II, the first king of unified Italy, was designed in 1878 by Giuseppe Sacconi. Work began in 1885 and the monument was inaugurated in 1911. In 1921 the Tomb of the Unknown Soldier was added, which led to the monument's nickname, Altare della Patria, or "Homeland's Altar." Its final exterior look was completed in 1927. It is made of bright white marble, in a strong (and criticized) contrast with the more typical, warmer Roman travertine. It has been compared to a wedding cake and a typewriter, and has few admirers. The statue is so big that when it came out of the foundry, a celebration meal was held inside, with 21 people.

Walking Tour 1:

The Roman Ghetto

By Sarah Morgan

I t is said that the Roman Jews are "more Roman than the Romans," given that they've been present in the city for more than two thousand years. And the quarter they have occupied for nearly a millennium is one of the oldest and most fascinating, combining a history that is written in stone and earth but also in the collective memory of its inhabitants. This is a part of Rome with a strong identity and a tangible sense of community, a place where the inhabitants and others gather and exchange gossip, or sit out on summer nights to catch a breeze from the Tiber. Where you can sample Roman kosher food and where the dominant commercial activities still hark back to the regulations imposed in the 16th century that limited Jews to the sale of fabrics, clothing, and old iron.

For more than three hundred years, the Ghetto was an enclosed place bounded by gates and high walls; a tiny strip of land between the Tiber and the Via del Portico di Ottavia. Since then it has grown to encompass roughly the area that lies between Via delle Botteghe Oscure, the Theater of Marcellus, the Tiber, and Via Arenula. Almost nothing remains visible of these gates and walls today but the Tempietto del Carmelo of 1759 in Piazza Costaguti, an abandoned edifice with a half-domed roof, now colonized by pigeons, where papal guards controlled one of the five entrances to the Ghetto.

Walk on into the Via del Portico di Ottavia, which serves as the Ghetto's main "piazza." This end of the street is the bustling center of Ghetto life and has been a meeting place for local inhabitants for many centuries. Until the walls and gates were demolished, this area—then a small piazza with a fountain lying just outside of the Ghetto—was where the Jews congregated during the daytime.

Looking toward the Tiber, all the turn-of-the-century buildings up to the river delineate the area of the enclosed Ghetto that was razed at the end of the 19th century. In some cases this radical "making good" was not completely carried

Portico di Ottavia

through; notice how the street ahead ends abruptly with the buttressed remnants of a half torn-down building.

But the northern side of the Via del Portico di Ottavia preserves its original flavor. No. 1, now housing the famed Pasticceria Boccione, is also known as the House of Lorenzo Manilio, built in 1468 as the long, low entablature inscription testifies. Its facade is randomly decorated with Roman reliefs, and at the far end a row of four busts stares out at passersby—a much eroded fragment of a Roman sarcophagus, no doubt found on or near the site.

At the far end of the street, the monumental atrium of the **Portico di Ottavia** rises dramatically against the backdrop of the massive brick arches of the Theater of Marcellus, and the cobbles give way to a current archaeological site where you can observe what is being uncovered. Large parts of the Ghetto overlie significant archaeological remains. The Portico of Octavia, built by Augustus in honor of his sister Octavia in the early 1st century B.C. and rebuilt after damage by fire 200 years later, was one of the most impressive buildings in ancient Rome. A vast rectangular colonnade extended far behind the portico—which is all that is visible today—and enclosed two temples, dedicated to Jupiter and Juno.

The excavations currently underway around the portico have revealed the stratifications of centuries: 19th-century debris lies over medieval tiles which cover ancient amphorae, then the base of the pillars of the portico, well below the present ground level. And further down archaeologists are presently uncovering the remains of still older buildings, probably belonging to the period of Republican Rome.

In the Middle Ages a fish market was established in the ruins of the portico which remained active until the end of the 19th century. (Eighteenth-

century drawings show how marble slabs were used to spread out the catch.) You can still see to the right of the portico the marble block with the Latin inscription used for measuring the size of the fish: the largest fish went to the conservators of Rome, the city's magistrates. (The block has been temporarily removed due to excavation).

Built into the remains of the portico's colonnade is the **Church of Sant'Angelo in Pescheria**, named after the nearby fish market. The church (which must have been a refuge from all the cries and smells of the market outside) was rebuilt in the 16th century but originally dated back to 770. An aquatic theme is reflected in the interior, and there is a detached fresco of the Madonna and angels by the school of Benozzo Gozzoli (15th century) and a 16th-century Saint

Sant'Angelo in Pescheria

Palazzo Mattei di Giove

Andrew said to be by Vasari. Continue past No. 29, the so-called Vallati House of the 14th century, where an inscription facing the street records the fact that on October 16, 1943, the SS entered the Ghetto at this point and deported 1,091 Jews.

At the end of the street, flanking the Lungotevere, stands the early-18th-century Church of San Gregorio della Divina Pietà a Ponte Quatto Capi (closed to the public). This small church once stood in a piazza that held another entrance to the Ghetto. The present structure is of the early 18th century, but there was a church on the site since at least the 12th century. On the facade an inscription in Latin and Hebrew refers to Jews who refused to convert to Christianity: "I HAVE SPREAD OUT MY HANDS ALL THE DAY UNTO A REBELLIOUS PEOPLE, WHICH WALKETH IN A WAY THAT WAS NOT GOOD, AFTER THEIR OWN THOUGHTS; A PEOPLE THAT PROVOKETH ME TO ANGER CONTINUALLY TO MY FACE" (Isa. 65:2–3). Above the door is an 18th-century painting of the Crucifixion by Etienne Parrocel. Jews were forced to attend mass here on Sundays in the hope that they would convert, but many defiantly stuffed their ears with wax so they would not hear the preaching.

Cross the street to the **Synagogue** or Tempio Maggiore, which dominates the area with its large, squared, aluminium-covered dome. The building was designed by Osvaldo Armanni and Vincenzo Costa in an Art Nouveau, Neo-Assyrian style and inaugurated in 1904. Ever since 1982 when a child was killed here as a result of a Palestinian extremist attack, the carabinieri patrol outside day and night. The entrance to the **Museo d'Arte ebraica** is on the Lungotevere. A fee of €5 includes a guided visit of the synagogue, the airy centrally planned interior of which is decorated with scriptural inscriptions and symbolic palms and cedars. Situated on two floors, the museum displays sacred objects and furnishings of the 16th and 17th centuries, as well as exhibits that recount the history of the Jews in Rome, including old photographs and prints of the Ghetto, a copy of the papal bull of 1555 ordering that the Jews be enclosed, and material relating to the German occupation.

Walk back along the shady tree-lined Lungotevere, and turn right onto Via del Tempio. Passing the newer buildings on either side that rise above the original Ghetto, stop to browse in the Libreria Menorah or return directly to the main piazza and cut across to the left and the tiny entrance to Via della Reginella.

OUR PICK

In 1823 Pope Leo XIII allowed the Ghetto to be enlarged toward Piazza Mattei. Via della Reginella was thus absorbed into the Ghetto and today is one of the most typical of its streets, with its medieval narrowness and uneven cobbles, the shaded buildings giving off a musty odor of crumbling age. Explore around the nearby streets and you will find little courtyards that recall the original Ghetto.

The street opens onto the charming Piazza Mattei, with its beautiful and delicate **Fountain of the Tortoises**. The fountain, a happy accumulation of additions, was commissioned by the Mattei family in the 1580s and designed by Giacomo della Porta. Taddeo Landini added the four bronze youths, and a century later a third sculptor who may or may not have been Gian Lorenzo Bernini, completed the composition with the tortoises tipping off the central bowl.

The area outside the enclosed Ghetto was once occupied by some of the great Roman families. The Mattei were most dominant in the area: theirs were the mid-15th-century Palazzo Mattei di Paganica opposite the entrance to Via della Reginella and the 16th-century **Palazzo Mattei di Giove** on the corner of Via dei Funari and Via Caetani. Enter the courtyard of the latter at Via dei Funari and you will see the impressive array of classical statues, busts, and bas-reliefs displayed around the walls of the building. This was how noble families of the Renaissance period liked to show off their extensive collections of Roman antiquities. If you walk up the magnificent stairway to the loggia on the first floor, you have an even better view of the courtyard.

Exiting to the right onto Via Caetani you find yourself catapulted into the recent past: on the wall opposite you a bronze plaque is placed in memory of Aldo Moro, the Italian statesman who was kidnapped and killed by the Brigate Rosse and whose body was found in this spot on May 9, 1978.

Further Information

**Fontana delle Tartarughe
(Fountain of the Tortoises)**
Piazza Mattei

Palazzo Mattei di Giove
Via Caetani, on the corner of
Via dei Funari

Portico di Ottavia
Via del Portico di Ottavia, on
the corner of Via Sant'Angelo
in Pescheria

Sant'Angelo in Pescheria
Via Portico di Ottavia; open: daily
7 A.M.–noon, 4–7 P.M.

**Sinagoga e Museo d'Arte ebraica
(Synagogue and Museum of
Jewish Art)**
Lungotevere dei Cenci; tel.: 06-
68400661; open: Mon.–Thurs.
9 A.M.–4:30 P.M., Fri. 9 A.M.–2 P.M.,
Sun. 9 A.M.–12:30 P.M.; closed: Sat.
and Jewish holidays; admission: €5.

FOCUS: LARGO ARGENTINA

By Aaron Gatti

The Area Sacra of Largo Argentina takes its name from the nearby tower in Via del Sudario, once the property of Giovanni Burcardo. Born in Argentoratum, present-day Strasbourg, and master of ceremonies to Pope Alexander VI, Burcardo had given the name Argentina to the tower on his land.

The Area Sacra was uncovered during demolition work begun in 1926. Four temples are still clearly visible, labeled with the first four letters of the alphabet.

Toward the end of the 4th century B.C., Temple C, dedicated to Feronia, was constructed on what was the original ground level. Temple A, dedicated to Giuturna, was built midway through the 3rd century, and Temple D, dedicated to Lari Permarini, was added to the group at the start of the 2nd century B.C. The round Temple B, dedicated to Dea Fortuna, was built later in the space between A and C.

During the last century B.C., the area was caught up in radical changes that were to leave a mark in the entire center of the Campus Martius. These involved the construction of the Theater of Pompey, the porticoes to the west, and the Hecatostylum (the portico of a hundred columns) to the north (101 B.C.).

In A.D. 80 most of the Campus Martius, including this area, was burned to the ground. During the reign of the Emperor Domitian, the area underwent further radical alterations. In front of the temples the ground level was raised once again and paved with travertine slabs. The temples' facades were rebuilt, as was the surviving portico.

Following this period of renovation, the overall appearance of the square was to remain unaltered until late Roman times. The gradual urbanization of the area during the medieval period led to considerable changes, with buildings superimposed onto the Roman structures.

Between 1926 and 1929 the area was flattened to build two luxury complexes. Before work began, five columns of the round Temple B were already visible in a courtyard, adjacent to the old Church of San Nicolò de' Cesarini, and so were the remains of the rectangular Temple A, incorporated into the framework of the church. Demolition work brought to light the remains of two further temples opening onto an extensive paved quadrant. At that point it was decided to conserve this unique and precious leftover of Republican Rome in its entirety.

Area Sacra of Largo Argentina

Walking Tour 2:

Around the Pantheon

By Ruth Kaplan

Rome's monuments have had a tendency to swap parts over the years. Metal hooks from ancient structures got melted down to make weapons; marble was taken from one facade to make another; columns were uprooted from the ruins and recycled. The Pantheon and its surroundings have been a particularly rich area for this game of pilfering. The two black granite water-spitting lions at the base of the Capitoline Hill come from an ancient temple complex once located here, as does the giant bronze pinecone (*la pigna*) in the courtyard of the Vatican Museums. White travertine for the facade of the Church of Sant'Agostino was taken directly off the Colosseum, and two columns from the nearby Baths of Nero and Alexander ended up supporting the porch roof of the Pantheon itself.

A good place to start tracing this area's interwoven history is in the small Piazzetta di Santo Stefano del Cacco, a hidden square a few blocks southeast of the Pantheon. Like many of Rome's piazzas, this too has become a de facto parking lot, but still maintains a peaceful atmosphere. Two of the buildings that delineate the piazza glow in typical warm Roman tones of salmon and pumpkin. The other two are thickly covered with ivy, and the south wall has a little oratory to the Madonna lit with electric candles.

The 9th-century **Church of Santo Stefano del Cacco**, on the piazza's west side, is almost completely covered with ivy. It is officially open to the public only during mass, but you can visit at off hours by ringing the "Benedettini Silvestrini" buzzer, at No. 26 next door, and one of the Silvestran monks will let you in.

Two lines of multicolored oriental granite columns divide the asymmetrical interior into three unequal parts. The columns are thought to come from an enormous ancient Roman temple complex dedicated to the Egyptian gods Isis and Serapis that once had its epicenter in this piazza. In fact, the church gets its nickname, "del Cacco," from a huge canine-headed Egyptian statue that was excavated on the site and displayed here in the middle of the 14th century. Local residents thought its head resembled that of a certain type of macaco monkey: thus, the nickname "cacco." The church has kept the name, though the statue has since been moved to the Vatican Museums.

Various restorations have covered most of the church's original 9th-century structure. The dark, cramped interior has a notably well-preserved fresco from 1519 on the right wall, a fragment of the *Pietà* by Perin del Vaga. The rest of the wall is lined with small nichelike chapels, while the chapels on the left all have oval domes and natural light, creating an unusual aesthetic imbalance inside.

The small street leading north out of the piazza, Via Santo Stefano del Cacco, showcases a small piece of ancient Rome's grandeur: a yard-long marble human foot, the Piè di Marmo, that presumably used to be part of an enormous statue. Its toenails are worn down and it has clearly been broken and repaired over the years, but the straps and sole of an ancient Roman sandal are still visible crisscrossed over the foot. Giant statues of gods and emperors were not uncommon in ancient Rome, and this one probably came from one of the temples in the Isis and Serapis complex. These statues and others like it were usually painted, dressed, and covered with jewels and candles for display.

The excavations of the ancient Egyptian temple complex have left their mark all over this part of Rome. The obelisk that stands on the back of Bernini's elephant in Piazza della Minerva comes from the ancient religious site, as does the one in front of the Pantheon, the origins of which trace back to the ancient Egyptian city of Heliopolis.

Passing by the Pantheon's splendor and the thick lines of café tables filling the piazza, walk up Via Pantheon to the **Church of Santa Maria Maddalena**. The late baroque, curvy facade—a tall, concave surface with elaborate niches filled with statutes and laughing angel heads—was done in 1735 by Giuseppe Sardi. As early as 1320, the site was used as a chapel for an adjacent hospital, but the interior architecture reflects later renovations. The most notable architectural feature of the church is its elongated octagonal nave, with curving walls that narrow as they near the main altar. Many of the decorative surfaces copy the nave's wavelike lines, including the slightly concave bend to the side chapels, the confessionals, and the sweeping, non-rectilinear marble frames around various paintings in the chapels.

An unusual series of large white marble statues line the church's interior walls, placed there in the 17th century as part of Rome's Counter-Reformation. They are not the church's usual biblical figures but rather symbols of particular moral values: "Simplicity" has a dove in her hand, and "Discretion" holds a key to her lips.

Santa Maria Maddalena

To the right of the highly decorated altar and cupola is a beautiful wooden statue of Mary Magdalene from the 15th century, with elongated features and bold, simple suggestions of eyes and hair. Facing her is a 16th-century wooden crucifix that legend says once detached its arms from its cross and animatedly spoke to Saint Camillo, the mercenary-doctor-saint whose followers once owned the church and the hospital next door. Camillo is buried in the second chapel on the right in a gold and silver urn.

A famous Werle organ is installed over the church's main door and is still used for concerts. The elaborate porch surrounding the organ protrudes out over the nave floor, covered with twisting white marble figures and gold paint.

Continuing north away from the Pantheon, take a left on Via delle Coppelle, created as part of Pope Leo X's Renaissance urban expansion program in the 1510s and 1520s. The nearby Via della Scrofa and Via di Ripetta are also part of this planned "Renaissance Quarter." Midway down on the left is Piazza delle Coppelle, a small square shaded by tall six-story apartment buildings and filled with tables from nearby restaurants and cafés.

Farther down the street, at No. 35, is the classic Renaissance **Palazzo Baldassini**, one of the best examples of an early-16th-century Roman palazzo. Antonio Sangallo the Younger's design draws from the Florentine palazzo style. Each tier of the three-level brick building is shorter than the one below it, with slight variations in the shape of the windows and architectural detailing. The stately travertine door is flanked by hefty stone columns.

A variety of well-preserved frescoes remain intact in various rooms, including a finely detailed "grotesque" vaulted ceiling on the first floor and a series of wall and ceiling paintings on the second floor. The second-floor loggia opens onto the small, well-proportioned inner courtyard, which has been used over the years as a warehouse for citrus fruit and a paper collection center. Palazzo Baldassini is now home to a private research institute, but you can easily organize a guided visit (see Further Information).

Sant'Agostino

Straight across Via della Scrofa, Via di Sant'Agostino opens up onto Piazza Sant'Agostino, dominated by the staircase and wide, tall, white facade (using travertine blocks snatched from the Colosseum) of the **Church of Sant'Agostino**, devoted to Saint Augustine, author of the "Confessions." Built by Giacomo da Pietrasanta in the early 1480s, the church has retained its early Renaissance character despite major renovations in 1750.

Inside, the church is cavernous and colorful. Every inch of the upper walls and ceiling are frescoed, many of them executed by Pietro Gagliardi in 1855, including the portraits of the Old Testament prophets on the two rows of square pilasters dividing the nave, the figures seated and holding Hebrew scrolls. Gagliardi's subjects take their inspiration from Raphael's 1512 painting of the prophet Isaiah on the third pilaster on the left, which is much more concerned with the prophet's musculature than his modesty—his robes are pushed back to reveal an exaggerated, muscled knee.

Raphael's contemporary Andrea Contucci, known as Sansovino, carved the 1512 *Madonna and Child with Saint Anne,* the protruding marble relief on the nave's left wall. The much larger *Madonna of Childbirth* in the back of the church was done in 1521 by Jacopo Tatti, known as Sansovino. She is still venerated as the protectress of women in childbirth—the base of the statue is decorated with pink and blue ribbons and snapshots of newborn babies.

Sant'Agostino is also home to Caravaggio's *Madonna di Loreto.* The canvas has a barefoot Mary holding a large toddler in her arms. Two peasants kneel in the foreground, supplicating her and exposing the soles of their dirty feet to the viewer. There is clearly a heartfelt dialogue going on between the subjects in the painting, so much so that looking at it feels like spying on an intimate conversation.

Heading back to the Pantheon, keep your eyes open for various smatterings of Rome's ancient layer. Via di Sant'Eustachio, close to the famous café of the same name, has two enormous gray granite columns flanking the side of a church. They are remnants of the Baths of Nero and Alexander, which, in the 1st century, extended from the Pantheon to Corso del Rinascimento. A 1717 plaque attached to the wall behind it speaks of a less civilized time in the space's history, strongly prohibiting trash dumping in the piazza. The punishment? A fine of 10 *scudi* or "other punishments" to be decided on a case-by-case basis.

FURTHER INFORMATION

Palazzo Baldassini
Via delle Coppelle, 35; for an organized visit, contact: Patrizia Lupi, tel.: 06-6840421, Tues.–Fri.

Sant'Agostino
Piazza Sant'Agostino; tel.: 06-68801962; open: daily 7:45 A.M.– noon, 4–7:30 P.M.

Santa Maria Maddalena
Piazza della Maddalena, 53; tel.: 06-6797796; open: daily 7:30 A.M.– noon, 5–7:30 P.M.

Santo Stefano del Cacco
Via di Santo Stefano del Cacco, 26; tel.: 06-6793860; open: Sun. 1 A.M.– 12:15 P.M. (mass at 11:30).

FOCUS: San Luigi dei Francesi

Via Santa Giovanna d'Arco; tel.: 06-688271; open: 7:30 A.M.–12:30 P.M., 3:30–7 P.M.; closed: Thurs. afternoon.

By Ruth Kaplan

Rome's French community established its headquarters here with the construction of this church, devoted to their saintly King Louis. Ground was broken in 1518, but its blueprints were revised numerous times. It was finally completed by Domenico Fontana in 1588, after the Italian-born French queen, Catherine de' Medici, donated hefty sums of money and land to the project.

Caravaggio, The Calling of St. Matthew

San Luigi's squared, two-tiered facade was executed by Fontana from a design by Giacomo Della Porta. Statues of Charles the Great and King Louis stand in the travertine niches on the first level. The triangular tympanum displays a carved fleur-de-lis shield, the symbol of France. A central window and balcony on the upper level, plus the emphasis on French national heroes, make the facade seem more appropriate for a Renaissance palazzo than for a church.

Low lighting and high ceilings create a dramatic atmosphere in the three-aisled nave. Antoine Dérizet's richly colored marble panels, stucco angels, and intricate border decorations (1756–1764) cover the pilasters and walls. Golden organ pipes hang over the main entrance. The vaulted ceilings above the two aisles are particularly interesting, with a series of complex vaults made from multidirectional ribs. The tombs scattered throughout are devoted to notable French citizens.

A wide selection of painting styles by Italian and French artists decorate the church's ten side chapels. The Santa Cecilia Chapel, second on the right, has five frescoes by Domenichino (early 17th century) on the life of the saint, done in lucid pastel colors with smooth, porcelain features on its subjects. The oil altarpiece by Guido Reni was copied from a Raphael original now in Bologna. The next chapel up has a dramatic oil, *The Glory of Saint Joan,* by the Avignonese painter Etienne Parrocel (1742). Scaffolding currently blocks the view of the church's main altarpiece, Francesco Bassano's *Assumption*.

The chapel that gets, and deserves, the most attention is the fifth on the left, with three paintings done by Caravaggio in 1599–1602. In the first large oil panel, *The Calling of Saint Matthew,* Christ points out the future saint with a godlike hand while an infusion of light comes in from what seems to be a hidden chapel window. The altarpiece, *Saint Matthew and the Angel,* uses a stark but energetic composition to show a very intimate conversation between the two. *The Martyrdom of Saint Matthew* has the barely clothed saint sprawled on the floor, he is about to get stabbed to death. Caravaggio's superb handling of light and emotions comes through in all three canvases.

Other Points of Interest

Palazzo della Borsa
Piazza di Pietra

➤ Originally the Palazzo della Borsa was the Temple of Hadrian, and the 11 remaining columns belonged to the temple's right side. In the Middle Ages, the extreme metal shortage led the Romans to exploit remains from the ancient days of affluence, and the Temple of Hadrian became one such target. The visible holes in the columns are the result of medieval ravaging; the plunderers removed the iron clasps, which held together various marble sections.

In 1695 Carlo and Francesco Fontana transformed the building into the Dogana di Terra, the customs house. Later again, in 1879, the building became the Borsa Valori (stock exchange). On this occasion it was redesigned by Virginio Vespignani. The building is now used for exhibitions.

Piazza Sant'Ignazio
➤ Often compared to an urban theatrical stage, this square was designed by Filippo Raguzzini in 1727–1728. Despite being somewhat overwhelmed by the huge facade of the church, which was built taller than planned by mistake, it is one of the most unique piazzas in Rome.

Santa Caterina dei Funari
Via dei Funari

➤ The name of this church was inspired by the local rope-makers, or *funari*, who once worked behind the church, amidst ruins from the Theater of Balbo. Both the church and the bell tower were built by Guidetto Guidetti, in 1560–1566. When the church was restored, an elegant travertine facade, inspired by the Church of Santo Spirito in Sassia, was added. The famous painting of Saint Margaret is by Annibale Carracci (1600) and can be found in the first chapel on the right.

Santa Maria in Campitelli
Piazza di Campitelli, 9; tel.: 06-68803978; open: daily 7:30 A.M.–noon, 4–7 P.M.

➤ In the large square next to the Theater of Marcellus is the Church of Santa Maria in Campitelli, also known as Santa Maria in Portico. It was erected by Carlo Rainaldi in the years 1657–1659, in fulfillment of a vow made for the cessation of the great pestilence of 1656. Architecturally, the church is considered the most interesting baroque church in Rome. It is ornamented with 22 fluted Corinthian columns of marble.

Sant'Ignazio
Piazza di Sant'Ignazio; tel.: 06-6794406; open: daily 7:30 A.M.–12:30 P.M., 4–7 P.M.

➤ The church was dedicated by Pope Gregory XV to Saint Ignatius of Loyola, the founder of the Jesuits. Under the supervision of Carlo Maderno, work began on the church in 1626, but due to lack of funding, there was still no cupola in 1685. To compensate for this, the painter and mathematician Andrea Pozzo planned and completed a remarkable painting that used trompe l'oeil optical devices to create fictitious spaces. *Glory of Saint Ignatius* effectively imitates the lighting and profundity of a cupola, the gigantic canvas (its diameter is more than 50 feet) depicting a luxurious dome in the hollow that the real cupola should have filled. The facade of the church is inspired by that of the church of Il Gesù, as is the interior, which has a single nave and three chapels on each side. The fresco in the vault by Andrea Pozzo also offers an optical illusion of a breakthrough of the ceiling.

Sant'Ivo alla Sapienza
Corso del Rinascimento, 40; tel.: 06-6864987; open: Sat. 9 A.M.–noon, 6–8 P.M., Sun. 9 A.M.–noon; closed: months of July and Aug.

➤ Pope Urban VIII, of the Barberini family, decided to convert the small chapel of the University of Rome into a majestic church. He hired Francesco Borromini, who started working on it in 1642. With his bee-shaped plan, based on the symbol of the Barberini family, Borromini found the most unusual way to celebrate the famous papal family. The spiral of the cupola was supposed to be a mitre, the papal headdress adorned with precious stones. When the church was almost completed, the new pope, Alexander VII, of the Chigi family, decided to leave his own family mark and had the doves of his coat of arms included in the decoration.

Museums

BIBLIOTECA E RACCOLTA TEATRALE DEL BURCARDO (BURCARDO LIBRARY AND THEATER COLLECTION)

Via del Sudario, 44; tel.: 06-6819471; website: www.burcardo.siae.it; e-mail: burcardo@mclink.it; open: 9 A.M.–1:30 P.M.; closed: Sun. and holidays; admission: free.

➤ Theatrical costumes, texts, and scene and stage sketches. Famous library with over 40,000 volumes.

CRYPTA BALBI

Via delle Botteghe Oscure, 31; tel: 06-39967700; open: 9 A.M.–7:45 P.M.; closed: Mon.; admission: €4.

➤ Remains of the theater built by Balbus in 13 B.C. which, after the 4th century A.D. and throughout the Middle Ages, were used as tombs, artisans' workshops, and for religious purposes.

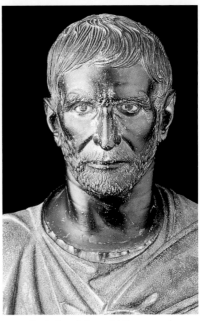

Bruto Capitolino, *Palazzo dei Conservatori*

MUSEI CAPITOLINI (CAPITOLINE MUSEUMS)

Piazza del Campidoglio; tel: 06-67102071; information and reservations: 06-39967800; open: 9:30 A.M.–7 P.M., Sun. 9:30 A.M.–11 P.M.; admission: €8.

➤ The Capitoline Museums is a complex of museums with a range of art and artifacts.

• PALAZZO DEI CONSERVATORI

The city government still uses this suite, which can be reached from the atrium of the Palazzo dei Conservatori. Inside are stuccoes by Luzio Luzi, relics from the monument of Marcus Aurelius, and frescoes by Cavalier d'Arpino (1595–1632). The gilded bronze *Hercules* after Lisippus (2nd century B.C.) and the remains of the colossal bronze statue of Constantine (4th century) are among the most important works in the Capitoline collection. Both are temporarily on display in the Sala degli Orazi e Curiazi. Other sculptures in bronze *(Spinario, Camiullus,* and the *Capitoline Brutus)* are in the Sala dei Trionfi. The Sala della Lupa (Hall of the She-Wolf) displays the *Lupa Capitolina,* the Capitoline she-wolf, a bronze 5th-century B.C. Etruscan statue. In 65 B.C. the statue, then in the Temple of Jupiter, was hit by lightning, which damaged part of the wolf and destroyed the twins beneath it. When the statue was moved to the Palazzo dei Conservatori in the 15th century, Antonio Pollaiolo added two new babies. Bernini's 1630 *Medusa's Head* is also in the neighboring Sala delle Oche (Hall of Geese). The sculpture group of Commodus with two tritons is in the Sala degli Arazzi (Hall of Tapestries).

• PINACOTECA CAPITOLINA

Founded by Pope Benedict XIV in 1748, the Pinacoteca Capitolina contains Italian and European art from the Middle Ages to the 18th century. It includes the following: Hall I—paintings from central Italy from the Middle Ages to the 1500s, including the *Death and Assumption of the Virgin* by Cola dell'Amatrice; Hall II—paintings by 16th-century artists from Ferrara, including Dosso Dossi, Garofalo, and Mazzolino; Hall III—work by Venetian artists of the 16th century, including *The Baptism of Christ* by Titian (1512) and *Portrait of Man with Crossbow* by Lorenzo Lotto (1551); Hall of Saint Petronilla—named after the great painting by Guercino, it displays *Romulus and Remus Suckled by the She-Wolf* (1617–1618) by Peter Paul Rubens, and the famous *Gypsy Fortune-Teller* (1595) and *Saint John the Baptist* by Caravaggio; Hall VI—dedicated to painters from Bologna, from Carracci to Guido Reni; Hall of Pietra da Cortona—works include *The Rape of the Sabine Women* and *The Sacrifice of Polyxena*.

The Palazzo dei Conservatori is connected to the Palazzo Nuovo by a gallery leading to the Tabularium that offers a superb view of the Roman Forum. Remains of the Temple of Veiove dating from the 2nd century B.C. are still visible by the Tabularium, beneath the Palazzo Senatorio. The ground level of the same structure also houses the remains of a building that pre-existed the Tabularium itself. One of the three rooms contains ancient floor mosaics dating from the 2nd century B.C. with irregular fragments of colored marble against a white background.

• PALAZZO NUOVO

To the right of the courtyard is the original equestrian statue of Marcus Aurelius, moved here from the Piazza del Campidoglio (substituted by a copy). On the ground floor statues, reliefs, and inscriptions, linked to Eastern cults prominent in the West during the Imperial Era, are displayed. The rooms to the right display statues, busts, and sarcophagi. On the first floor, there is a collection of Hellenistic sculptures and Roman copies of Greek originals.

Drunken Old Woman, dating back to the 3rd century B.C.; *Young Boy Portrayed as Hercules Choking the Snakes,* from the 2nd century A.D.; and *Hercules Killing the Hydra,* from the 2nd century, are all notable pieces of work. In the Sala delle Colombe (Hall of Doves) is a mosaic from Hadrian's Villa, a Roman copy of a Hellenistic original from the 2nd century B.C. The Gabinetto di Venere (Cabinet of Venus) holds *Capitoline Venus,* from an original by Praxiteles (4th century B.C.). The Sala degli Imperatori (Hall of Emperors) features 67 busts of Roman emperors arranged in chronological order. The Sala dei Filosofi (Hall of Philosophers) contains 79 busts of Greek and Latin philosophers, poets, and physicians. The huge Salone (Great Hall) also has many sculptures, including *Statue of a Young Centaur,* 2nd century A.D., signed by Aristeas and Papias and the famous *Wounded Amazon,* signed by Sosikles and copied from an original by Polykleitos from the 5th century B.C. Hellenistic school of art. The Sala del Fauno (Hall of the Faun) contains the *Satyr,* 2nd century A.D., from Hadrian's Villa in Tivola. The Sala del Gladiatore (Hall of the Gladiator) holds the famous *Dying Gaul* from a Pergamene original, the *Wounded Amazon* from an original by Phidias, and the *Statue of Cupid and Psyche,* from the 2nd century B.C.

View of the Sala degli Imperatori, Palazzo Nuovo

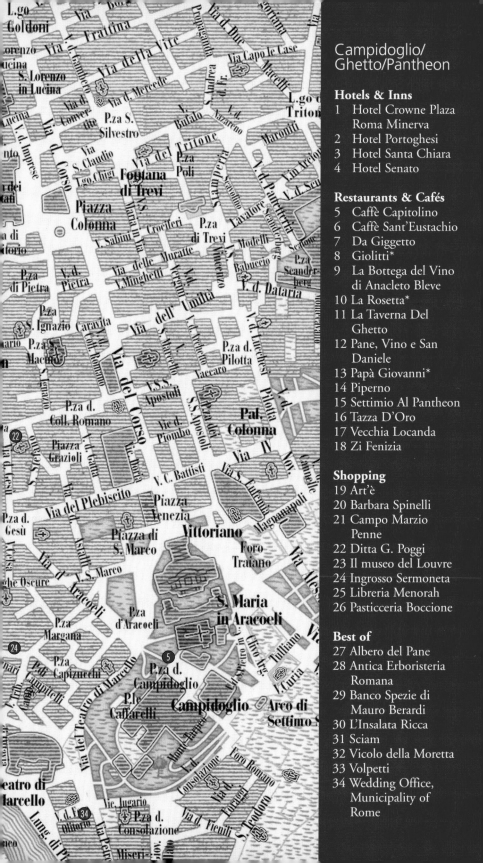

Campidoglio/ Ghetto/Pantheon

Hotels & Inns
1 Hotel Crowne Plaza Roma Minerva
2 Hotel Portoghesi
3 Hotel Santa Chiara
4 Hotel Senato

Restaurants & Cafés
5 Caffè Capitolino
6 Caffè Sant'Eustachio
7 Da Giggetto
8 Giolitti*
9 La Bottega del Vino di Anacleto Bleve
10 La Rosetta*
11 La Taverna Del Ghetto
12 Pane, Vino e San Daniele
13 Papà Giovanni*
14 Piperno
15 Settimio Al Pantheon
16 Tazza D'Oro
17 Vecchia Locanda
18 Zi Fenizia

Shopping
19 Art'è
20 Barbara Spinelli
21 Campo Marzio Penne
22 Ditta G. Poggi
23 Il museo del Louvre
24 Ingrosso Sermoneta
25 Libreria Menorah
26 Pasticceria Boccione

Best of
27 Albero del Pane
28 Antica Erboristeria Romana
29 Banco Spezie di Mauro Berardi
30 L'Insalata Ricca
31 Sciam
32 Vicolo della Moretta
33 Volpetti
34 Wedding Office, Municipality of Rome

HOTELS & INNS

Hotel Crowne Plaza Roma Minerva

Piazza della Minerva, 69; tel.: 06-695201/6794165; e-mail: minerva@hotel-invest.compronet.it; website: www.hotel-invest.com; category: ★★★★★; number of rooms: 134, including 20 suites; credit cards accepted: all major; access to internet: direct-line (US, UK) telephone jack in all rooms; €€€€*.

☛In this converted 17th-century palazzo, there is a grandeur rarely found in Rome's hotels. The main lounge area has a stained-glass roof and is lined with display cases with wares from some of the city's finest vendors. Rooms are comfortably large and many have views of Piazza della Minerva's church and elephant-obelisk statue. La Cesta restaurant offers both Italian and international dishes. In the summer months, the restaurant moves outdoors to the roof garden.

Hotel Portoghesi

Via dei Portoghesi, 1; tel.: 06-6864231/6876976; e-mail: info@hotelportoghesiroma.com; website: www.hotelportoghesiroma.com; category: ★★★; number of rooms: 28, including 6 suites; credit cards accepted: all major; access to internet: direct-line (US, UK) telephone jack in all rooms; €€.

☛Hotel Portoghesi stands in an area comprising Campo Marzio, Sant'Eustachio, and the Ponte district. The Sagnotti family turned the ancient building into a hotel about 150 years ago, maintaining intact furnishings and architectural quality and also making the necessary renovations to ensure that the hotel has modern comforts (such as air conditioning). You can enjoy breakfast on the roof garden.

Hotel Santa Chiara

Via Santa Chiara, 21; tel.: 06-6872979/ 6873144; e-mail: stchiara@tin.it; website: www.albergosantachiara.com; category: ★★★; number of rooms: 96; credit cards accepted: all major; access to internet: direct-line (US, UK) telephone jack in all rooms; most beautiful rooms: 407, 410, 451; €€–€€€.

☛The Hotel Santa Chiara is located right behind the Pantheon, facing Piazza della Minerva, and a short walk from Largo Argentina. The Corteggiani Family has owned the hotel since 1838, and the hotel is one of the oldest in Rome. It was completely refurbished in 1994. The rooms were redone and are comfortable, though some are aesthetically forgettable. The large, well-lit marble sitting room is a nice place to read.

Hotel Senato

Piazza della Rotonda, 73; tel.: 06-6784343/ 69940297; e-mail: book@albergodelsenato.it; website: www.albergodelsenato.it; category: ★★★; number of rooms: 56, including 6 suites; credit cards accepted: all major; access to internet: direct-line (US, UK) telephone jack in all rooms; €€€.

☛A fairly small hotel that faces right out onto the Pantheon and the fountain and café life of Piazza della Rotonda. Rooms are of average size, with wooden floors, and are beautifully furnished. Price is reasonable for the location.

RESTAURANTS & CAFÉS

Caffè Capitolino

Via delle Tre Pile; open: Tues.–Sun. 9 A.M.– 7 P.M.; closed: Mon.

☛Hidden away on a street off of Piazza del Campidoglio, this café offers one of the best views of Rome from its terrace. You can order coffee, juice, small sandwiches, gelato, or excellent pastries and eat inside at the counter or outside at tables. Even if you choose to eat inside (for about half the price) make sure to go on the terrace to gaze at the synagogue, Saint Peter's, the Aventine, and the Tiber River.

To get there, take a right onto Via delle Tre Pile (immediately after the top of the steps). The café is two flights up in the last building on the left and is unmarked.

Caffè Sant'Eustachio

Piazza Sant'Eustachio, 82.; tel.: 06-6861309; open: daily 8:30 A.M.–1 P.M.

☛One of Rome's top cafés since 1938, just one piazza away from the Pantheon. Many Romans believe that the best espresso in town is made here. Even if you're no connoisseur, you'll notice the rich but not

Restaurants & Cafés

bitter flavor of the espresso and the abundance of the *crema*, the creamy froth that floats on top. Ask for it *amaro* if you want it straight; otherwise they will put sugar in it for you. Try the *gran caffè speciale*, a double, creamy coffee invented by the house, or the parfait, a *granita* with whipped cream.

Da Giggetto
Via del Portico di Ottavia, 21A; tel.: 06-6861105; closed: Mon; €.
☛Serves all the staple Roman Jewish specialties. For those who prefer slightly lower prices or dining outside under one of the columns of the Portico di Ottavia.

Giolitti
Via Uffici del Vicario, 40; tel.: 06-6991243; open: daily 7:30 A.M.–midnight.
☛Some of the best gelato in the city is made at this century-old creamery that has maintained the elegance of its 1930s decor. Flavors range from standbys like chocolate and hazelnut to true-to-life flavors like pear and rice. You can taste the bubbles and alcohol in the champagne sorbet.

La Bottega del Vino di Anacleto Bleve
Via S. Maria del Pianto, 9/11; tel.: 06-6865970; open: Mon.–Sat. 8 A.M.–4 P.M., 5 P.M.–8 P.M.; open for lunch Mon.–Sat. 1 P.M.–3 P.M.; €.
☛Very popular and long-established wine bar serving delicious food (mainly cold cuts) with a first-rate wine list (also served by the glass).

Pane, Vino e San Daniele
Piazza Mattei, 16; tel.: 06-6877147; closed: Mon. evening and Sat. morning; €.

☛This wine bar is a recent addition to the Ghetto. All the wines are Friulian, and a variety of light meals are served including salads, soups, polenta, and the house speciality *fagottini alle melanzane*. Almost every dish incorporates the famous *prosciutto di San Daniele*.

Piperno
Monte de' Cenci, 9; tel.: 06-68806629; closed: Sun. evening and Mon.; €€.
☛The setting of Piperno is the main attraction, but when you climb up into this charming little hidden-away piazza, you can sample all the traditional specialities of Roman Jewish cuisine: *carciofi alla giudia, tegamino al cervello, trippa, coda e abbacchio*, and, to finish, the *palle del nonno* made from ricotta cheese.

Tazza D'Oro
Via degli Orfani, 84; tel.: 06-6789792; open: Mon.–Sat. 7 A.M.–8 P.M.; closed: Sun. (except in Dec.).
☛Another of Rome's top coffee bars. All the coffee *granitas* with whipped cream that you see people spooning out of plastic cups around the Pantheon come from here. Also well-known for its own line of roasted coffee beans.

Zi Fenizia
Via S. Maria del Pianto, 64/5; tel.: 06-6896976; closed: Fri. afternoon, Sat., and Jewish holidays.
☛A Ghetto institution—these kosher pizzas are among the best take-out pizzas in the city, with traditional toppings as well as kosher favorites: *aliciotti e indivia* or beef sausage, also *suppli* and hamburgers.

Specialty Shops

Art'è
Piazza Rondanini, 32; tel.: 06-6833907; open: Mon.–Sat. 9:30 A.M.–1 P.M., 3:30 P.M.–7:30 P.M.; closed: Mon. morning and Sun.
☛A Very sleek housewares store with museum-worthy Italian-designed kitchenware. There are at least ten beautiful retro toasters, half a dozen aerodynamic orange juicers, and infinite variations on stovetop

and electric espresso-makers in brightly colored enamel as well as the traditional chrome.

Barbara Spinelli
Via dei Prefetti, 25; tel.: 06-68301131; open: 10 A.M.–1:30 P.M., 3:30–7 P.M., Sat. 10 A.M.–7 P.M.; closed: Sun.
☛A kingdom of amber with one-of-a-kind

SPECIALTY SHOPS

pieces and rare stones like blue and red amber. Styles vary from ethnic with silver to classic with diamonds and emeralds. All handmade custom work.

Campo Marzio Penne

Via Campo Marzio, 41; tel.: 06-68807877; open: daily 10 A.M.–1 P.M., 2–7 P.M.

☛Pens of every type made as they were 50 years ago. Wax seals, inks in every color, address books, desk calendars, and diaries. Specializes in custom production of pens and in the repair of writing instruments.

Ditta G. Poggi

Via del Gesù, 74/75–Via Piè di Marmo, 38/41; tel.: 06-6784477; open: Mon.–Sat. 9 A.M–1 P.M., 4–7:30 P.M.; closed: Sun.

☛Many artists consider this the best art supply store in Rome. One part of the shop is loaded with a vast assortment of paints, brushes, and sketchpads, plus a nice selection of beautiful wooden boxed sets of drawing and painting materials. Entire shelves are filled with colored powder in clear plastic bags for mixing your own paints. You can even find chips and cement to do mosaic work. Paper, stationery, and portfolios are sold in the corner store across the street.

Il museo del Louvre

Via della Reginella, 28; open: Mon.–Fri. 10 A.M.–8 P.M.

☛This secondhand bookshop and gallery specializes in 20th-century literature and photography and is stacked with rare books, magazines, letters, and other curiosities. A space at the back of the shop houses exhibitions of photographs, prints, and drawings.

Ingrosso Sermoneta

Via dei Funari, 78; closed: Fri. afternoon, Sat., and Jewish holidays.

☛This amazing shop, walls lined with little drawers in the old style, will sell you any type of button, thread, hosiery, or underwear.

Libreria Menorah

Via del Tempio, 2; closed: Fri. afternoon, Sat., and Jewish holidays.

☛The only bookshop in Rome specializing in Jewish material, with books (some foreign language), old prints, music, videos, and CDs.

Pasticceria Boccione

Via del Portico di Ottavia, 1; closed: Fri. afternoon, Sat., and Jewish holidays.

☛More Roman Jewish specialities: the famous *pizze* made with candied fruits and pine nuts, almond biscuits, and *torte con ricotta e visciole.*

PROFILE

Aldo Giampieri: Crafting Religious Art

By Ruth Kaplan

In his 42 years of making religious ceremonial objects, 60-something craftsman Aldo Giampieri has developed highly specialized opinions on church decoration. Brass is better than bronze, for example. Because of its higher zinc concentration, brass is shinier and sturdier, he explains.

Giampieri is one of the last artisans left on Via dei Cestari. The short street connecting the Pantheon to Largo Argentina has long been full of shops selling religious statuary, ceremonial objects, and garments for men and women "of the cloth." But now most of the storefronts are only points of sale for objects made elsewhere. Giampieri knows of no other craftsman working in metal in the area.

Via dei Cestari, 39–40; tel.: 06-68802198.

Our Critic's Favorite Restaurants

La Rosetta

Via della Rosetta, 9; tel.: 06-6861002; closed: Sun; €€.

☛Over the years, La Rosetta has come to be considered the Eternal City's finest seafood restaurant. Owned by Massimo Riccioli, the restaurant is open at lunch as well, but with a smaller menu and lower prices—about 30 percent less than dinner. What better way to become familiar with the menu, which varies according to the season and features the best the seas have to offer. The oyster trio—raw, in green tea aspic and wrapped in spinach leaves—is a good starting point, as is the delicate Mediterranean sashimi with citrus fruit, red and green tomatoes, and herbs. A favorite entrée is the splendid dory filet with apples, shallots, and fennel.

La Taverna Del Ghetto

Via del Portico di Ottavia, 8; tel.: 06-68809771; open: daily noon–3 P.M., 6:30–11:30 P.M.; closed: Fri. evening; €.

☛With today's emphasis on the origins of many food products, kosher restaurants offer gourmet diners hygienic guarantees going back thousands of years. Frozen foods are prohibited, vegetables are sterilized, and meats and wines must first win the seal of approval of the rabbinical authorities. That said, tempting diners at Taverna del Ghetto are Jewish-Roman specialties such as the endive and anchovy torte and the stuffed zucchini, not to mention the famed Jewish-style artichokes. Homemade pastas and desserts are also available.

Papà Giovanni

Via dei Sediari, 4; tel.: 06-6865308; website: www.papagiovannirome.com; closed: Sun; €.

☛Fifty years ago, when carriage driver Papà Giovanni went to the Castelli Romani to pick up the wine for his little restaurant, he would never have imagined that one day his wine list would include 500 labels from all over the world and be acclaimed as the best in Italy. But this is precisely the opinion of the prestigious American magazine *Wine Spectator*. With room for no more than 40 diners, the restaurant may not be the place for large groups but is certainly the right address for an exceptional meal. Among the appetizers served are salads of mozzarella, truffle, and Parmesan, or artichokes, pecorino cheese, mint, and arugula. Pastas include *vermicelli cacio e pepe* and *tagliolini* with herbs and green tomatoes drizzled with olive oil. A popular second course and chef's suggestion is the house's stewed saltcod "Papà Giovanni" or the baked duckling with truffle, garnished with mixed greens or sautéed chicory. The house dessert is the *delizia romana*, a variation on the traditional Neapolitan *pastiera* cake but lighter. It's made with cow's milk ricotta, pine nuts, and grapes, and served warm. Diners can also opt for *profiteroles* prepared on the spot with pure, bitter, 70 percent cocoa. Reservations are required.

Settimio Al Pantheon

Via delle Colonnelle, 14; tel.: 06-6789651; closed: Sun., Mon; €.

☛Look no farther for authentic Roman cuisine: *amatriciana, gricia, cacio pepe,* and carbonara pastas; roast lamb, beans and pork skins; and stewed cuttlefish with peas. Also delicious is the grilled wild game. The atmosphere couldn't be more Roman either, with the good-natured staff's constant wisecracking in Roman dialect.

Vecchia Locanda

Vicolo Sinibaldi, 2; tel.: 06-68802831; closed: Sun; €.

☛The inspiring location on a pedestrian alley framed by an arch, together with the wonderful food, are convincing arguments for stopping to eat at this tranquil establishment hidden behind Largo Argentina. In addition to the classic pastas, the menu also includes radicchio ravioli and soups, and meat and seafood dishes from beef fillet in a radicchio cream sauce, to beef strips with porcini mushrooms, Vernaccia-sautéed gilt head (fish prepared with Italian wine), and grilled swordfish. An extensive wine list includes some 300 labels from all over Italy.

Piazza Navona/ Piazza Farnese

By Ruth Kaplan

ow filled with portrait painters, performers, and outdoor cafés, **Piazza Navona** still oozes with a baroque elegance that can be felt in the buildings and pedestrian lanes stretching out from it. The long, trim piazza gets its shape from the 1st-century-A.D. Stadium of Domitian that used to host games here. Bernini's 1651 masterpiece, the Fontana dei Quattro Fiumi, stands in the center. Bernini is also responsible for the playful Fontana del Moro on the southern end. Fontana del Nettuno dates from the previous century.

North of the piazza, in Piazza Sant'Apollinare, is the Renaissance **Palazzo Altemps**, home of the Ludovisi collection of classical art, with an obelisk-crowned lookout point on its roof. Pomarancio painted the frescoes in its first-floor chapel. On the other end of Piazza Navona is **Piazza di Pasquino**, with a worn-down torso from a Hellenistic statue group. From the 1500s on it was Rome's preeminent "talking statue"—a sort of public bulletin board where people anonymously aired their gripes in the form of verse and satire. Close by is the 18th-century **Palazzo Braschi**, home to the **Museo di Roma**'s extensive collection of paintings, drawings, and objects tracing Roman history from medieval times through the present (currently closed for restoration).

Across Corso Vittorio Emanuele II is the flamboyant facade of **Sant'Andrea della Valle**, famous for its elegant dome, the second largest in Rome after Michelangelo's dome at Saint Peter's. A few doors down is the handsome Renaissance building Piccola Farnesina, which contains the ancient sculpture collection of the **Museo Barracco**. Works of Egyptian, Sumerian, and Assyrian origin play a large role alongside classical and Etruscan pieces. To the right of the museum is the Florentine-influenced, 15th-century **Palazzo della Cancelleria**, with a remarkable courtyard edged by a double loggia. Very close to the palace is Campo de' Fiori, a favorite meeting place, with bars and restaurants lining the piazza. An outdoor produce and flower market is held here every morning.

Via dei Baullari connects over to Piazza Farnese, decorated with two huge tubs of Egyptian granite adapted into fountains. The piazza was built as a grounds for appreciating the magnificent **Palazzo Farnese**, home of the French Embassy since 1635. Antonio da Sangallo the Younger and Michelangelo both worked on the architecture. The gallery inside has excellent frescoes.

Left, Fontana di Quattro Fiumi (Fountain of the Four Rivers), Piazza Navona

CAMPO DE' FIORI

Piazza Campo de' Fiori

➤ A colorful and vibrant square in the middle of Rome, Campo de' Fiori, or "Field of Flowers," has been home to an open-air market since 1869. The square was once the plateau of the Theater of Pompey, the first brick theater built in Rome during the 1st century B.C. Nearby buildings have curved foundations inherited from the theater structure. A monument in the center commemorates Dominican monk and philosopher Giordano Bruno, accused of heresy and executed here in 1600. The name of the square derives from the late 14th century, when the spot was literally a field of flowers.

PALAZZO ALTEMPS (SEE MUSEUMS)

Piazza Sant'Appollinare, 4; tel.: 06-3974990.

➤ Construction of the Palazzo Altemps began in 1471 on an existing medieval site. It was constructed for Cardinal Girolamo Riario. Martino Longhi the Elder designed the great terrace with obelisks and a marble unicorn bas-relief that crowns the building, and completed the courtyard, started by Antonio da Sangallo the Elder and Baldassarre Peruzzi. In 1615 its beautiful chapel was decorated with paintings by Antonio Circignani, known as the Pomarancio.

Palazzo Braschi

In 1568 the building was bought by Marco Sittico Altemps, a cardinal of German origin (Altemps being an Italianization of the German family name Hohenems). Most of the artwork comes from the collections of noble Roman families, including the Ludovisis. The work was restored by Alessandro Algardi and Gian Lorenzo Bernini, and the palazzo itself was restored in 1837, 1949, and 1984.

PALAZZO BRASCHI (SEE ALSO MUSEO DI ROMA)

Piazza San Pantaleo, 10; tel.: 06-6875345.

➤ Built by architect Cosimo Morelli between 1790 and 1793, Palazzo Braschi was the last palazzo built for a papal family in Rome. It has a splendid *scalone* (a large staircase), considered the most beautiful in the city, if not in the world. It was designed and built by Giuseppe Valadier, with 18 columns of red granite taken from the Santo Spirito Hospital.

PALAZZO DELLA CANCELLERIA

Piazza della Cancelleria; tel.: 06-6989349; open: permit required from the Vatican (06-69893405).

➤ The Palazzo della Cancelleria is the epitome of the second generation of Roman Renaissance building. It was designed to be a cardinal residency and to incorporate a church. The two-story court is surrounded by arcades, and has 42 ancient granite pillars, whose graceful capitals are decorated with roses. The authorship is still debated, but Bramante, whose touch is clearly visible in the courtyard, is cited by Giorgio Vasari as one of the main contributors. Recently, however, it has been more preferably attributed to Antonio Bregno. The facade is extremely long with an elegant balcony overlooking Campo de' Fiori. In the basement of the palazzo are the remains of an ancient sepulcher and a section of the Euripus, a Roman canal.

Raffaele Riario—who became cardinal of the nearby Basilica of San Lorenzo in Damaso and took possession of the adjoining palazzo—decided to rebuild it as his own home. Work began in 1485 and was completed between 1511–1513. Immediately after completion, Riario was accused of plotting against Pope Leo X, so the building was confiscated and became

Palazzo Farnese

the house of the apostolic chancellery. In 1546 Vasari was involved in the latter stages of construction. He painted the Salone dei Cento Giorni (Hall of 100 Days), in 100 days. When Vasari made reference to his rapid work, Michelangelo allegedly retorted, "And it looks like it."

PALAZZO FARNESE
Piazza Farnese; closed to the public.

➤ Considered the most magnificent of all the Roman *palazzi*, Palazzo Farnese was built between 1517 and 1573, partly with plundered Colosseum materials, and at the hands of several architects and architectural styles. In 1517 Cardinal Alessandro Farnese commissioned the building to the architect Antonio da Sangallo the Younger. He wanted it to be erected near Campo de' Fiori, in what was the center of the administrative district. Elected as Pope Paul III, Farnese asked Sangallo to overhaul his original project and build a new, even more luxurious palazzo. After Sangallo's death in 1546, Michelangelo took over the project, adding an imposing roof cornice, a central balcony, and the third floor of the courtyard. Following the pope's death, the project was put on hold, however, and was eventually finished a quarter-century later by Giacomo della Porta, who followed Michelangelo's guidelines.

In 1635 the Farnese family gave the palazzo to the French government in order to avoid its huge maintenance costs. It has since been used as a home for the French Embassy, which, since 1874, has been paying a symbolic yearly rent to the Italian government, rather than paying for its maintenance.

On the facade, cornices decorated with Farnesian lilies separate the three floors. The first-floor windows are topped with alternate triangular tympanums, while the 13 third-floor windows have triangular and circular tympanums. The atrium, also by Sangallo, has a double line of red-granite columns and a collection of Roman busts. The courtyard contains two Roman sarcophagi. The decoration of the Salone dei Fasti dates to 1554. The frescoes are by Francesco Salviati and Taddeo Zuccari and were intended to celebrate the Farnese family and the Pope's political role. The Galleria dei Carracci tells of the consuming and sexual loves of the gods, and features the *Trionfo di Bacco e Arianna*. Completed in 1604 this masterpiece shows the decline of Renaissance decorative work, which gave way to a new pictorial language culminating in the baroque.

PASQUINO
Piazza di Pasquino

➤ In Piazza di Pasquino there is a small, incomplete marble statue that gave the square its name. The statue was found in 1501 and was probably a Roman copy of a Hellenistic statue from the nearby Stadium of Domitian. The name, according to one theory, derives from an outspoken local tailor, Pasquino, who used the statue as a place to post his criticisms of Roman society. Another theory suggests Pasquino worked for the papal courts and took it upon himself to inform his fellow Romans about all that was wrong in the Vatican. The statue became an important means of communication, used at night by people from the community to post messages about the aristocracy and the Church. This is why it became known as the "talking statue." Citizens began to use other statues in the city—Marforio (near the Campidoglio), Madama Lucrezia (near Piazza San Marco), the Facchino (on Via Lata), the Babuino (on Via del Babuino), and Abate Luigi (Piazza Vidoni)—for the same purpose, and these statues also started to "talk." In the 18th century, under Pope Benedict XIII, those found guilty of *pasquinate* could have incurred the death penalty.

PIAZZA NAVONA

➢ No other Roman piazza can rival the spectacular Piazza Navona, beloved by both Romans and visitors. This big, oblong square occupies the site of Domitian's Stadium Agonalis. With its

Sant'Agnese in Agone

three extravagant fountains—the Fountain of the Moor, the Fountain of the Four Rivers, and the Fountain of Neptune—and its ornate baroque churches, the piazza is one of Rome's more extraordinary sights. Foundations of the buildings around Piazza Navona originate from the vast stadium of Domitian, built before A.D. 86, which give a peculiar shape to the piazza. "Navona" is considered a corruption of the name of the athletic games that were held inside the stadium—changing from *agone* to *nagone* and then *navona*. However, *navona* also means "large ship" and the piazza's name could have derived from the historical flooding of the square on Saturdays in August—from the 17th century until the end of the 19th century—to allow for boat processions of royalty. It took two hours to flood the piazza.

The Fountain of the Four Rivers (Fontana di Quattro Fiumi) is probably the most famous and beautiful of the three fountains; it was designed by Gian Lorenzo Bernini in 1651. It consists of a pyramid rock foundation upon which a horse and a lion, both with long flowing tails, drink. In the corners, four prodigious, mythological personifications representing the four great rivers of the world—the Nile, Ganges, Danube, and Rio de la Plata—refer to the four continents: Europe, Asia, Africa, and America. The figures are seated on a triangular base of travertine rock designed by Bernini's assistants. The four continents hold up a Roman obelisk that once stood in the Circus of Maxentius and is surmounted by the dove of the Pamphilj family coat of arms. (The family's palace was in the square, where the Brazilian Embassy is located today.) According to an old myth, the statue that represents the Rio de la Plata river has a hand pointing toward the Church of Sant'Agnese in Agone, as if it is saying, "Please, don't collapse," while the statue representing the Nile covers its head, as if it is disgusted by the church designed by Borromini.

The Fountain of the Moor (Fontana del Moro), at the south end of the piazza, was designed by Giacomo Della Porta in 1576. It is named after the central figure of the Moor, who struggles with toothless dolphins and marine figures carved by Giovanni Antonio Mari.

Sant'Andrea della Valle

Sant'Agnese in Agone

Piazza Navona; tel.: 06-69205401; open: Tues., Wed., Fri. 2–6:30 P.M., Thurs., Sat. 4:30–7 P.M., Sun. 10 A.M.–1 P.M., 2–6:30 P.M.

➢ Built between the 8th century and 1123, this church was given its present appearance by the father-and-son architects Girolamo and Carlo Rainaldi in 1652. On the original site, an alleged brothel, Saint Agnes was pilloried nude to force her to renounce her faith. Her modesty was protected by the wondrous growth of her hair—a miracle depicted in Alessandro Algardi's marble relief on the altar.

The church was completed in 1653–1657 by Francesco Borromini. The concave facade has a single file of pillars and columns, surmounted by a dome and twin bell towers. Inside the cupola, which stands on eight columns, was frescoed with *Glory of Paradise* by Ciro Ferri in 1689, while the frescoes on the spandrels, Cardinal Virtues, were done by Baciccia in 1665.

In the underground chambers, entered through a door in the right wall of the second altar, are the ruins of the Stadium of Domitian, a Roman mosaic floor, and, on the wall, medieval frescoes. The church's foundations belong to the Stadium of Domitian, and the oldest structure goes back to the 8th century. The church was completely rebuilt by Innocent X, as a chapel for the Pamphilj family. The new facade is surmounted by a dome and twin side bell towers designed by Borromini and built by Antonio Del Grande and Giovanni Maria Baratta. Above the main entrance is a monument to Innocent X, who is buried in the crypt on the left of the main altar.

Sant'Andrea della Valle

Piazza Sant'Andrea della Valle; tel.: 06-6861339; open: daily 8 A.M.–12:30 P.M., 4:30–7:30 P.M.

➢ This church was built according to the plans of Carlo Maderno, who worked on them some time after 1608, basing his work on the late-16th-century plans of Pietro Paolo Olivieri. Maderno was also responsible for the remarkable cupola, built in 1622, which is the second highest in Rome after the dome of Saint Peter's. The fresco inside the dome, *Assunzione della Vergine*, by Giovanni Lanfranco, is extravagant and the plaudits he received brought out great jealousy in his coworker Domenichino, who was painting the spandrels at the same time. Frescoes in the apse include three beautiful scenes from the life of Saint Andrew, by Mattia Preti. The facade, made of travertine, by Carlo Rainaldi and Carlo Fontana, has a single central opening with two large niches on either side. The vast Latin-cross interior was arranged to resemble the interior of the famous Gesù. The decoration of the vault is the result of a restoration at the beginning of the 20th century. The second chapel on the right, Cappella Strozzi, was inspired by Michelangelo, and copies of works by Michelangelo, executed in bronze in 1616, confirm this. *Death of the Saint*, by Lanfranco in 1625, can be found in the Cappella di Sant'Andrea Avellino in the right transept. Above the entrance of the left circular chapel is the Tomb of Pope Pius II by a follower of Andrea Bregno (1470–1475). In the second chapel on the left is a tomb of Monsignor Giovanni della Casa, the author of a well-known 16th-century treatise on etiquette called *Il Galateo ovvero de' Costumi*. Among the statues in the side niches is *Saint John the Baptist* by Pietro Bernini, Gian Lorenzo's father. The Barberini Chapel, first on the left, is also called the Tosca Chapel because it provides the background to the famous Puccini melodrama.

Walking Tour 1:

The Quiet Streets West of Piazza Navona

By Sarah Morgan

West of Piazza Navona, in the northern part of the bulge where the Tiber loops past the densest area of monuments, government buildings, shoppers, and tourists, is a part of the historic city center that is a little more tranquil but no less rich historically and architecturally.

This area began to be built up from the late 11th century on, especially around the main thoroughfares that bore the faithful toward Saint Peter's and the Vatican—today's Via dei Coronari and Via del Governo Vecchio. These routes used to get dangerously crowded with people—in the Holy Year 1450, 200 people were crushed to death or drowned in the Tiber because a bottleneck of human traffic had formed along Via dei Coronari. Today the majority of tourists and pilgrims make their way to the Vatican by bus, and traffic is now funneled along the Corso Vittorio. Having lost their function as sole thoroughfare to Saint Peter's, these streets have become pleasantly quiet and pedestrian-friendly.

In the Middle Ages, the richer Roman families built towered palaces or fortresses here, some of which still remain, but the area is mostly characterized by its high concentration of Renaissance palaces and some beautiful examples of Renaissance ecclesiastical architecture.

Just behind Piazza Navona, on Via di Santa Maria dell'Anima, which lies parallel to its western side, you can admire the Renaissance facade in brick with travertine pillar strips (attributed to Giuliano da Sangallo) of the **Church of Santa Maria dell'Anima**. More often than not this entrance is closed and you have to skirt around to the right and enter at No. 20 on Via della Pace through a corridor and a little courtyard crowded with plants and jumbled pieces of classical marble. A pleasant, lofty space in the style of the late-Gothic German *hallenkirche* (in which aisles and nave rise to equal height) made rather heavy by the ceiling decoration, this was originally a German hospice for pilgrims. A church was founded on the site in 1386. Rebuilt in 1510 the church suffered severe damage during the Sack of Rome in 1527 and again in the late 18th century, so the restored version that we see today is mainly 19th century. For the last four centuries it has been the church of German-speaking Catholics. Notice to the right of the apse the beautiful tomb of the Dutch Pope Adrian VI (1522–1523), designed by Baldassare Peruzzi, a triumph of the pagan spirit of the Renaissance that, ironically, the pope condemned during his brief reign.

Right up against the back entrance to Santa Maria dell'Anima, in Vicolo dell'Arco della Pace, is another beautiful church, **Santa Maria della Pace**, whose dramatic baroque facade with semicircular portico dominates this end of the little piazzetta. Pope Sixtus IV had the original church built, possibly by Baccio Pontelli, in 1482. Allegedly he promised to dedicate the church to the Virgin if she would bring the war with Turkey to an end; hence *Santa Maria della Pace*, Our Lady of Peace. Inside, a short nave terminates in a domed octagon. The interior was decorated in the 16th century by various artists: Raphael painted the famous *Sybils* (1514–1515) above the arch of the first chapel on the right, but there are also works by Baldassare Peruzzi (in the Cappella Ponzetti on the left), Rosso Fiorentino, Jacopo Zucchi, and Orazio Gentileschi. In the mid-17th century Pietro da Cortona was commissioned to embellish the church in the baroque style, and it was he who reworked the interior, added all

Santa Maria della Pace

the stucco decoration, and also masked the 15th-century construction with the elaborate play of convexes and concaves of the facade. Bramante's fine cloister, to the left of the sacristy, should also be viewed (see Focus).

From the piazzetta, turn into the passageway to the left of the entrance to the Bramante cloister into the Arco della Pace, and then left into Via dei Coronari. In past centuries this long narrow street, known as the *Via Recta* (*recta* meaning straight), was one of the main routes toward Hadrian's Bridge and Saint Peter's, and connected Piazza Colonna with the Tiber. The street takes its present name from the sellers of rosaries (*coronari*) and other sacred objects who kept shop along the street and made their money from all the passing pilgrims. Now the dominant commerce has shifted to antiquities: almost every shop on the street is an antique shop of some sort. Note the beautiful Piazza Lancellotti (turn off to the right into Via Lancellotti) with its ancient olive tree.

Continuing down Via dei Coronari, to the right in the piazza of the same name stands **San Salvatore in Lauro**, one of the oldest churches in this part of Rome, though the neoclassical facade of 1862 belies this fact. A church of the same name was first recorded here in the 12th century, but was rebuilt in the 1400s, badly burned in 1591, and restored between 1594 and 1734. Tradition has it that the church takes its name from a forest of bay or laurel trees that stood here in antiquity. In the third chapel to the right is Pietro da Cortona's *Adoration of the Shepherds* (c. 1630), his first great altar-piece. The dramatic sunburst sculpture over the high altar frames a copy of the tiny statue of the Madonna of Loreto, and gold candlesticks and four sculpted heads of bishops contribute to the dazzling and theatrical effect. Note also the fine Renaissance cloister of **San Giorgio's Convent**, entered through a small door to the left of the church.

At the far end of Via dei Coronari, you will find yourself on Via del Banco di Santo Spirito. Cross over into the passageway, the Arco dei Banchi,

Cloister of San Giorgio's Convent

with its little shrine complete with lace and candles, and you will see a marble plaque inscribed in Latin set into the wall on the left-hand side. This is the oldest inscription of its kind to survive, and records the terrible flood of 1277, when the high altar inside the Pantheon was more than four feet under water.

Just past the Arco at No. 42 Via del Banco di Santo Spirito is the **Palazzo Gaddi** (not open to the public), which originally belonged to the Florentine Strozzi family and is said to have been enlarged by another Florentine, Jacopo Sansovino, for Luigi di Taddeo Gaddi (1528–1530). If you ask the *portiere*, or gatekeeper, he may allow you to view the courtyard. A long corridor with a decidedly telescopic effect takes you uphill to a small courtyard arrayed with an important collection of antique marbles. The palazzo has long been owned by Florentine families, and Michelangelo and Benvenuto Cellini are known to have stayed here.

At the corner of Via del Banco di Santo Spirito and Largo Tassoni, the wedge-shaped Palazzo del Banco di Santo Spirito stands adrift between the smaller, older streets and the noisy and congested Corso Vittorio. The upper stories of the facade were built by Antonio da Sangallo the Younger to resemble a Roman triumphal arch, and are crowned with two large baroque statues personifying Charity and Thrift. Built between 1521–1524, this palazzo was a bank, a hospital, and the papal mint all in one. The pope had the hospital built in order to convince the Roman people to deposit their savings in the bank. The palazzo was also the site of the Zecca Pontificia, or the papal mint, where the *paolo*, a gold coin that was circulated throughout Italy between the 16th and 18th centuries, was cast.

To the left of the old mint, Via dei Banchi Nuovi leads into Piazza dell'Orologio. This used to be called Piazza dei Rigattieri, after the vendors of used goods who sold their wares here. The piazza now takes its name from the clock tower designed by Francesco Borromini for the Convent of the Oratorians of San Filippo Neri (1647–1649), with its juxtaposition of concaves and convexes that is so recognizably Borrominian. Note the mosaic of the Madonna beneath the clock. The cloister of the convent is now given over to the Casa della Letteratura, a public library specializing in 20th-century literature. Take a look at the beautiful courtyard garden with orange trees and fountain.

Further Information

Palazzo Gaddi
(closed to the public)
Via del Banco di Santo Spirito, 42.

Santa Maria dell'Anima
Via della Pace, 24; tel.: 06-6828181;
open: daily 7:30 A.M.–7 P.M.,
Sun. 8 A.M.–1 P.M. and 3–7 P.M.

Santa Maria della Pace
Vicolo dell'Arco della Pace, 5;
tel.: 06-6861156; open: Mon.–Fri.
9 A.M.–noon.

San Salvatore in Lauro and
Cloister of San Giorgio's Convent
Piazza San Salvatore in Lauro, 15;
tel.: 06-6875187; open: daily 2–8 P.M.
and some mornings (call ahead).

FOCUS: Chiostro del Bramante

Via Arco della Pace, 5; tel.: 06-68809035; open: Mon., call ahead for hours; admission: €6.

By Sarah Morgan

One of the greatest architectural jewels of this part of Rome is the cloister of the Church of Santa Maria della Pace, built by Donato Bramante, the father of High Renaissance architecture. According to Vasari, this was Bramante's first commission in Rome, after he moved here from Lombardy just before 1500. Before becoming the official papal architect he worked for Oliviero Carafa, the cardinal of Naples, who commissioned this cloister in 1500. Building was completed in 1504, and in those years Bramante also worked on the study and measurement of ancient buildings in Rome, Tivoli, and Naples, recognizing the need to study and preserve what remained of ancient Rome.

The influence of this prolonged period of study is immediately apparent in this first Roman commission, which marks a significant change in his style. As well as incorporating building techniques he had learned from his study of ancient ruins, his work became more sober and restrained with greater attention to the arrangement of spaces and mass. The use of the heavier pilastered arcades on the lower story is much more "Roman" than his Milanese cloisters, for example. The apparent simplicity of the design, on a square plan with four bays to each side, conceals a very sophisticated play of space: while the lower story is heavy and grounded, the upper, in contrast, is lighter and more dynamic, with its slender columns and additional supports subdividing the spaces. The effect, standing in the courtyard, is that of being cut off from the rest of the city—and all the noises seem to die away, too—in this perfectly self-contained space, which is harmonious and delicate in its proportions.

Chiostro del Bramante

Walking Tour 2:

Via Giulia

By Amanda Castleman

Via Giulia slices through Rome's historic district in a strictly no-nonsense manner. It is a wide, straight, practical avenue, meant to lead the faithful to Saint Peter's. This Renaissance street was named for Pope Julius II (1503–1513), who replaced alleys where gangs of bandits and pickpockets would prey upon pilgrims, with a stretch of road, over a half-mile long, flanking the Tiber from the pedestrian Ponte Sisto to the Ponte Vittorio Emanuele II. In an effort toward French elegance—and architectural unity—Bramante was supposed to design all the buildings. This plan failed and a hodgepodge of palaces ended up lining the street.

At Via Giulia's debut, real estate prices were low—low enough even for artists. Cheeky goldsmith Benvenuto Cellini lived here, as did Sangallo the Younger, whose house at No. 79 served as the Tuscan Embassy before the unification of Italy. Raphael died before his rustic design at No. 86 was completed.

The **Palazzo Spada** anchors the southern end of the elegant corridor. Girolamo Capodiferro built this lavish white-stucco edifice, which was later acquired by Cardinal Bernardino Spada and finally by the Council of State.

OUR PICK

The ornate facade is guarded by statues of Roman patrons—such as Romulus, Numa, and Augustus—and faithful dogs. One inscription reads, "THE DICTATOR JULIUS CAESAR: HE FILLED THE WHOLE WORLD WITH HIS ENEMY'S GORE, AND AT THE END HE DRENCHED THE SENATE WITH HIS OWN BLOOD."

The Caesar motif is echoed within the Galleria Spada (see Museums). In the Hall of the Council of State there is a statue of Pompey that may have witnessed the dictator's assassination in 44 B.C. Experts disagree, but for some 20 years, until the last war, an elderly Frenchwoman appeared faithfully on the Ides of March and deposited a bouquet of scarlet carnations at the statue's feet.

The palazzo's best attraction remains free to the bold. Stride past the porter with an air of great resolve and efficiency, then pivot left to catch a glimpse of Borromini's perspective trick. The long colonnade stretches majestically into the distance—or at least *appears* to, thanks to a clever trompe l'oeil effect. In fact, the tunnel is a mere 30-feet long with a dinky two-foot statue. For a modest tip, the guard will sometimes escort sceptics behind the glass partition.

The Fontana del Mascherone—or "fountain of the giant mask"—decorates the same end of Via Giulia. Before Carlo Rainaldi's fountain was built, this site was the ferry landing. He combined two ancient sculptures: a vast marble basin and a grotesque face with a vacuous expression. The mask dribbles water from the Acqua Paola acqueduct, though for festivals it used to pipe red wine. Sadly, this tradition has fallen by the wayside.

Another victim of changing times and conservatism was the Arch of the Palazzo Farnese. Alessandro Farnese, one of the most blatantly rapacious rulers in papal Rome, disliked crossing the Tiber on public bridges, rubbing shoulders with the riffraff. He envisioned a private walkway connecting the palazzo with the Villa Farnesina: a mighty status symbol, the 16th-century equivalent of an executive heliopad. Michelangelo designed the graceful archway, now trailing with ivy, but the monument to Alessandro's ego stopped well short of the river.

The Farnese vanity contrasts badly with the humble hospices and confraternities in the area. Duck down the Via dell'Arco del Monte di Pietà, which runs into a tiny piazza, to find the **Church of Santissima Trinità dei Pellegrini**, by Paolo Maggi (1603–1616). The dingy ocher facade was added in 1723 by Francesco De Sanctis, the architect of the much more famous Spanish Steps, and the interior houses pieces by Guido Reni, Borgogone, and Cavalier d'Arpino.

This neighboring hospice, founded during the Holy Year 1575, was especially popular with English and Scottish pilgrims. Roman grandees would gather there to humbly wash the pilgrims' grubby feet—a ceremony that flourished until the 19th century. After the "hero's defense" of the city, Garibaldi's men recovered in the hospice, where the gallant poet and author of Italy's national hymn, Goffredo Mameli, died at the tender age of 22.

The **Church of Santa Maria dell'Orazione e Morte** was the headquarters of the Compagnia della Buona Morte, dedicated to burial of the poor. Inside, there used to be a spacious storage hall for corpses and easy access to the river, so floating bodies could be netted and hauled inside each morning.

The 1737 facade by Fernando Fuga reflects the morbid mission: gaping skulls with vegetal wings and spines flank the door. And the two plaques which invite alms are positively sinister. One image, black etched in ghostly white marble, shows a winged skeleton with a banner reading HODIE MIHI, CRAS TIBI (essentially, "you're next"). The other begs specifically for plague victims from the countryside, depicting a skeleton gloating over a human body.

After such brutal reminders of mortality, the neighboring **Palazzo Falconieri** seems cheerful, despite its austerity. Francesco Borromini was asked to unite two buildings in 1638. The result is an eye-strainingly massive building, now used as the Hungarian Academy. The narrow street hides the graceful marble top story—though if you back down the side street, stand on tip-toe, and crane your neck backward, a glimpse is possible. It's easier, and far less athletic, to simply admire the falcon heads on elongated female busts that peer from each side of the edifice.

Two churches nearby are worth a visit: **Sant'Eligio degli Orefici** and San Girolamo della Carità. Raphael began the former, the church of the gold and silversmiths, which is often considered one of the purest expressions of the Renaissance (1516). A cupola crowns this small beautiful building, laid out in an austere Greek cross plan. The church was heavily restored and is rarely open but is, nonetheless, one of the area's gems.

A cluster of churches grace the Piazza di Santa Caterina della Rota, including **San Girolamo della Carità** (usually closed, but try the bell and some charm at No. 63 Via San Girolamo). The architect transformed an awkward space into the lovely Capella Spada with polychrome marble and a unique angel balustrade. Many consider this another local example of Borromini's brilliance, but others favor Cosimo Fanzago. The late baroque Cappella Antamoro is also noteworthy for its subtle colored light, intimate scale, and unity—the fruit of a collaboration between Filippo Juvarra and the sculptor Pierre Legros.

The Via Giulia wasn't always the unobstructed avenue it is today. When the *Carceri Nuove*, or new prisons, were in use, this part of the street was cut off by two heavy chains and wrought-iron palings guarded by sentries. Pope Innocent X built the model prison "for a safer and more humane imprisonment of the guilty," as the inscription explains. At the end of the 19th century, it was replaced by the Regina Coeli Jail across the river. Now Valadier's structure houses, fittingly, the Criminology Museum (see Museums) (entrance at No. 29 Via del Gonfalone), full of antique papal torture instruments.

Detour down the whimsical Vicolo della Scimmia ("Monkey Lane") to visit the **Oratorio del Gonfalone**, a guild hall for medieval flag bearers. As

Interior, Oratorio del Gonfalone

Roman blood sports diminished in popularity, religious processions came in vogue. These lavish parades included floats and flags by competing confraternities. The guild's charitable work helped pay for medicine, burial costs, and dowries for poor spinsters.

Concerts are now held in the main oratory hall, which has a cycle of 12 beautiful frescoes of the Passion of Christ, including the *Crucifixion*, by Federico Zuccari.

Foot-sore tourists can relax on the flippantly nicknamed "Sofas of Via Giulia." These huge travertine blocks are the ground-floor remains of the unfinished court Bramante designed for Pope Julius II.

The northern tip of Via Giulia is Piazza d'Oro, a quiet cobbled wedge just off the wild traffic of the Lungotevere. Here stands the **Church of San Giovanni dei Fiorentini**, an architectural misadventure. Pope Leo X rejected plans by Michelangelo and Raphael, then hired and fired Sansovino. Two centuries after its inception, Corsini tacked on an uninspired 18th-century facade, now sprouted with weeds.

Ironically, the great aesthete Borromini is buried in this patchwork construction. His tomb is in the floor near the main altar: its simplicity reflects the shame of suicide. (The great architect had a messy, lingering death, which gave him time to repent, pass away in the "grace of God," and receive a Christian burial.) Under the high altar there is a crypt, designed by Borromini but never used because of past floods of the Tiber. Yet the basilica's modern notoriety comes from its pet masses, where Fido and Fluffy can receive blessings. It's an apt conclusion to the Via Giulia, which is full of august intentions tinted by quirky humanity.

FURTHER INFORMATION

Oratorio del Gonfalone
Via del Gonfalone, 32.

Palazzo Falconieri
Via Giulia, 1; tel.: 06-6889671;
open: Mon.–Sat. 10 A.M.–1 P.M.,
4:30–7:30 P.M.; closed: Sun.

Palazzo Spada
Piazza Capo di Ferro, 13; tel.: 06-6861158/32810; open: Tues.–Sat.
9 A.M.–7 P.M., Sun. 9 A.M.–1 P.M.;
closed: Jan. 1, May 1, Dec. 25.

San Giovanni dei Fiorentini
Via Acciaioli, 2; tel.: 06-68892059;
open: daily 8 A.M.–2 P.M., 4–7:30 P.M.

Sant'Eligio degli Orefici
Via di Sant'Eligio, 8A; tel.: 06-6868260; open: Mon.–Tues.
10 A.M.–1 P.M., Thurs.–Fri. 3–5 P.M.;
closed: month of Aug.

Santa Maria dell'Orazione e Morte
Via Giulia; tel.: 06-68802715; open:
Sun. and public holidays, mass 6 P.M.

San Girolamo della Carità
Via di Monserrato, 62A; tel.: 06-6879786; open: Wed. 10:30 A.M.–
noon, Sun. 10:30–11:30 A.M.

Santissima Trinità dei Pellegrini
Piazza della Trinità dei Pelligrini
(main entrance), side entrance: Via
dei Pettinari 36/A; tel.: 06-68451.

FOCUS: Santa Barbara dei Librai

Largo dei Librai, 85; tel.: 06-6833474 (visiting hours are erratic, call for further details); open: mass at 7 P.M. (8 P.M. in July and Aug.).

By Amanda Castleman

Bustling, bright Via dei Giubbonari spokes out from the Campo de' Fiori. Clothing boutiques, bars, and gourmet groceries line the cobbled street. And tucked away among all the lights and crowds is the quirky Church of Santa Barbara dei Librai.

Santa Barbara dei Librai

SANTA BARBARA DEI LIBRAI

The often-overlooked church was built in the 11th century on the ruins of the Theater of Pompey, near the site where Julius Caesar was assassinated. It is one of the most ancient churches dedicated to Saint Barbara, the beautiful daughter of the 3rd-century aristocrat Dioscorus. He locked her in a luxurious tower to better worship pagan gods without distraction—yet Barbara discovered Christianity. She was decapitated by her father, who was immediately struck down by lightning. This vengeful bolt led to widespread veneration of Saint Barbara; she is invoked in times of thunderstorms, fires, explosions, and sudden death. She is the patroness of artillery-men, firemen, carpenters, and miners.

In the Middle Ages, the humble premises fell into disrepair, until the Guild of Booksellers formed and began restoration in 1601.

The facade is squeezed between flanking buildings. Two orders fight for stability, burdened by curlicues, scallops, and columns. Yet inside, the petite scale is charming and intimate. Any larger and the swirl of pastels and patterns would be overwhelming.

Faux marbling blankets the walls: aqua stripes, violet blotches, yellow mosaic, green flecks, and what truly resembles a brown leopard print. The intricate large altar is nearly lost amid the riotous color. Look closely, though, at the inlaid agate, ivory, and mother of pearl.

Santa Barbara has four chapels in the Greek cross pattern. The Cappella del Crocifisso contains an unusual 14th-century wooden sculpture of Jesus, flanked by Luigi Garzi's later fresco of the Madonna and Saint John at the foot of the cross. A superb 15th-century triptych decorates the right-hand chapel, depicting the Madonna, child, and saints in rich scarlet and umber on wood. Inscriptions recognize the University of Typesetters, booksellers, librarians, and the "spiritual bond" among those who print, sell, and preserve books. The rare 21-pipe organ is also noteworthy, sporting only 45 keys of boxwood and ebony.

The church's themes were all drawn together in a Claude Mellan painting: Mary and the Christ child, Saint Barbara, Saint John the Divine, and Thomas Aquinas all beam down upon the soberly dressed and pious Guild of Booksellers, who are encouraging children to worship.

Other Points of Interest

ORATORIO DEI FILIPPINI

Piazza della Chiesa Nuova; tel.: 06-68802662; open: by appointment only.

➤ This wonderful example of Borromini architecture was built on the site of the old Santa Cecilia a Monte Giordano, which was destroyed to make space for the new building. The square in front is considered a masterpiece, carrying the partial asymmetry that is Borromini's trademark. Originally built in 1637, it has been used to hold concerts since 1922. In one of the palace's three courtyards is a magnificent washbasin of marble and *cipollino*, of Borromini's design.

PALAZZO MASSIMO ALLE COLONNE

Corso Vittorio Emanuelle II, 141; tel.: 06-48903500; open: Tues.–Sun. 9 A.M.–7 P.M.

➤ This palazzo was built in 1532–1536 by Baldassarre Peruzzi over Domiziano's Odeon. The ground floor has a central portico with six Doric columns. In the courtyards are some interesting fragments of bas-reliefs, and a 17th-century nymphaeum. The *Salone d'ingresso*, or entrance hallway, on the first floor has a frieze painted by Daniele da Volterra. The Sala degli Arazzi has some beautiful examples of Flemish tapestry. The chapel on the second floor is located in the bedroom where San Filippo Neri brought the young Paolo Massimo back to life. A 19th-century painting recalls the miracle.

SAN CARLO AI CATINARI

Piazza B. Cairoli; tel.: 06-68803554; open: Mon.–Sat. 7 A.M.–noon, 4:30–7 P.M., Sun. mass only.

➤ The church is named after the basin-makers district, or *catinari*, in which it stands. It was built in 1612–1620 under the auspices of Rome's Milanese congregation to commemorate one of the most important figures of the Catholic Reformation, Cardinal Carlo Borromeo. The architect Rosato Rosati presided over

185

Santa Maria in Vallicella/Chiesa Nuova

the construction of the church and its dome. The sober facade, in travertine, was added in 1636–1638 by the architect G. B. Soria. It presents three main doors and a balcony. Its soaring dome, finished in 1620, is considered one of the most beautiful in Rome. The interior is noteworthy for Domenichino's *Cardinal Virtues*, in the spandrels of the dome, and for the altar designed and executed by Martino Longhi the Younger. The altarpiece, *Charles Borromeo Carries the Holy Nail in Procession*, is by Pietro da Cortona (1650). In the vault of the apse is Giovanni Lanfranco's *Glory of Saint Charles*, while Guido Reni's *Charles Borromeo in Prayer* is in the choir.

Santa Maria di Monserrato

Via di Monserrato; tel.: 06-6865861; open: Sun. mass only, 10 A.M.–1 P.M.

➣ The national church of the Spaniards was built with alms from Aragon and Catalonia after 1518; the architect was Antonio da Sangallo. Its pavement of white marble and many of its monuments formerly belonged to the Church of San

Fiorenzo di Lorenzo, San Sebastiano, *Galleria Spada*

Giacomo in Piazza Navona. In the cloister at the back of the church, there is a collection of monuments and fragments of sculptures, also taken from San Giacomo. The lower part of the facade is by Francesco da Volterra. A young Bernini sculpted the bust of Cardinal Pietro Montoya.

Santa Maria in Vallicella (also known as Chiesa Nuova)

Piazza della Chiesa Nuova; tel.: 06-687528; open: daily 8 A.M.–noon, 4:30–6:30 P.M.

➣ The so-called Chiesa Nuova or "New Church" was built in 1575, over an older church, Santa Maria in Vallicella, which originated in the 12th century.

The interior is richly decorated with the work of Pietro da Cortona and a young Peter Paul Rubens. Cortona is the author of the large fresco of the ceiling and the one in the apse. Rubens painted the *Angels and Cherubs Adoring the Madonna and Child* above the main altar and the two compositions of *Santi Domitilla, Nereo and Achilleo* and *Santi Gregorio Magno, Mauro and Papia* on the two sides of the presbyterium. The dome, designed by Martino Longhi, has no tambour and opens directly into an interior space, which is lavishly decorated by Cortona in triumphant baroque style.

The ground-floor sanctuary can only be entered on the feast of Saint Philip, May 25–26. The church is dedicated to the life of Filippo Neri, who founded the oratory in 1552.

Museums

Galleria Spada (Spada Gallery)

Vicolo del Polverone, 15/B; tel.: 06-6861158; on-line booking: www.ticketeria.it; open: 8:30 A.M.–7:30 P.M., holidays 8:30 A.M.–6:30 P.M.; closed: Mon.; admission: €5.

➣ The Spada Gallery, where Borromini designed the Perspective Gallery, is housed in the palace of the same name. The collection includes paintings by Titian, Andrea del Sarto, and Pieter Brueghel, among many others, as well as an important sculpture of Pompey, who many scholars now believe represents Domitian.

Palazzo Altemps

Museo Barracco (Barracco Museum)

Corso Vittorio Emanuele II, 168; tel.: 06-68806848; open: 9 A.M.–7 P.M.; closed: Mon.; admission: €2.50.

➤ At the end of the 19th century, Baron Giovanni Barracco assembled a precious collection of ancient sculptures and in 1904 he donated it to the city of Rome, to be set aside in the Barracco Museum. Underneath the portico of the museum, in a Renaissance-style courtyard, is the marble sculpture of the torso of a seated Apollo. In Hall I is a sarcophagus from the 4th century. On the second floor there are Phoenician art objects from 3000 to 30 B.C., Etruscan artifacts, and Cypriot limestone sculptures. The third floor houses collections from the classical period, the Hellenistic era, and some Roman statues.

Museo Criminologico (Criminology Museum)

Via del Gonfalone, 29; tel.: 06-68300234; e-mail: museo.criminologico@giustizia.it; open: Tues.–Sat. 9 A.M.–1 P.M., Tues., Thurs. also 2:30–6:30 P.M.; closed: Mon. and holidays; admission: €2.

➤ The collections illustrate the history of crime and criminology with sections devoted to torture, capital punishment, criminal anthropology, and the history of modern prisons.

Museo di Roma (Museum of Rome)

Palazzo Braschi, Piazza San Pantaleo, 10; tel.: 06-6875880.

➤ The museum contains around 40,000 objects, including sculptures, paintings, marble pieces, and mosaics dating from the Middle Ages to 1870.

Museo Napoleonico (Napoleonic Museum)

Piazza Ponte Umberto I, 1; tel.: 06-68806286; website: www.comune.roma.it/museonapoleonico; e-mail: napoleonico@comune.roma.it; open: 9 A.M.– 7 P.M., Sun. 9 A.M.–1:30 P.M.; closed: Mon.; admission: €3.

➤ The museum retraces the story of the Bonaparte family, from the last decades of the 18th century to the Roman period, ending with the Second Empire.

Palazzo Altemps/Museo Nazionale Romano

Piazza Sant'Apollinare, 44; tel.: 06-6833759; open: 9 A.M.–7:45 P.M.; closed: Mon.; admission: €5.

➤ The collection includes *Athena Parthenos* by Antiochos, a copy from the 1st century B.C. of Fidia's original; a wonderful painted loggia on the first floor; the *Ludovisi Throne*, a Greek original from the 5th century B.C.; the sculpture *Gaul Killing Himself with His Wife*, known for the concentrated expression and exact anatomical work; and the massive *Head of Juno*, from the 1st century B.C.

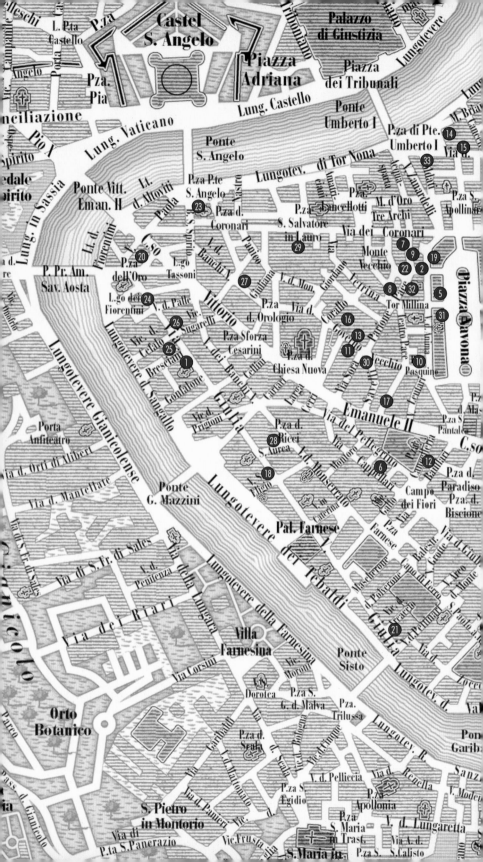

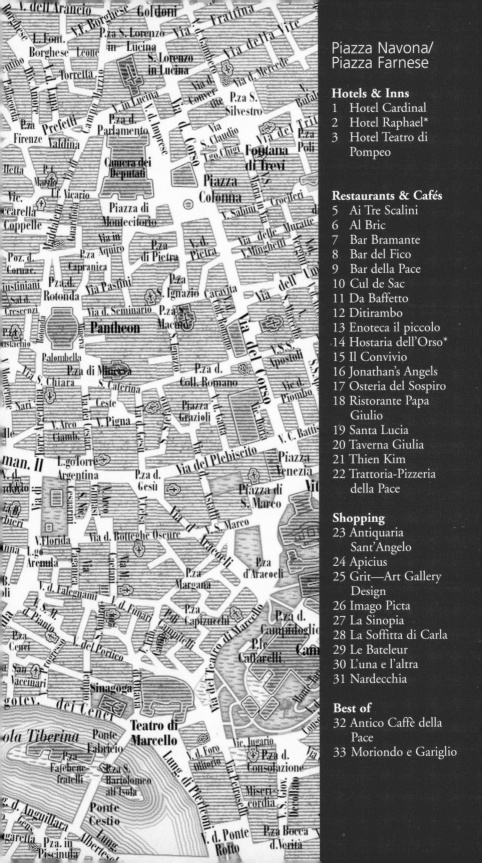

Piazza Navona/
Piazza Farnese

Hotels & Inns
1 Hotel Cardinal
2 Hotel Raphael*
3 Hotel Teatro di
  Pompeo

Restaurants & Cafés
5 Ai Tre Scalini
6 Al Bric
7 Bar Bramante
8 Bar del Fico
9 Bar della Pace
10 Cul de Sac
11 Da Baffetto
12 Ditirambo
13 Enoteca il piccolo
14 Hostaria dell'Orso*
15 Il Convivio
16 Jonathan's Angels
17 Osteria del Sospiro
18 Ristorante Papa
   Giulio
19 Santa Lucia
20 Taverna Giulia
21 Thien Kim
22 Trattoria-Pizzeria
   della Pace

Shopping
23 Antiquaria
   Sant'Angelo
24 Apicius
25 Grit—Art Gallery
   Design
26 Imago Picta
27 La Sinopia
28 La Soffitta di Carla
29 Le Bateleur
30 L'una e l'altra
31 Nardecchia

Best of
32 Antico Caffè della
   Pace
33 Moriondo e Gariglio

HOTELS & INNS

Hotel Cardinal

Via Giulia, 62; tel.: 06-68802719; fax: 06-6786376; category: ★★★★; access to internet: none; most beautiful rooms: those with terrace with view of the historic center; €€–€€€

☛The building was designed in 1400 by Renaissance architect Donato Bramante. The main wall of the bar is original and is made of granite stones taken from the Roman Forum. Archaeological finds are located in the breakfast room gallery.

Hotel Raphael

Largo Febo, 2; tel.: 06-682831/6878993; e-mail: info@raphaelhotel.com; website: www.raphaelhotel.com; category: ★★★★; number of rooms: 69, including seven with terrace; credit cards accepted: all major; facilities: sauna, fitness center, transport from airport; access to internet: computer, with internet access, available to guests in the lounge; most beautiful rooms: 418, 507, 508, and 509; €€€€*.

☛Located just off Piazza Navona, the Raphael is one of the most popular hotels in Rome, with elegant and comfortable rooms. During summer, hotel guests can dine on the roof terrace, a fully furnished bar with a great sunset view of the city.

Hotel Teatro di Pompeo

Largo del Pallaro, 8; tel.: 06-68300170/ 68805531; e-mail: hotel.teatrodipompeo@ tiscalinet.it; website: web.tiscali.it/hotel_ teatrodipompeo; category: ★★★; number of rooms: 12; credit cards accepted: all major; access to internet: direct-line (US, UK) telephone jack in all rooms; €€.

☛Near Campo de' Fiori and Piazza Navona, this small hotel has 12 very charming rooms. It is built right next to the arched walls of the Theater of Pompey, where Caesar was stabbed in 44 B.C.

RESTAURANTS & CAFÉS

Ai Tre Scalini

Piazza Navona, 26–27; tel.: 06-6865609.

☛Only the lactose intolerant could pass up the chance to eat homemade ice cream while sitting directly in front of Bernini's masterpiece, the Fountain of the Four Rivers, in Piazza Navona. Ai Tre Scalini, a gelaterie famous for its rich chocolate *tartufo* (truffle), also serves food. And to top it off, Ai Tre Scalini is housed in a palazzo designed by Borromini and built in 1645. Rarely does one get to soak in such cultural riches while slurping an ice cream cone. For those who don't like chocolate, there are over 20 other flavors to choose from.

Al Bric

Via del Pellegrino, 51; tel.: 06-6879533; open: Tues.–Sat. 7:30–11:30 P.M., Sun. 12:30–2:30 P.M., 7:30–11:30 P.M.; closed: Mon.

☛Via del Pellegrino, once the street of goldsmiths, hosts this osteria and wine bar that seats about 40. The pleasant atmosphere, characterized by light wood tables and walls decorated with wine labels and historic cartoons, is certainly an advantage, but this osteria-wine bar also boasts gourmet food.

Bar Bramante

Via della Pace, 25; tel.: 06-68803916.

☛A magnet for actors, actresses, and celebrities of Rome. Unlike its rival, Bar della Pace, this bar also serves dinner—quite an elegant affair.

Bar del Fico

Piazza del Fico, 26; tel.: 06-6865205.
☛Full of Rome's social butterflies, drawn here in part because of the undeniably beautiful setting.

Bar della Pace

Via della Pace, 26; tel.: 06-58333920.
☛Famous throughout Rome. Clients sit, or rather, lounge, drinking cocktails for hours.

Cul de Sac

Piazza Pasquino, 73; tel.: 06-68801094; open: daily noon–4 P.M., 7 P.M.–1:30 A.M.; closed: Mon. lunch; credit cards accepted: all major.
☛This celebrated wine bar claims to be Rome's first. Steps away from Piazza Navona, Cul de Sac has tables both inside and outside under oversized umbrellas. The wine list reads like a who's who of vineyards. The menu has snacks, like sliced cheeses and cured meats, as well as more sophisticated items: swordfish carpaccio, onion soup, and homemade pâté.

Da Baffetto

Via del Governo Vecchio, 114; tel.: 06-6861617; open: daily 6:30 P.M.–1 A.M.; credit cards accepted: none.
☛Perhaps Rome's best-known pizzeria named after a man with a mustache, Da Baffetto is a pizza-pie institution. The always crowded eatery has overly quick service, but the bruschetta and thin-crust pizza are fantastic. Come very early or very late, or expect a line.

Enoteca il piccolo

Via del Governo Vecchio, 74–75; tel.: 06-68801746; open: daily 10:30 A.M.–3:30 P.M., 5:30 P.M.–1 A.M.
☛This cozy wine bar serves excellent food at lunch, and in the evening offers sangria with *frutti di bosco, fragolino,* and good red wines.

Il Convivio

Via dell'Orso, 44; tel.: 06-6869432; open: daily 7 P.M.–midnight; closed: Sun.; credit cards accepted: all major; €€.
☛It's not easy to find this small restaurant north of Piazza Navona, but it's worth the search. Chef Angelo Troiani creates innovative dishes based on fish and simple ingredients. Try the *rollè di agnello farcito con frittatine alle erbe* (lamb roll stuffed with herbs) or the *soufflè di crema di mandorle e prugne profumato di arancia* (almond and prune soufflé with essence of orange).

Jonathan's Angels

Via della Fossa, 16; tel.: 06-6893426.
☛If you want to escape the preening on Via della Pace, go to nearby Jonathan's Angels. This bar has an unusual claim to fame—its bathrooms. In the *Kitsch Dictionary of the World,* the bathrooms of Jonathan's Angels deserve their very own page. They are quite large, dimly lit, and covered from floor to ceiling with religious paraphernalia and other incongruous odds and ends. Outside the magnificent bathrooms you will find a young and lively crowd. The intriguing owner of Jonathan's Angels, Nino Medras, is an ex–stunt man and acrobat.

Osteria del Sospiro

Vicolo della Cancelleria, 13; tel.: 06-68803786; closed: Mon.; €.
☛This friendly restaurant serves high-quality food at reasonable prices. Specialties include *baccala affumicato* (smoked cod) and the unusual and delicious *tagliatelle 'del sospiro'* made with fresh anchovies, cherry tomatoes, pecorino romano, and *finocchietto.*

Ristorante Papa Giulio

Via Giulia, 14; tel.: 06-68135920; closed: Sun.; credit cards accepted: all major; €.
☛The decor is straight from a *film noir:* tall dark leather banquettes, smoky old mirrors, crisp white linen, glass goblets. And the food lives up to the elegance.

Santa Lucia

Largo Febo, 12; tel.: 06-68802427; closed: Tues.; €.
☛Spectacular location, especially when eating outside in the raised triangular piazza. Serves quality Neapolitan cuisine.

Taverna Giulia

Vicolo dell'Oro, 23; tel.: 06-6869768; closed: Sun.; credit cards accepted: all major; €.
☛Frequented by celebrities, this taverna is the standard-bearer of Ligurian food in Rome. Specialties include *mosciame e trenette al pesto, tripe alla genovese,* artichokes, and flank roast.

RESTAURANTS & CAFÉS

Thien Kim

Via Giulia, 201; tel.: 06-68307832; open: 7:30–11:30 P.M.; closed: Sun.; credit cards accepted: all major; €.

☛Thien Kim is a quiet haven near the bustle of the Lungotevere, serving up delicate Vietnamese cuisine. The mixed starters and soups are renowned.

Trattoria-Pizzeria della Pace

Via della Pace, 1; tel.: 06-6864802; open: May–Sept. 8 P.M.–1 A.M.; closed: Mon.; credit cards accepted: all major, except American Express.

☛Owner Bartolo also runs the Antico Caffè della Pace (No. 5 Via della Pace) and has single-handedly transformed this picturesque corner of Rome into one of its trendiest scenes. Seeing and being seen is as important as home cooking and Neapolitan-style pizzas at this always crowded restaurant. And although he doesn't take reservations, waiting for the hearty fare based on recipes from Sicily is a worthy trade-off. A combination of public relations savvy and a central location make it a favorite dining spot for Italian TV personalities—and a hunting ground for paparazzi.

SPECIALTY SHOPS

Antiquaria Sant'Angelo

Via del Banco di S. Spirito, 61; tel.: 06-6865-944; open: Mon.–Fri. 10 A.M.–1 P.M., 4–8 P.M.

☛In this antique shop opposite the Ponte Sant'Angelo, you can browse amongst a wealth of prints, books, and paintings.

Apicius

Via Giulia, 86; tel.:06-68309404; open: 10 A.M.–9 P.M.; closed: Mon. morning and Sun.

☛This small elegant shop bears the name of a celebrated epicure in the time of Tiberius. Exotic variations of olive oil and vinegar are its speciality, as well as pâté, and marmalade.

Grit—Art Gallery Design

Via Giula, 73; tel.: 06-68301217; open: Mon., Sat. 3–7 P.M., Tues–Fri. 10 A.M.–7 P.M., Sun. in Dec.

☛A flowing path sweeps through this gallery, surrounded by ceramics, translucent magazine stands, and a high-end bean bag (€180).

Imago Picta

Via Giulia, 70.

☛The shop is eye candy, a doll's house full of Pompeii-style wall paintings, mosaics, mirrors, and other decorative motifs.

La Sinopia

Via dei Banchi Nuovi, 21c; tel.: 06-6872869; open: Mon.–Sat. 10 A.M.–1 P.M., 4–7:30 P.M.; credit cards accepted: none.

☛This is more than an antiques shop—although beautiful objects are for sale—because the store's staff also offers expert advice, appraisals, and design hints, plus courses in restoration and gilding.

La Soffitta di Carla

Via Tancredi Cartella, 49; tel.: 06-43533956; open: 10 A.M.–1 P.M., 4:30–7:30 P.M.; closed: Sun.

☛Furniture, photographs, and every other kind of object dating from the late 19th century to 1930.

Le Bateleur

Via S. Simone, 71; tel.: 06-6544676; open: Mon.–Sat. 10 A.M.–7:30 P.M.; credit cards accepted: all major.

☛Located in an 11th-century sacristy just off the Via dei Coronari, this is the ultimate curiosity shop. It's packed with vintage and collectible objects.

L'una e l'altra

Via del Governo Vecchio, 105; tel.: 06-68804995.

☛Women's clothing by up-and-coming designers. Strong on the minimalist look.

Nardecchia

Piazza Navona, 25; tel.: 06-6869318; open: Mon.–Sat. 10 A.M.–7:30 P.M.; credit cards accepted: all major.

☛A large selection of ancient and modern etchings and prints.

PROFILE

Tracking Down Treasures in Rome's Watery Underbelly

By Laura Collura Kahn

Carlo Pavia

When Carlo Pavia wants to visit his favorite part of Rome, he gets up at dawn, packs a bag with a diving suit, a camera, and a few tools, and sets off for a drain hole. For more than two decades, Pavia, the owner of a photography shop in Piazza della Cancelleria, has been exploring the entrails of the capital.

For Pavia, scrutinizing the "belly of Rome," is like digging up the various fragments of a mosaic and gradually finding the right place for them in the overall design. Through his works, he discovers fascinating tidbits about Rome's past. By piecing them together, he forms a better understanding of Rome and its history.

He is now working on his 25th publication, a book called *Oddities of Ancient Roman Times*, an exploration of the city's hidden side. His research has uncovered more intriguing trivia about Rome. For example, he has discovered where the only gray column of the Pantheon comes from—a place in Egypt, near Hurghada, called Umm Dikal that was once a hard-labor site, where prisoners would carve granite columns that were then sent off to Rome.

OUR CRITIC'S FAVORITE RESTAURANTS

Ditirambo

Piazza della Cancelleria, 74; tel.: 06-6871626; open: 1–3:30 P.M., 8–11:30 P.M.; closed: Mon. for lunch; €.

☛The cozy setting and imaginative but well-balanced Mediterranean cuisine have made reservations *de rigueur* for anyone interested in dining in this popular restaurant just off Campo de' Fiori. Some of the temptations include yellow polenta with salt-cod mousse and handmade ricotta-and-almond-flour pasta, in addition to vegetarian dishes and meat entrées. Desserts and cookies are made on the premises. Solid wine list.

Hostaria dell'Orso

Via dei Soldati, 25/C; tel. 06-68301192; closed: Mon. at lunchtime and Sun.; €€€€.

☛Italian superchef Gualtiero Marchesi came to Rome to revitalize one of the temples of Roman food. A five-star restaurant housed in a splendid medieval building (three floors, a piano bar, and a discothèque), the Hostaria offers a combination of typical Marchesi dishes—like his famous gold-and-saffron risotto, served with an edible gold leaf—and creative versions of traditional regional cuisine, such as Guidìa-style artichokes; *rigatoni all'Amatriciana*; fresh pasta bits with cheese fondue; *paccheri* with shrimp tails; roast baby lamb, and roast baby pork. For dessert, there is Catalan cream with lemon and ginger, green tea sorbet, and Italian-style meringue. Try the gourmet experience either by ordering one of four set menus (from €74 to €130) or à la carte. The wine list offers some 430 labels from all over the world, including rare vintage wines and collectors' bottles.

Vatican

By Ruth Kaplan

The best approach to **Basilica di San Pietro** is by Via della Conciliazione. You will be passing by the 15th-century Palazzo dei Penitenzieri, on the left, and then, once in **Piazza San Pietro**, you will see hundreds of saints looking down on you from atop the two arms of Bernini's layered colonnade. Bernini and Maderno created the two fountains on either side of the Egyptian obelisk and sundial. The cavernous basilica is fitted with Michelangelo's 435-foot-high dome. The top offers excellent views. His **Pietà** sits just inside the main doors of the church. Bernini's gilded bronze baldacchino covers the papal altar, and his multifigured Tomb of Pope Alexander VII is inset into a left wall.

It's a ten-minute walk to the entrance of the Vatican Museums, which host some of the most important works of art in the world, including a collection of ancient Egyptian and Etruscan art. The most famous works of the Vatican Museums are the frescoes by Raphael and Michelangelo that were created especially for these buildings. The **Raphael Rooms** were decorated by the master and his students. The **Stanza della Segnatura** contains *The School of Athens*, a crystallization of Renaissance approaches to composition and perspective, as well as Renaissance interest in secular, classical subjects. Frescoes on the other walls include the famous *Disputation of the Holy Sacrament* and *Parnassus*. The grand finale is Michelangelo's **Cappella Sistina** ceiling, which he completed alone over the course of four years. The central panels document the creation of man and other scenes from the book of Genesis, while the side panels consist of portraits of the prophets and sibyls. Exiting the museum takes you by Bernini's perspective-tweaking staircase, the Scala Regia.

To the right of the main door of Basilica San Pietro is the beginning of *Il Passetto*, a fortified corridor built during medieval times to link the Vatican safely to the fortress of **Castel Sant'Angelo** on the banks of the Tiber. The circular fortress began as emperor Hadrian's mausoleum and has been reincarnated as part of the Aurelian Wall, a prison, and a papal residence in times of political upheaval. The adjacent pedestrian bridge, **Ponte Sant'Angelo**, was built by Hadrian and revamped by Bernini, who designed the ten angel statues glancing down at passersby.

Left, View from Ponte Sant'Angelo

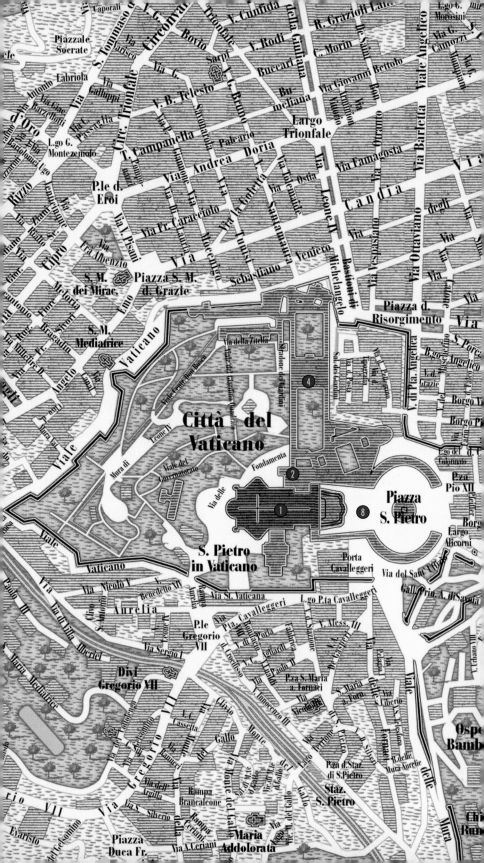

Vatican

PIETÀ

Michael Angelo's ineffable *Pietà* lurks obscurely in a
side-chapel—indeed to my sense the rarest artistic combination
of the greatest things the hand of man has produced.

—Henry James, *Italian Hours*

BASILICA DI SAN PIETRO (SAINT PETER'S BASILICA)

Piazza San Pietro; tel.: 06-69884466/
69883712; open: daily 7 A.M.–7 P.M.
(Oct.–March: closes at 6:00 P.M.).

➤ Saint Peter's Basilica, the center of
the Catholic Church, is 717-feet long; the
diameter of the dome is 140 feet; and
the top of the cross on the dome is 448 feet
above ground. The basilica has 46 altars
and 233 windows. The bronze baldacchino
by Bernini is sustained by four columns,
whose bases, in white Carrara marble, were
sculpted by Borromini. In the eight coats
of arms belonging to popes of the
Barberini family, Borromini sculpted the
face of a young woman in various phases of
conception and birth, until the smiling
head of a child appears. It symbolized the
supremacy of the Roman Church as the

Michelangelo, Pietà

Mother Church. To finance its construction, Pope Leo X introduced a special tax
on all Roman courtesans. The tax brought
in 20,000 ducats, four times the amount
normally produced by indulgences. The
nave is 613-feet long, 81-feet wide, and
133-feet high. The columns are all made of
one piece, except two columns to the sides
of the altar of Navicella. The size of the
portico is enormous, measuring 468-feet
long, with five broad entrances that lead to
a spacious hall. Inside the porch, over the
central arch, is the fragment of Giotto's
famous mosaic, the *Navicella,* done by the
artist in 1289 and preserved at the time of
the demolition of Old Saint Peter's. Five
huge doors give access to the basilica. The
bronze doors in the center belonged to Old
Saint Peter's, and were designed by Filarete
and Simone Baldi, the brother of
Donatello. The bas-reliefs of the panels
represent the martyrdom of Saints Peter
and Paul; those upon the framework introduce mythological subjects. The fifth door
to the right, the Porta Santa, is opened
only in Jubilee years.

Crowning all stands Michelangelo's
wondrous dome, the mightiest effort of a
master hand. As one gazes upward, the
feeling is one of bewilderment—it's incon-
ceivable how workers could have lifted
and poised such a prodigious cupola.
Stones, bricks, timber, cement, and water
all had to be lifted to the height of 400 feet
by over 600 skilled workmen. Twenty-
seven chapels and altars are contained
within the aisles, apse, and transept. They
include the Chapel of the Pietà, with
Michelangelo's sculpture; the Gregorian
Chapel, whose altar dates from 1118 and
belonged to Old Saint Peter's; the altar of
Saints Peter and Paul, with the monument
of Alexander VII by Bernini; and the altar
of the Transfiguration, with the finest
mosaic in the basilica. It is only by the

closest inspection and at a specific angle in certain light that one can detect that they are not paintings but mosaics executed in exceedingly small particles. This is a copy of Raphael's *Transfiguration,* and is said to have occupied ten men for nine years. In the apse at the end of the basilica is a gigantic chair of gilded bronze designed by Bernini. It contains the chair supposedly used by Saint Peter as bishop of Rome.

• THE BALDACCHINO

➢ Overshadowing the papal altar, Bernini's colossal baldacchino, with its four spiral columns of exceptional bronze work, soars to a height of 95 feet from the base of the pillars to the top of the cross that surmounts it. The weight of this mighty canopy is said to be 93 tons.

• CRYPTS

➢ The entrance is by a narrow stair, at the foot of one of the four great piers of the dome. At the bottom of the steps, a narrow passage leads to a small oratory in the form of a cross. The crypts, due to the different level between the old and the new basilica, are divided into Grotte Nuove, the part under the dome, and Grotte Vecchie, under the nave, made of three huge naves with big pilasters. The floor of the ancient basilica has medieval tombs, ancient mosaics, and fragments of precious marble work, in fact, nearly all that remains of the treasures of art that adorned Old Saint Peter's. The exquisite beauty of some of the fragments of sculpture preserved in this space (several from the hand of Mino di Fiesole and Donatello) makes one regret Bramante's decision to demolish Constantine's building.

CAPPELLA SISTINA (SISTINE CHAPEL)

Città del Vaticano, Viale Vaticano; tel.: 06-69884466; open: Mon.–Fri. 8:45 A.M.–3:20 P.M., Sat. and the last Sun. of every month 8:45 A.M.–12:20 P.M.; closed: public and religious holidays.

➢ The Sistine Chapel was built at the request of Pope Sixtus IV between 1475 and 1481, when the papacy was a powerful political entity. The chapel is a huge rectangular room with six large windows on each of the massive walls, covered by a barrel vault—which represented a blue sky bejeweled with golden stars—and a mosaic made in the 15th-century Cosmatesque style. An exquisite marble screen divides the room into two unequal parts consisting of a larger choir and a small nave. A striking work of Renaissance art, it is the Pope's official private chapel and is also the place where cardinals of the Catholic Church congregate to elect a new pope. The ceiling of the Sistine Chapel, commissioned by Julius II, along with Michelangelo's *Last Judgment,* are together arguably the greatest masterpiece of Western art and probably the largest body of painting executed solely by one man. They are also possibly the most-viewed paintings in the world, with an average of about 15,000 people visiting on any given day. Between the years 1481 and 1483, Pope Sixtus IV, using the church's huge influence, commissioned some of the finest artists of the time—Perugino, Sandro Botticelli, Luca Signorelli, Cosimo Rosselli, Domenico Ghirlandaio, and Pinturicchio—to fresco the side walls and also those facing the altar. Pope Julius II continued the task of

---

CAPPELLA SISTINA

Until you have seen the Sistine chapel, you can have no adequate conception of what man is capable of accomplishing. One hears or reads of so many great and worthy people, but here, above one's head and before one's eyes is living evidence of what one man has done. . . . At present I am so enthusiastic about Michelangelo that I have lost all my taste for Nature, since I cannot see her with the eye of genius as he did. If only there were some means of fixing some images in one's memory!

—Goethe, *Italian Journey*

decorating the chapel in 1508, assigning Michelangelo to fresco the vault, completed in 1512, and the far wall, completed under the papacy of Pope Paul III in 1534–1549. The frescoes represent parallel events in the lives of Moses, on the left wall, and Christ, on the right wall. Reflecting the trend of the time, each fresco contains a series of scenes with hidden meanings and symbols, which connect with those of the opposite wall.

• LEFT WALL

➢ From the altar is Perugino's *Moses and Zipporah* (Zipporah was Moses' wife in Egypt), which depicts the circumcision of their son. On the second panel is *The Burning Bush* by Botticelli, with Moses slaying the Egyptian and driving the Midianites from the well. It represents Moses as both temporal and spiritual leader, calling for the wrath of God to be unleashed on anyone who challenged his decisions, conceivably a preview of the similar powers later bestowed on popes. In the painting *Crossing of the Red Sea* by Cosimo Rosselli, which commemorates the papal victory at Campomorto in 1482, the sea is literally red. *The Giving of the Tablets of the Law on Mount Sinai* is also by Rosselli. In *The Punishment of Korah, Dathan, and Abiram,* on the fifth panel, Botticelli himself appears as the second to last figure on the right. The fresco depicts the famous Arch of Constantine in the background. *Moses Giving his Rod to Joshua,* by Luca Signorelli, depicts the mourning of Moses.

• RIGHT WALL

➢ Starting at the altar are the *Baptism of Christ* by Perugino and Pinturicchio, and Botticelli's *Temptations of Christ,* with the devil disguised in the habit of a Franciscan monk. The *Calling of Peter and Andrew* is by Domenico Ghirlandaio. The fourth panel is the *Sermon on the Mount* by Rosselli. *The Handing Over of the Keys to Saint Peter,* by Perugino with the help of Luca Signorelli, represents Christ bestowing spiritual and temporal power on Saint Peter by giving him the keys to both the kingdoms of Heaven and Earth. The *Last Supper* by Cosimo Rosselli is a masterpiece. The *Resurrection* is by Domenico Ghirlandaio, with additions by Arrigo Van der Broeck

(1572), and *Saint Michael Defending the Body of Moses* was painted by Signorelli, with additions accredited to Matteo da Lecce (1572). In the niches between the windows are 28 different portraits of the first popes by Fra Diamante, Ghirlandaio, Botticelli, Rosselli, and many others.

• THE VAULT

➢ Michelangelo frescoed the ceiling for Pope Julius II between 1508 and 1512, working on specially designed scaffolding. This enormous pictorial series occupies the entire surface, fusing architectural elements with bright and beautiful coloring. The immensely intricate composition can be separated into three different elements: the center of the vault has nine scenes from Genesis, from Creation to events in the life of Noah, surrounded by subjects from the Old and New Testaments. Beginning at the altar are the *Separation of Light from Darkness,* the *Creation of the Stars,* the *Separation of the Waters,* the *Creation of the Fishes and Birds,* the *Creation of Adam,* and the *Creation of Eve.* The *Temptation and Expulsion from Paradise,* the *Sacrifice of Noah, The Flood,* and the *Drunkenness of Noah* are all framed by decorative pairs of nudes, Michelangelo's *Ignudi,* his personal trademark of the ceiling. In the lunettes over the windows are some of the ancestors of Christ, including: *Hezekiah with Parents, Josiah with Parents, Solomon with his Mother,* and *Rehoboam with Mother.*

• THE ALTAR WALL

➢ Michelangelo worked alone for seven years, until its completion in 1541, on the massive—66 by 33 feet—extraordinary, and alarming *Last Judgment* on the altar wall, commissioned by Pope Paul III. A new wall was constructed that slanted inwards to stop any dust from settling on what is considered to be the masterpiece of his mature years. The painting is a dynamic composition of nude characters in motion, set against a seemingly infinite space. The strong color of the background was produced by the artist's liberal use of lapus lazuli. In the upper center is Christ the Supreme Judge, an athletic, muscular figure that dominates the painting. In the left central zone, probably as a warning to

Castel Sant'Angelo and bridge

Catholics about the dangers of straying from their faith, the select blessed souls ascend into heaven. In the center is a group of angels with trumpets, while the unfortunate, damned souls are thrust helplessly towards Hell with no mercy being shown by Christ, and are eagerly welcomed by the Dante-inspired Charon and Minos—a rather unusual subject for an altar decoration. Within this scene a famous figure, known as Disperato, looks pathetically down into the abyss. The nude figures were covered with cloth painted by Daniele da Volterra following orders of Pope Pius IV, who protested and saw the nudes as an utter disgrace.

CASTEL SANT'ANGELO

Lungotevere Castello, 50; tel.: 06-6819111, reservations: 06-39967600; open: Tues.–Sun. 9 A.M.–8 P.M., ticket office closes 7 P.M.; admission: €5, €3 students; credit cards: none.

➢ This castle has seen several remodelings and different uses. It has been a mausoleum, a fortress, a prison, and a papal residence. Despite these changes, the original architectural lines of the monument can be easily observed. Emperor Hadrian built it in A.D. 123 as a mausoleum and tomb for himself and his successors. He also erected the Pons Aelius, or the Sant'Angelo Bridge, as the main entrance. The mausoleum had a square basement of 282 feet, which corresponds to today's enclosure walls. In the basement, a cylindrical structure was erected whose diameter was an outstanding 210 feet. At the basement's corners were groups of statues, while inside were three superimposed huge rooms, still intact, which contained the imperial tombs. In 275 it was included in the Aurealian Wall, thus becoming a fortress that resisted the assaults of the Visigoths in 410 and the Ostrogoths in 537. Emperor Theodoric first used it as a prison even though it continued to serve as a fortress. With the transfer to Rome of the papal authority, Boniface IX and the architect Nicolò Lamberti transformed it into a still more effective fortress to protect popes who, when in danger, used to hide in the huge papal apartment where the Vatican archives and treasures were stored. The papal apartment is at the peak of a square tower on top of the original cylindrical structure. Pope Nicholas V built three corner bastions while Pope Alexander VI erected the fourth. Castel Sant'Angelo was located in a strategic position, a crossroads between the ancient and medieval cities and the Vatican, which had been growing around Saint Peter's Square. The christening of the castle occurred in 590 when the archangel Gabriel allegedly announced to Pope Gregory the end of a plague epidemic. The bronze statue on the terrace depicts the angel sheathing his sword. Today the castle hosts the National Museum of

Castel Sant'Angelo, which displays collections of arms and papal apartments with outstanding decorations, stuccoes, frescoes, and ceramics.

Musei Vaticani (Vatican Museums)

Viale del Vaticano, 13; tel.: 06-69883333/ 69884466/69884947; open: Mon.–Fri. 8:45 A.M.–1:45 P.M., visitors allowed in until 12:45 P.M. (Jan., Feb., Nov., Dec.), 8:45 A.M.– 4:45 P.M., visitors allowed in until 3:45 P.M. (March–Oct.), Sat 8:45 A.M.–1:45 P.M.; closed: Sun., Jan. 1 and 6, Feb. 11, March 19, Easter Monday, May 1, June 29, Aug. 14 and 15, Nov. 1, Dec. 8, 25, and 26, and other religious holidays.

➢ Housed inside the Palazzi Vaticani— originally the Vatican papal palaces of the Renaissance popes—is one of the world's most compelling and exhaustive art collections. The museums are important in their display of classical statuary, Renaissance painting, Etruscan relics, and Egyptian artifacts, not to mention the furnishings and decoration of the palace itself. At the end of the 18th century, Popes Clement XIV and Pius VI began to establish proper museums for the papal collections. Until that time, the collections were arranged in accordance with Renaissance style, in the octagonal courtyard and Palazzetto dei Belvedere, as well as the Casina di Pio IV. Other museums include the Chiaramonti Museum built by Pius VII, the Egyptian Museum and the Etruscan-Gregorian Museum built by Gregory XVI, and the Scala Pia built by Pius IX. The Vatican Palace holds a collection of museums on diverse subjects and once inside there is a choice of routes, but the outstanding features that merit observing are the Stanze di Raffaello, or Raphael Rooms, and the Sistine Chapel.

• Pinacoteca

➢ This museum contains a collection of paintings that include: *The Transfiguration* by Raphael, the most renowned of all his oil paintings, begun for the Cathedral of Narbonne; *St. Jerome* by Leonardo, so famous that it is frequently loaned to exhibitions abroad; *Descent from the Cross* by Caravaggio; and Domenichino's painting *The Last Communion of Saint Jerome*, ordered by the Franciscans of the Church

Raphael, The Transfiguration, *Pinacoteca*

of Santa Maria in Aracoeli, who, disliking it, quarreled with the master, paid him only 50 scudi, and threw his work in a lumber room.

• Museo Pio-Clementino (Pio-Clementino Museum, or Palazzetto del Belvedere)

➢ Built for Innocent VII on the highest spot of the Vatican, and transformed into a museum at the end of the 18th century. Next to the palazzetto is the tower built by Bramante to contain the first spiral staircase in Rome, designed to facilitate entry into the garden from the palazzetto. Next to the staircase, to the east, is the Fountain of the Galley, built by Carlo Maderno. In the museum are many famous ancient sculptures: the *Apoxyomenos* from Lisippo's bronze; the *Apollo Belvedere*, a 2nd-century Roman copy; and the impressive group of the *Laocoonte (Laocoön)* found in 1506 on the Esquiline Hill, near the Golden House of Nero.

• The Raphael Rooms

➢ From the Sala dell'Immacolata, you enter four of the state rooms belonging to the old Vatican palace, known as the Raphael Rooms, which contain the foremost creations of this great master, rivaled by no other works of art except the ceiling of the Sistine Chapel. These four rooms took Raphael more than 12 years of work, from 1508 to 1520; he died before they were completed.

The first room, Stanza dell'Incendio di Borgo, contains four large frescoes. The second room, the Stanza della Segnatura, is so-called because papal briefs were once signed and sealed in it. This was actually the pope's private library, and the frescoes on the wall represent the subjects that determined the ordering of libraries in ancient times (philosophy, theology, poetry, law). The Stanza della Segnatura contains two of his most splendid works: *La Disputa* and *The School of Athens.* In the lower part of *La Disputa,* saints, doctors, and laymen are assembled around an altar, and are engaged in investigating the tenets of the Church. In the upper part of the painting the heavens are opened, and Christ, overshadowed by the Holy Ghost, stretches out His arms to offer Himself as a sacrifice for sin. *The School of Athens,* depicting an assembly of scholars, is a representation of philosophy in contrast to religion as portrayed in *La Disputa.* The two central figures in the background are Plato and Aristotle. In the foreground Pythagoras is engaged in writing, while Empedocles and others are represented watching him. The third room is the Stanza d'Eliodoro, containing four frescoes by Raphael: *Heliodorus Driven from the Temple by Angels,* the meeting of *Saint Leo the Great and Attila,* the *Miracle of the Blessed Sacrament at Bolsena,* and the *Deliverance of Saint Peter from Prison.* In the fourth room, the Sala di Costantino, the frescoes were begun by Raphael, but were almost entirely executed after his death (1520) by his pupils. The subjects of the four large paintings are scenes from the life of Constantine: the *Apparition of the Cross to Constantine,* the *Baptism of Constantine,* the *Donation of Constantine* to the popes, and the *Victory of Constantine over Maxentius* on the Tiber bank beside the Milvian bridge.

PIAZZA SAN PIETRO (SAINT PETER'S SQUARE)

➤ The new facade was inaugurated in 1606, when the five naves and the atrium of the old basilica were finally taken down. It also underwent a dramatic restoration in the Jubilee Year 2000, revealing hidden colors under what was for a long time only white. The colonnade of the square—intended to embrace the entire world and used by the pope for outdoor masses—was built by Bernini between 1656 and 1667. It has four lines of 284 columns and is decorated with 140

Raphael, The School of Athens, *Raphael Rooms*

statues of saints. If you stand in either of the two spots, one on each side, marked by round marble disks next to the fountains, you will see only one line of columns instead of four. The red-granite obelisk in the center of the square comes from Egypt. Erected in Heliopolis by Pharaoh Pheros, it was transported to Alexandria by Augustus and then brought to Rome by Caligula, who placed it in his circus, not far from the present sacristy. According to a legend, the bronze globe that surmounted it was supposed to hold the remains of Caesar. In 1586 Pope Sixtus V decided to place the obelisk where it is now. During the move, the bronze globe was removed and examined for traces of Caesar remains, but it turned out to be made of solid bronze. Pope Sixtus gave the ball to the city of Rome, then decided to keep it in the Palazzo dei Conservatori; a bronze cross replaced it on top of the obelisk. The two fountains, in line with the obelisk, are equidistant from the colonnade. The left fountain was designed by Gian Lorenzo Bernini, the right one by Carlo Maderno.

PONTE SANT'ANGELO

➤ This bridge was built by the Emperor Publius Aelius Hadrianus to connect his mausoleum with the city in 136, and was named after him: Pons Aelius. The statues of Saints Peter and Paul, at the south end of the bridge, were erected by

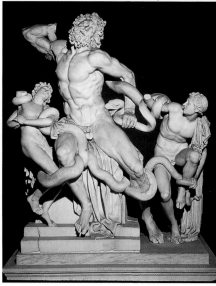

Lacoonte (Laocoön), *Museo Pio-Clementino*

Clement VII on the site of two chapels, memorials of a tragedy that took place here in the Jubilee Year of 1450. A dense crowd of pilgrims was crossing the bridge when some horses and mules took fright. Many pilgrims were pushed down and trampled under foot and many fell into the Tiber; 128 people died. On the parapet of the bridge are statues of angels holding different instruments of the Passion. They were designed by Bernini and executed by his scholars. The drapery of the figures is bizarre, and suggests that a high wind is blowing.

Basilica and Piazza San Pietro

BASILICA DI SAN PIETRO

Taken as a walk not less than as a church, St. Peter's of course reigns alone. Even for the profane . . . it serves where the Boulevards, where Piccadilly, and Broadway, fall short, and if it didn't offer to our use the grandest area in the world, it would still offer the most diverting. Few great works of art last longer to the curiosity, to the perpetually transcended attention. You think you have taken the whole thing in, but it expands, it rises sublime again, and leaves your measure itself poor . . . . The place struck me . . . as a real exaltation of one's idea of space; so that one's entrance, even from the great empty square which either glares beneath the deep blue sky or makes of the cool far-cast shadow of the immense front something that resembles a big slate-colored country on a map, seems not much a going in somewhere as a going out. The mere man of pleasure in quest of new sensations might well not know where to better his encounter there of the sublime shock that brings him, within the threshold, to an immediate gasping pause. . . . Then you have only to stroll and stroll and gaze and gaze; to watch the glorious altar-canopy lit its bronze architecture, its colossal embroidered contortions, like a temple within a temple, and feel yourself, at the bottom of the abysmal shaft of the dome, dwindle to a crawling dot.

—Henry James, *Italian Hours*

Museums

MUSEO NAZIONALE DI CASTEL SANT'ANGELO (NATIONAL MUSEUM OF CASTEL SANT'ANGELO)

Lungotevere Castello; tel.: 06-6819111; open: 9 A.M.–7 P.M.; closed: Mon.; admission: €5.

➤ Built by the emperor Hadrian as a mausoleum for himself and his successors, Castel Sant'Angelo was later transformed into a fortress and then into a prison. Today it holds an important art and military museum.

MUSEO STORICO NAZIONALE DELL'ARTE SANITARIA (NATIONAL HISTORIC MUSEUM OF THE MEDICAL ARTS)

Lungotevere in Sassia, 3; tel.: 06-68352353; open: Mon., Wed., Fri. 10 A.M.–noon; admission: €3.

➤ Curios of the medical arts from the Roman age up to the present day, ex-votos, and surgical instruments.

MUSEO STRUMENTALE DELL'ACCADEMIA NAZIONALE DI SANTA CECILIA (MUSEUM OF MUSICAL INSTRUMENTS OF THE NATIONAL ACADEMY OF SAINT CECILIA)

Via della Conciliazione, 4; tel.: 06-328171; e-mail: archivi_biblioteca@santacecilia.it; open: 10 A.M.–6 P.M.; admission: free.

➤ The collection includes 255 musical instruments. Note the Stradivari violin of 1690.

Walking Tour

Vatican Museums

By Gordon Ramsey

Over the centuries, the Vatican has acquired an extraordinary collection of art. But often visitors to Saint Peter's and the Sistine Chapel ignore the treasures that are on display in the museum and galleries. Here's an easy itinerary that can help you discover these masterpieces of sculpture and painting.

The Vatican's **Egyptian Museum** is a good place to begin. The collection has everything amateur Egyptologists crave: lots of tablets with hieroglyphics, golden sarcophagi, and, of course, the obligatory mummy. However, many of the most interesting works don't date from the time of the pharaohs, but from the glory days of imperial Rome. An entire room is reserved for the pseudo-Egyptian statues carved from glossy black basalt that decorated Hadrian's Villa near Tivoli.

The collection also includes statues from temples built during the Roman Empire for the worship of Egyptian gods. One of the most striking pieces is the figure of an elegant dog-headed man dressed in a Roman toga. This 2nd-century A.D. work found near Anzio, represents Anubis, the Egyptian god responsible for guiding dead souls to the underworld.

Halfway through the Egyptian Museum you come to the Terrace of the Hemicycle, which is dominated by a colossal bronze pinecone flanked by two bronze peacocks. Dating from the 1st or 2nd century A.D., the giant pinecone, *pigna*, was found near the Baths of Agrippa, in a neighborhood of Rome still known as Pigna. Once used to decorate the atrium of the original Saint Peter's Basilica, it was moved to its present location in 1608, while the new Saint Peter's was under construction. The peacocks (reproductions) were also used in the old basilica, but in all likelihood they originally came from Hadrian's Mausoleum (now Castel Sant'Angelo).

When you reach the end of the Egyptian Museum, having passed through some smaller rooms with Mesopotamian and Assyrian artifacts, you arrive at the entrances of the Vatican's two principal collections of classical statuary, the Chiaramonti and Pio-Clementino Museums.

The **Chiaramonti Museum** consists of a long corridor with a daunting collection of statues, urns, pagan altars, and sarcophagi, as well as lots of portrait busts of emperors, senators, and their wives. The museum, whose layout was arranged under the direction of the neoclassical sculptor Antonio Canova, has remained largely unchanged since it opened in 1808.

It is the **Pio-Clementino Museum** that contains the Vatican's most important works of classical statuary. In fact, its Octagonal Courtyard represents the heart and soul of the entire Vatican collection. The courtyard was intended to provide an exhibit space for Pope Julius II's (1503–1513) private collection of antique statuary. It was designed by Donato Bramante at the very end of the 15th century and integrated into the already existing Palazzetto dei Belvedere, a papal summer residence built several years earlier by Innocent VIII (1484–1492).

The first work placed in the courtyard was a Roman copy of a Greek statue of Apollo, which became widely known as the *Apollo Belvedere*. The 16th-century art critic and great champion of neoclassicism Johann Joachim Winckelmann wrote of this piece, "Of all the works of antiquity that have escaped destruction, the statue of Apollo represents the highest ideal of art."

However, most visitors will prefer the much more dramatic statue of Laocoön and his two sons. Laocoön was a Trojan priest who warned his countrymen not to take the Greeks' giant wooden horse into the city walls. But his countrymen refused to believe him, and he and his sons were killed by giant snakes sent by Athena. The sculpture shows the father and sons struggling and screaming in the coils of the great serpents. Unearthed in 1506 on the Esquiline Hill near the Golden House of Nero, it was transported to the courtyard under the watchful eye of Michelangelo himself.

Originally square, the courtyard was transformed by architect Michelangelo Simonetti in 1772 by adding an octagonal portico. This transformation was part of a process initiated by Pope Clement XIV (1769–1774) and continued by Pius VI (1775–1799) that turned the Vatican's collection into a public museum. It is from these two popes that the museum gets its name. Simonetti worked under both of them and he is responsible for the museum's impressive neoclassical rooms.

The Octagonal Courtyard, with its serious subjects taken from mythology, connects to the much lighter Room of the Animals, a kind of marble menagerie with dozens of animal sculptures. From there, you enter the Room

Octagonal Courtyard, Museo Pio-Clementino

of the Muses, where the famous *Belvedere Torso* is displayed. As with the *Apollo Belvedere,* this particular hunk of broken statuary made a deep impression on artists and art historians over the centuries. Michelangelo made many studies of it and it can be clearly seen in his beefy and muscular Christ in the Sistine Chapel's *Last Judgment.*

The exhibits in the Pantheon-inspired Round Room center around a great porphyry basin taken from the Golden House of Nero. It is the largest-known piece of sculpture carved from a single block of porphyry. The last stop in the Pio-Clementino Museum is the Greek Cross Room, which houses two immense porphyry sarcophogi, one belonging to Constantine's mother, Helena, the other to his daughter Costanza.

From the Pio-Clementino Museum, a staircase leads up to the Vatican's **Etruscan-Gregorian Museum**. This collection includes the *Mars of Tody,* a very rare 4th-century B.C. bronze Umbro-Etruscan statue. However, the collection of artifacts pales in comparison to Rome's other Etruscan museum at Villa Giulia, and you may prefer saving your energy and concentration for the Vatican's **Pinacoteca**, a relatively small painting gallery with 15 rooms containing stunning works by many of history's greatest artists.

R.
OUR PICK

One of the most impressive of the gallery's early works is an image of the *Last Judgment* done in Rome some time during the second half of the 12th century by the painterly duo known simply as Niccolò and Giovanni. As with most *Last Judgments*, it contains some amusingly grotesque scenes of the torments of hell.

The Pinacoteca's second room is dominated by a large two-sided triptych painted by Giotto and his assistants. Executed around 1315, it originally graced the high altar of Old Saint Peter's Basilica.

Fifteenth-century Renaissance painters are represented by such notables as Fra Angelico, Filippo Lippi, and Melozzo da Forlì. But it is the works of Venetian painter Carlo Crivelli that stand out, especially his unusual and emotionally intense *Pietá*. In Crivelli's painting, the Virgin Mary looks strangely demented as she both smiles and cries while staring into the face of her dead son. On the left, Mary Magdalene wails with her eyes fixed on Christ's pierced hand, while Saint John the Evangelist screams toward heaven.

The entire scene is bathed in a soft golden light and is set against a wallpaper-like background of angel heads and wings (cherubs on clouds). Crivelli's attention to decor and his use of very strong lines, especially in the hair, give the work a strikingly modern look, almost art nouveau.

The largest room, the one that literally marks the gallery's turning point, is dedicated

Nicolò e Giovanni, The Last Judgment

Bellini, Deposition

to the work of Raphael. Dim lighting protects the tapestries hanging on the walls. Based on Raphael's designs, these tapestries were woven in Brussels in 1515 and originally decorated the Sistine Chapel's presbytery.

The three large paintings in the Raphael room date from distinct periods of the artist's brief but brilliant career. On the right is the *Coronation of the Virgin*, one of the artist's earliest works. Painted in 1503 when Raphael was 20 years old and working in Perugia, it clearly shows the influence of Perugino, his teacher, whose *Resurrection of Christ* hangs in the previous room, as does a work by Raphael's father, Giovanni Santi.

On the left is the *Madonna of Foligno*, which was painted in 1512 after Raphael had come to Rome and had begun work on the frescoes in the Apostolic Palace. It was originally placed in the Church of Santa Maria in Aracoeli on the Capitoline Hill.

The central and most powerful work is Raphael's famous *Transfiguration*. Completed in 1520 for the Church of San Pietro in Montorio, it was his final painting and it testifies to the tremendous impact Michelangelo's Sistine Chapel frescoes had on other artists of the day.

This immense painting actually depicts two scenes: the *Transfiguration,* when Christ appeared before Peter, James, and John beside Moses and Elijah, and an episode from the Gospel of Matthew in which a possessed child is taken to the apostles to be healed. An extremely complex image, with many hands pointing in different directions and alarmed faces looking wildly about, it demands considerable attention. Happily, cushioned benches line the back wall and offer the opportunity for some comfortable contemplation and a little rest.

Of the two works on display in the next room, one is often a photographic reproduction (due to frequent loans to exhibitions abroad) of an unfinished sketch of Saint Jerome done around 1480 by Leonardo da Vinci. The other, Giovanni Bellini's *Deposition*, finished in 1471, may be the Pinacoteca's most beautiful painting. Bathed in a clear light, suggesting the influence of Piero della Francesca, Bellini shows Mary Magdalene holding Christ's limp hand and tenderly touching his wound. A somber and stoic Nicodemus stands straight and tall above them, while Joseph of Arimithea, his face partly hidden by Christ's, gently lays him in the tomb.

Moving on, the *seicento* (1600s) is represented by several notable artists, including Guido Reni and Nicholas Poussin, and by Caravaggio's version of the *Deposition*. Another work, an extremely interesting representation of *Peter's Denial of Christ*, is attributed to the school of Caravaggio.

Finally, if open, the small room of Byzantine icons is also well worth a visit.

FOCUS: VATICAN NECROPOLIS

By Gordon Ramsey

Necropolis

Few people are aware that Saint Peter's is built on top of an ancient city of the dead. The Necropolis, dating from the 1st to 4th centuries, can be visited by making reservations with the Vatican (see Further Information). To get to the excavations, you pass through an entrance in the thick foundation walls of the original Saint Peter's Basilica. This basilica, erected by Constantine but completed after his death in c. 349, was demolished in 1506 to make way for the construction of the current Saint Peter's.

Under the floor of the old basilica, archaeologists have unearthed a street lined with mausoleums. These burial chambers, richly decorated with fine stucco work, frescoes, and mosaics, testify to the wide range of gods that were worshipped in ancient Rome. Dionysius is the most commonly represented god, but there are also images of Jupiter and Minerva. One chamber shows an Egyptian deity holding the ahnk. Another mausoleum, built for a pagan family that later converted to Christianity, has a well-preserved mosaic of Christ pictured as a sun god driving a chariot.

The road rises as you walk west until you almost reach the level of the floor of Constantine's basilica. Here, lights illuminate a barely discernable and humble spot considered to be the grave of Saint Peter. Around A.D. 67, Peter is said to have been crucified upside down in Nero's Circus, which was located just to the south of the Necropolis. About a century later, a small funeral monument referred to as a trophy was erected on the site. However, it is now almost entirely hidden from view. The apse of Constantine's great basilica was built around the small monument, which was enclosed on three sides by marble slabs and remained visible to the congregation. During the building's later phases of construction, three altars were built over this shrine. The last one, built in 1615 for the new basilica, is called the Confession Altar and is located right under Bernini's grandiose canopy.

The tour ends when you pass through a door leading into the Vatican Grottoes, the chambers situated between the floor of the Old Saint Peter's Basilica and the nave of the new one. You can also reach the grottoes, where many popes are buried, from inside Saint Peter's through a passageway in the pillar of Saint Longinus under the dome.

FURTHER INFORMATION

Visits to the Necropolis under Saint Peter's require a little extra effort. You must make a reservation by fax or e-mail addressed to the Ufficio degli Scavi, Fabbrica di San Pietro, indicating the dates you would be available to take the tour, the number of people in the tour, the language of preference, and a contact number in Rome to confirm the booking. If you're going to be in Rome for a little while, you can make a reservation in person. To get to the booking office, walk through the Arch of the Bells on the left side of the basilica. Tell the Swiss Guard on duty that you want to go to the Soprintendenza degli Scavi.

The groups are small, and demand is high, so you are advised to book well in advance. The cost is €7.50 per person for a tour, which lasts about an hour and 15 minutes. Tours do not run on Sundays.

Reverenda Fabbrica di San Pietro
Basilica di San Pietro in Vaticano; tel.: 06-69885318; fax: 06-69885518; e-mail: uff.scavi@fabricsp.va.

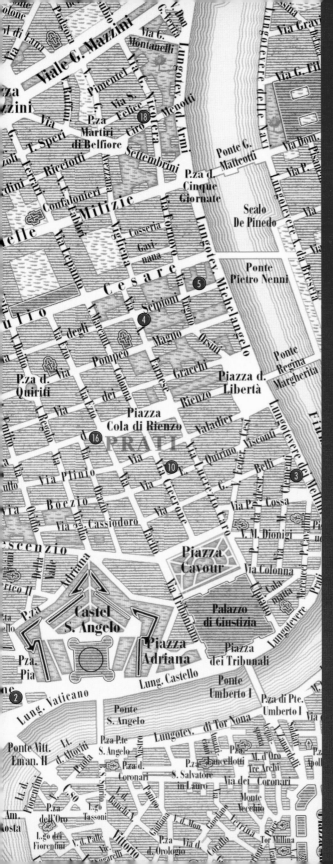

Vatican

Hotels & Inns
1 Hotel Atlante Garden
2 Hotel Columbus
3 Hotel dei Mellini
4 Hotel Farnese
5 Hotel Giulio Cesare
6 Hotel Sant'Anna

Restaurants & Cafés
7 Il Matriciano
8 Nuvolari
9 La Veranda dell'Hotel Columbus
10 Le Bouchon
11 Taverna Angelica*

Best of
12 Castroni, Via Cola de Rienzo, 196
13 De Carolis
14 La Tradizione
15 Ottaviani
16 Pellacchia
17 Rome Cavalieri Hilton
18 Tastevin

Hotel Atlante Garden

Via Crescenzio, 78/A; tel.: 06-6872361; e-mail: atlante.garden@atlantehotels.com; website: www.atlantehotels.com; category: ★★★★; number of rooms: 54; credit cards accepted: all major; facilities: parking (€35 a night); access to internet: direct-line (US, UK) telephone jack in all rooms; most beautiful rooms: 334 (single), 236 (double); €–€€.
☛Very elegant and comfortable. Its roof garden has a spectacular view of the city.

Hotel Columbus

Via della Conciliazione, 33; tel.: 06-6865435/ 6867796; e-mail: hotel.columbus@alfanet.it; category: ★★★★; number of rooms: 92, including 2 suites; credit cards accepted: all major; facilities: free parking; access to internet: a computer in the hotel can be used for internet; most beautiful room: 702; €€€.
☛Located in the 15th-century Palazzo Rovere, a medieval mansion of princes and cardinals transformed into a comfortable hotel. The rooms and salons have vaulted ceilings, wooded beams, and stuccoes, and are elegantly decorated.

Hotel dei Mellini

Via Muzio Clementi, 81; tel.: 06-324771/ 32477801; e-mail: info@hotelmellini. com; website: www.hotelmellini.com; category: ★★★★; number of rooms: 80, including 13 suites; credit cards accepted: all major; facilities: roof garden, parking (€25 a night), wheelchair access, no smoking floor; access to internet: fax, computer hook-up, and internet connection in all rooms; most beautiful rooms: 412 (double), 410 (suite); €€€–€€€€.
☛The hotel is located in a recently restored 19th-century building not too far from Saint Peter's Basilica. The furniture, decorations, and paintings provide elegance and comfort.

Hotel Farnese

Via Alessandro Farnese, 30; tel.: 06-3212553/ 3215129; e-mail: info@hotelfarnese.com; website: www.travel.it/roma/hotelfarnese; number of rooms: 23, including 1 suite; category: ★★★★; credit cards accepted: all major; facilities: free parking; access to internet: direct-line (US, UK) telephone jack in all rooms; most beautiful rooms: 46 (double), 45 (suite); €€–€€€.
☛What used to be an aristocratic residence is now the site of the Hotel Farnese, a quiet and homey hotel in the heart of Prati, one of Rome's most elegant residential districts. The palazzo, dating back to 1906, has been completely renovated. The hotel has an atrium lobby, an elegant hall featuring period furniture, and a breakfast lounge. Guest accommodations are spacious and offer modern amenities. Some rooms feature a private terrace.

Hotel Giulio Cesare

Via degli Scipioni, 287; tel.: 06-3210751/ 3211736; e-mail: giulioce@uni.net; website: www.hotelgiuliocesare.com; category: ★★★★; number of rooms: 90; credit cards accepted: all major; facilities: free parking; access to internet: direct-line telephone jack in all rooms; most beautiful rooms: 300 and 315; €€€.
☛A former residence of a countess, the hotel is decorated with antique furniture and tapestries. Breakfast is served in the beautiful garden, weather permitting.

Hotel Sant'Anna

Borgo Pio, 133; tel.: 06-68801602/68308717; e-mail: santanna@travel.it; website: www.hotelsantanna.com; category: ★★★; number of rooms: 20; credit cards accepted: all major; access to internet: direct-line (US, UK) telephone jack in all rooms; most beautiful rooms: third-floor rooms have terraces; €€.
☛In a recently restored, 16th-century palazzo, 100 yards from Saint Peter's Square.

Restaurants & Cafés

Il Matriciano

Via dei Gracchi, 55; tel.: 06-3212327; open: 12:30–3 P.M., 8–11:30 P.M.; closed: Wed. in the winter and Sat. in the summer; credit cards accepted: all major; €.

☛Located in the Prati neighborhood, it features *rigatoni all'amatriciana*, of course, but also water buffalo mozzarella, fried broccoletti, zucchini flowers, and *suppli* (rice dumplings) for appetizers. Traditional but good cuisine.

Nuvolari

Via degli Ombrellari, 10; tel.: 06-68803018; open: 6:30 P.M.–2 A.M.; closed: Sun.

☛On the corner of Via degli Ombrellari, named for the umbrella-makers that once populated the street, sits the bar Nuvolari, named for the famous race-car driver, Tazio Nuvolari, whose photo hangs from one of the bar's walls. It is both a wine and cocktail bar, with a good selection of vintages. Food is also served and with your drink you can have soup, carpaccio, salads, cheese, or sandwiches. With a candle on every table and jazz or blues playing (the music is neither too loud nor too soft), Nuvolari has an intimate and relaxing atmosphere.

Taverna Angelica

Borgo Vittorio, 14; tel.: 06-6874514; open 7:30 P.M.–midnight every day; closed: Sun.; €.

☛Each dish that leaves the kitchen of the Taverna Angelica receives lavish attention. To spend an evening there is to taste a bit of culinary heaven. In the summer you will find lighter dishes and more fish on the menu, including the *tagliolini* with squid and seafood. For dessert in the summer you should try the fresh dates with coffee cream. The menu is meatier and heavier during the colder winter months; their incredibly tender version of duck *à l'orange* is not to be missed. Call to reserve a table, especially on weekends.

Our Critic's Favorite Restaurants

Veranda dell'Hotel Columbus

Via della Conciliazione 33, tel.: 06-6865435; fax: 06-6864874; open: 12:30–3:30 P.M., 7:30–11:30 P.M. every day; €.

☛This restaurant owes its charm to the lovely namesake veranda in Palazzo della Rovere, with tables flanked by fruit trees. Diners will be no less impressed by the elegant windows on the courtyard. Dinner is served by candlelight in front of a fresco attributed to Pinturicchio. The menu includes an interesting mix of creative cuisine like zucchini blossoms stuffed with lobster, risotto with lamb and greens, and a cured pork *lonza* stuffed with beans. Among the sweets, top honors go to the chocolate flan with citrus garnish.

Le Bouchon

Via Cicerone, 55/C, tel.: 06-35761; open: Mon.–Sat. 12:30–3 P.M., 7:30 P.M.–midnight; €.

☛Hotel Cicerone's Le Bouchon has a Mediterranean menu, with Chef Giuseppe Settimi preparing his "seasonal temptations" in the summer. The variegated menu ranges from a selection of salads to creative dishes like the macaroni fritter with pesto and scamorza cheese, chicken and eggplant strudel with green bean ragu, and zucchini stuffed with beef and olives.

A Modern Mosaicist
By Laura Collura Kahn

Roberto Grieco's lucky break came 23 years ago, thanks to his mother. On her way to the Vatican to buy coins and stamps for her collections, she would walk through the mosaic workshops there. On every visit, she would beg the chief master to hire her son, a graduate of the Fine Arts Academy. After several months of such visits, the master caved in and granted a trial period. That was in 1978, and Roberto Grieco has worked there ever since. Now 45, Grieco works six days a week, eight hours a day, in the Vatican workshop, and also runs his own mosaic store on the Via Sistina in the afternoon.

He is fortunate enough to work for what is arguably the most prestigious mosaic workshop in the world: the Studio Vaticano del Mosaico, founded in the late 16th century, when Pope Gregory XIII ordered the decoration of the Gregorian Chapel in Saint Peter's Basilica.

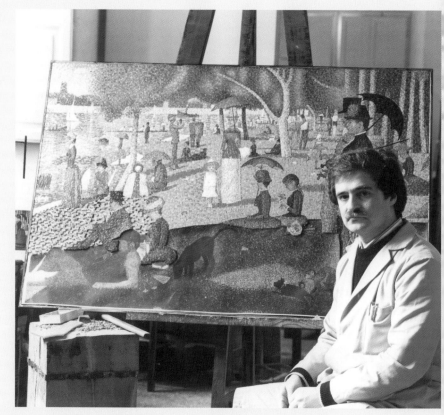

Grieco in front of one of his works

Over the decades, the studio grew into a precious warehouse of mosaic enamel glass, as the artists working there were encouraged to experiment and created every conceivable hue of every color. In the 1600s, for example, a variety of yellow shades was created. In the 1700s, some 80 types of red saw the light, and the secret formula was deposited in the Vatican archives. As a result, the studio can now draw on a supply of some 28,000 colors, many of which were made centuries ago.

Grieco considers himself very lucky. The type of work that is produced at the studio would be unthinkable anywhere else. The artisans work with the traditional techniques—no computers or modern materials. The methods are virtually unchanged from the 19th century.

The original site was turned into a garage, so the studio is today an austere laboratory tucked in a building next to the Vatican's famed Paolo VI Hall, where the pope holds important ceremonies.

Though it sells its work to a few select clients, the studio primarily produces mosaic landscapes or portraits for the pope, who uses them as gifts for heads of state and other personalities he visits with or who visit him at the Vatican. These are mainly reproductions of famous works of art by masters such as Caravaggio, Raphael, or Guercino, or even the 19th-century Impressionists. Also, the pope often brings views of Rome in mosaic form as presents, and those, too, are done by the studio.

In addition, the Vatican workshop makes marble mosaics, fashioned in the style of ancient Rome, that are normally sold and used as tables.

PAVLVS QVINTVS PONTIFEX MAXIMVS
AQVAM IN AGRO BRACCIANENSI
SALVBERRIMIS E FONTIBVS COLLECTAM
VETERIBVS AQVAE ALSIETINAE DVCTIBVS RESTITVTI
NOVISQVE ADDITIS
XXXV AB MILLIARIO DVXIT

IO DOMINI MDCXII PONTIFICATVS SVI SEP

Trastevere/ Gianicolo

By Ruth Kaplan

Rome's Trastevere neighborhood (literally, "across the Tiber") is a densely populated network of crisscrossed alleys known for being both traditional and trendy. The quiet residential streets east of Viale di Trastevere are centered around the **Santa Cecilia in Trastevere**, a church and convent known for its peaceful courtyard and remains of Pietro Cavallini's spectacular 1293 fresco of the *Last Judgment*. Across the viale, the **Santa Maria in Trastevere** church and piazza constitute the social and religious heart of the neighborhood. Founded in the Roman era, the church has been a destination for pilgrims throughout the centuries. Its 13th-century outdoor mosaics glimmer over the piazza, whose central fountain and sheer size make it one of Rome's most inviting.

Just beyond Trastevere is the Janiculum Hill, now a green network of parks and monuments with one of the best views of Rome's skyline. On the way uphill is **San Pietro in Montorio**, an early medieval oratory rebuilt in the late 15th century. Next door is the **Tempietto di Bramante**, a well-balanced, domed structure designed by Bramante on the supposed site of Saint Peter's crucifixion.

Near San Pietro in Montorio the **Fontana dell'Acqua Paola** (see American Academy entry), or simply the "Fontanone," as it is commonly called, marks the first great spot to view the city down below. The fountain was built in 1610 to celebrate the renovation of Trajan's aqueduct, and incorporates columns from Old Saint Peter's Basilica.

The curved piazza leads into the wooded park on the **Passeggiata del Gianicolo**, the long stretch of road that cuts across the Janiculum ridge all the way back to the Tiber. This path leads through tree-lined lawns to the enormous equestrian statue honoring Giuseppe Garibaldi, who fought here in the 19th century to make Rome the capital of a united and independent Italy.

Some of the oldest bridges crossing the Tiber are only open to pedestrian traffic. The flagstone-paved **Ponte Sisto** is one of the most picturesque, built in the 3rd century and redone in the 15th. In Piazza Trilussa, facing Ponte Sisto, is the other Fontana dell'Acqua Paola, known as the Fontanone di Ponte Sisto.

One river crossing takes you onto the **Isola Tiberina**, an island in the middle of the Tiber with an active hospital and church on it. The 1st century B.C. **Ponte Fabricio** links the island to the Jewish Ghetto on the east side of the Tiber. There are views here of **Il Ponte Rotto**, a one-arched fragment of a 179 B.C. bridge that once spanned the river.

Left, Fontana dell'Acqua Paola

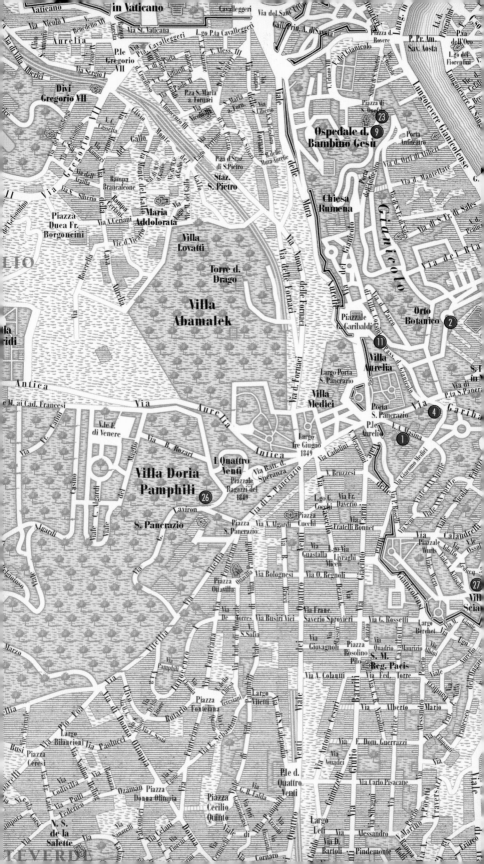

Ponte Fabricio and Isola Tiberina

Isola Tiberina (Tiber Island)

➤ This small island of volcanic origin in the middle of the Tiber was of exceptional relevance to the birth and development of Rome. According to tradition, the island was formed by the grain from the royal properties in Campus Martius (Field of Mars) that were thrown into the river by the people as a sign of contempt for the last king, who was overthrown.

In the 3rd century B.C., the island became the center of worship of Aesculapius, the god of medicine. The temple erected in his honor was located on the present site of the Church of San Bartolomeo and was flanked with porticoes in which the sick awaited healing. Its detached position from the rest of the community made the island an ideal destination for a place of healing. The Fatebenefratelli Hospital, opened in 1548, remains on the island today.

In the 1st century B.C. the layout of the island was modified and artificially molded into the shape of a ship. A section of the prow is still visible on the side facing the valley. Two bridges connecting the island to the mainland were built in the same period. The Ponte Fabricio is still intact; the Ponte Cestio—originally built in 46 B.C. by Lucius Cestius—was restored

in the 4th century by the emperors Valentinian, Valente, and Gratian, and completely redone at the end of the 1800s.

Passeggiata del Gianicolo (Janiculum Promenade)

➤ The road traveling over the Janiculum Hill is lined with statues, shrubs, and well-kept gardens, and affords delightful views of Rome. An equestrian statue of Giuseppe Garibaldi crowns the summit of the hill overlooking the city.

Ponte Fabricio

➤ This is the oldest bridge in Rome built with blocks of tufa and peperino. It was built in 62 B.C. by Lucius Fabricius, the commissioner of roads, and remains virtually intact, although in the 2nd century it was restored by replacing the original travertine facade with bricks. It is also known as Ponte dei Quattro Capi, literally "the bridge of four heads," because of the two four-faced sculptures that decorate the parapets. Below the parapets, on both sides, are carved inscriptions praising Fabricius. It has been restored several times as it was repeatedly damaged by floods. During the Middle Ages, it was called Pons Judaeorum, Jews' Bridge, after the nearby Ghetto.

Il Ponte Rotto (The Broken Bridge)

➢ Il Ponte Rotto was the first stone bridge in Rome. Started in 181 B.C., it was completed in 142 B.C. Restored and overhauled on several occasions, it finally collapsed in 1598. In 1886, two of the three surviving arches were destroyed to allow the construction of a new bridge, the Ponte Palatino.

Ponte Sisto

➢ Pope Sixtus IV ordered the Ponte Sisto built in 1474 and paid for it with taxes paid by prostitutes. (During the Renaissance, Rome had a huge number of prostitutes. According to historians, in 1490, the number of official prostitutes, not including concubines, totaled 6,800, in a city of 50,000 people.) The previous bridge, built by Emperor Antoninus Caracalla and restored by Valentinian in 366–367, had been destroyed by floods. Architect Baccio Pontelli incorporated in the first arch, on the side of Trastevere, the remains of Pons Aurelius. In the center of the bridge there is a big, round hole that Romans call the *occhialone*, that served to alert the city of coming floods. Whenever water reached it, it meant that the river passed the safety level.

San Pietro in Montorio

Piazza San Pietro in Montorio, 2; tel.: 06-5813940; open: daily 7:30 A.M.–noon, 4–6 P.M.; if closed, ring bell at door to right of church.

➢ The earliest mention of San Pietro in Montorio occurs in the 9th century. For many centuries, this was venerated as the place of Saint Peter's martyrdom. The present church was built at the close of the 15th century by Ferdinand and Isabella of Spain, following the plans of architect Baccio Pontelli. In 1849, it was restored again. The name derives from the ancient Latin name for the Janiculum Hill—Mons Aureus, Mount of Gold, so-called because of the yellow sand that could be seen at twilight.

The facade of the church—typical of a time when crisp, geometrically inspired classical architecture was fashionable—has a Gothic rose window. Inside, there is a single nave with three bays and two main

chapels. The following works are worth noting: *The Flagellation of Jesus,* in the first chapel on the right, by Sebastiano del Piombo (1518) probably based on an initial drawing by Michelangelo; *Conversion of Saint Paul* by Giorgio Vasari—who depicted himself as the figure in black on the left edge—in the fourth chapel on the right; and *Saint Francis Transported by Angels* by Francesco Baratta, which can be found on the altar of the second chapel on the left. The altar balustrade has some superb columns of *giallo antico* found in the House of Sallust, near the Porta Salaria. The view of Rome from the front of the church is enchanting, and tempts one to linger in this beautiful spot.

Santa Cecilia in Trastevere

Piazza di Santa Cecilia; tel.: 06-5899289; open: daily 9 A.M.–1 P.M., 2–7 P.M.; admission: €2.

➢ Initially the house of Cecilia, the young martyr who lived in the 3rd century A.D., and her husband Valerian, also a saint and a martyr, the Church of Saint Cecilia in Trastevere was built by Pope Paschal I in 821 and embellished between the 11th and 13th centuries with a bell tower, a cloister, part of the convent, the frescoes on the inside facade, and the ciborium. It was built around the remains of a *caldari-*

San Pietro in Montorio

um, a room with hot baths. It was in this room that Saint Cecilia was placed and exposed to steam for three days in an attempt to suffocate her. She refused to die and sang throughout the terrible ordeal—thus becoming the patron saint of music—until she was finally beheaded. Her body was found in 1595 and immortalized in the famous statue beneath the altar by sculptor Stefano Maderno in 1600.

An entrance believed to have been designed by the Florentine architect Ferdinando Fuga leads into a huge courtyard extending before the church. The portico of the church extends in front of the facade and still has a 12th-century mosaic frieze. Inside the church, on its left wall, there is a vestibule with a monument to Cardinal Nicolò Forteguerri by Mino da Fiesole. From the right aisle (through a frescoed corridor) you reach a room believed to be the *caldarium,* which contains paintings by the Bolognese painter Guido Reni. On the altar of this room is Reni's *The Decapitation of Saint Cecilia.* In the center of the presbytery is the ciborium, or altar canopy, by Gothic sculptor Arnolfo di Cambio, signed and dated 1293. In the apse, the outstanding 9th-century mosaic of Saint Paul, Saint Cecilia, Pope Paschal I, Saint Peter, Saint Valerian, and Saint Agatha flanking Christ giving a benediction was commissioned by Pope Paschal I. The splendid *Last Judgment,* a huge fresco by Pietro Cavallini (1289–1293), can be admired by entering the choir of the nuns. The fresco is the greatest masterpiece of Roman medieval painting and marks the passage from the great Byzantine tradition to the birth of Giotto's modern style.

SANTA MARIA IN TRASTEVERE

Piazza Santa Maria in Trastevere; tel.: 06-5814802; open: daily 7:30 A.M.–1 P.M., 4–7 P.M.

➤ The history of Santa Maria in Trastevere reaches further back than the time of Constantine. The historian Lampridius relates that during the pontificate of Callistus I, the Christians were in possession of a place of assembly in Trastevere, their rights to which, however, were disputed by the corporation of *popinarii,* or tavern-keepers. The question was brought before the emperor Alexander

Santa Maria in Trastevere

Severus, who decided in favor of the Christians, saying that it was better that God should be worshipped there, in whatever fashion it might be, than that the place should be given over to revelry.

The original oratory was erected in the 3rd century by the pope Saint Callixtus I. Pope Julius I rebuilt it on a larger scale in c. 340, and this Julian basilica was restored and adorned with frescoes by Pope John VII (705–707). It was re-erected in its present form by Innocent II in 1140.

The mosaic in the facade is from the 13th to 14th centuries. It represents the Virgin Mary and child enthroned, with female figures approaching them. Almost at the top of the bell tower is a small mosaic of the Madonna and child, probably also of the 12th century. The altar, which is of the time of Innocent II (1130–1143), is overshadowed by an arcaded canopy resting on four columns of porphyry. The beautiful mosaics of the apse were also commissioned by Innocent II. He was a member of the Papareschi family, whose palace was located in Trastevere. There are also seven mosaic pictures illustrating subjects from the life of the Virgin Mary, a 13th-century work of Pietro Cavallini, who displays a level of absolute novelty and excellence here. At the end of the right aisle is the Chapel of Our Lady di Strada Cupa, named after the street where Perugino's picture was formerly venerated. Domenichino designed the chapel and painted in the vaulting the charming figure of a child scattering flowers. Domenichino is also responsible for the ceiling of the basilica with the Assumption painted on copper at the center.

TEMPIETTO DI BRAMANTE

Piazza San Pietro in Montorio; tel.: 06-5813940; open: daily 8 A.M.–noon, 4–6 P.M.
➤ The Tempietto di Bramante, designed by Donato Bramante, was built between 1502–1507 to commemorate the place of Saint Peter's martyrdom. In 1605 the roof was redesigned and modified, while Gian Lorenzo Bernini, in 1628, designed the entrance to the crypt. The harmony of Tempietto's volume, proportions, and dimension made it a model for 16th-century buildings in Rome. Bramante's outstanding handling of the geometric elements of the circle and cylinder is regarded as the epitome of the synthesis between the Renaissance and ancient Rome. Inside, on the altar, stands a 16th-century statue of Saint Peter. At the end of Bernini's stairs is the place where Saint Peter's cross is said to have stood. It is surrounded by a stucco decoration by Giovanni Francesco Rossi, which narrates the saint's life.

Tempietto di Bramante

Walking Tour 1:

Exploring Trastevere and Its Churches

By Beagan Wilcox

Trastevere, one of Rome's most picturesque and beloved neighborhoods, sits on a bend in the Tiber River's winding course. The name, Trastevere, which means "across the Tiber," also gives one an idea of the ancient Romans's geographical orientation. Trastevere lies across the river from the heart of the city, where the city government—in all its various forms throughout the ages—has always been situated.

But the *Trasteverini*, inhabitants of the riverbank neighborhood, have never gazed enviously across the Tiber's waters at the other side. On the contrary, historically they have been fiercely proud, to the extent of isolationism. Into the 14th century, contact between *Trasteverini* and people from across the river was limited. Even in the 1800s, some *Trasteverini* liked to claim that they had never crossed the Tiber.

Since 1870, when a wide thoroughfare running right through the center of the neighborhood was built (and appropriately called Viale Trastevere), the divided halves of Trastevere have slowly acquired different characters, like twins who have grown apart in their later years. The northern part, which lies closer to the Vatican, has become a hub of social activity, attracting many tourists and boasting an active nightlife. The southern part does not receive the same number of visitors. In the evening, it is still possible to walk the area's cobbled streets without jostling against other strollers or the wares of the numerous street peddlers who flock to the piazzas and streets on the northern side of Viale Trastevere.

During the day, one can wander the neighborhood's quiet streets, peeking into artisans' workshops and bakeries—the doors are often flung wide open. The area is

San Crisogono

also home to several of Rome's loveliest small churches, which feel unexpectedly intimate amidst the intimidating grandeur of many of Rome's other, larger churches.

A Romanesque campanile (bell tower), jutting into the sky above the church, reveals that **San Crisogono** has older origins than its baroque facade suggests. Inside, baroque mingles with Romanesque, giving the church a solemn but colorful air. Light streams through several of the high windows, falling in patches on the splendid, bright Cosmatesque pavement from the 12th century. In contrast, the ceiling, a royal blue with ornate gold-leaf design, is from the 1620s; at the very center lies a copy of Guercino's *Triumph of San Crisogono*, now in London. The apse contains a mosaic fragment of the *Virgin and Child between the Saints Crisogono and Giacomo*, dating from the 13th century, in the style of Cavallini.

The front and side doors of the church constantly swing open and closed as numerous parishioners dart into the church for a moment of repose while going about their daily business. Once inside, the loud honking and zooming of traffic on Viale Trastevere is drowned out by the church's cloak of hushed silence.

Excavations begun in 1907, and continued sporadically throughout the century, have revealed the church's ancient foundations; these paleo-Christian remains can be seen by going to the sacristy at the far left end of the church and then descending into the musty depths. After making a small donation, without which one will remain in the dark, visitors can see part of the ancient church, with traces of frescoes dating from the 8th to the 11th centuries, and some inscriptions believed to be from the cemetery of Pancrazio on via Aurelia.

Viale Trastevere will seem unusually loud after emerging from a visit to Rome's dark netherworld below San Crisogono. Quickly cross the street, headed toward the cinema, and duck into the calmer, narrow Via della Lungaretta. A less-prominent campanile, that of the **Church of Santa Maria della Luce**, rises there above the orange-tiled roofs on Via della Lungaretta. The church's facade lies on Vicolo della Luce, which intersects with Via della Lungaretta on the right. A small plaque at the entrance informs visitors of the church's brief visiting hours (see Further Information). However, on weekdays, those who want to see the church can ring the bell at No. 22A on Via della Lungaretta. After a few minutes, a clergy member will appear and usher visitors through a courtyard and into the church.

As its name suggests, light fills the small church. The central nave curves elegantly upward to a large oval window located directly above the pews. Two smaller naves flank the larger one, holding some interesting works of art, including a 16th-century representation of the Madonna della Luce. With its cream-colored, luminous late-baroque interior, the church feels cheerful and welcoming.

Originally, the church was named for Saint Salvatore. But, as legend has it, in 1730 a blind man suddenly regained his sight while praying before a painting of the Madonna close to the church. The man yelled, "Light, light!," and the faithful quickly gathered around. From then on, the church parishioners have addressed their prayers not only to Saint Salvatore but to the

Bernini, Ludovica Albertoni

Madonna as well. A leaflet about the church explains that other miracles followed that first divine illumination.

Via della Lungaretta opens into one of the few large piazzas in the area—Piazza in Piscinula, named for the ruins of some classical baths which supposedly still lie beneath the cobblestones. The tiny **Church of San Benedetto in Piscinula**, at the far end of the long, rectangular piazza, is said to sit atop the remains of the Domus Aniciorum, the luxurious residence of the important Anicii family. In the late Middle Ages, according to legend, Saint Benedict lived for a time with this noble family.

The church's modest neoclassical facade was designed by Pietro Camporese the Younger in 1844, replacing the former baroque design. The small campanile holds two bells, one of which is believed to be the smallest in all of Rome; it is also almost 2,000 years old, according to an inscription on its body dated 1069. To enter the church, one must ring the bell at No. 40. A nun will come to the door and escort visitors through a small, dark vestibule where, according to legend, Saint Benedict prayed and slept.

Usually one immediately looks upward in a church—toward the altar and stained glass—but in the shadowy chapel of San Benedetto in Piscinula, one is first compelled to look at the bright oranges, yellows, and pinks of the remaining patches of 12th-century pavement, with its beautiful serpentine design. The eye then slowly travels to the chapel's vaulted ceiling, supported by antique columns. A single altar is adorned with a 14th-century painting of Saint Benedict. An early 14th-century Venetian Madonna and child on the altar itself is especially adored, because it is believed that Saint Benedict prayed before the painting.

It is the traveler's instinct to purposely wander off course and the beautiful streets between the Church of San Benedetto in Piscinula and that of San Francesco a Ripa lend themselves to such exploration. One street along the way—Vicolo dell'Atleta—deserves particular attention. Located behind the

Church of San Benedetto in Piscinula, it is usually quiet and empty. Named for a Greek statue of an athlete unearthed there in 1844 (now in the Vatican Museums), the street is lined with well-maintained medieval, Renaissance, and modern buildings. On one corner, at No. 14, is a marvelous brick medieval building. It is believed to have been a synagogue, the oldest of the many once located in the area which was home to a flourishing Jewish population until 1555, when the city's Jews were ordered by papal edict to move across the river (to what became known as the Ghetto).

At the end of Vicolo dell'Atleta, turn to the right onto Via dei Genovesi, and then to the left onto Via Anicia, which leads to the spacious Piazza San Francesco d'Assisi, a square filled with large potted palms. Saint Francis lodged in the Saint Biagio hospice that adjoins the church, but **San Francesco a Ripa** was actually founded by Count Pandolfo dell'Anguillara and given to the Franciscan order in 1229. In 1682 it was completely rebuilt by Mattia De Rossi.

Near the sacristy is a series of beautiful 15th-century tombstones of the Anguillata family, while the Pallavicini-Rospigliosi Chapel, in the right transept, has an unusual example of late-baroque sculpture, representing a macabre dance with skeletons that play with the tombstones and the portraits of the dead.

The church has gained renown because it houses the statue of the Blessed Ludovica Albertoni, one of Bernini's famous late works, executed in 1671–1675. The statue rests in the last chapel of the left aisle; the supple folds of Ludovica's marble robes and her expression of ecstasy continue to awe the many art historians who flock to the church. A more recent addition to the church is the Tomb of Giorgio De Chirico (1888–1978), found at the other end of the left aisle and adorned with the words *"Pictor Optimus."*

Like most places of worship run by the Franciscans, the church has a tranquil, almost homey feeling. A cat sleeps in a square of sun behind the wooden pews. According to the afternoon custodian, an older and chatty woman, the tiger cat, named *Briciola,* (crumb), also attends morning mass, placing herself directly beneath the altar. The legacy of Saint Francis lives on.

Further Information

San Benedetto in Piscinula
Piazza in Piscinula, 40; tel.: 06-5818297; open: Nov. 1–Mar. 31, 7–10 A.M., 4:30–5:30 P.M., Apr. 1–Oct. 31, 4:30–6:30 P.M., Weekday mass: 8 A.M., Sun. and public holidays: 9 A.M.

San Crisogono
Piazza Sonnino, 44; tel.: 06-5818225; open: Mon.–Sat. 7 A.M.– 7:30 P.M., Sun. 8 A.M.–1 P.M., 4:15–7:30 P.M.

San Francesco a Ripa
Piazza San Francesco d'Assisi, 88; tel.: 06-5819020; open: daily 7:30 A.M.–noon, 4–7 P.M.

Santa Maria della Luce
Via della Luce; open: Sat.–Sun. 11 A.M.–6 P.M. and Sat. evenings, on weekdays ring the bell at Via della Lungaretta, 22A.

Chiostro della confraternita di San Giovanni Battista dei Genovesi, Via Anicia, 12; tel.: 06-5812416.

By Beagan Wilcox

Cloister of San Giovanni

A small plaque attached to the door of No. 12 Via Anicia informs visitors of the cloister's odd visiting hours: Tuesdays and Thursdays from 3:00 to 6:00 P.M. (Note that the cloisters are closed the entire month of August.) Ring the bell during those hours and the guardian will slowly swing back the heavy doors, allowing visitors to enter the verdant confines. This exquisitely beautiful cloister was built in the second half of the 15th century probably by Baccio Pontelli. During the hot summer months, the cloister offers a cool oasis of shade and calm from the hot streets of Rome.

Octagonal columns support a double loggia which surrounds a well-kept garden with orange trees standing at the periphery close to the columns and rose bushes, rosemary, and palms interspersed throughout. Two paths crisscross the garden, but unfortunately, visitors are not allowed to walk on them. However, there are several benches surrounding the garden, providing resting places for the weary.

At the center of the garden is a well from the 1400s, flanked by two Ionic columns from which hangs its dipper. Water from the well is now used only for the garden's plants, which seem to have enjoyed persistent attention throughout the centuries. A column a few yards to the right of the entrance bears a Latin inscription that records the 1588 planting of a palm in the cloister by P. A. Lanza of Savona.

Every year, on June 24, the cloister opens to the public for an entire day for the *festa* of the patron saint, Saint John the Baptist. In the early evening there is a short performance in the usually off-limits garden, followed by a reception.

Walking Tour 2:

The Treasures of the Janiculum Hill: Villa Sciarra & Rome's Botanical Gardens

By Beagan Wilcox

Villa Sciarra and Rome's Botanical Gardens, formerly Villa Corsini, both on the Janiculum Hill, are less well-known—and less frequently visited—than the larger and grander Villa Borghese or Villa Pamphilj. Yet, their quiet charms and startling beauty will enchant even the most demanding connoisseur of Rome's parks.

Tucked away in a quiet part of Trastevere, the entrance to the **Botanical Gardens** is found at the end of Via Corsini. A one-euro ticket is required to enter, but with this fee comes a map of the garden and a partial list of species found in each area. The Botanical Gardens is home to over 3,500 species of flora, many of which are well marked.

Only since 1883 has the swath of land on the Janiculum Hill been home to Rome's Botanical Gardens, which were formerly located on the Esquiline Hill. Prior to that the area was the grounds of the nearby villa owned first by the Riario family—who cultivated a vineyard there—and then by the Corsini family.

Walking into the Botanical Gardens, one slowly leaves behind the tumult of the outside world, only reminded of its existence by the occasional whine of a distant siren. In the morning, loud whining or cries may sometimes arise from within the Botanical Gardens because of the many toddlers brought there by their mothers or nannies. For the most part, though, the sounds of birds twittering and the gurgle of fountains prevail.

Near the entrance, on the right, is an area that was once used to exercise the Riario and Corsini families' horses, who ran laps around what is now a tangled bed of prickly pears and other cacti. Continuing along the path, one comes upon the Monumental Greenhouse, which houses a magnificent collection of orchids and a small collection of carnivorous plants.

The Corsini Greenhouse, which lies adjacent to the larger Monumental Greenhouse, was built in the early 1800s and was the first heated greenhouse on the villa's grounds. Inside is the succulent plant collection. Several plants grow from an enormous marble tub that is believed to have been used by Queen Christina of Sweden, the villa's most infamous inhabitant.

Queen Christina, who gave up her throne at the age of 27 and was received into the Roman Catholic Church, rented the villa from the Riario family in 1659 until her death there in 1689. Known for her wit and intelligence, she frequently donned male attire and took delight in shocking people with her sexual exploits. Indeed, it is believed that she ordered the construction of the Monumental Staircase found in the middle of the Botanical Gardens in order to more easily reach a small love nest—the Casino del Gianicolo, the scene of her seductions—perched on the upper part of the Janiculum. The casino was destroyed in the early 1900s and replaced by a statue of Garibaldi; however, one of the enormous plane trees near the Monumental Staircase past which Christina led her lovers is still there. It is 350 to 400 years old—one of the oldest plane trees in Rome.

The desire to climb the Monumental Staircase may not be as urgent for many visitors as it was for the Queen of Sweden. Instead, following the path from the base of the staircase to the right, one finds a forest of towering oaks and maples with patches of sunlight straining through the branches. It is believed to be the last remnant of the forest once covering all of Rome. The path winds through the forest and to the top of the Botanical Gardens, where there are splendid views of the city. At the very top there is a Japanese garden, complete with a small pagoda, ideal for resting from the climb. Going back down the Janiculum Hill, the path curves through a large shady bamboo stand, past a rose garden and a small garden for the blind that has aromatic plants with Braille labels.

Villa Sciarra

Benches are strategically scattered throughout the Botanical Gardens and it is one of the most pleasant places in Rome to spend several hours reading, writing, or simply enjoying the beauty and tranquillity.

Shady **Villa Sciarra** has steep slopes, with a lower part where the grass grows long and wild, and an upper part, which is more manicured and populated by numerous statues and fountains of fauns, centaurs, satyrs, and nymphs who lend the place a playful and mysterious air.

The villa owes its name to the Sciarras of Carbognano, who owned the land from 1749 until the mid-1800s, when Maffeo Sciarra made a series of faulty financial speculations and had to sell off

Botanical Gardens

parcels of the family's property. In 1849 Garibaldi's troops battled in the villa and several of the walkways bear the names of those valiant patriots.

After passing though the hands of various owners, Villa Sciarra was bought by the American diplomat George Wurts, known for his passion for Italian art. With the help of his wealthy wife, Henrietta Tower, Wurts transformed the place with rare plants, a flock of peacocks, and his own rich collection of art. He also filled the villa with the fountains and statues we find there today, all brought from a Lombard villa.

Upon the death of his wife, Wurts donated Villa Sciarra to the Italian state in 1930. Thirteen years later, during the October 1943 deportation, some of Rome's Jews found refuge in the depths of the villa while the Nazis searched for them throughout the city.

Next to a small merry-go-round, where children gleefully play attended by their *nonni* or grandparents, are some quiet echoes of Villa Sciarra's splendid past: Twelve statues representing the months of the year, each with its own distinct character, emerge behind a half circle of hedge. Farther up, a romantic walkway along the very top of the villa is lined with cypress trees on one side and roses on the other.

In the farthest corner of Villa Sciarra, pomegranate, orange, and almond trees are the remaining traces of the period in the early 1700s when many kinds of fruit were cultivated there for market. Far below, with Piazza Venezia in the distance and the green of the Aventine Hill across the way, lies the spectacular panorama of the rooftops of Rome.

FURTHER INFORMATION

Botanical Gardens/Villa Corsini
Largo Cristina di Svezia, 24; tel.: 06-49917107; open: 9:30 A.M.–6:30 P.M. (summer); 9:30 A.M.–5:30 P.M. (winter); closed: Sun., Mon., and month of Aug.; admission: €2.

Villa Sciarra
Open: sunrise to sunset.

Largo 3 Giugno 1849; open: sunrise to sunset.

Villa Pamphilj

By Beagan Wilcox

Joggers are dogged athletes, and the beauty of their activity is the possibility of practicing anywhere. But in Rome the streets are busy, the sidewalks are narrow, and the exhaust gas from cars and mopeds abundant. So, our suggestion is: when in Rome, do as the Romans do and go jogging in the parks.

Villa Pamphilj, located on the very top of the Janiculum Hill, is Rome's largest park and a favorite destination of the city's joggers. Starting under the dusty pink archway of its entrance, we suggest you follow the curving path down to the left, where you will run past the ivy-covered remains of an aqueduct built by Pope Paul V in the 17th century. The path remains on high ground, while below you will see a wild profusion of green, the "Valley of the Deer," to the left, fenced off from the public. A water fountain on the left is the first of several scattered throughout the villa.

After a short distance, you will pass through another smaller gateway with wrought-iron doors. A long, shady, narrow avenue lies in front of you, lined with olive, oak, and palm trees. As the path opens into a wider space, turn right onto the Avenue of the Fountain of Venus. The tall walls of the Casino del Bel Respiro (or, roughly, the "House of Fresh Air") rise on the right, with cheerful potted orange trees on top of the walls and young sapling orange trees growing below. The Fountain of Venus lies within a small grotto at the original entrance to the estate; bubbling water and the play of shimmering light on the ceiling of the grotto soothe the senses.

Enclosed within high walls and iron gates, the casino is off-limits to the public, but after climbing two long flights of stairs to a large plateau of playing fields, you should stop for a moment to look back at it from above, and admire its beds of elegant parterre gardens and its small lily-padded pond.

Continue to the right on the dusty but shady path that runs along the entire edge of the playing fields. Leaving them behind, you will come to a junction in the path, presided over by a waterless fountain with Neptune, lying on his side, clasping a small city in his arms. If you go straight you will run through a less-traveled area, suited for long-distance runners. Veering to the left you will catch sight of a green glimmer below—the Lago del Giglio, or "Lake of the Lily," where hundreds of little turtles skim the surface of the water.

The path hugs one side of the lake (the other side is forest) and then starts to climb a small hill. Once you reach the top, you will find yourself back at the playing fields, above the Casino del Bel Respiro.

Other Points of Interest

AMERICAN ACADEMY

Via Angelo Masina, 5; tel.: 06-58461; fax: 06-5810788.

➢ The American Academy, situated on the top of the Janiculum Hill, consists of 10 buildings and 11 acres of beautiful gardens. Villa Aurelia, built in 1650, hosts academy conferences and meetings, while Casa Rustica, a small farmhouse built at the end of the 16th century, offers a prime place to study. To the west of the academy is Porta San Pancrazio, the 17th-century gate, which replaced the ancient Porta Aurelia. To the east is the Fontana dell'Acqua Paola, built on a panoramic terrace by Flaminio Ponzio.

PALAZZO CORSINI (SEE MUSEUM ENTRY FOR GALLERIA NAZIONALE D'ARTE ANTICA)

Via della Lungara, 10; tel.: 06-6880232.

➢ Originally commissioned by Cardinal Raffaele Riario in 1511, Palazzo Corsini became the residence of Swedish Queen Christina in the 17th century. Christina encouraged the development of an artistic culture. In 1690, poet Agostine Taia mentioned the idea of "renewing the spirit of Arcadia," a pastoral region in ancient Greece, while at the palace with the former queen. She took him up on it, deciding to create a new literary academy called Accademia dell'Arcadia. In 1738, two years after the Corsini family acquired the building, architect Ferdinando Fuga built a new facade. The Galleria Nazionale d'Arte Antica is located in the palace and houses works by Beato Angelico, Murillo, Caravaggio, Guido Reni, Rubens, and Salvator Rosa.

Besides the Galleria, the palazzo is home to the Biblioteca Corsiniana, known for its refined collection of scripts, and the Accademia Nazionale dei Lincei, the most prestigious Italian academy, founded in 1603 by Federico Cesi.

SAN BARTOLOMEO ALL'ISOLA

Isola Tiberina; tel.: 06-6877973.

➢ On the ruins of the temple of Aesculapius, the church was erected in the 10th century at the request of the Holy Roman Emperor Otto III. Only the well, located on the steps of the presbytery, and the capitals in the crypt remain as evidence of Otto's church.

It was rebuilt in 1583–1585, possibly by Martino Longhi the Elder, after the flood of 1557. It was further renovated, baroque style, in 1623 and most recently in 1973–1976. The facade, credited to either Orazio Torriani or Martino Longhi the Younger, has a fragment of a mosaic dating from the period of Pope Alexander III, in the late 12th century. The bell tower, one of the most harmonious of the Romanesque period, dates from 1113, when the church was first restored by Pope Pascal II. The nave and the two columns are lined with pillars, probably from the ancient temple. At the center of the stairs in the presbytery, either by Nicolò di Angelo or Pietro Vassalletto, the marble well head was probably used as a health-giving spring. A porphyry basin near the altar has the remains of the apostle and martyr Bartholomew, most famous for his miraculous healing during his evangelist work. On the right of the presbytery, a niche contains a 10th-century bronze basin of probable Arab manufacture. The pair of lions on the steps date from the 12th century and were originally located at the sides of the entrance door.

Palazzo Corsini

View of frescoes, Villa Farnesina

SAN COSIMATO
(CURRENTLY THE FUNERARY CHAPEL OF THE OSPEDALE NUOVO REGINA MARGHERITA)

Piazza di San Cosimato

➤ Built in the 10th century, the church was restored in 1475. The Romanesque bell tower, dating from the end of the 11th century, is among the oldest in the city. The complex includes two cloisters, one of which, with its 250 small columns, is the largest in Rome. The main altar has a beautiful 13th-century painting of the Virgin and child that originally belonged to Old Saint Peter's Basilica. The *protiro* in front of the church dates from the 12th century.

SANT'ONOFRIO AL GIANICOLO

Piazza di Sant'Onofrio, 2; tel.: 06-6864498; open: Mon.–Fri. 7 A.M.–1:30 P.M., Sat. 8:30 A.M.–2 P.M., Sun. for mass only; closed: month of Aug., except saint's feast day on Aug. 12.

➤ This picturesque building was erected in 1439 in honor of Saint Onuphrius, an Egyptian monk who lived in the wilderness for 60 years. A series of frescoes in the cloister, painted in 1600, represents the legendary stories of his life: the rejection by his father, the King of Persia; becoming a hermit when he was a boy; giving a little

loaf to the child Jesus and receiving it back enlarged tenfold; his holy death; and his burial in a grave, scooped out by two lions, in the sand.

In the lunettes of the portico, in front of the entrance to the church, are three frescoes by Domenichino, representing incidents in the life of Saint Jerome. On the front of the richly decorated Chapel of the Rosary are the *Sybils* by Agostino Tassi. The altar of the church has some beautiful paintings by Baldassare Peruzzi, while the first right chapel has an Annunciation by Antoniazzo Romano. The tomb of the famed Renaissance poet Torquato Tasso is in the first chapel on the left. His death occurred just as he was to have been solemnly crowned on the capitol as "Prince of Poets." The room in which he died may be visited in the adjoining monastery.

VILLA FARNESINA

Via della Lungara, 230; tel.: 06-68801767; open: Mon.–Sat. 9 A.M.–1 P.M.; admission: €4; students, €3.

➤ Commissioned by banker and art patron Agostino Chigi, Villa Farnesina was erected between 1507 and 1509 by Baldassarre Peruzzi. In 1580 the villa was purchased and named after the Farnese family. The building, the epitome of a 16th-century city palazzo, was the center of Roman Renaissance cultural life, as Chigi enjoyed being surrounded by artists, intellectuals, politicians, and ambassadors. Domenico Beccafumi, Sebastiano del Piombo, Giovanni Antonio Bazzi (known as Il Sodoma), and Peruzzi painted the sumptuous frescoes, inspired by mythological and astrological subjects. The ceiling of the Loggia of Psyche was designed by Raphael and painted by Giulio Romano, Giovanni da Udine, and Giovanni Francesco Penni. The Loggia of Galatea contains works by Peruzzi, Sebastiano del Piombo, and Raphael himself, who painted the *Triumph of Galatea* (1514). This can be considered one of his more classic works, due to the subject, the formal structure, and color.

The garden was inspired by Chigi's request to create a "harmonious composition." This beautiful garden was destroyed in 1878–1880 when the course of the Tiber was changed, and a small shaded park is now in its place. Today it is the home of the Accademia Nazionale dei Lincei, Italy's most illustrious Italian art academy.

The Loggia of Psyche frescoes in Villa Farnesina were restored between 1989 and 1997 by the Istituto Centrale del Restauro, in collaboration with five of its former pupils.

Museums

GALLERIA NAZIONALE DI PALAZZO CORSINI (NATIONAL GALLERY OF PALAZZO CORSINI)

Via della Lungara, 10; tel.: 06-68802323; website: www.ticketeria.it; open: 8:30 A.M.– 7 P.M.; closed: Mon.; admission: €4.

➤ Seat of the Arcadian Academy of Queen Christina of Sweden, the gallery contains Roman finds of the Imperial Age as well as 16th- and 17th-century paintings.

MUSEO DEL FOLKLORE (FOLKLORE MUSEUM)

Piazza S. Egidio, 1/B; tel.: 06-5816563; open: 9:30 A.M.–8 P.M.; closed: Mon.; admission: €3.

➤ Original documents and reconstructions of environments illustrate the everyday life of Rome during the last centuries of papal power.

MUSEO DI TORQUATO TASSO (TORQUATO TASSO MUSEUM)

Piazza Sant'Onofrio, 2; tel.: 06-6828121; admission: free; groups by appointment only.

➤ Housed in the convent where the poet died, it contains ancient editions of his works and other memoirs.

SANT'ONOFRIO AL GIANICOLO

Here—almost like pearls in a dunghill—are hidden mementos of two of the most exquisite of Italian minds. Torquato Tasso [the famed Italian poet] spent the last months of his life here, and you may visit his room and various warped and faded relics. . . . In a little shabby, chilly corridor adjoining is a fresco of Leonardo, a Virgin and Child, with the donatorio. It is very small, simple and faded, but it has all the artist's magic, that mocking, illusive refinement and hint of a perfection of irony or the perfection of tenderness? What does he mean, what does he affirm, what does he deny? Magic wouldn't be magic, nor the author of such things stand so absolutely alone, if we were ready with an explanation.

—Henry James, *Italian Hours*

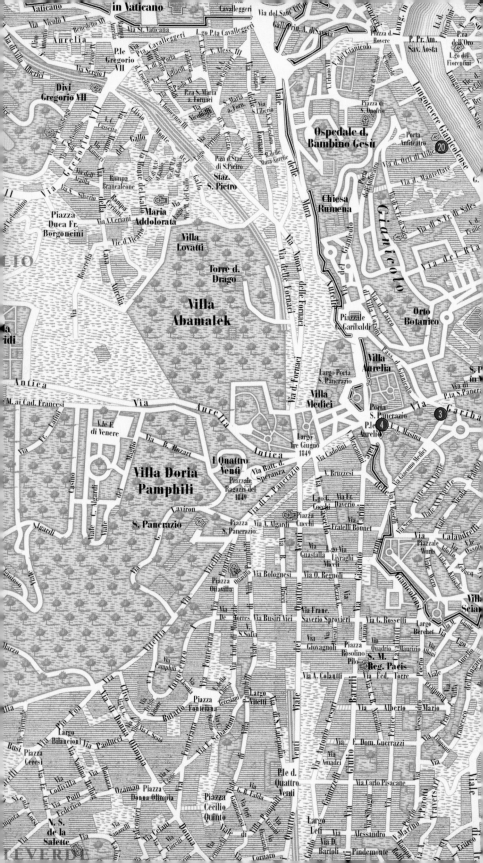

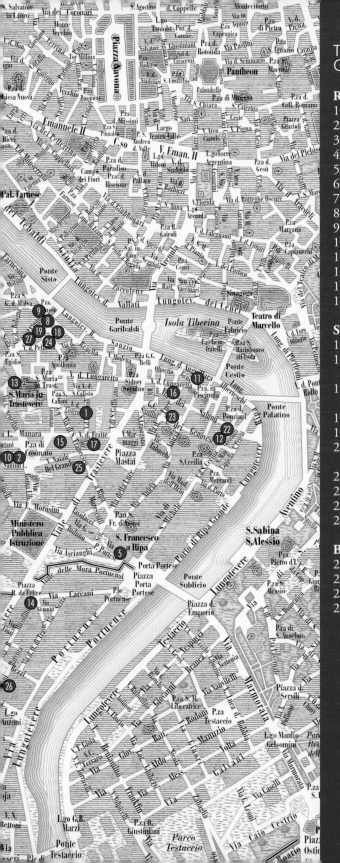

Trastevere/ Gianicolo

Restaurants & Cafés
1 Ai Fienaroli*
2 Alberto Ciarla*
3 Antica Pesa
4 Antico Arco
5 Antico Tevere
6 Atm Sushi Bar
7 Da Lucia
8 Ferrara*
9 Friends
10 Galeone Corsetti
11 La Gensola
12 L'Asinocotto
13 La Tana dei Noantri
14 Riparte Caffè

Shopping
15 Americana Vintage
16 Antico Forno di
   Trastevere
17 Azzurra Alto
   Artigianato
18 Corner Bookshop
19 Forno La Renella*
20 Laboratorio Ilaria
   Miani
21 La Bottega Artigiana
22 Le Cugine
23 Panificio Boldrini
24 Polvere di Tempo

Best of
25 Bar Cecere
26 Jaiya Sai Ma
27 Michele Tricarico
28 Porta Portese

Editor's Note:

While Trastevere is a beautiful part of the city, its hotel offerings are limited and not particularly noteworthy. For this reason, we have not included any listings.

Antica Pesa

Via Garibaldi, 18; tel.: 06-5809236; closed: Sun.; €.

☛Solid cuisine, very well known in the area.

Antico Arco

Piazzale Aurelio, 7; tel.: 06-5815274; open: 7:30–11:30 P.M.; closed: Sun.; credit cards accepted: all major; €€.

☛A small dining room in an 18th-century palazzo on top of the Gianicolo hill, this restaurant is one of the most refined in the neighborhood. While a bit noisy, the atmosphere is friendly and the cuisine is creative and nicely complemented with very good wines (the list is plentiful). Some of the specialties include flan of asparagus ravioli filled with calamari, *risotto al castemagno* (a cheese from Piedmont) in wine sauce, crunchy fried zucchini flowers, pheasant breast with couscous in a potato crust, and mozzarella made from buffalo milk. For dessert they offer an excellent pear tart with a whisky-based sauce and *tarte tatin*.

Atm Sushi Bar

Via della Penitenza, 7 (corner Via della Lungara); tel.: 06-68307053; open: 8 P.M.–12 A.M.; closed: Mon.; credit cards accepted: all major; €.

☛The first sushi bar in Rome. The atmosphere is intimate with diffused light shining on the predominantly blue and gray color scheme, and lots of wood, steel, iron, and leather. Typical dishes are sushi, sashimi, and tempura accompanied by excellent tea and pleasant background music.

Da Lucia

Vicolo del Mattonato, 2B; tel.: 06-5803601; open: 12:30–3 P.M., 7:30–11 P.M.; closed: Mon. and for 3 weeks in Aug.; €.

☛Da Lucia is located on one of Trastevere's most picturesque alleys. The small but neatly furnished establishment boasts old paintings and photos on its walls and maintains an informal but reserved atmosphere thanks to its few tables—making reservations a good idea. A perfect synthesis of Roman cuisine, the menu offers *spaghetti alla gricia* (black pepper, pecorino, and guanciale), *penne all'arrabbiata* (spicy tomato sauce), and *spaghetti cacio pepe* (grated pecorino and black pepper), together with seconds like beef shoulder and onions, Roman-style tripe, rabbit *alla cacciatore*, and cuttlefish with peas. Owner Renato Bizzarri also respects tradition and serves gnocchi with tomato sauce on Thursday, and pasta and broccoli in stingray broth followed by stewed salt-cod on Fridays. Regional cheeses and desserts like bananas with maraschino, chocolate mousse, and crème caramel top off the meals. The wine list includes about 30 carefully chosen labels.

Ferrara

Via del Moro, 1A ; tel.: 06-5803769; closed: Sun.; €.

☛Ferrara's attentive staff describes bottles of wine as if they were talking about close friends. Some of those bottles may indeed be from close to home, seeing as Ferrara serves exclusively Italian wines and a few French champagnes. It is a treat to read the carefully compiled wine list, or rather, book (of epic proportions), but in the end you will probably need your waiter or waitress's expert guidance in making your choice. The spacious and elegant restaurant is located on three exquisitely renovated floors of a palazzo built in the 1600s. Ferrara's creative menu also includes exceptional homemade desserts—a rarity in Rome.

Friends

Piazza Trilussa, 34; tel.: 06-5816111; open: Mon.–Sat. 6:30–1:30 A.M., Sun. 6 P.M.–1:30 A.M.; credit cards accepted: none.

☛Cocktail bar with music and aperitifs.

La Gensola

Piazza della Gensola, 15; tel.: 06-5816312; €.

☛Great Sicilian cuisine. Specialties include pasta with sardines and steamed shellfish.

RESTAURANTS & CAFÉS

La Tana dei Noantri

Via della Paglia, 1-2-3; tel.: 06-5806404; €€€

☛A traditional Roman trattoria with *cucina casalinga,* homemade cuisine. Not far from the American Academy. A great location for outdoor eating. Specialties include antipasti, *gnocchi alla romana*, and artichokes.

Riparte Caffè

Via degli Orti di Trastevere, 3; tel.: 06-5861852; reservations: 06-5861816; closed: Sun., Mon.; credit cards accepted: all major.

☛A restaurant and café that offers a mix of art exhibits, photography, and food. The dishes served are all made with ingredients grown or raised on the owners' private farm. Try pasta with sausages and raisins, carpaccio, and buffalo caciottina cheese with honey. Live music on Friday and Saturday nights: jazz, swing, and ragtime.

SPECIALTY SHOPS

Americana Vintage

Via Manara, 5; tel.: 06-5810797; open: 10 A.M.–1 P.M., 4 P.M.–8 P.M.; closed: Sun.

☛The only store in Rome with vintage guitars. Items date from the 1930s to 1960s.

Antico Forno di Trastevere

Via della Lungaretta; tel.: 06-5814650; open: daily 10:30 A.M.–8 P.M.

☛The tantalizing display of cookies in this bakery's window catches the eye of many a passerby. Further investigation will not disappoint—the cookies are as good as they look. A deli and other specialty items are also available.

Azzurra Alto Artigianato

Via Fratte di Trastevere, 44e; tel.: 06-5806303; open: daily 10:30 A.M.–8 P.M.

☛This Trastevere shop sells hand-embroidered towels, tablecloths, and sheets as well as handbags and other items.

Forno La Renella

Via del Moro, 15; tel.: 06-5817265.

☛An extraordinary variety of pizzas and breads come out of its wood oven. It serves the restaurants and homes of the entire neighborhood.

Laboratorio Ilaria Miani

Via Orti d'Alibert, 13A; tel.: 06-6861366; open: 10 A.M.–1 P.M., 4–8 P.M.; closed: Sat., Sun.

☛A store located in a beautiful corner of Rome, at the foot of the Janiculum Hill. It sells lamps and lampshades, paintings, and all sorts of decorative objects.

La Bottega Artigiana

Via Santa Dorotea, 21; tel.: 06-5882079; open: 9:30 A.M.–1:30 P.M., 3:30–7:30 P.M.; closed: Sun.

☛Sells fine ceramics from various areas of Italy, including Deruta, Faenza, and Vietri. Particular attention to design.

Le Cugine

Via dei Vascellari, 19; tel.: 06-5894844; open: 10 A.M.–8 P.M.; closed: Mon.

☛Named for the two cousins who own it, this store has an eclectic selection of antiques. Sabrina Alfonsi, one of the cousins, graciously guides visitors through the collection, which focuses on second-hand objects culled from the houses of Rome. It's a cheerful hodgepodge of 19th-century birdcages, grandma's cups and saucers, dressers, and lace.

Panificio Boldrini

Via dei Genovesi, 11; tel.: 06-5881616; open: daily 6 A.M.–8:30 P.M.

☛En route between the Churches of San Benedetto in Piscinula and San Francesco a Ripa, this tiny bakery and pizza place is a local favorite. No awning or bright sign announces its presence, but a small crowd gathers inside around lunchtime, waiting for pizza hot from the oven.

PROFILE

Judging a Book by Its Cover
By Amanda Castleman

Daniele Bevilacqua at work

Daniele Bevilacqua, one of the last book-binders in Rome, practices a centuries-old art that survived the success of printing presses and remains defiant after the advent of the e-book. In his small work-shop in Monteverde, the 80-year-old arti-san restores battered antique volumes, and also creates new books from scratch.

Raw materials clutter the narrow space: tottering stacks of paper, rusty scissors, scrolls of cloth, scraps of leather and vellum, a plastic sack of glue, and a knobby boars'-hair brush. Fierce old machines — dark with oil and time—stand guard. He darts over to one, used for chopping uni-form paper edges. This particular model is over 100 years old and lacks the safety features of modern machines.

His wooden sewing frame stands near the shop entrance. The instru-ment is a simple one, which tightly clamps the book as the *rilegatore* stitches. Three strands of cotton twine run from top to bottom. This durable tech-nique, dating back to the 12th century, leaves bands on the spine—a true mark of excellence.

Bevilacqua binds and restores books mainly for foreign academies in Rome—the American, British, French, Dutch, and Finns—and once bound a volume for Pope John Paul II, but he also tackles small projects, such as dis-sertations, photo albums, and collections of magazines.

His bookbinding career began at age 14 in Trastevere, his local neighbor-hood. After World War II, he became a bookbinder for the Italian navy, where he spent 38 years restoring books, while also maintaining his Monteverde workshop.

Italy has always been renowned for its bookbinding. It pioneered limp binding, an early form of paperback, as well as gold embossing. Its elegant marbled paper has been exported for endpaper since the 17th century. And many of the classic bookbinding styles—spare and simple Aldine, classical Etruscan, and ornate Maioli—began on this peninsula.

The technique has not changed drastically with time, according to Bevilacqua. The materials have evolved slightly. Harmful acids and dyes are no longer used, and new materials, like inexpensive plastic-coated paper, are often used. Yet, leather remains Bevilacqua's material of choice. He works with the full range: goatskin (known as morocco); calfskin, with its rich brown tones; poorer quality sheepskin; and vellum. His books are works of art—inside and out.

Legatoria Monteverde, Via Francesco Daverio, 28, tel.: 06-5806579/5810345.

SPECIALTY SHOPS

Polvere di Tempo

Via del Moro, 59 (right across the street from Ferrara); tel.: 06-5880704.

☛A tiny but elegant store with sundials, sand clocks, and many handmade items, including copper and silver rings and leather address books.

The Corner Bookshop

Via del Moro, 48 (across the street from the Forno La Renella); tel.: 06-5836942; open: Mon.–Sat. 10 A.M.–1:30 P.M., 3:30–8 P.M., Sun. 11:30 A.M.–1:30 P.M., 3:30–8 P.M.

☛A small bookstore with English-language hardcovers, paperbacks, fiction, non-fiction, and general interest books.

OUR CRITIC'S FAVORITE RESTAURANTS

Ai Fienaroli

Via dei fienaroli, 5; tel.: 06-5884474; closed: Sun; €.

☛Mediterranean tradition plus some creative ideas: marinated chicken with balsamic vinegar, tuna tartare, mussels with curry sauce, rice with sepia ink and shellfish. The homemade fruit sorbets are good, and the wine selection is carefully put together.

Alberto Ciarla

Piazza S. Cosimato, 1; tel.: 06-5884377; open: evenings only; closed: Sun.; €€.

☛Former rugby player Alberto Ciarla is now known as the guru of seafood cuisine. In the heart of Trastevere, his restaurant offers dishes approaching legend, like spaghetti with bass, shellfish and seafood "panacea," shrimp salad, and an endless variety of recipes that highlight the freshness of the ingredients and the flavors from the sea.

Antico Tevere

Via Portuense, 45; tel.: 06-5816054; closed: Sun. at lunch; €.

☛While the cuisine offers solid renditions of Mediterranean-style seafood, this restaurant's trump card is its privileged position on a lovely terrace facing the Tiber near Porta Portese. In addition to the live music in the evenings, another aspect that can't go unnoticed is the availability of parking, not an easy thing to find in the capital. Dishes to taste are the octopus in *bella vista*, the *orecchiette* with fresh clams and squash, and the fresh *strozzapreti* pasta.

Galeone Corsetti

Piazza San Cosimato, 27; tel.: 06-5816311; closed: Wed. at lunch; €.

☛Since 1927, the Corsetti family has been offering typical Roman cuisine like *bucatini all'amatriciana* and roast lamb, together with a selection of seafood dishes. Among the latter are the *spaghetti alla Corsetti*, prepared with seafood and scampi in a delicate non-tomato sauce. Second courses include broiled turbot filet with pâté and John Dory filets with porcini mushrooms.

L'Asinocotto

Via dei Vascellari, 48; tel.: 06-5898985; closed: Mon.; €.

☛Amidst the narrow streets of Trastevere, home to true Roman cooking, L'Asinocotto pays homage to its location with a menu offering traditional cooking reworked in a creative tone and split equally between seafood specialties and the fruits of the earth. The *garganelli* pasta with lamb ragu is a wonderful first course. Among the second courses, the swordfish prepared with capers and citrus fruit is a house favorite. There's a solid wine list with a selection of labels also served by the glass.

Northern Rome

By Ruth Kaplan

utside the northern perimeter of the Aurelian Wall, the city seems to take a deep breath and stretch out, devoting generous space to museums, parks, and villas. Some of the city's most upscale residential property radiates outward from the **Villa Borghese**, a large public park that was built as a private residence and garden in the 17th century. A series of paved pathways takes walkers, cyclists, and rollerbladers past the villa's lawns, fountains, and even a now-defunct racetrack. There is also a zoo and movie theater inside the park. The artistic gem of the villa is the **Galleria Borghese**, a well-chosen display of Renaissance and classical works from the collection of Cardinal Scipione Borghese. A half-dozen masterpieces by Bernini are there, including *David* and *Pluto and Proserpina* (also known as the *Rape of Proserpina*), as well as paintings by Caravaggio and Raphael.

Villa Borghese's green carries over its northern boundary into the Valle Giulia, an area named after Pope Julius III, whose private residence, the **Villa Giulia**, once stretched out from here all the way north to the Milvian Bridge. The villa itself, built in the 16th century, now houses the Museo Nazionale Etrusco, with a large collection of pre-Roman works from Lazio and Southern Umbria. Many of the ceramics, bronzes, and stone carvings date back to as early as the 9th century B.C.

The Viale delle Belle Arti leads down from the Villa Giulia, bringing you forward three thousand years in art history to the neoclassical **Galleria Nazionale d'Arte Moderna**, a comprehensive collection of 19th- and 20th-century Italian art, including works by de Chirico, Boccioni, and Morandi. The museum also has a well-stocked collection of paintings, prints, and drawings by artists of the same period from other European countries. A new wing is devoted to contemporary art exhibitions.

Left, Bernini, Pluto and Proserpina, *Galleria Borghese*

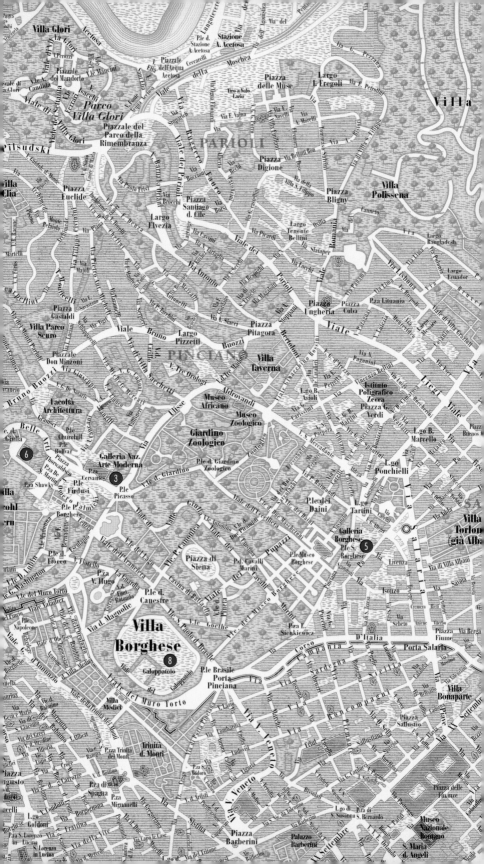

VILLA BORGHESE

Open: park open dawn to sunset.

➤ The Villa Borghese's perimeter is 4 miles long and has seven gates. Its origins go back to Pope Paul V, of the Borghese family, who sponsored his nephew Cardinal Scipione Borghese's desire to build a large villa. Between 1608 and 1615, the cardinal accumulated more land around a lot his family had owned since 1580. He also had a "small" house that now hosts the Galleria Borghese. The facade was originally richly decorated with busts, statues, and bas-reliefs—a total of 523 pieces. Most of them were taken away and sold to France in 1807. The park was enlarged and altered between 1770 and 1793, when it was transformed by garden expert Jacob Moore into an English-style park. One of the best-known parts of the villa is Piazza di Siena, named after the city that the Borghese family came from in the second half of the 16th century.

Museums

GALLERIA NAZIONALE D'ARTE MODERNA (NATIONAL GALLERY OF MODERN AND CONTEMPORARY ART)

Viale delle Belle Arti, 131; tel.: 06-322981; reservations: 06-3234000; open: 8:30 A.M.– 7 P.M., Sun. 9 A.M.–8 P.M.; closed: Mon.; admission: €6.

➤ An impressive collection of paintings, sculptures, and prints, largely by Italian artists, dating from the 1800s to the present.

Carlo Carrà, Ovale delle Apparizioni, *Galleria Nazionale d'Arte*

MUSEO DELLA CASINA DELLE CIVETTE (MUSEUM OF THE CASINA DELLE CIVETTE)

Villa Torlonia, Via Nomentana, 70; tel.: 06-44250072; open: 9 A.M.–7 P.M. (summer), 9 A.M. –5 P.M. (winter); closed: Mon.; admission: €3.

➤ A fanciful building on the grounds of Villa Torlonia with several splendid Art Nouveau polychrome leaded-glass windows produced between 1908 and 1930.

MUSEO E GALLERIA BORGHESE (BORGHESE MUSEUM AND GALLERY)

Piazzale del Museo Borghese; tel.: 06-8417645; website: www.ticketeria.it; open: 9 A.M.–7 P.M.; closed: Mon.; reservations: 06-328101, strongly recommended (entrance granted to a limited number of people every two hours); admission: €7.

➤ In the recently and splendidly restored villa (1613–1614), Cardinal Scipione Borghese collected paintings and sculptures, both ancient and of his time, thus creating an extraordinary collection with masterpieces by Bernini, Canova, Caravaggio, Titian, Rubens, and other outstanding artists.

MUSEO NAZIONALE ETRUSCO DI VILLA GIULIA (VILLA GIULIA NATIONAL ETRUSCAN MUSEUM)

Piazzale di Villa Giulia, 9; tel.: 06-3226571; open: 8:30 A.M.–7:30 P.M.; closed: Mon., Jan. 1, and Dec. 25; admission: €4.

➤ Housed in the splendid villa of Pope Julius III, the Villa Giulia was founded in 1889 to hold all pre-Roman antiquities of the regions of Latium, southern Etruscan and Umbria. The original collection was greatly expanded by the acquisition of the Barberini collection in 1919, and the Pesciotti collection in 1972. Material from ongoing excavations is added periodically. The museum is reputed to have the best Etruscan collection in the world and one of the best collections of Greek pottery. In addition to the exquisite jewelry and the extraordinary technical instruments—doctors' scalpels, cooking tools, massaging utensils— note the nearly life-size *Sarcofago degli Sposi* (Bride and Groom Sarcophagus).

Walking Tour

Outside the Walls on Via Salaria and Via Nomentana

By Gordon Ramsey

Visiting the quiet, mainly residential neighborhoods on the Via Salaria and Via Nomentana outside Rome's walls isn't on everyone's to-do list when they come to the Eternal City. Many people don't realize that lying under the sprawling villas and wide, shady boulevards of the Salaria/Nomentana districts are hundreds of thousands of graves. Because of this, the area is home to some of Rome's most significant art treasures.

The Via Salaria and the Via Nomentana have been leading people in and out of Rome for thousands of years. The Via Salaria, which gets its name from the salt (*sale*) that was brought to the city from the mines in the northeast, was the road the Romans are said to have taken on their way to rape the Sabine women. The Via Nomentana connected Rome to the ancient city of Nomentum (now Mentana).

The Jews and Christians of ancient Rome, forbidden to bury their dead within city walls, dug catacombs along all the major roads leading out of the city. The catacombs on the Via Salaria and the Via Nomentana may not be as famous as those along the Via Appia, or Appian Way, but they deserve equal attention.

Several catacombs have been excavated in the area, including Jewish catacombs under Villa Torlonia. However, only two are open to the public: the Catacombs of Priscilla on Via Salaria and the catacombs under the Church of Sant'Agnese fuori le Mura on Via Nomentana. These two sites are within easy walking distance of each other and both are located near large public parks (for those who also want to escape the noise and traffic of downtown).

With eight miles of galleries and more than 40,000 tombs, the **Catacombs of Priscilla** on the Via Salaria is one of the largest and oldest burial sites in Rome. Known as the Queen of the Catacombs, hundreds of martyrs and seven popes were buried there. The catacombs are named after the woman who donated the land to the Christian community some time in the 2nd century A.D.

As with all of Rome's catacombs, the galleries and shelves (*loculi*) for the dead were dug out of *tufo*, a volcanic rock that is soft to dig but hardens when it comes in contact with the air. The corpses were wrapped in cloth, covered with quick lime, and sealed in the *loculi* behind marble slabs or terra-cotta tiles.

These white marble slabs, wet and shiny from the humidity, can't fail to catch your eye as you walk through the dark *tufo* galleries. The crude etchings on these slabs, the earliest of Christian tombstones, provide a quick lesson in early Christian iconography, but they also offer glimpses into the lives of ordinary people.

Mosaic in Sant'Agnese

For example, on the grave of his eight-year-old daughter Dora, a shoemaker carved the word *dulce* (sweet) with the *L* made in the shape of a sandaled foot.

What truly distinguishes the Catacombs of Priscilla from the rest of Rome's catacombs are its fine frescoes. Included among its many paintings are illustrations of familiar (and perhaps not-so-familiar) stories from the Old Testament: Jonah and the Whale, Noah and the Ark, Abraham's Sacrifice of Isaac, Susanna and the Elders, and the Three Hebrews in the Fiery Furnace. There are a couple of scenes from the life of Christ: the Raising of Lazarus and the Visit of the Magi.

But Santa Priscilla's most famous fresco is of the Virgin Mary. Painted at the beginning of the 3rd century, it is considered to be the oldest-known representation of Jesus' mother. Mary is depicted sitting with the infant Jesus on her lap. Beside her, a prophet, identified as Balaam, points to a star.

After visiting the dark and cramped catacombs you may want to cross the Via Salaria and enjoy the wide-open spaces of Villa Ada, once the private residence of Italy's first king, Vittorio Emanuele II. From the Catacombs of Priscilla it's an easy walk southwest to the **Church and Catacombs of Sant'Agnese fuori le Mura** on the Via Nomentana.

Saint Agnes was a Christian virgin who was publicly stripped, mutilated, burned, and beheaded for refusing to marry a Roman pagan. Because of her impressive martyrdom, she became an immensely popular cult figure and many of Rome's early Christians sought to be buried near her.

The body of Saint Agnes lies in the catacombs directly below the Church of Sant'Agnese fuori le Mura—right under the altar in fact. And although these catacombs are not as impressive as those at Priscilla (there are no frescoes), they contain touching images of everyday life in ancient Rome. One grave is marked with a picture of a nice round prosciutto. Another has a rough etching of one of that period's most unpleasant occupations: a digger of catacombs.

The Church of Sant'Agnese was originally constructed in the 4th century, rebuilt by Pope Honorius I in the 7th century, and has been renovated many times since. Its most noteworthy feature is the large apsidal mosaic, one of the finest works of Byzantine art in Rome. The simplicity of its composition attests to the deep devotion and respect the locals felt for Saint Agnes. She is shown standing against a gold background between Pope Symmachus and Pope Honorious I (who would later be condemned as a heretic). Although said to be only 13 when she was martyred, Saint Agnes is dressed as a Byzantine empress in golden robes and jewelry. According to legend, this is how she appeared to the world eight days after her death. Only her rosy, apple-dumpling cheeks betray her youth.

The only indications of her brutal martyrdom are some puny red flames at her feet and a very small sword in her hand. The hand of God himself comes down from the sky to crown her head with laurels. This powerful image is a far cry from later Christian iconography, which often depicts her as a demure maiden holding her severed breasts on a platter.

The great architectural wonder at Sant'Agnese fuori le Mura is the **Mausoleum of Saint Costanza**, located less than 650 feet to the right of the church entrance. Built by Emperor Constantine for his daughters Costanza and Elena, the mausoleum, as with all Roman mausoleums, is circular in form. Twelve pairs of slender marble columns encircle the central domed space, which is lit from above by 12 windows. A barrel-vaulted walkway runs around the building's perimeter. The smooth curves and elegant proportions instill an immediate sense of calm.

Mausoleum of Saint Costanza

The walkway's ceiling is covered with magnificent 4th-century mosaics. Divided into three sets of paired panels, some are decorated with delicate geometric motifs, others with images suggesting a sumptuous banquet: flagons of wine, game birds and animals, and musical instruments.

The two most interesting panels depict scenes of wine making. Little blue men lead oxcarts laden with grapes to be crushed by more little blue men, already exuberantly stomping. If you look carefully, you may notice that occasionally the oxen are somewhat less than willing to be led by the nose. In the center of these lively scenes are the portraits of Costanza and her first husband, Annibaliano. Elegant and serene, joyous and ancient, the mausoleum (converted into a church in 1254) has become one of the city's most popular wedding spots.

Further Information

Catacombs of Priscilla
Via Salaria, 430; tel.: 06-86206272; open: Tues.–Sun. 8:30 A.M.–noon, 2:30–5 P.M., closed: Mon., Jan., Easter, Christmas; admission: €5; (€3 reduced fare).

Church and Catacombs of Sant'Agnese fuori le Mura
Via Nomentana, 349; open: 9 A.M.–noon, 4–6 P.M.; closed: Mon. afternoon, Sun., holiday mornings; admission: €4 (€2 reduced fare); tours given in a variety of languages and include visit to Mausoleum of Saint Costanza (no audiocasettes).

By Gordon Ramsey

Villa Torlonia, a large public park filled with exotic plants, is a sort of 19th-century Disneyland. With fake Egyptian obelisks, a fake medieval castle, a fake temple to Saturn, fake ruins, a fake Moorish green house, it has everything you need to have a truly good time.

The villa is the product of several generations of the Torlonia family's extravagance. In 1806, Giovanni Torlonia (1755–1829), the founder of a banking empire closely connected to the Vatican, began muscling his way into Roman nobility and bought the villa. Torlonia hired Giuseppe Valadier, the neoclassic architect responsible for the design of Piazza del Popolo, to start work on an estate to rival any in Rome.

Coppedé neighborhood

But the villa, as it currently stands, largely reflects the work of architects hired by Giovanni's son, Alessandro (1800–1886), while its true crown jewel, the Casina delle Civette (The Owl Palace), is an architectural folly created by Alessandro's gloomy and misanthropic nephew, Prince Giovanni Torlonia.

The building's decoration reflects the prince's love of the occult and the macabre. The owl is one of the most common decorative motifs, hence the building's name. But you will also find an impressive menagerie of other creepy creatures. Outside, you can spot stone snakes, snails, and strange birds. Inside, don't miss the chorus line of bats on the starry ceiling above the chandelier in the prince's bedroom.

Although Prince Torlonia's tastes have a certain endearing kitschiness, there's no question that the artists and craftspeople responsible for creating the decor in his home were of the highest order. In recognition of this, the restored Casina delle Civette now houses a museum of stained glass—a unique gallery featuring fine stained-glass works and sketches by early-20th-century masters.

If you walk back down Via Nomentana to Viale Regina Margherita and walk or take the 3 streetcar a few stops west you'll reach Piazza Buenos Aires. A couple paces north on Via Tagliamento brings you to the strange land known as the Quartiere Dora. Built between 1921 and 1926 by the Florentine architect Gino Coppedè (1886–1927), the neighborhood is often referred to simply as the Coppedè.

Piazza Mincio marks the screaming high note in Gino Coppodè's wild Roman opera. The piazza's central feature is the Fountain of the Frogs. A circle of frogs lines the fountain's basin, which is supported by spouting young men holding giant clam shells.

All the buildings in the piazza are dripping with ornament. Wherever you look there is something to attract the eye. Balconies with twisting columns hang off walls decorated with motifs drawn from every period imaginable: Assyrian, Babylonian, Byzantine, medieval, Renaissance, Norse.

Like many architects of the time, Coppedè drew on a wide range of decorative arts—mosaics, ironwork, frescoes, stone carvings—to make innovative and personal architectural statements. However, through the sheer brute force of relentless excess, he managed to transcend early-20th-century eclectic traditions to create a truly distinctive, if futureless, architectural style.

Focus

253

FURTHER INFORMATION

Villa Torlonia

Via Nomentana, 70; tel.: 06-44250072; open: April 1–Sept. 30, 9 A.M.–7 P.M., Oct. 1–March 31, 9 A.M.–5 P.M.; closed: Mon.; admission: €2.50, under 18 and over 65 enter free.

Northern Rome

Hotels & Inns
1 Hotel Turner

Restaurants & Cafés
2 Capo Boi
3 Ceppo
4 Dai Toscani
5 Ezio le Scalette
6 Loreto
7 Mariano
8 Semidivino
9 Trimani, Via Goito*

Best of
10 Aldovrandi Palace
11 Antiquariato a Piazza Verdi
12 Gay Odin
13 Il Mercantino del Borghetto Flaminio
14 Il Tiepolo
15 Parco dei Principi
16 Ponte Milvio
17 Ruggero Gargani
18 San Filippo
19 Trimani, Via Cernaia

HOTELS & INNS

Hotel Turner

Via Nomentana, 29; tel.: 06-44250077/ 44250165; e-mail: info@hotelturner.com; website: www.hotelturner.com; category: ★★★; number of rooms: 47, including 4 suites; credit cards accepted: all major; facilities: parking nearby (€13 a night), jacuzzis (€16 a night); access to internet: direct-line (US, UK) telephone jack in all rooms; most beautiful room: 522; €€–€€€.

☞Elegant hotel on 19th-century street, right off Via Veneto. The lobby is decorated with 18th-century furnishings. A marble staircase leads to the breakfast room. The rooms, all individually decorated, are spacious with *bois de rose* furniture.

RESTAURANTS & CAFÉS

Capo Boi

Via Arno, 80; tel.: 06-8415535; closed: Sun.; credit cards accepted: all major; €.

☞A lively Sardinian seafood place offering a plentiful selection of antipasto and a wide variety of fresh fish. The anchovy salad is highly recommended. Make sure to save some room for the Sardinian desserts. It's a good idea to make a reservation. The kitchen closes around midnight.

Ceppo

Via Panama, 2; tel.: 06-8419696; fax: 06-85301370; closed: Mon. and month of Aug.; credit cards accepted: all major; €.

☞Elegant restaurant located in the Parioli area. Ingredients are always excellent. Best selections include sautéed squids with spelt salad, parmesan *zabaione* (a sort of eggnog dessert made with sugar and egg yolks), and a whole-grain lasagna with mushrooms. Tempting sweets. Good selection of wines.

Dai Toscani

Via Forlí, 41; tel.: 06-44231302; closed: Sun.; credit cards accepted: all major; €.

☞A casual restaurant serving Tuscan cuisine. Who can resist bruschetta with lard? The ice cream is homemade and the specialty is hazelnut. Kitchen closes at midnight.

Ezio le Scalette

Via Chiana, 89–91; tel.: 06-8411714; fax: 06-8540467; closed: Sat. for lunch, Sun., and all of Aug.; credit cards accepted: all major; €.

☞The owner's three great passions are Tuscan cigars, fish, and hunting, and it is best not to question him about them. Though apparently grumpy, the owner is a very good restaurateur. The location is modern and is divided into different rooms "furnished" with aquariums that are home to lobsters, seabass, and moray eels. Revised traditional Sardinian cuisine. Very good seabass and prawns, and baby octopus; excellent *spaghetti alla bottarga*; and a not-to-be-missed Catalan lobster. Very good and very expensive selection of wines.

Loreto

Via Valenziani, 19; tel.: 06-4742454; open: 12:30–3 A.M., 7:30 A.M.–1 P.M.; closed: Sun. and month of Aug.; €€

☞Elegant restaurant known for its fish and seafood. Specialties include *cannolicchi alla "Loreto,"* *rigatoni agli scampi* (shrimp pasta), and *sorbetto di lamponi* (raspberry sorbet).

Mariano

Via Piemonte, 79; tel.: 06 4745256; closed: Sat., Sun., and month of Aug.; €.

☞Simple but good cuisine at this restaurant specializing in game. A reasonable wine selection. Specialties include *Tortelli con brodo di fagiano* (large tortellini in pheasant broth) and *risotto con tartufo* (truffle risotto).

Semidivino

Via Alessandria, 230; tel.: 06-44250795; closed: Sun., Sat. at lunch.

☞A small wine bar for a light seasonal meal and good wine. Each day a selection of about a dozen wines is available by the glass. The complete list includes around 500 wines. There's also a large selection of cheeses, pâtés, salami, and smoked meat and fish.

RESTAURANTS & CAFÉS

Trimani
Via Goito, 20; tel.: 06-4469661; closed:
Sun.; credit cards accepted: all major.
☛Rome's oldest enoteca, located near the Termini train station, was founded in 1821 by Francesco Trimani and is still under family management. Bottles fill wooden shelves lining the inside of the store and the musty cantina smell lures curious pedestrians and die-hard wine lovers alike.

PROFILE

Enrico Jovane at work

Enrico Jovane, the Spiderman of Monument Restoration
By Laura Collura Kahn

Enrico Jovane, 38, is no maverick protester in search of a photo-op. He is Rome's one and only urban climber. After he took up mountain climbing, people began to request his help at first with cats stuck on windowsills and then, gradually, with more difficult types of work. After a while, he realized he could make a career out of his mountain-climbing skills, and he could do so in an urban setting. Initially, he carried out simple tasks, but over time the tasks grew more acrobatic—and spectacular.

Jovane devised creative ways to access difficult spots and was able to reach places that others couldn't. For example, at the Church of Ariccia, in a town in the Lazio region, he was hired to clean the dome and install a protective structure on the inside to stop pieces of window glass from falling to the floor below. By dangling from a cable stretched across the dome's diameter, he was able to scale it from the inside without putting up any kind of scaffolding.

His gear bag includes a helmet, some nylon cable, a climbing harness, and two or three snap-hooks, each able to hold up to 5,500 pounds. Once he has hoisted himself up into a cranny or onto a roof, Jovane puts on his restorer's cap. Before embarking on a job, experts illustrate the technique he should use. Through experience, though, he has learned a great deal about restoration and can often handle a project on his own.

When the actual restoration procedure requires special skills, Jovane takes an expert up with him, be it an engineer or a professional restorer, who bravely scales walls and climbs great heights alongside Jovane. Although Jovane has carried out high-profile jobs, like installing a lightning rod on the roof and a huge fly-curtain around the courtyard of the Palazzo Altemps museum, he doesn't turn down more menial tasks—like cleaning window panes. He has one such contract with the Scuderie del Quirinale, the former stables of the presidential palace in Rome, recently turned into a museum.

Southern Rome

By Ruth Kaplan

he archaeologically rich southern section of Rome includes remains of ancient tombs and temples, early Christian catacombs, and countrylike stretches of greenery. The area's most central point starts just south of the Circus Maximus with the sprawling **Terme di Caracalla**, once Rome's largest public bath complex. Completed in A.D. 217, the baths served as an important meeting place for 300 years, with a series of heated pools, gymnasiums, and Greek and Latin libraries. Much of the original brick structure and detailed mosaic pavement are still intact.

From the baths, Via di Porta di San Sebastiano passes through the Aurelian Wall and leads to the **Via Appia Antica**, the Old Appian Way. Linking Rome with nearby cities, the Via Appia was the most important of the ancient city's consular roads, both for moving armies off to war and bringing in goods from around the Mediterranean. Roman law dictated that the dead be buried outside the city limits, and the Via Appia once served as the city's most prominent burial ground. Its early Christian sites include the **Catacombe di San Callisto**, with walls full of burial niches on four different underground levels. Many of the early popes were buried here, as well as Saint Cecilia. Further down the Via Appia are the **Catacombe di San Sebastiano**, which mark the site of a 4th-century basilica. Graffiti on the catacomb walls heavily references Saints Peter and Paul, whose remains are thought to have been brought here during a time of Christian persecution by the Romans.

Gated villas and scattered remains of anonymous tombs lead down to the **Circo di Massenzio**, a 546-yard-long racetrack built by the emperor Maxentius in memory of his son Romulus, whose grave, the **Mausoleo di Romolo**, is on the same site.

Another noteworthy tomb is the huge drum-shaped **Tomba di Cecilia Metella**, burial site of the daughter of an important Republican-era citizen. Its rich frieze contains fragments of marble statuary. Smaller tombs continue to dot the Via Appia as it opens up into larger tracts of land, including the extensive brick ruins of the **Villa dei Quintili**, an ancient residence.

Off the Via Appia are the **Basilica di Santi Nereo e Achilleo** and the **Catacombe di Domitilla**, the largest underground burial site in Rome, which contains many pre-Christian tombs from the 1st and 2nd centuries A.D.

West of the Via Appia, in a densely populated neighborhood, is the grand church of **San Paolo fuori le Mura**, a reconstruction of a 4th-century basilica that stood on this site, where Saint Paul is thought to have been buried.

Left, Interior of San Paolo fuori le Mura

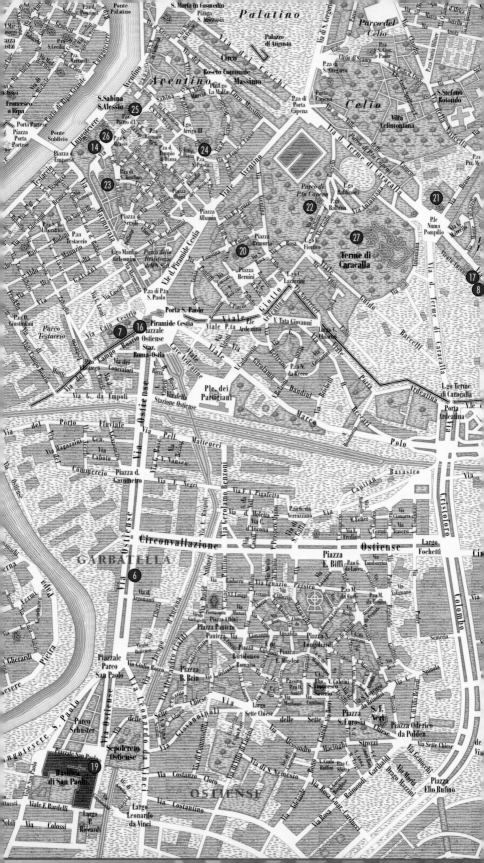

Southern Rome

Catacombe di Domitilla

Basilica di Santi Nereo e Achilleo and Catacombe di Domitilla (Basilica of Saints Nereus and Achilleus and Catacombs of Domitilla)

Via delle Sette Chiese, 283; tel.: 06-5110342; open: 8:30 A.M.–noon, 2:30–5:30 P.M. (Oct.–March: closes at 5 P.M.); closed: Tues. and month of Jan.

➤ The Catacombs of Domitilla are the largest and most extensive subterranean cemetery complex in all of Rome. The network of catacombs, developed between the 3rd and the 5th centuries, consists of 900 inscriptions and nearly 9 miles of tunnels. The catacombs are located on an estate that once belonged to Flavia Domitilla, the granddaughter of the emperor Vespasian.

The site also includes a pagan burial ground, called the Hypogaeum of the Flavians, which was later occupied by Christians. Inside, the burial chambers are adorned with both classical and Christian frescoes, including an early depiction of Christ as the Good Shepherd.

The catacombs can be entered through the Basilica of Saints Nereus and Achilleus, a 4th-century structure, which was built on the tombs of martyrs persecuted by Emperor Diocletian. The basilica was discovered in 1874.

Catacombe di San Callisto (Catacombs of Saint Callistus)

Via Appia Antica, 110; tel.: 06-51301580/ 5130151; open: 8:30 A.M.–noon, 2:30–5:30 P.M. (Oct.–March: closes at 5 P.M.); closed: Wed., Jan. 1, Easter Sunday, Dec. 25, and months of Feb. and Mar.

➤ Created around the end of the 3rd century from a Christian cemetery, these catacombs became the official cemetery of the Church. Sixteen popes and over 50 martyrs were buried in the 12-mile-long galleries. The catacombs today consist of five levels.

On the first level is the basilica, which is now a museum that exibits fragments and inscriptions of Saints Sixtus and Cecilia. A staircase, built in A.D. 380 leads to the second level, where the Crypt of Popes (3rd century A.D.), a rectangular hall, served as the burial ground for nine popes and several high church officials. At the end of the 2nd-century gallery is the entrance to Cubicula of the Sacraments (3rd century A.D.). The frescoes with baptism and Eucharist scenes are among the earliest examples of Christian painting. In the Saint Eusebius and Saint Gaio area are two crypts containing the ashes of the two martyrized popes. The Crypt of Saint Cecilia has, 5th-, 6th-, and 9th-century frescoes depicting her, Pope Urban, and Christ. Pope Saint Cornelius's tomb, in a remote part of the catacombs, has beautiful Byzantine-style frescoes depicting Popes Cornelius and Sixtus II and two African cardinals. The so-called Crypts of Lucina, decorated with ancient paintings of unique beauty, complete the Regione of Cornelius.

The Catacombs of Saint Callistus were discovered in 1849 by the archeologist De Rossi. They are named after Pope Callistus I, who died in 222 and was the first administrator of the church's cemetery.

Catacombe di San Sebastiano (Catacombs of Saint Sebastian)

Via Appia Antica, 136; tel.: 06-7850350; open: 8:30 A.M.–noon, 2:30–5:30 P.M.; closed: Sun. and from Nov. 15–Dec. 15.

➤ Although they were restored in the early 17th century, the Catacombs of Saint Sebastian are the product of artistic and engineering efforts from the first four centuries after Christ's death.

The plastered walls present hundreds of examples of 3rd- and 4th-century graffiti crying out to Saints Paul and Peter for help. Under the exterior of the basilica is the *Platonia*, the 4th-century Tomb of Saint Quirinus; the Chapel of Honorius III; and a cubiculum which, according to graffiti, was temporarily Saint Peter's tomb. The large villa, built in the 2nd century, contains two rooms and a courtyard, which is paved with a white mosaic. Paintings, such as a fine marine set in the main room, date from the 1st and 2nd centuries.

There are also three mausoleums, built in the 2nd century and later used by Christians. The first on the right has an inscription stating the name of the owner, Marcus Clodius Hermes. Inside are various decorations and a frescoed vault. Also inside are niches for cremations and loculi for bodies. The second mausoleum is the Mausoleum of the Innocentiores, named after the guild or funerary club that owned it. Early Christian symbols such as fish are scratched into the walls of the lower cell. On the left is the Mausoleum of the Ax, named after the image of an ax on the exterior. The Crypt of Saint Sebastian was built in the 4th century, but was later remodelled.

Mausoleo di Romolo (Mausoleum of Romulus)

Villa di Massenzio, Via Appia Antica; open: 9 A.M.–6:30 P.M. (summer), 9 A.M.–4:30 P.M. (winter); closed: Mon.

➤ The circular tomb that commemorates the emperor Maxentius's son Romulus was also used to bury other members of the imperial family. There is a corridor that runs around a central pillar in which there are niches for the burial urns to rest.

San Paolo fuori le Mura

Via Ostiense, 186; tel.: 06-5410341; open: daily 7 A.M.–7 P.M. (summer), 7 A.M.–6:30 P.M. (winter).

➤ San Paolo fuori le Mura was built by Constantine on the site of the Tomb of the Apostle. With time, the basilica grew bigger than Old Saint Peter's and was decorated with splendid works, such as the mosaics of the apse by Cavallini. On July 15, 1823, a fire destroyed 15 centuries of treasures. Through the negligence of some workmen employed to do repairs in the roof, the basilica caught fire. The flames raged with such fury that all the marble columns, except 40 in the side aisles, were completely calcined, and the porphyry columns surrounding the Tomb of the Apostle split into fragments.

Catacombe di San Callisto

SAN PAOLO FUORI LE MURA

The restored basilica is incredibly splendid. It seems a last pompous effort of formal Catholicism, and there are few more striking emblems of later Rome. . . . It rises there, gorgeous and useless, on its miasmatic site, with an air of conscious bravado, a florid advertisement of the superabundance of faith. Within it's magnificent, and its magnificence has no shabby spots, a rare thing in Rome. Marble and mosaic, alabaster and malachite, lapis and porphyry, incrust it from pavement to cornice and flash back their polished lights at each other with such a splendor of effect that you seem to stand at the heart of some immense prismatic crystal.

—Henry James, *Italian Hours*

Pictures, marbles, mosaics, and monuments were all damaged. The only portions spared by the flames were the western facade, with its mosaics of the 13th century; the great arch of Galla Placidia, with its splendid mosaics of the 5th century; the mosaics of the apse from the 13th century; and some of the mosaic portraits of the popes.

After the disastrous fire, steps were taken at once to restore the basilica, and contributions were sent from all the Catholic countries in Europe. The top of the facade of the present basilica was decorated with mosaics in imitation of the original. Five large doors correspond to the same number of aisles in the interior. The second door from the right includes parts of the ancient bronze door built in Constantinople in 1070 and brought to Rome for the original basilica. Inside is a linear forest of 80 gigantic granite columns, each formed out of a single block. The roof is of carved woodwork, coffered and richly gilt. The walls on all sides, encrusted with precious marbles, glow with color. Like a long frieze, along the entire central nave, there is a series of mosaic medallions with the faces of all the popes since Saint Peter. The triumphal

Terme di Caracalla

Tomba di Cecilia Metella

many as 10,000 people at once, they were started by Septimius Severus in A.D. 206 and mostly completed by his son, Caracalla between 211 and 216. Additional structures were erected later, probably before A.D. 235. They operated until 537 and include an open-air, Olympic-size swimming pool (*natatio*), covered cold hall (*frigidarium*), some small intermediary warm rooms (*tepidarium*), and a huge hot hall (*caldarium*). Surrounding these were the exercise room (*palestra*), changing rooms, and lounges. The facilities also included Greek and Latin libraries as well as a stadium. This arrangement was symmetrically duplicated on the other side. The Baths of Caracalla presented an innovation from previous baths, namely the circular shape—some 112 feet in diameter—of the *caldarium*. Rooms were decorated by mosaics, frescoes, and statues. Small parts of these decorations are now displayed at the Vatican Museums, Piazza Farnese (two granite basins), and the Archaeological Museum in Naples.

arch, which survived the fire of 1823, is decorated with 5th-century mosaics. The mosaics of the apse were done by artisans sent by the Doge of Venice in 1220. From the transept you can best admire the 13th-century mosaics by Pietro Cavallini that once decorated the facade of the old basilica. The altar stands over the Tomb of the Apostle. The altar has a Gothic canopy made by Arnolfo di Cambio (1285), resting on four columns of red porphyry and surmounted by a baldacchino upheld by four columns of oriental alabaster. The bases are inlaid with malachite. The marble Easter candlestick on the right of the altar belonged to the previous basilica, and is a unique specimen of medieval sculpture.

TERME DI CARACALLA (BATHS OF CARACALLA)

Viale delle Terme di Caracalla, 52; tel.: 06-5758626/39749907; reservations 06-39967700; open: Tues.–Sun. 9 A.M.–1 hour before sunset, Mon. 9 A.M.–2 P.M.; closed: Jan. 1, May 1, Dec. 25; admission: €4.

➢ As the area around Via Appia was cramped by too many monuments and buildings, the Baths of Caracalla were built on a new parallel street, created to accommodate developments. They are the best-preserved baths in Rome. Hosting as

TOMBA DI CECILIA METELLA (TOMB OF CECILIA METELLA)

Via Appia Antica, 161; tel.: 06-7802465; open: Mon.–Fri. 9 A.M.–1 hour before sunset, Sat., Sun. and public holidays 9 A.M.–1 P.M.; admission: €2.

➢ One of the most important Roman monuments and the best-known landmark along the Via Appia is the massive drum-shaped tomb built around 50 B.C. for the noblewoman Cecilia Metella. She was the daughter of Metellus, conqueror of Crete, and wife of Crassus, one of Caesar's generals. The tomb comprises a huge cylindrical structure—almost 100 feet in diameter—covered in travertine, and a burial chamber that is still visible from the inside. The construction rests on a square base and is decorated by a frieze with garlands and bucranes that, in the Middle Ages, gave the name "Capo di Bova" (Bull's Head) to the entire surrounding area. The frieze breaks off with the relief of a trophy of arms and a barbarian prisoner. In 1302 it was donated to the family of Pope Boniface VIII, who transformed it into a tower to keep watch over their nearby castle.

TOMBA DI CECILIA METELLA

Today I visited . . . the tomb of Metella, which made me realize
for the first time what solid masonry means. These people built
for eternity; they omitted nothing from their calculations except
the insane fury of the destroyers to whom nothing was sacred.

—Goethe, *Italian Journey*

VIA APPIA ANTICA (OLD APPIAN WAY)

➤ Old Appian Way, known as *regina viarium,* or "queen of roads," is the most famous of all Roman consular roads. It was built in 312 B.C. by Appius Claudius, who straightened and widened an ancient road, creating Rome's link with its expanding empire and an axis of communication southward and eastward that was vital for Roman economic development. Mostly abandoned after the 6th century and then restored by Pope Pius VI in the 18th century, it is lined with ruined family tombs, while beneath the fields on either side lay a labyrinth of catacombs.

VILLA AND CIRCO DI MASSENZIO (VILLA AND CIRCUS OF MAXENTIUS)

Via Appia Antica, 153; tel.: 06-7801324; open: 9 A.M.–7 P.M. (summer), 9 A.M.–5 P.M. (winter); closed: Mon.; admission: €3.

➤ The Villa and Circus of Maxentius is a complex of extensive ruins, built in A.D. 309 by Emperor Maxentius. It includes the ruins of a palace, a circus, and a mausoleum that Maxentius built in honor of his son Romulus.

Work on the circus began in the 4th century B.C. and the grounds were continually enhanced until A.D. 549, when the last of the chariot races were held here. The circus, which was the private property of the emperor, was approximately 558 yards in length and 90 yards wide, and was capable of holding up to 10,000 spectators. In the middle, the *spina,* which separated the two chariot tracks, was just under 300 yards in length. In 10 B.C., Emperor Augustus built an imperial box and adorned the spina with the obelisk of Domitian that Bernini later erected in Piazza Navona.

VILLA DEI QUINTILLI

Via Appia Nuova, 1092; tel.: 06-4824181/ 4815576; open: 9 A.M.–1 hour before sunset; closed: Mon.; admission: €4.

➤ The Villa dei Quintili, the largest villa of the Roman countryside, is located five miles from the center of the city. The complex—you can see the ruins of a nymphaeum, a peristyle, large halls with windows, and the arches of the aqueduct—is named after the wealthy brothers who became its owners under Emperor Commodius, who had them executed. It has been the source of countless art treasures since the reign of Hadrian.

Villa dei Quintilli

Walking Tour 1:

Navigating Ancient Walls, Roads & Gates

By Ruth Kaplan

M odern Rome has no real name for the swath of land south of the Baths of Caracalla. It's a semicircular patch bounded by the ancient city walls and by an imposing four-lane road leading out of town. What it does offer is a beautiful hour-long walk that takes you past quirky Renaissance chapels, through ancient Roman arches, and up on the southernmost ramparts of the Aurelian Wall.

Start at the beginning of Via di Porta San Sebastiano, a narrow cobblestone road just down from the Baths of Caracalla. This was once the urban stretch of the ancient Appian Way, but it now feels anything but urban. On Sundays it is closed off to motor vehicles, and you are likely to hear birds, and even roosters, rather than cars. Near the corner on the right is the entrance to

House of Cardinale Bessarione

OUR PICK

the Parco San Sebastiano, a sprawling stretch of green with rolling walking paths, benches, and an elementary school on its grounds. Next door is the tall, narrow stucco facade of the **Church of San Cesareo in Palatio**. Built in the 8th century, it was heavily restored in the 16th century and has some of Rome's most intricate Cosmatesque tile work, transferred here from the old Basilica of San Giovanni in Laterano. Underground are some 2nd-century black-and-white mosaics of sea animals and gods, which may have been part of Roman baths on this site. The church is often closed, but it is possible to arrange a visit by either calling or talking to the custodian who lives next door.

The gated complex next to San Cesareo is the House of Cardinal Bessarione, a 15th-century humanist scholar who summered here. Though closed to the public, you can see through the gate to the elegant raised porch decorated with frescoes from that era.

The rest of the road is quiet, with the occasional private residence popping up in breaks in the stone wall. A 3rd-century burial site, the Tomb of the Scipio Family, is marked on the left. Cars still drive through the Arch of Drusus, a large carved decorative arch near the end of the road. Just beyond that is the imposing Aurelian Wall, the 12-mile protective ring around the city built by Aurelian and Probus in A.D. 270–282. Heavily rebuilt after the Visigoth invasions of the 4th century, the wall was used defensively up through 1870, when the army of the kingdom of Italy managed to breach through and conquer Rome.

The sturdy square gate leading through the wall is known as the Porta San Sebastiano, named for the Church of Saint Sebastian a little more than a mile outside the wall. In pre-Christian times, the gate was known as the Porta Appia, after the Appian Way that ran through it.

The Porta San Sebastiano is the largest and best-preserved passage of the whole Aurelian Wall, with two stories of rooms and walkways above the gate itself. The interior has been restored and is now home to the **Museum of the Walls of Rome**, a museum chronicling the history of the wall and an overall history of Rome's defensive constructions. The exhibition explains and illustrates the full range of Roman stone- and brick-building techniques, all the way back through the 7th century B.C. Arched windows in the museum space itself provide good views of the green Appian Way.

As you walk through the gate, notice the decorative carvings and the keystone on the inner arch with a Greek inscription dedicating the rebuilt gate to God and the saints.

Take a left after passing through the gate, and follow the wall as it curves toward the next gate, the Porta Latina. Much smaller than the Porta San Sebastiano, the Porta Latina was the first gate built in the Aurelian Wall. From here the lush Via di Porta Latina stretches back into the center of the city.

The petite, barrel-shaped chapel just inside the gate is the **Oratory of San Giovanni in Oleo**, a 16th-century building marking the spot where Saint John the Evangelist is supposed to have escaped unharmed from a cauldron of boiling oil. The building has ancient origins, but it is unclear whether it is built on the spot of an early Christian oratory or a pagan mausoleum, which would date to before the construction of the Aurelian Wall. It is also unclear who designed

Arch of Drusus

the present chapel: Bramante was once assumed to be its main architect, but likely candidates also include Antonio da Sangallo the Younger or Baldassarre Peruzzi. Borromini led a restoration of the oratory in 1658, adding the circular frieze in dark cement that still hugs the bottom of the chapel's domed roof.

Ring the doorbell at No. 17 across the street for access to the chapel, which is usually locked. Someone is there during church hours to open the door for you or just give you the keys to open it yourself. Inside the tiny octagonal interior is a white altar that takes up almost half of the floor space. The walls sport a five-panel fresco cycle of the life of Saint John, done in the 1660s by Lazzaro Baldi, a student of Pietro da Cortona. Its large panels depict the wise-looking, muscle-bound saint tied up in chains, and later being put into a pot of boiling oil while two cherubs look down on him.

Further down Via di Porta Latina on the right is the handsome medieval **Church of San Giovanni a Porta Latina**. Small yellow signs point to it, tucked away at the end of a quiet cul-de-sac. This church was built in the 5th century, restored in 772 and again in the 12th century, and has held on to its late-medieval look. An enormous, ancient cedar tree shades the grassy yard out front. The garden's highlight is an ancient well made of worn-away white marble, flanked by two miniature columns. Its marble facing is carved in an unusual pattern of circular swirls. Four mismatched ancient columns were used to build the tall, breezy porch. There is also an elegant six-tiered Romanesque campanile to the left of the portico.

The interior of the church has a classic three-aisle basilican form, with tall, bare walls and two rows of ancient columns splitting the nave. Restorations in 1940 brought some life back to the 12th-century frescoes that decorate the space between the column capitals and the ceiling. Many of their biblical themes are instantly recognizable: the Creation of Man, the Temptation, and the Expulsion. The paintings on the other wall seem to have been done by a different artist, though all share the cartoonish simplicity of medieval composition and proportion. The priest's lectern at the head of the church is made out of two ancient marble slabs, and the slightly raised floor below it is done in a Cosmatesque checkered pattern.

As you continue on the ten-minute stroll down Via di Porta Latina you will see exquisite private residences and once-glamorous abandoned villas.

View of vault, San Sisto Vecchio

When the street ends, cross over back toward the Baths of Caracalla to **San Sisto Vecchio**, the rebuilt version of an important 13th-century church. It is not open to the public, but ring the buzzer—you might get a friendly nun to escort you around. The elegant Romanesque bell tower and fragments of 13th- and 14th-century frescoes in the presbyterium are all that remains of the old church where Saint Dominic once lived. Try to convince the nuns to let you see the remains of the fresco cycle on the curved walls behind the apse. Snatches of the original groundwork are also visible in the convent's modern cloister.

FURTHER INFORMATION

Museo delle Mura di Roma (Museum of the Walls of Rome) (see also museum entry)
Via di Porta San Sebastiano; tel.: 06-70475284; open: Tues.–Sun. 9 A.M.–7 P.M.

Oratory of San Giovanni in Oleo
Via di Porta Latina, immediately before the Aurelian Walls.

San Cesareo in Palatio
Via di Porta San Sebastiano, 4; tel.: 06-7009016.

San Giovanni a Porta Latina
Via di San Giovanni a Porta Latina; tel.: 06-70491777; open: daily 7 A.M.–noon, 3–6 P.M.

San Sisto Vecchio
Piazzale Numio Pompilio, 8; tel.: 06-77205174.

Piazza di Santa Balbina, 8; tel.: 06-7808756; open: Sat., Sun. 8:30–11:30 A.M.

By Ruth Kaplan

The church and former convent of Santa Balbina stands on a flattened stretch of ground on the road leading uphill from the Baths of Caracalla toward the Piccolo Aventino, the little sister of the Aventine Hill. Built in the 5th century A.D., it was devoted to the 2nd-century virgin martyr Saint Balbina. The church has since been rebuilt, but still prominently displays a mix of ancient and medieval decorations.

From the man-made flattened Piazza di Santa Balbina, a short staircase leads up to the church's portico, with a high, sloping roof and three wide arches built in brick. Three arched windows repeat the portico's look in the brick upper level.

You might have to let yourself into the church by sliding back the iron bolt that locks the main door. Inside is an open nave with simple niches as side chapels. The space is well lit from a stretch of arched herringbone-cutout windows on the upper reaches of the cream-colored walls.

One of Santa Balbina's most interesting decorative features is a half-dozen or so 1st-century-A.D. Roman mosaics that were found in 1939 and subsequently inlaid into the floor. They depict the signs of the zodiac calendar and birds, an incongruous pre-Christian addition to the church. A few ancient amphorae lining the front wall add some further ancient flair.

The beautiful Tomb of Cardinal Stefanus de Surdis, in the back right corner, was done in 1303 by Giovanni di Cosma, a member of the family for which the Cosmati style is named.

Traces of Byzantine-style paintings remain on the walls of the first and third chapels on the right, including fragments of a Mother and child surrounded by various saints. The apse fresco, the *Glory of Christ* by Anastasio Fontebuoni (1523), is in much better condition. Under it is a colorful 13th-century episcopal chair with intricate mosaic inlays. More frescoes are visible in the last chapel on the left, including a stolid Saint Peter suffering through his upside-down crucifixion. A piece from the church's original 5th-century stone altar is on display there in a glass box.

The best-preserved fresco is in the second left chapel: a Madonna and Child flanked by saints, with a floating bust of Christ above them. It is attributed to the 13th-century school of Pietro Cavallini.

Santa Balbina

Walking Tour 2:

2,000 Years of Religious History on the Aventine Hill

By Ruth Kaplan

The Aventine has not changed its character very much, ever since the Roman emperor Trajan chose to build his home on the Aventine Hill, breaking from the more mainstream Palatine as the preferred location of Rome's most powerful citizens. It is still overwhelmingly residential, and still known as the home of the wealthier, if not the most powerful, segment of Rome's population.

One of the seven original hills of the ancient city, the Aventine has a long history as a place of religious worship. The Temple of Diana was once located here, and is still recalled in a street name. Three of the area's most famous churches have been in their current locations since the times of early Christendom. Nowadays, the Benedictine Order has its world headquarters and its principal university here.

Luckily for its residents and visitors, the area is blissfully free of traffic; every day feels like Sunday, with the majority of parked cars coming from wedding guests at the various churches. Public transportation is plentiful on the four stretches that flank the Aventine: the Circus Maximus to the north, Viale Aventino to the east, the Lungotevere hugging the Tiber to the west, and to the south, the vibrant Testaccio neighborhood, filled with restaurants and clubs.

Approaching the Aventine Hill from Viale Aventino, start by going up Via di Santa Prisca. A few hundred yards up on the right is the small **Church of Santa Prisca**, set back from the street with a ramp and stairs to approach it. Archaeologists believe that there has been a church of the same name on this location since the 4th century A.D. Before that, the site was used as a place of worship for the pagan Mithraic cult.

Santa Prisca's brick and marble facade is squeezed between two protruding buildings, giving the church an air of modesty. Inside, a wooden entryway and balcony with an organ break away from the traditional stone architecture of Rome's churches, almost giving the place the feel of a Protestant church. A fading sea of frescoes from the 17th century covering the apse are unfortunately poorly lit. To the left of the nave in a little side chapel there is an unusual series of panels with the Lord's Prayer printed elaborately in nine languages, including the unlikely Hebrew, Samaritan, and Esperanto.

Try to make your visit fall on the second or fourth Sunday of the month, when the excavated depths under the church are open for an informative guided tour. The visit starts by going around the back of the church and down into the vaulted antechamber of an ancient *domus,* or private Roman mansion, discovered and excavated by a group of Dutch archaeologists in the 1930s. A short hallway decorated with ancient sculptural fragments leads to what used to be Saint Prisca's crypt, a large, well-lit room teeming with colorful frescoes painted by the same artist who decorated the nave upstairs. Two out-of-use curving stairwells leading up to the church are still visible.

The core of interest on the underground level starts with the small 3rd-century antechamber of what was used in early Christian times as a place of worship for the pagan Mithraic cult. Brought back from Persia by Roman soldiers in the 1st century B.C., the cult blossomed to include an estimated 2,000 Mithraea throughout Rome at its height in the 3rd century A.D. Forty of the places of worship are now accessible. The god Mithras was honored for bringing civilization into existence by slaying a bull, whose blood enriched the earth's soil and made it arable. The antechamber at Santa Prisca's Mithraeum contains a red-painted stone block used for animal sacrifices—because of the size, it was probably only used for pigs and sheep, rather than actual bulls. A long, rectangular chamber follows, with an expressive and nearly life-size ancient bas-relief depicting the muscular Mithras killing a bull, with an enormous bearded god reclining at his feet, possibly the god Saturn. Now-faded frescoes line the walls, and long countertops were used to serve a common meal, an important element of Mithraic worship. At least three adjoining rooms are visible through arched doorways, but are temporarily off-limits due to water damage.

Continue up Via di Santa Prisca, keeping left of the grassy park on Via G. Berniero. You'll find yourself facing a 12th-century stone wall that used to be the fortified quarters of the adjoining Savelli family castle, of which only a small tower remains. Inside the walls is Rome's Parco Savello, better known as the Giardino degli Aranci, or the "Park of the Orange Trees." Filled with rows of the short, leafy fruit trees and punctuated by looming, thin Italian pines, the small park is full of shade and is a haven for those stuck in the city on a

Santa Prisca

SANTA SABINA

[It's] a very fine old structure of the fifth century, moldering in its dusky solitude and consuming its own antiquity. What a massive heritage Christianity and Catholicism are leaving here! . . . It has a noble nave, filled with a stale smell, which brought tears to my eyes, and bordered with twenty-four fluted marble columns of Pagan origin. The crudely primitive mosaics along the entablature are extremely curious.

—Henry James, *Italian Hours*

blistering day. A lookout point with stone benches offers a wide-angle view stretching from the Capitoline Hill and the Vatican down to the southern reaches of the Tiber River.

The park's gate leads out to the impressive church-and-monastery complex of **Santa Sabina**. Founded by Peter of Illyria, a priest from Dalmatia (now southern Croatia), in A.D. 422, the church has undergone a series of renovations approximately every 400 years, all of which have left their architectural and decorative marks. The main entrance, flanked by ancient Roman columns, leads straight into the side of the wide, spacious nave. Light pours in from the high 9th-century windows, with colorless glass fitted into inventive geometrical cutouts. The pulpit and low-walled choir in the front of the church come from the same 9th-century renovation. A single Roman column emerges from below the floor on the right side of the nave, a possible remnant of the original house of the Roman matron Sabina, for whom the church was named, or the nearby Temple of Juno. Baroque touch-ups added the Elci chapel on the left side of the nave, containing the delicate *Madonna of the Rosary with Saints Dominic and Catherine* by 17th-century painter Sassoferrato.

The most impressive remnant of the 5th-century construction is the spectacular lapis lazuli mosaic over the main door in the side of the church. Gold-tiled letters are strung together to form a long inscription, which is largely indecipherable due to the lack of spaces between words, as was common in Latin text. Two finely detailed female figures flank the stretch of blue tile, both representing converts to Christianity: one symbolizing converted Jews, the other converted pagans.

Santa Sabina's layered architectural history continues in its hushed medieval cloister, up a short inclined hallway from the church's main entrance. Thin, short, elegant columns separate

Cloister of Santa Sabina

the walkway from a little interior garden, with four bushy cypresses surrounding a dry well. The covered pathway is strewn with some intricately carved, double-arched medieval window frames, more decorative than functional. Dominican friars still live in the rooms surrounding the cloister.

As you walk out of the cloister, take a look at the well-preserved 5th-century carved wooden doors leading into the church. They are paneled with fanciful scenes from the Bible, including what is believed to be one of the earliest depictions of the Crucifixion.

Continuing down Via di Santa Sabina in the opposite direction of the Giardino degli Aranci, the street ends in the elaborately decorated Piazza dei Cavalieri di Malta. Built by the artist and architect Giovanni Battista Piranesi in 1765, the piazza consists of two high whitewashed walls bursting with a range of cryptic symbols—shields, two-headed eagles, and a special eight-pointed cross—relating to the Knights of Malta, a religious order whose world headquarters have been located here since their expulsion from the isle of Rhodes in the 16th century. The piazza is best known for the optical-illusion keyhole in the door at No. 3, through which you can see a surprisingly large Saint Peter's Basilica framed by a line of cypress trees. It is also the only keyhole in the world that gives you a view of two different countries—the Sovereign Military Order of Malta and the Vatican—while standing in yet another one—Italy.

Behind Piranesi's obelisk-adorned walls is the Benedictine **Church of Sant'Anselmo**, home to the most important center for Benedictine study. Monks from all over the world come here to study theology and philosophy. The Benedictines are the heirs to the musical tradition of the Gregorian chant and from October to June anyone going to their vesper service (at 7:15 P.M.) can enjoy a trip back in time listening to their choir. A great gift shop filled with Benedictine products is also part of the church-and-university complex (see Specialty Shops).

Although the actual Church of Sant'Anselmo is a mere hundred years old and is architecturally overshadowed by its neighbors, the tree-filled grounds make a pleasant place to sit, with two little bench-filled gardens in the middle of the cypresses. Between the thick greenery, the height and quiet of the location, and the pious studiousness exuded by the monastic university, Sant'Anselmo is a microcosm of the religiosity and calm that pervade the whole Aventine Hill.

FURTHER INFORMATION

Sant'Anselmo
Piazza di Sant'Alessio; open: all day from Sept.–June, flexible hours during the summer.

Santa Prisca
Piazza di Santa, Prisca and Via di Santa Prisca; tel.: 06-5743798; open: 8 A.M.–noon, 2–7 P.M.; Mithraeum open: tours at 4 P.M. every second and fourth

Sunday of the month; admission: €4; note: Tours meet at door marked No. 13 next to the church. Tours are usually in Italian, but group visits can be arranged in other languages by calling 06-4815576.

Santa Sabina
Piazza Pietro d'Illiria; tel.: 06-5743573; open: 6:30 A.M.–12:45 P.M., 3:30–7 P.M.

FOCUS: San Saba

Via di San Saba; tel.: 06-5743352; open:
daily 7 A.M.–noon, 4–6 P.M.

By Ruth Kaplan

San Saba

Founded in the 7th century by
monks fleeing the Arab invasions
of Jerusalem, San Saba has always
been one of Rome's most prominent
churches. The monks living there
served as papal diplomats to the East
in the 8th century, and by the 9th
century the church on the "Piccolo
Aventino" was recognized as one of
the most important in Rome.

Enter the walled complex
through the small *protiro*, or col-
umn-edged doorway, that looks
down onto Via di San Saba. Inside
is a small garden with orange trees.
The brick portico and arched loggia
above it date from 1463, one of the
many additions to the church since its inception as an oratory.

A rich collection of marble altars and sarcophagi are shown on the
portico walls, including a piece found in the 1909 excavations of the oratory—
a relief of a man on horseback holding a falcon. Another wall is covered with
terra-cotta pieces stamped with the insignias of various builders. Stairs in the
left corner show the recessed ground level of the original church.

The nave is almost as wide as it is long, due to the addition of an unusual
fourth aisle on the left. Seven aged granite columns line both sides of the nave.
The floor is paved in a colorful Cosmati checkerboard with five swirling discs on
its spine. Gold-and-blue Cosmati mosaic work also covers a tall panel running
along half the right wall. A collection of 9th- and 10th-century frescoes from
this site hang on display in a corridor off to the right, leading to the sacristy.

With the exception of the 13th-century Crucifixion, the rest of the apse
frescoes were executed in the 15th century, though stylistically they resemble
the medieval mosaic, with orderly rows of the 12 apostles as both men and
sheep flanking a large figure of Christ. The dark marble *ciborio*, or four-poster
altarpiece, is topped by an octagonal, colonnaded roof.

Extending out from the original church walls is the curious fourth aisle,
originally built to link the adjacent monastery to the church. Its well-lit 13th-
century frescoes depict the life of Saint Nicholas of Bari, here presumed
(wrongly) to be the Saint Nicholas of Christmas. One panel shows him giving
a mysterious gift to three sleeping girls. All three frescoes show an interesting,
though unsuccessful, attempt to create a three-dimensional effect around
their arched borders.

SAN PAOLO ALLE TRE FONTANE

According to the legend these Tre Fontane (three fountains) sprang up from the blood of St. Paul when he was beheaded, and have been running ever since. [The church's] greatest attractions are the life-size figures of Christ and the Apostles, painted on the pillars of the nave after drawings by Raphael. In other places he treated the Twelve as a group, all dressed alike, but here this extraordinary genius depicted them separately and [has] given each his distinctive attributes, not as if he were following the Master, but as though, after the Ascension, he had to stand on his own feet and work and suffer alone.

—Goethe, *Italian Journey*

Other Points of Interest

ABBAZIA DELLE TRE FONTANE (ABBEY OF THE THREE FOUNTAINS)
Via di Acque Salvie

➤ This sanctuary is on the site of Saint Paul's martyrdom. According to Christian tradition, the three fountains sprang forth in each of the three spots where his severed head touched the ground after he was beheaded.

The group of buildings that form the sanctuary lies concealed amid eucalyptus trees and is now a Trappist monastery. The Trappists took over the site in 1867, planting it and making a then-marshy land habitable. The Trappist store, outside the entrance of the abbey, is well known for its homemade chocolate and eucalyptus liqueur.

Three churches are grouped together within the monastic enclosure: the Church of San Paolo, the Church of Santi Vincenzo e Anastasio, and that of Santa Maria Scala Coeli.

• SAN PAOLO
➤ The oldest of the three churches located in the complex of the Abbazia delle Tre Fontane. First built in the 6th century, San Paolo was completely rebuilt by Giacomo Della Porta between 1599 and 1600. The church floor features a polychromatic Roman mosaic of the four seasons, which came from Ostia.

• SANTA MARIA SCALA COELI
➤ Santa Maria Scala Coeli was first built in the 12th century, then rebuilt by Giacomo Della Porta in 1583. The floor of the crypt belongs to the original church. The apse has a beautiful mosaic by Francesco Zucchi (1595).

• SANTI VINCENZO E ANASTASIO ALLE TRE FONTANE
➤ The Church of Santi Vincenzo e Anastasio was built in 1221. The three-nave interior and large portico are simple and unadorned, with whitewashed walls, timber roofs, and windows of perforated marble. The church walls also contain some remains of 16th-century frescoes.

CIMITERO PROTESTANTE (NON-CATHOLIC CEMETERY)
Via Caio Cestio, 6; tel.: 06-5741900; open: Tues.–Sun. 9 A.M.–4:30 P.M. (Oct.–Mar.), Tues.–Sun. 9 A.M.–5:30 P.M. (April–Sept.); admission: free.

➤ This cemetery was opened at the end of the 18th century. In those days, non-Catholics in Rome could have their houses of worship only outside the Aurelian Wall, and could not have access to the church cemeteries. So the Vatican decided not to oppose the request for a non-Catholic cemetery next to the Pyramid of Caius Cestius, in an area far from the center of town. The old cemetery is in a quiet, beautiful garden with large pine trees. The new cemetery is much more crowded. Among the most illustrious people buried here are the Romantic poets Keats and Shelley, who died in La Spezia and

CIMITERO PROTESTANTE

I spent an hour at the little Protestant Cemetery, close to St. Paul's Gate,
where the ancient and the modern world are insidiously contrasted.
They make between them one of the solemn places of Rome. . . .
Shelley's grave is here, buried in roses—a happy grave every way for the
very type and figure of the Poet. Nothing could be more impenetrably
tranquil than this little corner . . . . where a cluster of modern ashes is
held tenderly in the rugged hand of the Past.

—Henry James, *Italian Hours*

whose ashes were buried here by Lord Byron; the American explorer Thomas Jefferson Page; and Italian Communist Party founder Antonio Gramsci.

PYRAMID OF CAIUS CESTIUS
Piazzale Ostiense

➤ This imposing pyramid, veneered in bright white marble, stands 118-feet high with a base that is 72-feet square; it is possibly one of the best-preserved monuments of ancient Rome. It was built as a funerary monument for the senior Roman magistrate and member of the college of Roman priests Caius Cestius in merely 330 days—a fact recorded in the inscription on the facade that overlooks Piazzale Ostiense. The internal frescoed funeral chamber is not open to the public. The pyramid is an unmistakable landmark and

was probably viewed as inappropriate when it was built after the death of Cestius in 12 B.C.—as it does today.

SANTI BONIFACIO E ALESSIO
Piazza di Sant'Alessio, 23; tel.: 06-5743446; open: daily 9 A.M.–noon, 3:30–6 P.M.

➤ In the 4th century, a church in honor of Saint Boniface was built here. Honorius III rebuilt it in 1216, and dedicated it to Saint Alexius and Saint Boniface. Of that building only the bell tower and mosaic pavement remain. In 1750 the church was modernized, and nearly all its ancient features were sacrificed. The entrance leads through a courtyard. The doorway has a rich mosaic border, probably the work of Honorius III. The altar is covered by a beautiful baldacchino resting on four columns of *verde antico*. In the choir,

Pyramid of Caius Cestius

Model of Imperial Rome, Museo della Civiltà Romana

behind the altar, is a rich episcopal throne flanked by two marble columns inlaid with mosaic. An inscription on one of these states that there were originally 19 similar columns around the apse. At the foot of the left aisle the wooden stair under which Saint Alexius is said to have died is preserved. The mosaic pavement dates from the 13th century.

Museums

CENTRALE MONTEMARTINI

Via Ostiense, 106; tel.: 06-5748030; open: 9:30 A.M.–7 P.M.; closed: Mon.; admission: €4 (includes entry to the Capitoline Museums).

➤ The Acea Art Center is located in the Centrale Montemartini, the first publicly owned power plant to generate electricity in Rome, in disuse since the 1960s. This museum, a rare and successful example of industrial-archaeological recovery, combines ancient statues with the power plant's industrial architecture and imposing machines. The numerous, splendid works on display include the terra-cotta decoration of the archaic sanctuary of Fortuna and Mater Matuta, by the Church of Saint Omobono in the Foro Boario (7th to 6th century B.C.), the famous funerary bed from Amiterno plated with bronze (1st century), and the so-called *Togato Barberini*, holding the portrait busts of his father and grandfather (1st century B.C.).

MUSEO DELLA CIVILTÀ ROMANA (MUSEUM OF ROMAN CIVILIZATION)

Piazza G. Agnelli, 10; tel.: 06-5926041; open: Mon.–Sat. 9 A.M.–6:45 P.M., Sun. 9 A.M.– 1:30 P.M.; closed: Mon.; admission: €4.

➤ The museum traces the history of Rome through its efforts to civilize the world. The magnificent model of imperial Rome on the scale of 1 to 250 is not to be missed.

MUSEO DELLE MURA DI ROMA (MUSEUM OF THE WALLS OF ROME)

Via di Porta San Sebastiano, 18; tel.: 06-70475284; open: 9 A.M.–7 P.M.; Sun. 9 A.M.– 5 P.M.; closed: Mon.; admission: €3.

➤ Located at the beginning of the Old Appian Way, inside Porta San Sebastiano, the museum highlights the architectural history of Rome's fortified surrounding walls and allows access to the only section of the wall open to the public.

MUSEO NAZIONALE dell'ALTO MEDIOEVO (NATIONAL MUSEUM OF THE EARLY MIDDLE AGES)

Viale Lincoln, 3; tel.: 06-54228199; open: 9 A.M.–8 P.M.; closed: Mon.; admission: €2.

➤ This recently founded museum (1967) contains archaeological material from excavations and collections belonging to the period spanning from late antiquity to the height of the Middle Ages (4th to 13th centuries).

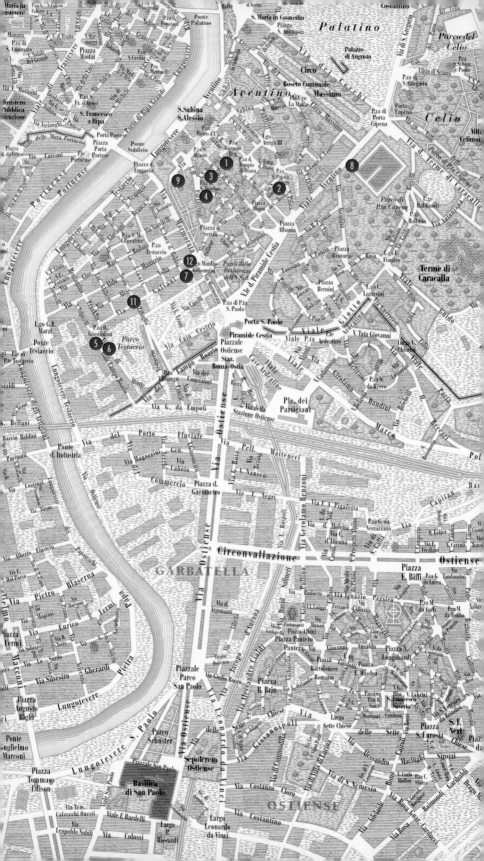

Southern Rome

Hotels & Inns
1 Hotel Aventino
2 Hotel Domus
   Aventina
3 Hotel Sant'Anselmo
4 Hotel Villa San Pio

Restaurants & Cafés
5 Al Regno di Re
   Ferdinando II
6 Checchino, dal 1887*
7 Da Oio a Casa Mia
8 Ristorante Cinese
   Court Delicati

Shopping
9 Badia Primaziale di
   Sant'Anselmo—
   Negozio Benedettino

Best of
10 Il Gelato di San
   Crispino
11 Il Seme e la Foglia
12 Volpetti

HOTELS & INNS

Hotel Aventino

Via San Domenico, 10; tel.: 06-5745231;
e-mail: info@aventinohotels.com; website:
www.aventinohotels.com; category: ★★;
credit cards accepted: all major; €€.

☞Hotel Aventino is the more modest sibling of Villa San Pio and Hotel Sant'Anselmo, with large but simple rooms. The building itself is set back from the street the way the Aventine's private residences are, and guests must ring the bell to be buzzed in. Beautiful garden area in the back.

Hotel Domus Aventina

Via di Santa Prisca, 11/B; tel.: 06-5746135/
57300044; e-mail: domus.aventina@flashnet.it;
website: www.domus-aventina.com; category:
★★★; number of rooms: 26; credit cards
accepted: all major; access to internet: direct-
line (US, UK) telephone jack in all rooms;
most beautiful rooms: 20, 21; €€.

☞In the quietest of Rome's seven hills, the Aventine, the Hotel Domus Aventina is perfect for those who desire an oasis of peace. Most rooms face the 17th-century cloister of the Church of Santa Prisca. Some have balconies with a view.

Hotel Sant'Anselmo

Piazza Sant'Anselmo, 2; tel.: 06-5743547/
5783604; e-mail: info@aventinohotels.com;
website: www.aventinohotels.com; category:
★★★; number of rooms: 147; credit cards
accepted: all major; facilities: free parking;
access to internet: direct-line (US, UK) telephone jack in all rooms; most beautiful
room: 529; €€.

☞The Hotel Sant'Anselmo is a small, exclusive hotel located across a grassy piazza from Sant'Anselmo's Benedictine college. The ground floor of this converted villa consists of multitiered, cozy lounge areas with ornate Victorian furniture. The vine-covered arbor in the back garden frames carved stone tables and chairs. The rooms are small but comfortable and some on the upper floors overlook the city. Some rooms also have balconies.

Hotel Villa San Pio

Via Sant'Anselmo, 19; tel.: 06-5783214/
5783604; e-mail: info@aventinohotels.com;
website: www.aventinohotels.com; category:
★★★; number of rooms: 78; credit cards
accepted: all major; facilities: limited free
parking, roof garden, solarium, health and
fitness center, access for disabled; access to
internet: direct-line (US, UK) telephone jack in
the three-star deluxe rooms; most beautiful
room: 529; €€.

☞Hotel Villa San Pio belongs to the same hotel complex of the Sant'Anselmo, in the exclusive Aventine Hill. It consists of two buildings with a quiet lawn/breakfast area between the two, and has a more modern feeling than the Sant'Anselmo. The elegant rooms range in size, and are all outfitted with period furnishings. Some rooms have balconies overlooking the well-kept garden.

RESTAURANTS & CAFÉS

Checchino, dal 1887

Via di Monte Testaccio, 30; tel.: 06-5746318;
open: 12:30–3 P.M., 8 P.M.–midnight; closed:
Sun., Mon., one week at Christmas, and the
month of Aug; €€€€.

☞The main, non-smoking dining room of Checchino is carved out from the ancient ceramics heap known as Monte Testaccio. It is still run by the same family who opened a wine-and-cheese eatery here in 1870. In front of the old slaugh-terhouse, the restaurant is renowned for its reworking of the "fifth quarter," or less-prized butcher cuts: oxtail, offal, and tripe. High-end Roman specialties such as *tonnarelli* with oxtail sauce and *rigatoni* with baby veal tripe are among the top dishes. Seasonal favorites like fried arti-chokes and *pasta e ceci* (pasta with chick-peas) are also good. Over 600 wines are kept in the ancient wine cellar, which may be visited on request. The 40 cheeses on the menu and a range of sweets are paired up with dessert wines suited to their flavor. There are also outdoor tables.

Da Oio a Casa Mia

Via Galvani, 43/45; tel.: 06-5782680; open: 12:30–3 P.M., 7:30 P.M.–midnight; closed: Sun.; credit cards accepted: all major; €.

☛Specialties of the house at this 60-year-old Roman trattoria are *rigatoni con cacio e pepe* (pasta with grated sheep's-milk cheese and black pepper) and *pajata* (lamb intestines with milk inside). Typical second courses include oxtail or tripe sautéed with onion, wine, and celery in a tomato sauce. Roomy, pleasant tables outside.

Ristorante Cinese Court Delicati

Viale Aventino, 39–41; tel.: 06-5746108; open: noon–2:45 P.M., 7:30–11 P.M.; closed: Mon.; credit cards accepted: all major; €.

☛This excellent restaurant tends to surprise everyone who eats here, showing how delicate Chinese food can be. Steamed dishes come to the table in traditional bamboo steamers: simple dumplings with chopped shrimp mixed into the dough, or a whole steamed trout stuffed with scallions and dressed with a vinegar-soy sauce and strips of fresh ginger. Try the fresh mango salad in a fiery hot pepper-lemongrass dressing. Ginseng and ginger grappas are served as after-dinner drinks.

SPECIALTY SHOPS

Badia Primaziale di Sant'Anselmo—Negozio Benedettino

Piazza Cavalieri di Malta, 5; tel.: 06-5791365; open: Tues.–Sun. 10 A.M.–noon, 4–7 P.M.; closed: Aug. 5–25.

☛The wine section of this unique shop highlights award-winning cabernet from the Muri-Gries monastery in the northern Italian region of Alto Adige. Gregorian chants are featured on CDs recorded in Germany, France, and the United States. And the herbal cures department offers natural concoctions using recipes that date back to medieval times. "The idea behind this store is to showcase the products made by Benedictine monks and nuns from all over the world," explains Claudio Bruno, the store's manager. And the results have been impressive: On Saturdays and Sundays, the store often sees up to 400 customers.

OUR CRITIC'S FAVORITE RESTAURANT

Al Regno di Re Ferdinando II

Via di Monte Testaccio, 39; tel.: 06-5783725; closed: Sun., Mon. at lunch; €.

☛At this bit of Naples tucked into the Roman area of Monte Testaccio, Pippo Sanfilippo prepares the great classics of Neapolitan cuisine with passion and skill. Diners can choose from three first courses that vary daily (don't miss the rice *sartù* on Tuesdays or the cavatelli in seafood stew on Fridays) or select among the meat or seafood second courses like the potato cake, Neapolitan meatballs, or fresh sardines stuffed with provola cheese. The wine list includes Campania labels for accompaniments.

AIR TRAVEL

Airports

Aeroporto Leonardo da Vinci (better known as Fiumicino) is 20 miles/35 km southwest of Rome.

Tel.: 06-65951; for arrival and departure info.: 06-65953640; Alitalia: 06-65631; website: www.adr.it.

From Fiumicino to the center of Rome, a taxi ride takes about 45 minutes and costs €45, plus a tip if you have baggage.

There are two trains that depart from an elevated railway station in the airport (look for train signs). One train is a shuttle called Airport-Termini Express (marked FS) that leaves from the airport and goes to Termini Station every 30 minutes from 6:37 A.M. to 10:37 P.M. and from Termini Station to the airport every 30 minutes from 5:51 A.M. to 10:51 P.M. It costs €9. It takes 30 minutes, non-stop, from the airport to Termini Station where you can get a bus, train, or taxi to your specific destination.

The other train runs between the airport and Tiburtina Station every 15 minutes from 6:27 A.M. to 10:27 P.M. and from Tiburtina Station to Fiumicino airport every 15 minutes from 5:26 A.M. to 9:26 P.M. It costs €4.50 and also stops in Trastevere and Ostiense Stations.

All train tickets must be stamped at gate.

There is also a night bus service that costs €4. It leaves from Fiumicino airport to Tiburtina station every hour from midnight to 5 A.M. and from Tiburtina to Fiumicino airport every hour from 1 A.M. to 4 A.M.

Aeroporto Ciampino is 9 miles/15 km south of downtown Rome. Tel.: 06-794941, for general information or information on arrivals and departures. From Ciampino to the center of Rome a taxi ride takes about 30 minutes and costs about €35, plus a tip if you have baggage.

COTRAL buses go to the Anagnina Station of Metro Linea A where you can transfer to a subway. They leave every half-hour between 7 A.M. and 11 P.M. and cost €1 (COTRAL: 06-7222153).

Lost Luggage

If you lose your baggage at Fiumicino and you are on any airline but Alitalia, call 06-65956777 or 06-65954252. If you are on Alitalia, call 06-65631.

If you lose your baggage at Ciampino, call 06-79494225.

Within Italy

The main airlines in Italy are Alitalia (tel.: 06-65642), Airone (tel.: 06-48880001) and Meridiana (tel.: 06-478041). There are usually special weekend rates, family discounts, and reduced prices for young people.

CARS

Car rentals are great for exploring the countryside, but not necessary for city driving. Rentals cost between €300 and €400 for a medium-sized car for a week.

Some major agencies are: Avis (tel.: 06-65011531/199-100133); Hertz (tel.: 06-542941); Maggiore National (tel.: 06-65011508), and Travel Car (tel.: 190-180180). They all have offices at Fiumicino and at Termini Station. You need a credit card, passport, and license to rent a car, and you must be 25 years old.

Driving in Italy is on the right and regulations are similar to those in the United States. There are certain towns where the horn is forbidden (this is indicated by a sign saying ZONA DI SILENZIO). Speed limits are 130 kph (80 mph) on the *autostrade* and between 70 and 90 kph (43 and 56 mph) on smaller roads unless otherwise marked. There are large fines for drinking and driving which may include the suspension of a license and the possibility of six months imprisonment. There is a network of *autostrade* (toll-highways) as well as *superstrade* (free expressways). When you enter an *autostrade,* you are issued a ticket and you must return that ticket when you exit and pay a toll. On some shorter highways, a toll is paid on entry.

Gas stations on the autostrade are open 24 hours a day. Gas (*benzina*) generally costs €1.10 per liter. Street parking in Rome is difficult. It is usually recommended to park in a garage.

Autostrade Information: 06-43632121 (24 hours a day); website: www.autostrade.it.

TRAIN TRAVEL

For information on schedules and ticket costs, you can refer to www.fs-on-line.com or call 147888088 from 7 A.M.–9 P.M.

There are a few types of trains on the Italian railway (Ferrovie dello Stato-FS). The fastest is the Eurostar, which operates on many main lines including Rome-Florence-Milan. A trip from Rome to Venice, reservations and *supplemento* (supplement) included, is about €40. The Intercity (IC) trains cost less but are slower. Reservations are always advisable.

You can buy tickets in the ticket office, or *biglietteria,* or in one of the self-ticketing machines at the station. You can also buy them at a travel agent with an FS sticker. Tickets can be purchased up to two months before travel but must be stamped immediately before boarding at orange machines located at the beginning of the tracks. There is a fine for unstamped tickets. Note that in Rome there are two main stations: Tiburtina, in the eastern part of the city, and Termini, in the center. Make sure to confirm which station you want.

CREDIT CARDS

To report lost or stolen credit cards, call the appropriate number for your card carrier: American Express (tel.: 800-874333), MasterCard (tel.: 800-870866), or Visa (tel.: 800-877232). American Express also has an office in Rome: Piazza di Spagna, 38; tel.: 06-67641.

CURRENCY EXCHANGE

You can change currency at any bank or you can withdraw money from ATMs (there is usually a fee of $1–$5 for a withdrawal and a withdrawal limit of $500 per day). Most U.S., Canadian, or U.K. bank cards, Mastercards, and VISAs can be used at ATMs in Rome.

CUSTOMS AND DUTIES

When shopping, keep receipts for all of your purchases. To get a V.A.T. (Value-Added Tax) refund (about 12% of the cost of your pur-chase), you must spend more than €150 at a store and request a V.A.T. form at the store where you purchase the goods. At the airport, get your form stamped by Italian customs, who will give you specific information about receiving your refund. If you paid by credit card, you will get the reimbursement credited to your card; if you paid by cash, you will get a check sent to your home address.

As a resident of the U.K., you do not have to pass through customs to reenter your home country.

As a U.S. resident over 21 years old, you can bring in 200 cigarettes, 50 cigars, or 2 kilograms of tobacco; 1 liter of alcohol; and gifts worth $100. Prohibited items include meat products, seeds, and plants.

As a resident of Canada, you can bring in C$500 worth of duty-free goods if you have been away for more than 7 days, C$200 if you've been away between 48 hours and 7 days, and C$50 for less than 48 hours.

HOURS

Business hours vary depending on the stores and the season, but most stores are open Mon.–Sat. 9 or 9:30 A.M.–1 P.M. and then 3:30 or 4 P.M.–7 or 7:30 P.M.

In more touristy areas of Rome, some stores stay open throughout lunch time and may be open for limited hours on Sunday.

Museum hours vary greatly, but most are open from 8:30 or 9 A.M. until 5 or 6 P.M. without a break. It is best to call the museum to check the specific hours. Many museums are also closed one day a week, usually on Mondays.

Banks are open weekdays 8:30 A.M.– 1:30 P.M. and 2:45 P.M.–3:45 P.M.

Churches are usually open from early morning until noon or 12:30 P.M. They open again in the afternoon until about 7 P.M. Major cathedrals are open all day.

INFORMATION BOOTHS

There are 12 information booths located around the city. They have maps; schedules for the theater, opera, and museums; and information on guided tours. The people running the booths speak English. You can also call 06-36004399 for information in English.

INTERNET CAFÉS

Internet cafés are located all around the city, especially around Piazza Venezia, Termini Station, the Trevi Fountain, and in Trastevere. The cost is about €4 an hour. We suggest: ☛Internet Café, Via Cavour, 213; tel.: 06-47823051. ☛Internet Point, Via Gatea, 25; tel.: 06-47823862. ☛TreviNet Place, Via in Arcione, 103; tel.: 06-69922320.

MAIL

Postcards and letters to the United States and Canada cost €0.77. Postcards and letters to the U.K. cost €0.44. You can buy stamps (francobolli) at a tobacco store (tabacchi), recognizable by the black "T" sign.

Post offices are open Mon.–Fri. 8 A.M.–2 P.M. and Sat. 8:30 A.M.–noon. Main offices at Termini, Piazza and San Silvestro, and the airport are open Mon.–Fri. 8:30 A.M.–6:30 P.M. and Sat. 8:30 A.M.–1 P.M.

PASSPORTS AND VISAS

United States citizens do not need a visa to visit Italy unless they plan to stay longer than three months, in which case they must apply for a permesso di soggiorno. Contact the Italian Consulate closest to you for further information. U.K. citizens only need a passport.

PETS

Most animals can enter Italy if they are accompanied by their owner and a certificate of good health issued by a certified veterinarian in the country of origin no more than 30 days before the departure date. These certificates are available on the internet (www.italemb.org) or can be requested from the closest Italian Consulate. The certificate does not need to be authenticated by the embassy.

SCOOTERS

Scooters can be rented all over Rome. They usually cost between €30–35 a day.
You can rent scooters at:
☛Scoot-a-long, Via Cavour, 302; tel.: 06-6780206.
☛Scooters for Rent, Via della Purificazione, 84; tel.: 06-4885485.
☛St. Peter's Moto, Via Fosse di Castello, 7; tel.: 06-6875714.

TAXIS

If taxis are available, they will usually stop when hailed in the street. They also can be found at special taxi stands around the city, or can be called by phone (in which case there is a supplement). There is also a supplement for night service, Sundays, holidays, and baggage. You can call a cab at 06-3570, 06-8822, 06-6645, 06-4994, 06-5551, 06-4157, or 06-88177.

You do not need to tip unless you have baggage.

TELEPHONES

Telephone cards (carta telefonica) can be purchased at a tabacchi. To call the U.S. or Canada, dial 001 then the number. To call the U.K., dial 00 44 then the number. To use a calling card, deposit a token and then dial the international number for your calling card and you will be connected with an operator. (AT&T, tel.: 172-1011; MCI, tel.: 172-1022; and Sprint, tel.: 172-1877.)

Tipping

There is a service charge included in most restaurants, but it is customary to leave an additional 5–10% tip, depending on the quality of the service. We suggest a tip of 10% for up to €50 bill, and 5% over €50. Tip a chambermaid a minimum of €1 per day and the bellhop or porter €1 per bag. Tip €.10 for drinks at the counter of a bar and €.50 for a round of drinks.

TRANSPORTATION AROUND ROME

Tickets for the metro or the bus must be stamped at a machine upon entering the metro station or the bus. Bus tickets can be purchased at tabacchi, while subway tickets can be purchased at the metro station. Maps can be purchased at newsstands (giornalai) around the city and at some bookstores.

LATE-NIGHT PHARMACIES

☛Farmacia Internazionale Barberini, Piazza Barberini, 49; tel.: 06-4825456.
☛Farmacia Cola di Rienzo, Via Cola di Rienzo, 213; tel.: 06-3243130.

Acknowledgments

This has been a collective effort by the staff of the Italian supplement of the *International Herald Tribune*, many of its regular contributors, and a number of other people and organizations.

We would like to thank: all the authors whose bylines appear in this guidebook; food critic Domenico Nucera for his restaurant reviews; Aaron Gatti for the months he spent photographing Rome; Andrea Rossi and Justine Kahn for their photographs; Luisa Milanese, Sarah Leiwant, Massimiliano Giamprini, and Marco Gallucci for their contributions as researchers and writers; Joan Pra Levis for her advice with the graphics; and Luigi Sinigaglia of LS Cartography for his outstanding work on the maps.

We would also like to thank Guido Improta and the Azienda di Promozione Turistica of Rome, Rome's tourist board. (Their offices are located on Via Parigi, 11 and their telephone number is 06-488991. Their very informative web site address is www.romaturismo.it.) In the course of the last four years covering Italian affairs for the Italian supplement of the IHT, we have had many opportunities to work with Italian institutions, but Mr. Improta's is exceptional for its professionalism and efficiency. When we approached them for help in researching photographs and obtaining images from various local, state, and Vatican agencies, we feared that time restraints would limit their contribution. In fact, Mr. Improta and his team—in particular the head of the Images division Adriana Amici and art historian Claudia Viggiani—spent months working with and for us, and managed to provide an extraordinary amount of help in a short amount of time. Ms. Viggiani also reviewed the entire manuscript for historical accuracy—a considerable task given the time frame. Their commitment to this project was exemplary. And for that, we are very grateful.

Finally, we would like to thank: graphic artist Lisa Vaughn for her creative contribution; editorial assistant Tiffany Sprague for her consummate attention to detail; and our editor, Isabel Venero, whose patience, artistic eye, insights, and dedication made this guidebook much better than it would have been otherwise.

Claudio Gatti
John Moretti

AMANDA CASTLEMAN

Amanda Castleman is a freelance journalist, specializing in travel, the environment, and women's issues. Her features have appeared in the Italian supplement to the IHT, as well as the *Daily Mail, Wired, Salon,* and the *Oxford Times.* Oblivious to the tech slump, she continues developing www.expatter.com, an online magazine for expatriates. Her travel writing career began at age 16, drafting brochures for the family business: walking and backpacking tours in the Pacific Northwest. Two years later, she became a full-time journalist and funded a degree in Classics by reporting and editing at *The Daily* in Seattle, where she won several national awards. Amanda lives in Oxford, England, on a traditional narrow boat, but has spent the last two years swilling espresso at the American Academy in Rome. She is married to Ancient Greek musicologist John Curtis Franklin.

LAURA COLLURA KAHN

Laura Collura Kahn was born and raised in Rome. She attended an American school, where she learned English and developed a passion for the United States — which never became strong enough to make her leave Italy. She began her career as a journalist in 1992 at the Italian daily *L'Indipendente.* In 1998 Laura moved to Milan to work for the Italian supplement to the IHT as a reporter. In 2000 she became the paper's deputy editor, and in 2001 she moved back to Rome, which she missed terribly.

RUTH KAPLAN

Ruth Kaplan grew up in Providence, Rhode Island. A craving for culture led her to New York City, where she got her bachelor's degree in English at Columbia University. It was in her role as chief food critic for her college newspaper that she first discovered how to legitimately combine journalism and the *dolce vita.*

Her obsessive appreciation for Dante's *Divine Comedy* led her ultimately to Rome, where she lived for two years. There she wrote for the Associated Press, Dow Jones Newswires, the Italian supplement to the IHT, and *ESN,* a European computer magazine. The most glamorous of her other eight jobs abroad was leading deluxe bike tours in Italy's remote countryside.

Ruth's restless side has brought her to Belize, Bogotá, and most corners of Europe, returning many times to Berlin, Croatia, and Sicily.

She is currently living and working in New York City.

JOHN MORETTI

John Moretti, 30, has lived in Italy for five years. He is originally from Boston and has worked as a journalist at *The Addison Independent* in Middlebury, Vermont; the Associated Press in Rome; and the Italian supplement to the IHT in Milan. He has also been a contributor to several magazines and newspapers, including *The Independent on Sunday; Time Out;* and Ft.com, the online edition of the *Financial Times.*

Business and leisure have taken him to more than 40 countries: to Russia as a student; to Northern Australia as a cattle rancher; and to Cleveland, Ohio as an entrepreneur. He speaks French, Italian, Spanish, and Russian. When in Rome, and tired of sightseeing, John would recommend eating *pajata* in Testaccio, renting rollerblades in the Villa Borghese, or catching an A.S. Roma match at the Stadio Olimpico. John is currently the features and web editor for the Italian supplement to the IHT.

SARAH MORGAN

Sarah Morgan has a Ph.D. from Cambridge University and has lectured in Italian studies at the University of Bristol. She has published a number of essays on the Italian Resistance and the problem of post-war violence and is currently working on a book, *The Schio Killings: From Civil War to Cold War, Myth and Memory of the Resistance,* to be published this year by Bruno Mondadori. She now works on a freelance basis as a journalist and for radio.

DOMENICO NUCERA

A native Roman, Nucera was one of the cofounders of the city's Libreria del Viaggiatore, or Travelers' Bookstore. He has published widely on the subjects of food and travel, and has produced documentaries and food and wine stories for television. He contributes regularly to Italy's leading magazines and, since 2000, writes restaurant reviews for *Corriere della Sera's* Rome metro section. In 2003, he published the *EAT Guide* to Rome restaurants, coauthored with Giulia Collina and Luca Zanini.

ELISABETTA POVOLEDO

Elisabetta Povoledo's special interest in art, history, and cultural phenomena are the natural consequence of her post-secondary education. She has a masters degree in art history from McGill University and studied art at the University of Rome and in Urbino.

Born on Lake Maggiore, she grew up in Canada and moved to Rome to pursue her studies. Attracted by visions of facile success and lured by its glossy glamour, she turned to journalism. During her 12 years in Rome she worked for Italian state radio and for several American daily newspapers; she currently works for the Italian supplement to the IHT. She enjoys writing about culture, the occult, and UFOs.

GORDON RAMSEY

Prize-winning journalist Gordon Ramsey has prowled the streets of Rome since 1997, scouting out their secrets and hidden soul. His offbeat reporting evolves from personal interests in the history of Rome and its art and architecture.

Gordon has a master's degree in French literature from the University of Montreal, Canada, and has been working in the field of international development and communications.

MARGARET STENHOUSE

Like many young people of the 1960s, Scots-born Margaret Stenhouse was planning to work her way around the world. Rome was her first stopover, and she fell in love with the city. The upshot was that she stayed on…and on. A lifetime living in the Eternal City has not dimmed her fascination, she says. "I still get a thrill from strolling through Roman Forum and discovering some half-forgotten work of art in a church tucked up a side street."

Trained as a journalist with Scottish publishing house D.C. Thomson's, Margaret has had a long career as a travel writer and newspaper correspondent. She has also written a book about the mysteries of Lake Nemi, an important cult center near Rome dedicated to the goddess Diana and the inspiration for Frazer's Golden Bough. She is currently involved in a project to have Nemi recognized as a UNESCO World Heritage Site.

BEAGAN WILCOX

After graduating from Bard College, Beagan Wilcox lived and worked in Rome for four years. Although she contemplated becoming a taxi driver in Rome (because she knew the city better than many of her Roman friends), she returned to the United States to go back to school. In 2002 she completed a dual master degree program in international affairs and journalism at Columbia University.